THE MODERN PRACTICE
OF ADULT EDUCATION

THE MODERN PRACTICE OF ADULT EDUCATION

From Pedagogy to Andragogy

REVISED AND UPDATED

Malcolm S. Knowles

Association Press
Follett Publishing Company/Chicago

Designed by Donna Cook

Library of Congress Cataloging in Publication Data

Knowles, Malcolm Shepherd, 1913–
 The modern practice of adult education.

 Bibliography: p.
 Includes index.
 1. Adult education. I. Title.
 LC5215.K62 1980 374 80–14344
 ISBN 0–695–81472–9

First Printing

Contents

Exhibits

1
Preparing Yourself
to Inquire

Setting a Climate for Inquiry

This book, if it practices what it preaches, should be a good adult-learning experience for you, the reader. Since I believe that the single most effective teaching device available to teachers is the example of their own behavior, I shall do my best to make this book a good example of an adult-learning experience.

But this goal won't be easy to attain, because at its best, an adult-learning experience should be a process of self-directed inquiry, with the resources of the teacher, fellow students, and materials being available to the learners but not imposed on them. The learners should be active participants, discovering for themselves those things they are ready to discover at a particular phase of their personal development. But people typically don't read books in this spirit. They read books as they listen to lectures—to get answers to questions the author thinks are important rather than to explore questions and answers in a spirit of mutual inquiry. This is the problem: most people have been trained to *read* books rather than to *dialogue* with them.

So if this book is to serve as a learning experience for you, we must at the outset establish a climate of mutual inquiry. And as we shall see later, I believe that this is the first step in developing any learning experience.

Now what, exactly, is involved in establishing a climate of mutual inquiry in a book? I'm not sure I know. Plato did it by actually writing in the form of dialogues between teachers and students. But this technique seems more appropriate to philosophical inquiry than to the more technological inquiry covered in this book.

Perhaps for this kind of book the most important aspects of the climate are the attitudes of the author and reader. Speaking for myself, my attitude is that of a helper to you, not as your teacher in the traditional sense. I perceive you as coming to this book for help in discovering better ways to perform whatever adult-educational functions you are responsible for at this time and perhaps in the future. For some readers these functions will be different from those of others, and I shall try to resist the temptation to put you all in the same mold. I also perceive you as bringing a variety of experiences, previous training, and points of view about society and education to the reading of this book. I bring my experience, training, and point of view to the writing of it. I shall present my ideas with conviction and enthusiasm, not with the attitude that they are the truth or the best ideas but in the hope that they will provide a framework with which you can compare and test your own ideas. My attitude is that I am sharing my experience, training, and point of view with you rather than imposing them on you.

This set of attitudes on my part sets up some requirements regarding your attitudes, though, if our climate of mutual inquiry is to come off. First and foremost, this book presupposes that you will come to it with an attitude of inquiry rather than one of dependent edification. By this I mean that I am expecting you to look to this book to help you formulate questions about your practices as an adult educator to which you will then seek answers from many sources, including this book, other books, training programs, colleagues, and above all, your own experimentation. An attitude of gentle skepticism would probably also be helpful. I shall feel less inhibited about expressing my ideas, assumptions, and convictions clearly and forcefully if I can rely on you to test them against your experience, to adopt those that make sense to you, and to build on them creatively.

Another aspect of the climate of this mutual inquiry that I think is important for us to agree on is the relatively pioneering nature of our undertaking. Although the education of adults is as old as civilization, and adult education as an identifiable field of study and practice has celebrated its silver anniversary, the notion that there is a distinct and different technology for adult learning is in its very beginning stages of development. Consequently, what we know about how to help adults learn is largely the product of artistic experience, and our theories about the phenomena of adult learning are highly speculative. Even the labels we give these phenomena and the categories we use to organize them (such as the typology of techniques in Chapter 11) are crude and constantly changing. We must await a good deal more research before we can start talking about the scientific foundation of our technology of adult education. But for adventurous souls with a high tolerance for ambiguity, this is the most exciting phase in the evolution of a new discipline. So our climate must be characterized by a willingness to take risk, to experiment, to learn from our mistakes, and to construct theories that we know will have to be modified. People who need pat answers, neat categories, and proved theories will be uncomfortable in the climate required by this book—or, indeed, by the field of adult education as it is now.

How the Inquiry Is Organized

This inquiry is organized into three parts. Part I attempts to bring out into the open certain assumptions about the emerging role and technology of adult education on which the rest of the book is based. Chapter 2 explores the meaning of "modern practice." Chapter 3 presents assumptions about who adult educators really are (including the assumption that there are many more of us than any statistics show), what their mission is as social practitioners, and what their role is becoming and must become in our changing society. Chapter 4 is a highly personal statement of a beginning theory about adult learning for which I have borrowed the label "andragogy" from my European colleagues. I am not sure, of course, that all the assumptions in Part I are right. But they are there to be challenged, tested, and modified through the process of your inquiry. I can testify, though, that they have made a difference in my own practice, have given me the security of knowing what I am doing and why I am doing it, and have brought a sense of consistency to my actions.

Part II constitutes a kind of how-to-do-it manual for applying the principles of andragogy to the organization and administration of comprehensive programs of adult learning. There is one chapter for each phase of the andragogical process: establishing a climate and structure, assessing needs and interests, defining purposes and objectives, constructing a design, operating the program, and evaluating the results. This section is liberally illustrated with examples of materials developed by a variety of institutions, not all of which are equally congruent with andragogical principles—a fact that presents the reader with the opportunity to take a clinical rather than an imitative stance toward the illustrations.

Part III traces the application of the same basic process of adult education to the designing and managing of particular learning activities, in the andragogical spirit of helping adults learn, in contrast to the pedagogical spirit of teaching adults. Chapter 11 carries the full weight of this part of the inquiry.

Several appendices have been added to provide illustrative material that might interfere with the flow of the text if included in the chapters. Because *andragogy* is a new word to American readers and has such a central place in this book, and because etymologists tend to take a critical stance toward the formation of new linguistic forms, I have included in Appendix A a reproduction of my correspondence with the publishers of Merriam-Webster dictionaries regarding "andragogy."

Where to Start

There are several ways you can go about using this book as a resource for your own self-directed inquiry, with you taking the initiative to get what will be useful to you rather than passively letting it tell you what it assumes you ought to know.

One way is to think of questions you would like to get answers to or problems you would like to find better solutions to. You might find that simply scanning the Table of Contents will give you an overview of the kinds of information the book contains and will stimulate questions or remind you of problems. Then for each question or problem pick a key word, find it (or a synonym) in the Index, and turn to the pages in the book indicated by the Index. For example, you might be curious to know what motivates adults to want to learn. If you look in the Index under "Motivation," "Needs," and "Participation," you will find several places in the book that deal with this question. Or you might be having a problem getting people to come into your program. If you look in the Index under "Program, promotion of" or under "Promotion" you will find where in the book this problem is dealt with.

Another way to use this book is as a resource for improving specific competencies. Turn to Appendix B and you will find a model of competencies for performing the roles of learning facilitator, program developer, and administrator. Instructions are in Appendix B for you to rate each competency in terms of its importance to your career goals as compared with its present level of development. By going through this self-diagnostic process you will emerge with a profile showing the gaps between where you are now and where you want to be in regard to these competencies. You can select those competencies in which there are substantial gaps, pick out key words in each competency statement, and look them up in the Index. You could, if you wanted to construct a systematic learning plan for yourself, even draft a learning contract as described in Chapter 11.

For Your Continuing Inquiry . . .

Knowles, Malcolm S. *Self-Directed Learning: A Guide for Learners and Teachers.* Chicago: Association Press/Follett, 1975.

National Center for Higher Education Management Systems. *Adult Learning Activities: A Handbook of Standard Terminology for Classifying and Describing Learning Activities of Adults.* National Center for Education Statistics Handbook No. 9. Washington, D.C.: Government Printing Office, 1979.

The Emerging Role and Technology of Adult Education

Part I

2
What Is Modern Practice?

In a World of Accelerating Change

As I reflect back on nearly five decades as a worker in the vineyards of adult education, it is clear to me that each decade witnessed more changes in the theoretical framework, organizational structure, personnel, clientele, methods, techniques, and materials of our field than the preceding decade. Adult educators who used the practices in the seventies that they had learned in the sixties were ineffective and archaic. "Modern" is thus a very temporary state. My own assessment is that the half-life of current practices is about a decade—that half of the practices become outdated over the course of ten years. So about half of this book had to be rewritten when I revised the 1970 edition.

One of the reassuring features of this process of change, however, is that the basic concepts and assumptions about adult learners and adult learning that have been flowing through our stream of thought for half a century have remained intact; it is remarkable that the propositions made by Eduard C. Lindeman in 1926 in his *The Meaning of Adult Education* have been largely supported —and enriched—by experience and research ever since.

What are the main ideas that are influencing—or will influence—adult-education practices in the eighties and nineties? I can observe several in my field of vision.

A New Conception of the Purpose of Education

Perhaps most fundamental of all the current thrusts on our thinking is the re-examination of our notions about the very purpose of education. The dominant conception about the mission of education until recently has been to produce what in the literature is most often called "the educated man." In our era of Women's Lib we would prefer the terminology "the knowledgeable person." The faith has been that if we simply pour enough knowledge into people: 1) they will turn out to be good people, and 2) they will know how to make use of their knowledge. This faith may have been justified, or at least understandable, in an era of relative stability in which knowledge and technology changed very gradually and in an era in which education was considered a right and privilege for essentially an elite leisured class.

But in an era of knowledge explosion, technological revolution, and a social policy of equality of educational opportunity, this definition of the purpose of education and this faith in the power of transmitted knowledge are no longer appropriate. We now know that in the world of the future we must define the mission of education as to produce *competent* people—people who are able to apply their knowledge under changing conditions; and we know that the foundational competence all people must have is the competence to engage in lifelong self-directed learning. We now know, also, that the way to produce competent people is to have them acquire their knowledge (and skills, understandings, attitudes, values, and interests) in the context of its application.

Hence the accelerating spread in the seventies and eighties of competency-based education. (I tend to agree with Cyril Houle that a more descriptive label would be "performance-based education"; but it is "competency-based education" that has caught on.) Not only are competency models beginning to replace content-transmission objectives as the basis for organizing curricula, but self-paced individualized learning modules (or learning packages) and learning contracts are replacing course outlines as the modes for structuring learning experiences. This new way of thinking about education has drastic implications for the education of children and youth, but it seems to be especially relevant to a field of practice that has responsibility to help adults live productively in a world of accelerating change.

From a Focus on Teaching to a Focus on Learning

A second thrust in our thinking is a shift in our research and practice away from a focus on teaching to a focus on learning. Until quite recently most educational psychologists (with the exception of Piaget and Bruner) gave their attention almost exclusively to studying the reactions of children to teaching, and schools of education gave their attention primarily to training teachers how to control students' reactions to their teaching. With Piaget's and Bruner's discoveries that children have a natural ability to conceptualize and Tough's finding that adults go through a natural sequence of steps when they undertake to learn something on their own, we began to be interested in finding out more about the natural processes of learning—focusing on what happens inside the learner rather than on what the teacher does. Out of this line of thinking came a new emphasis on education as a process of facilitating self-directed learning and a redefinition of the role of teacher as a facilitator of self-directed learning and a resource to self-directed learners.

Lifelong Learning

A third thrust is the injection into our thinking of the concept of lifelong learning as the organizing principle for all of education. The basic premise underlying this line of thought is that in a world of accelerating change learning must be a lifelong process. Therefore, schooling must be concerned primarily with developing the skills of inquiry, and adult education must be primarily concerned with providing the resources and support for self-directed inquirers.

New Delivery Systems

Influenced strongly by all of these forces is a fourth thrust—a concern for developing new ways to deliver educational services to individuals so that they can go on learning throughout their lives at their convenience in terms of time and place. Among the labels being given to these new delivery systems are "nontraditional study," "external degrees," "multimedia learning systems," "community education," "learning communities," "learning resource centers," "educational brokering agencies," and "learning networks." These labels represent more than just a random series of innovative experiments; they point to a new direction in our thinking about how and where learning takes place. Education is no longer seen as the monopoly of educational institutions and their teachers. We now perceive that resources for learning are everywhere in our environment and that people can get help in their learning from a variety of other people. The modern task of education, therefore, becomes one of finding new ways to link learners with learning resources.

For Your Continuing Inquiry . . .

Regarding Contemporary Change and the Future

Bennis, Warren G., and Slater, Philip E. *The Temporary Society*. New York: Harper & Row, 1968.
Daedalus. *Toward the Year 2000*. Cambridge, Mass.: Journal of the American Academy of Arts & Sciences, 1967.
De Chardin, Pierre Teilhard. *Future of Man*. New York: Harper & Row, 1964.
Dumazedier, J. *Toward a Society of Leisure*. New York: The Free Press, 1967.
Fromm, Erich. *The Revolution of Hope: Toward a Humanized Technology*. New York: Harper & Row, 1968.
Fuller, R. Buckminster. *Operating Manual for Spaceship Earth*. Carbondale: Southern Illinois University Press, 1969.
Gardner, John. *Self-Renewal: The Individual and the Innovative Society*. New York: Harper & Row, 1963.
Harrington, Fred H. *The Future of Adult Education*. San Francisco: Jossey-Bass, 1977.
Michael, Donald N. *On Learning to Plan and Planning to Learn: The Social Psychology of Changing Toward Future-Responsive Societal Learning*. San Francisco: Jossey-Bass, 1973.
_____. *The Unprepared Society: Planning for a Precarious Future*. New York: Basic Books, 1968.
O'Toole, James. *Work, Learning, and the American Future*. San Francisco: Jossey-Bass, 1977.
Rubin, Louis (ed.). *The Future of Education: Perspectives on Tomorrow's Schooling*. Boston: Allyn & Bacon, 1975.
Sarason, Seymour B. *The Creation of Settings and the Future Societies*. San Francisco: Jossey-Bass, 1972.
Schon, Donald A. *Beyond the Stable State*. New York: W. W. Norton, 1971.
Toffler, Alvin. *Future Shock*. New York: Random House, 1970.
_____. *Learning for Tomorrow: The Role of the Future in Education*. New York: Random House, 1974.

Regarding the Purpose of Education

Bergevin, Paul. *A Philosophy for Adult Education*. New York: Seabury Press, 1967.
Eble, Kenneth E. *A Perfect Education*. New York: Macmillan, 1968.
Gessner, Robert (ed.). *The Democratic Man: Selected Writings of Eduard C. Lindeman*. Boston: Beacon Press, 1956.

Illich, Ivan. *Deschooling Society.* New York: Harper & Row, 1970.

———. *Tools for Conviviality.* New York: Harper & Row, 1973.

Kidd, J. Roby. *Relentless Verity: Education for Being-Becoming-Belonging.* Syracuse: Publications in Continuing Education, Syracuse University, 1974.

Lindeman, Eduard C. *The Meaning of Adult Education.* Montreal: Harvest House, 1961.

Nash, Paul. *Models of Man: Explorations in the Western Educational Tradition.* New York: John Wiley & Sons, 1968.

Nyberg, David (ed.). *The Philosophy of Open Education.* Boston: Routledge & Kegan Paul, 1975.

Postman, Neil, and Weingartner, Charles. *Teaching as a Subversive Activity.* New York: Delacorte Press, 1969.

Tolley, William P. *The Adventure of Learning.* Syracuse: Syracuse University Press, 1977.

Whitehead, Alfred N. *The Aims of Education and Other Essays.* New York: Macmillan, 1959.

Regarding Competency-Based Education

Davies, Ivor K. *Competency-Based Learning: Management, Technology, and Design.* New York: McGraw-Hill, 1973.

Grant, Gerald, et al. *On Competence: A Critical Analysis of Competence-Based Reforms in Higher Education.* San Francisco: Jossey-Bass, 1979.

Hall, G. E., and Jones, H. L. *Competency-Based Education: A Process for the Improvement of Education.* Englewood Cliffs, N.J.: Prentice-Hall, 1975.

Houston, W. Robert. *Exploring Competency Based Education.* Berkeley, Ca.: McCutchan Publishing Co., 1964.

Pinto, Patrick R., and Walker, James W. *A Study of Professional Training and Development Roles and Competencies.* Madison, Wis.: American Society for Training and Development, 1978.

Torshen, Kay P. *The Mastery Approach to Competency-Based Education.* New York: Academic Press, 1977.

Woditsch, Gary A. *Developing Generic Skills: A Model for Competency-Based General Education.* Bowling Green, Ohio: Bowling Green State University, 1977.

Regarding Learning

Bruner, Jerome S. *Toward a Theory of Instruction.* Cambridge, Mass.: Harvard University Press, 1966.

Cross, K. Patricia. *Accent on Learning.* San Francisco: Jossey-Bass, 1976.

Furth, Hans G. *Piaget for Teachers.* Englewood Cliffs, N.J.: Prentice-Hall, 1970.

Gross, Ronald. *The Lifelong Learner: A Guide to Self-Development.* New York: Simon & Schuster, 1977.

Hilgard, Ernest R., and Bower, Gordon H. *Theories of Learning.* New York: Appleton-Century-Crofts, 1966.

Houle, Cyril O. *Continuing Your Education.* New York: McGraw-Hill, 1964.

———. *The Inquiring Mind.* Madison, Wis.: University of Wisconsin Press, 1961.

Howe, Michael J. A. *Adult Learning: Psychological Research and Applications.* New York: John Wiley & Sons, 1977.

Kidd, J. Roby. *How Adults Learn.* New York: Association Press, 1973.

Knowles, Malcolm S. *Self-Directed Learning: A Guide for Learners and Teachers.* Chicago: Association Press/Follett Publishing Co., 1975.

_____. *The Adult Learner: A Neglected Species.* Houston, Texas: Gulf Publishing Co., 1978.

Knox, Alan B. *Adult Development and Learning.* San Francisco: Jossey-Bass, 1977.

Loevinger, Jane. *Ego Development: Conceptions and Theories.* San Francisco: Jossey-Bass, 1976.

Maslow, Abraham. *Motivation and Personality.* New York: Harper & Row, 1970.

Rogers, Carl R. *Freedom to Learn: A View of What Education Might Become.* Columbus, Ohio: Charles E. Merrill, 1969.

Silberman, Melvin L.; Allender, Jerome S.; and Yanoff, Jay M. *The Psychology of Open Teaching and Learning: An Inquiry Approach.* Boston: Little, Brown, 1972.

Tough, Allen. *The Adult's Learning Projects.* Toronto: Ontario Institute for Studies in Education, 1971.

_____. *Learning Without a Teacher.* Toronto: Ontario Institute for Studies in Education, 1967.

Regarding Lifelong Education

Cropley, A. J. *Lifelong Education: A Psychological Analysis.* New York: Pergamon Press, 1977.

Dave, R. H. *Lifelong Education and School Curriculum.* Mono. No. 1. Hamburg, Germany: UNESCO Institute for Education, 1973.

_____ (ed.). *Reflections on Lifelong Education and the School.* Mono. No. 3. Hamburg, Germany: UNESCO Institute for Education, 1975.

_____. *Foundations of Lifelong Education.* New York: Pergamon Press, 1976.

Draves, William. *The Free University: A Model for Lifelong Learning.* Chicago: Association Press/Follett, 1980.

Faure, Edgar, et al. *Learning to Be: The World of Education Today and Tomorrow.* Paris: UNESCO, 1972.

Hesburg, T. M.; Miller, P. A.; and Wharton, C. R., Jr. *Patterns for Lifelong Learning.* San Francisco: Jossey-Bass, 1973.

Husen, Torsten. *The Learning Society.* New York: Harper & Row, 1974.

Jessup, Frank W. (ed.). *Lifelong Learning: A Symposium on Continuing Education.* New York: Pergamon Press, 1969.

Lengrad, Paul. *An Introduction to Lifelong Learning.* London: Croom Helm, 1975.

Ohliger, John, and McCarthy, Colleen. *Lifelong Learning or Lifelong Schooling?* Syracuse, N.Y.: Syracuse University Press, 1971.

Peterson, Richard, et al. *Lifelong Learning in America.* San Francisco: Jossey-Bass, 1979.

Regarding New Delivery Systems

Bailey, S. K., and Macy, F. U. *Regional Learning Services: A Design for Educational Flexibility.* Syracuse, N.Y.: Policy Institute of Syracuse University Research Corporation, 1973.

Basking, Samuel (ed.). *Organizing Nontraditional Study.* New Directions for Institutional Research, No. 4. San Francisco: Jossey-Bass, 1974.

Berte, Neal R. *Individualizing Education by Learning Contracts.* New Directions for Higher Education, No. 10. San Francisco: Jossey-Bass, 1975.

Chickering, Arthur W. *An Introduction to Experiential Learning*. New Rochelle, N.Y.: Change Magazine Press, 1977.

Commission on Non-Traditional Study. *Diversity by Design*. San Francisco: Jossey-Bass, 1973.

Cross, K. Patricia. *The Missing Link: Connecting Adult Learners to Learning Resources*. Princeton, N.J.: College Board Publications, 1979.

Cross, K. Patricia, and Valley, John R. (eds.). *Planning Non-Traditional Programs*. San Francisco: Jossey-Bass, 1974.

Gould, Samuel B., and Cross, K. Patricia. *Explorations in Non-Traditional Study*. San Francisco: Jossey-Bass, 1972.

Harman, David (ed.). *Expanding Recurrent and Nonformal Education*. New Directions for Higher Education, No. 14. San Francisco: Jossey-Bass, 1976.

Hartnett, R. T., et al. *The British Open University in the United States*. Princeton, N.J.: Educational Testing Service, 1974.

Heffernan, James M.; Macy, Francis U.; and Vickers, Donn F. *Educational Brokering: A New Service for Adult Learners*. Syracuse, N.Y.: National Center for Educational Brokering, 1976.

Houle, Cyril O. *The External Degree*. San Francisco: Jossey-Bass, 1973.

Keeton, Morris T., and Tate, Pamela J. *A Boom in Experiential Learning*. New Directions for Experiential Learning, No. 1. San Francisco: Jossey-Bass, 1978.

Keeton, Morris, et al. *Experiential Learning: Rationale, Characteristics, and Assessment*. San Francisco: Jossey-Bass, 1976.

Miller, Ronald, et al. *Planning for a Statewide Educational Information Network*. Princeton, N.J.: College Board Publications, 1978.

Milton, Ohmer. *Alternatives to the Traditional*. San Francisco: Jossey-Bass, 1973.

Perry, Walter. *The Open University*. San Francisco: Jossey-Bass, 1977.

Rust, Val D. *Alternatives in Education: Historical and Theoretical Perspectives*. Beverly Hills, Cal.: Sage Publications, 1977.

Sarason, Seymour B., et al. *Human Services and Resource Networks*. San Francisco: Jossey-Bass, 1977.

Sarason, Seymour B., and Lorentz, Elizabeth. *The Challenge of the Resource Exchange Network*. San Francisco: Jossey-Bass, 1979.

3
What Is the Role and Mission of the Adult Educator?

What Is an Adult?

I am often asked, especially by teachers in high schools, community colleges, universities, and professional schools, "How do you define 'adult' when you talk about adult education?"

There are, of course, many definitions in current usage. There is the dictionary definition: "fully developed and mature: GROWN-UP" (*Webster's New Collegiate Dictionary*, 1973, p. 17). But this isn't very helpful in the absence of definitions of "fully developed," "mature," and "grown-up." Then there is the physiological definition: achievement of the ability to reproduce—which varies from era to era, culture to culture, and individual to individual (and probably from sex to sex). And there are various legal definitions—voting age, driving age, drinking age, juvenile delinquent versus adult criminal age, age of consent, and the like. But there is a wide variation among governments and eras in these definitions, as well.

From the point of view of determining what individuals should be treated as adults educationally, it seems to me the two critical questions that should be asked are: 1) who behaves as an adult—who performs adult roles? (a social definition) and also 2) whose self-concept is that of an adult? (a psychological definition). Both questions can probably be answered only as a matter of degree. Applying the first criterion, a person is adult to the extent that that individual is performing social roles typically assigned by our culture to those it considers to be adults—the roles of worker, spouse, parent, responsible citizen, soldier, and the like. Applying the second criterion, a person is adult to the extent that that individual perceives herself or himself to be essentially responsible for her or his own life.

We have a holdover from a long tradition, however, that complicates this picture, which is that historically the role of student has been defined as a role appropriate for childhood and youth. Accordingly, many of the policies, rules and regulations, entrance requirements, financial arrangements, physical facilities, curricula, instructional strategies, and graduation requirements of our educational institutions are geared to the characteristics of children and youth. As adults have returned to academia in increasing numbers to study part-time while working or homemaking full-time, they have experienced culture shock in being treated as children.

Furthermore, even children and youth are likely to be adult to some degree. A high school student who is working part-time or taking care of the household of an ill parent or editing a school newspaper is performing adult roles to a degree. And many youth are taking a high degree of responsibility for their own lives outside of school and resent being given little responsibility for their lives in school.

What Is Adult Education?

People have little difficulty getting a clear picture of what elementary education is (it is what goes on in the red brick building with little children) or what secondary education is (it is what goes on with adolescents in those bigger buildings near the football stadium) or what higher education is (it is what goes on in those enormous college and university complexes, with youth). But adult education is much harder to picture. It takes place in all sorts of buildings and even in no buildings at all, involves all sorts of people, has no set curriculum, and often isn't even labeled "adult education," but such things as "staff development," "manpower development," "developmental education," "inservice education," "continuing education," "lifelong education," and many others.

One problem contributing to the confusion is that the term "adult education" is used with at least three different meanings. In its broadest sense, the term describes a process—the process of adults learning. In this sense it encompasses practically all experiences of mature men and women by which they acquire new knowledge, understanding, skills, attitudes, interests, or values. It is a process that is used by adults for their self-development, both alone and with others, and it is used by institutions of all kinds for the growth and development of their employees, members, and clients. It is an educational process that is often used in combination with production processes, political processes, or service processes.

In its more technical meaning, "adult education" describes a set of organized activities carried on by a wide variety of institutions for the accomplishment of specific educational objectives. In this sense it encompasses all the organized classes, study groups, lecture series, planned reading programs, guided discussions, conferences, institutes, workshops, and correspondence courses in which American adults engage.

A third meaning combines all these processes and activities into the idea of a movement or field of social practice. In this sense "adult education" brings together into a discrete social system all the individuals, institutions, and associations concerned with the education of adults and perceives them as working toward the common goals of improving the methods and materials of adult learning, extending the opportunities for adults to learn, and advancing the general level of our culture.

Another problem contributing to the confusion is that adult education is such a relatively new field of social practice that it is still in the process of forming an identity that is separate from youth education, social work, counseling, and related fields of social practice. Although the education of adults has been a cultural function since ancient times, it was not until the founding of the American Association for Adult Education in 1926 that adult education was conceived of as a delineated field in this country. Since then the field has been growing and changing so dynamically that it has been almost impossible to keep up with its statistics or its character. Indeed, institutionally sponsored adult education is the fastest growing aspect of our national educational enterprise in the last quarter of this century. And it is growing not only horizontally—reaching a greater and greater proportion of our adult population, but vertically—taking over institutions that heretofore served only youth. In many colleges and universities and in most community colleges, over half of the enrollments are by adults who are working full-time and studying part-time, and those institutions are becoming essentially adult-educational institutions.

Who Is an Adult Educator?

Many more people are adult educators than know they are. If "adult educator" is defined as one who has some responsibility for helping adults to learn, look at how many people in this country are entitled to bear this hallmark:
—hundreds of thousands of program chairmen, education chairmen, and discussion leaders in such voluntary associations as women's clubs, men's clubs, service organizations, religious laymen's organizations, PTA's, professional societies, civic clubs, labor unions, trade associations, farmers' organizations, and the like;
—tens of thousands of executives, training officers, supervisors, and foremen in business and industry, government, and social agencies;
—thousands of teachers, administrators, and group leaders in such educational institutions as public schools, colleges and universities, libraries, and commercial schools;
—hundreds of program directors, writers, and editors in the educational aspects of such mass media as newspapers, magazines, radio, and television;
—a few score full-time, professional adult educators who have been trained specifically for this vocation and who are making their permanent career in it.

But relatively few of this vast corps are conscious that they are performing the increasingly precisely defined role of "adult educator." Few of them are aware that there is a growing body of knowledge and techniques that they can learn to help them perform this role better. The reasons for this condition are not hard to surmise. In the case of the myriad of volunteer leaders, the assignment is to do a specific job in a finite period of time: "to serve as the program chairman of the XYZ club for one year." In the case of the executives and supervisors the assignment tends to be in terms of particular processes in particular companies: "sales manager, Parts Division." In the case of teachers the assignment tends to be in terms of subject matter: "instructor of mathematics." The fact is, though, that to the extent that all of these assignments involve helping other adults to become more competent, they have a common element—what we might call an adult-education component. And to this extent all the people carrying these kinds of assignments are partly adult educators.

What Does an Adult Educator Do?

What are the functions an adult educator performs? To answer this question it is probably necessary to distinguish among several levels of the adult-education role.

At the firing-line level are the teachers, group leaders, and supervisors who work directly with adult learners on a face-to-face basis. Among their functions are: 1) helping the learners diagnose their needs for particular learnings within the scope of the given situation (the diagnostic function); 2) planning with the learners a sequence of experiences that will produce the desired learnings (the planning function); 3) creating conditions that will cause the learners to want to learn (the motivational function); 4) selecting the most effective methods and techniques for producing the desired learnings (the methodological function); 5) providing the human and material resources necessary to produce the desired learnings (the resource function); 6) helping the learners measure the outcomes of the learning experiences (the evaluative function).

At the program-director level are the committee chairmen, training directors, evening-school principals, extension deans, and other administrators who are responsible for planning and operating broad programs consisting of a variety of adult-educational activities. Their functions include: 1) assessing the individual, institutional, and societal needs for adult learning relevant to their organizational settings (the diagnostic function); 2) establishing and managing an organizational structure for the effective development and operation of an adult-education program (the organizational function); 3) formulating objectives to meet the assessed needs and designing a program of activities to achieve these objectives (the planning function); 4) instituting and supervising those procedures required for the effective operation of a program, including recruiting and training leaders and teachers, managing facilities and administrative processes, recruiting students, financing, and interpreting (the administrative function); 5) assessing the effectiveness of the program (the evaluative function).

At the professional-leadership level are the small group of career adult educators who are responsible for such functions as developing new knowledge, preparing materials, inventing new techniques, providing leadership for coordinative organizations, training adult-education workers, and generally promoting the further development of the field of adult education.

What Is the Adult Educator's Mission?

At first sight the mission of the adult educator seems simple: to operate successful educational activities for mature men and women, success being defined in terms of the numbers and enthusiasm of the participants. But a reading of the history of the adult-education movement in this country indicates that the mission of adult educators is much greater than this. In fact, this mission can best be described in relation to satisfying three distinct sets of needs and goals: 1) the needs and goals of individuals, 2) the needs and goals of institutions, and 3) the needs and goals of society.

The Needs and Goals of Individuals

The primary and immediate mission of every adult educator is to help individuals satisfy their needs and achieve their goals. Usually if an individual is asked what these are, he or she will respond in terms of the acquisition of some specific competence, such as "being able to speak in public" or "knowing mathematics." Or the person might go one level of abstraction higher to such objectives as "being able to make more money" or "being able to get along with people better." These, to be sure, are important incentives to learning, but in this book they are treated as "interests" rather than "needs," a distinction that will be discussed more fully in a later chapter. Interests are relevant to the adult educator's technology, but in relation to this mission we are talking about something different and more fundamental—indeed, about something of which individuals are less conscious than they are of their interests. We are talking about the more ultimate needs and goals of human fulfillment.

One such need can be stated negatively as the prevention of obsolescence. This need arises from the fact that most adults alive today were educated in their youth according to the doctrine that learning is primarily a function of youth and that the purpose of education is to supply individuals in their youth with all the knowledge and skills they will require to live adequately for the rest of their lives. But the rapidly accelerating pace of change in our society has proved this doctrine to be no longer valid. Facts learned in youth have become insufficient and in many instances actually untrue; and skills learned in youth have become outmoded by new technologies. Consequently, adult years become years of creeping obsolescence in work, in play, in understanding of self, and in understanding of the world.

The problem is that education is not yet perceived as a lifelong process, so that we are still taught in our youth only what we ought to know then and not how to keep finding out. One mission of the adult educator, then, can be stated positively as helping individuals to develop the attitude that learning *is* a lifelong process and to acquire the skills of self-directed learning. In this sense, one of the tests of everything the adult educator does—whether it be to conduct a course in hatmaking, a human-relations workshop, or a staff meeting—is the extent to which the participants leave a given experience with heightened curiosity and with increased ability to carry on their own learning.[1]

Another ultimate need of individuals is to achieve complete self-identity through the development of their full potentialities. Increasing evidence is appearing in the psychological literature that complete self-development is a universal human need, and that at least a feeling of movement in this direction is a condition of mental health.[2] A. H. Maslow, for example, arranges human needs in the hierarchical order shown in Exhibit 1.

Exhibit 1

MASLOW'S HIERARCHY OF HUMAN NEEDS

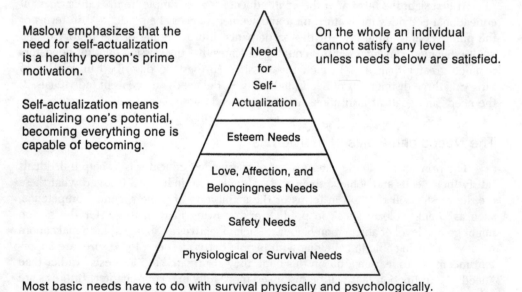

Maslow emphasizes that the need for self-actualization is a healthy person's prime motivation.

Self-actualization means actualizing one's potential, becoming everything one is capable of becoming.

Need for Self-Actualization

On the whole an individual cannot satisfy any level unless needs below are satisfied.

Esteem Needs

Love, Affection, and Belongingness Needs

Safety Needs

Physiological or Survival Needs

Most basic needs have to do with survival physically and psychologically.

---

[1]For an elaboration of this idea, see Cyril O. Houle, *The Inquiring Mind* (Madison, Wis.: University of Wisconsin Press, 1961).

[2]See Gordon Allport, *Becoming: Basic Considerations for a Basic Psychology of Personality* (New Haven: Yale University Press, 1955); Erik H. Erikson, *Childhood and Society* (New York: W. W. Norton, 1950); Kurt Lewin, *A Dynamic Theory of Personality* (New York: McGraw-Hill, 1955); Gardner Murphy, *Human Potentialities* (New York: Basic Books, 1958); and Carl R. Rogers, *On Becoming a Person* (Boston: Houghton Mifflin Co., 1961).

He then proposes the following principles of operation for these needs: 1) gratification for the needs on each level, starting with the lowest, frees a person for higher levels of gratification; 2) those persons in whom a need has been satisfied are best equipped to deal with deprivations of that need in the future; 3) healthy persons are those whose basic needs have been met so that they are principally motivated by their needs to actualize their highest potentialities.[3] This concept implies that the adult educator's mission is to help individuals learn what is required for gratification of their needs at whatever level they are struggling. If they are hungry, we must help them learn what will get them food; if they are well-fed, safe, loved, and esteemed, we must help them explore undeveloped capacities and become their full selves.

A third ultimate need of individuals is to mature. Harry Overstreet equated maturity with "linkages with life" as follows:

> A mature person is not one who has come to a certain level of achievement and stopped there. He is rather a *maturing* person—one whose *linkages with life* are constantly becoming stronger and richer because his attitudes are such as to encourage their growth. . . . A mature person, for example, is not one who knows a large number of facts. Rather, he is one whose mental habits are such that he grows in knowledge and the wise use of it.[4]

The idea of maturity as a goal of education must be defined more specifically than this, however, if it is to serve as a guide to continuous learning. Out of the psychological literature comes the notion that there are several dimensions of the maturing process, each with its own unique cycle of development. If the really critical dimensions of the maturing process could be identified, then adult educators would have some reliable yardsticks against which to measure the accomplishment of their mission. As a starting point, the fifteen dimensions in Exhibit 2 are nominated for consideration. (Note that these dimensions describe directions of growth, not absolute states to be achieved.)

Exhibit 2

DIMENSIONS OF MATURATION

From	Toward
1. Dependence	Autonomy
2. Passivity	Activity
3. Subjectivity	Objectivity
4. Ignorance	Enlightenment
5. Small abilities	Large abilities
6. Few responsibilities	Many responsibilities
7. Narrow interests	Broad interests
8. Selfishness	Altruism
9. Self-rejection	Self-acceptance
10. Amorphous self-identity	Integrated self-identity
11. Focus on particulars	Focus on principles
12. Superficial concerns	Deep concerns
13. Imitation	Originality
14. Need for certainty	Tolerance for ambiguity
15. Impulsiveness	Rationality

[3] A H. Maslow, *Motivation and Personality* (New York: Harper and Brothers, 2nd ed., 1970).
[4] Harry A. Overstreet, *The Mature Mind* (New York: W. W. Norton, 1949), p. 43.

Perhaps the meaning of this conception of dimensions of maturing can be made clearer by brief elaborations on them.

1. *From dependence toward autonomy.* All human beings enter this world in a completely dependent condition; their every need must be fulfilled by someone else. One of the central quests of their lives is for increasing self-direction (although the opposite of dependence in our complicated world may not be independence so much as self-directing interdependence). The fact is that every experience we have in life tends to affect our movement from dependence toward autonomy; and to the extent that a given experience helps us to move away from dependence it can be said to be educational, while to the extent that it tends to keep us dependent or make us more dependent, it can be said to be antieducational. Think of the effects on this dimension of maturing of the traditional conceptions of the roles of teacher, parent, minister, boss, and leader, which tend to put the individual in an essentially dependent role.

2. *From passivity toward activity.* Throughout childhood individuals who are maturing become increasingly active in exploring the world about them and tend to engage in an expanding number of its activities. In adulthood the emphasis is likely to shift from quantitative activity to qualitative activity, but whether on a qualitative basis or a quantitative basis, maturing individuals tend to be participating individuals. And the way they are taught to participate in school and in other educative experiences— whether they are put in the role of passive recipients of knowledge or in that of active inquirers after knowledge—will greatly affect the direction and speed of their movement in this dimension of growth.

3. *From subjectivity toward objectivity.* It is a universal characteristic of infancy that the world revolves around "me," takes on its meaning from "my" perception of it, and is subject to "my" commands. One of the most difficult adjustments people have to make in life is to move themselves out of the center of the universe and to discover where they really fit into it. The extent to which each experience in life helps them to look at themselves realistically, and to maintain self-respect in the process, is certainly one of the tests of its educational quality.

4. *From ignorance toward enlightenment.* It is in this area of maturing that schooling has traditionally placed its emphasis. But are we clear about what "enlightenment" really is? Certainly it can't be knowing everything—the volume of modern knowledge is too vast for any individual to encompass it. In his *Some Things Worth Knowing*, Stuart Chase poses this as one of the most pressing problems our civilization must solve, and he suggests one possible line of attack. He proposes that every individual should be perceived as being both a specialist and a generalist. As specialists, people need to master deeply the knowledge and skills of their vocation. But as generalists they need to master and keep up to date on a core of knowledge from all those specialities that bear on the practical problems of life—thus suggesting a kind of "core curriculum" for adult education, which would consist of a distillation of the essential elements from every discipline that all citizens should know. Only through such a process as this, Chase argues, can true enlightenment be achieved.

5. *From small abilities toward large abilities.* There is a tendency in human nature, once we have learned to do something well, to take pride in that ability and to rest on the laurels it wins us. Since each newly developed ability tends to be learned in its simplest form, this tendency can result in individuals becoming frozen into the lowest level of their potential performance. A skillful facilitator of learning helps each individual to glimpse higher possible levels of performance and to develop continually larger abilities.

6. *From few responsibilities toward many responsibilities.* Another curious tendency in human nature, especially among parents, teachers, and supervisors, is to underestimate the amount of responsibility a child, student, and subordinate can carry. And so the maturation process is frequently retarded by the parent retaining responsibility the child is prepared to take over, the teacher making decisions the students are ready to make, and the supervisor carrying functions the subordinates are ready to have delegated to them.

7. *From narrow interests toward broad interests.* The child's world starts with a field of interests that is bounded by the crib, and one significant sign of a person's continuing maturation is the extension of this field in ever-widening circles for the rest of life. Anything that causes an individual's field of interests to become fixated within a given circle or to recede to smaller circles is interfering with an important dimension of maturation. This dimension has special relevance to work with older people, in which the myth is widely held that it is natural for interests to diminish with age. Gerontologists who have made the opposite assumption—that older people are able to develop new interests and are healthier if they do—have had spectacular results.

8. *From selfishness toward altruism.* We come into the world in a state of total self-centeredness, and one of our central tasks for the rest of our lives is to become increasingly able to care about others. Conditions that induce a spirit of rivalry toward others rather than helpfulness toward others—such as the competition for grades promoted by traditional schooling—interfere with maturation in this dimension. Incidentally, there are some psychiatrists (e.g., Franz Alexander) who hold that altruism is the single best criterion of mental health.

9. *From self-rejection toward self-acceptance.* While children's first impression of themselves is probably that they are kings or queens of the mountain, they soon learn that much of their natural behavior (making noise, getting into things, not eating correctly, etc.) is "bad." And so their attitude quickly changes from one of self-adulation to one of self-rejection. But mature persons are those who accept themselves as persons of worth (which, incidentally, is a prerequisite to being able to accept others as having worth). And so the extent to which subsequent life experiences help the individual move from self-rejection toward self-acceptance will largely determine whether an individual matures in this dimension or not.

10. *From amorphous self-identity toward integrated self-identity.* Erik Erikson has provided the deepest insights concerning this dimension of maturation, mapping out its course through the "eight ages of man," as follows:

   a) *Oral-sensory,* in which the basic issue is trust vs. mistrust.
   b) *Muscular-anal,* in which the basic issue is autonomy vs. shame.
   c) *Locomotion-genital,* in which the basic issue is initiative vs. guilt.
   d) *Latency,* in which the basic issue is industry vs. inferiority.
   e) *Puberty and adolescence,* in which the basic issue is identity vs. role confusion.
   f) *Young adulthood,* in which the basic issue is intimacy vs. isolation.
   g) *Adulthood,* in which the basic issue is generativity vs. stagnation.
   h) *Maturity,* in which the basic issue is ego-integrity vs. despair.[5]

Although no stage is completely fulfilled at any point in life—and we continue to actualize each stage further throughout life—if development in a given stage is mostly

---

[5]Erik H. Erikson, *Childhood and Society* (New York: W. W. Norton, 1950), p. 273. See also his *Identity and the Life Cycle,* International Universities Press, *Psychological Issues,* Vol. 1, No. 1 (1959).

frustrated, an individual is likely to remain fixated at that stage. Erikson's concepts of the process of identity formation are far too complex and provocative to be described in this book. But perhaps this taste is sufficient to indicate that the dimension of maturation from "I don't know who I am" toward "I know clearly who I am" is a delicate and crucial one.

11. *From focus on particulars toward focus on principles.* To a child's mind each object is unique and each event is unconnected with any other. The discovery of principles enabling a person to group objects and connect events is the essence of the process of inquiry. One of the tragic aspects of traditional pedagogy is that it has so often imposed principles on inquiring minds and has therefore denied them the opportunity to mature in the ability to discover principles.

12. *From superficial concerns toward deep concerns.* The young child's world is an existential world; all that matters is the enjoyment of pleasure and the avoidance of pain at the moment. One dimension of maturing consists of gaining perspective on what mattered more deeply in our past and is likely to matter more deeply in our future—and, having accomplished this feat, gaining perspective on what matters in the past and future of others. Too often this process is retarded by society's trying to impose its deep concerns on us before we have discovered our own.

13. *From imitation toward originality.* The child's first technique of learning and adapting is that of imitation. The adult world has long tended to accept this method of learning as not only natural but *best*, and has geared much of its educational system to produce conformity through imitation. The consequence has been the retardation of generations of human beings in their maturation toward the more self-fulfilling end of this dimension, originality.

14. *From the need for certainty toward tolerance for ambiguity.* The basic insecurity of the child's world imposes a deep need for certainty. Only as our experiences in life provide us with an increasing sense of security and self-confidence will we be able to move in the direction of a mature tolerance for ambiguity—a prerequisite for survival in a world of ambiguity.

15. *From impulsiveness toward rationality.* Traditionally, the naturally impulsive behaviors of children have been controlled through systems of reward and punishment—with emphasis on the latter. Too often the consequence of this policy is reactions of irrationality—rebellion, withdrawal, and fantasy. True maturing toward rationality requires self-understanding and self-control of one's impulses.

Perhaps there are other dimensions of the maturing process that ought to be added or that ought to replace some of these dimensions, and certainly, until further research is done on this important aspect of human development, we shall have to regard any such formulation as highly tentative. Meantime, the general notion that one of the missions of the adult educator is to assist individuals to continue a maturing process throughout life provides some useful guidelines for the development of a sequential, continuous, and integrated program of lifelong learning.

A few implications of this multidimensional theory of maturation can be suggested to illustrate this point:

1) Every educational activity provides an opportunity for growth by each individual in *several* dimensions. For example, although focusing on stimulating growth toward increased enlightenment, a course on world affairs can be planned so as to stimulate growth toward greater independence of thought, broader interests, greater objectivity, and tolerance for ambiguity.

2) The dimensions of maturation tend to be interdependent, so that changes in one dimension have an effect on other dimensions. For example, considerable growth toward enlightenment might be produced by methods (such as those used in the traditional lecture course) which cause the student to become increasingly dependent on the teacher. Although a choice may sometimes have to be made between such values, a truly artistic teacher will try to induce positive growth in all dimensions.

3) All human beings move on a scale from zero to infinity in each dimension throughout life, and tend to incorporate learning from a given experience in proportion to its relevance to their stage of development on the scale at that moment. For example, in a group of fifteen adult students, the individuals would be ready to take fifteen different degrees of responsibility for their own learning; and if the learning experience is to be optimally useful, provision must be made for this range of differences.

No doubt other ultimate needs could be identified, but these serve to illustrate the point that the adult educator's mission in helping individuals is far more complex and significant than it might appear on the surface. Perhaps the classic summary of individual needs and goals that define the adult educators' mission and challenge their art is contained in these words of Eduard Lindeman:

> In what areas do most people appear to find life's meaning? We have only one pragmatic guide: meaning must reside in the things for which people strive, the goals which they set for themselves, their wants, needs, desires, and wishes. Even here our criterion is applicable only to those whose lives are already dedicated to aspirations and ambitions which belong to the higher levels of human achievement. . . . Viewed from the standpoint of adult education, such personalities seem to want among other things, intelligence, power, self-expression, freedom, creativity, appreciation, enjoyment, fellowship. Or, stated in terms of the Greek ideal, they are searchers after the good life. They want to count for something; they want their experiences to be vivid and meaningful; they want their talents to be utilized; they want to know beauty and joy; and they want all of these realizations of their total personalities to be shared in communities of fellowship. Briefly they want to improve themselves; this is their realistic and primary aim. But they want also to change the social order so that vital personalities will be creating a new environment in which their aspirations may be properly expressed.[6]

The Needs and Goals of Institutions

Much adult education takes place under the auspices of institutions, and adult educators are employed by institutions. These institutions, too, have needs and goals that help to define the adult educator's mission. At least three sets of these needs and goals can be served, and in some ways served best, by adult-educational means:

1. *The development of individuals in the institution's constituency in the direction of the institution's goals for them.* Most institutions with adults in their constituencies have some sort of image of the kind of people they want to influence their members to become. For example, labor unions want their members to understand and support the cause of unionism, appreciate its historical role, participate effectively in the activities of their union, understand their legal rights and obligations, exert influence on public policy, be wise consumers, and enjoy the cultural life of their communities. Religious institutions have various ways of describing their goals for their members, but they

---

6Eduard C. Lindeman, *The Meaning of Adult Education* (Montreal: Harvest House, 1961), pp. 13–14. By permission.

tend to converge on a conception of "committed" members who believe and live according to the creed propounded by the institution. A public school's image for its adult constituents is likely to be flavored by such symbols as "responsible citizen," "efficient worker," or "good parent"; that of a university, by "intellectual leader" or "professional leader"; that of a trade association, by "industrial statesman"; and so on. Institutional leaders expect adult-educational programs to help to produce these kinds of qualities in their constituents, and they evaluate the programs at least partly on the basis of their effectiveness in doing so.

Even in institutions whose constituents are primarily children and youth, adult education is perceived as an instrument for helping them improve the quality of education of the young. Public schools, for example, are devoting increasing energy to improving the educative quality of the home environments of their children through courses, study groups, and lecture series on child development and home and family living for parents, parental counseling, and extracurricular activities for parents and children together. Many voluntary youth agencies, such as the Boy Scouts, Girl Scouts, YMCA and YWCA, Sunday schools, and 4-H clubs, perceive the training of volunteer adult leaders as the critical element in their accomplishing their character-building goals with youth.

Not infrequently the needs and interests of individuals come into conflict with the needs and interests of their institutions, as when a member develops an independence of thought that contradicts the established doctrine of the institution. In such cases the adult educator may have to make a choice as to which mission to serve: helping individuals to grow or helping the institution to survive. Increasingly, however, adult educators are resolving such conflicts between education and indoctrination by taking the institution as their client and helping its leaders to engage in a process of self-study, as a result of which the institution's educational goals are often broadened to provide wider areas of freedom for individual growth.

2. *The improvement of institutional operation.* A growing number of institutions—especially in industry and government—have come to recognize that one of the most efficient means for increasing the effectiveness of their operation is the continuing education of their employees. This recognition has reached such a point in industry, in fact, as to move two serious students of the phenomenon to describe the educational activities of American industry as a third great educational force on a par with our public school and higher-education systems.[7]

What industry has discovered is equally applicable to every other institution—namely, that adult-education processes are basic tools of organizational growth and development. These processes are now used routinely for the orientation of new employees, for on-the-job training in technical skills, for the preparation of personnel for advancement, for executive development, for supervisory training, for the improvement of interpersonal relations within the organization, and for the improvement of the institution's public relations. Increasingly these same processes are coming to be used for the planning and guiding of long-run institutional change.

One of the missions of adult educators, then, is to help institutions become increasingly effective as institutions. In this sense, institutions are their clients as well as

---

[7]Harold F. Clark and Harold S. Sloan, *Classroom in the Factories* (Rutherford, N.J.: Fairleigh Dickinson University, 1958).

individuals, and part of their art is helping various target populations within institutions—governing boards, administrators, supervisors, departmental personnel, members, and the like—to learn new behaviors that will produce stronger institutions. In carrying out this mission adult educators may take the role of direct instructor or trainer, but more frequently their role will be that of planner, consultant, or "change agent"—a specialized role to which modern adult-education literature is devoting increasing attention.

3. *The development of public understanding and involvement.* An institution can build good public relations through either a Madison Avenue type of sales approach or through involving its public in the serious study of public needs, problems, and goals. Although each approach has its place, the adult-educational approach tends to produce deeper and more lasting understanding and caring.

In the case of public schools, for example, it is ironic that although one of the first contributions of adult education was the education of the public about childhood education,[8] this potentially invaluable function was largely neglected until the past few years. During the years following World War II, when expanding enrollments and rising costs were causing school budgets to be scrutinized critically by the various watchdogs of the public treasuries, school superintendents in a number of cities found that their most effective supporters came from among the adult citizens who had participated in their evening programs for adults. But the Seattle Public Schools proved in a dramatic experiment in 1957–58 that adult education processes were even more effective in mobilizing public support when used directly for this purpose. After a series of setbacks in school-levy elections in the early 1950s, in spite of all-out publicity campaigns, a Citizens School Levy Committee in 1957 organized a citywide program of citizen conferences and study groups in which information about the needs and program of the schools was presented and discussed. When the school levy was again presented to the people in March, 1958, it was approved—a result credited largely to the educational approach taken.[9]

The periodical literature of adult education contains other reports of the use of adult-education processes to produce public understanding of such diverse institutions as the armed services (exhibits, documentary films, guided tours), universities (public lectures, cultural events, citizen advisory councils), the March of Dimes (which preceded its nationwide campaign of Salk vaccination with community-by-community educational programs), and the United States National Commission for UNESCO (which sponsored nationwide citizen discussion programs). In general, these programs succeeded in producing real public understanding to the extent that they were informative rather than indoctrinational and to the extent that they involved citizens in meaningful participation in the work of the institution.

It is a legitimate mission of adult educators to use their art to bring about a better understanding of their institutions, but theirs is a mission requiring the highest ethical commitment, for the line of demarcation between education and propaganda is a fine one.

---

[8]The lyceum movement, which flourished in the 1830s, had as its objective "the advancement of education, especially in the common schools." It succeeded in mobilizing public opinion in favor of tax-supported public schools. See Carl Bode, *The American Lyceum* (New York: Oxford University Press, 1956).

[9]See Donald Nylen and Dale Coss, "We Heard a Knock at the Door," *Adult Leadership*, Vol. vii (September, 1958), pp. 61–69.

The Needs and Goals of Society

Every society has used adult-education processes to continue the development of the kind of citizens visualized to be required for the maintenance and progress of that society; and the perception of the kind of adult required is different for each society. For example, the perception in Soviet society is quite different from the perception in Western society; the perception in urban society is different from that in rural society; the perception in Jewish society is different in some respects from the perception in Catholic or Protestant societies; the perception in professional society is different from that in industrial society; and so on. The challenging fact is that adult educators are the agents of several different societies whose needs they are expected to serve simultaneously. And one of the measures of their artistry is the extent to which they are able to understand and serve these differing needs.

But there are more general needs of American society, perhaps even of world society, that define an even broader mission for the adult educator.

A society whose central dynamic change—economic and technological, political, social, cultural, and even theological—requires a citizenry that is able to change.[10]

A society whose elements—geographic, economic, intellectual—are becoming increasingly complex and interdependent requires a citizenry with broader knowledge, less parochial values, more tolerant attitudes, and greater skill in human relations than past societies demanded.

A society in which machinery is doing more and more of the work of man requires a citizenry capable of performing increasingly complicated occupational roles and capable of creatively using more leisure time.

A society in which gaps between people (youth vs. adult, black vs. white, East vs. West, rich vs. poor) are becoming better defined and less tolerable requires a citizenry that is liberated from traditional prejudices and is able to establish open, empathic, and collaborative relationships with people of all sorts.

A strong case can be made for the proposition that the greatest danger to the survival of civilization today is not atomic warfare, not environmental pollution, not the population explosion, not the depletion of natural resources, and not any of the other contemporary crises, but the underlying cause of them all—the accelerating obsolescence of man. The evidence is mounting that man's ability to cope with a changing world is lagging farther and farther behind the changing world. The only hope now seems to be a crash program to retool the present generation of adults with the competencies required to function adequately in a condition of perpetual change. This is the deep need—the awesome challenge—presented to the adult educator by modern society.

The Changing and Challenging Role of Adult Educators

As the mission of adult educators has become more complex and more significant, the character of their role has been gradually changing. The demands on them to prepare more carefully for performing the role have increased proportionately.

---

[10]See *Daedalus,* "Toward the Year 2,000," Vol. 96, No. 3 (Summer, 1967); John Gardner, *Self-Renewal* (New York: Harper & Row, 1963); Donald A. Schon, *Beyond the Stable State* (New York: W. W. Norton, 1971); Alvin Toffler, *Future Shock* (New York: Random House, 1970).

For many years it was assumed that the principles and techniques used in the education of children would be equally effective in helping adults learn. People were therefore recruited to direct institutional programs of adult education on the basis of having had experience in directing programs of youth education; teachers of children were recruited as teachers of adults; and it was taken for granted that any reasonably well-educated person would know how to do a good job as program chairman or study-group leader of a voluntary organization.

But as knowledge accumulated both from experience and from research in adult education and related social sciences, it became increasingly apparent that adults were more than just grown-up children, that they possessed certain unique characteristics as learners that required different principles and techniques from those employed with children. And with this new knowledge, which the rest of this book is concerned with describing, came the insight that good adult educators don't just happen; they become good by learning these principles and techniques. As a result, the role of adult educator has moved gradually away from that of willing amateur toward that of trained specialist, and opportunities have multiplied for the requisite training to be obtained at all levels: for the firing-line leaders and teachers, through short-term institutes and literature; for program directors, through summer workshops, courses, and literature; and for professional leaders, through master's and doctoral programs in graduate schools of education.

Another way in which the role of adult educators has been changing is in its basic theoretical conception.

Initially, adult educators were conceived loosely as "those who educate adults," in the sense of transmitting knowledge to them, telling them what they ought to know, or at best enticing them to learn. Their clientele was perceived as consisting mostly of underprivileged adults, and their function was perceived as being primarily remedial—helping individuals catch up to the average. In recent years, however, adult educators are referred to increasingly in the literature as "change agents" and as performing "helping roles." Their clientele is perceived as consisting of all types of individuals (indeed, it is the better-educated persons who now predominate in adult-education enrollments), institutions, and communities. Their function has moved increasingly away from being remedial toward being developmental—toward helping their clients achieve full potential.

As agents of change their responsibilities now extend far beyond the routine scheduling of activities in response to cursory expressions of interest. Their responsibilities entail, rather, the involvement of clients in a penetrating analysis of higher aspirations and the changes required to achieve them, the diagnosis of obstacles that must be overcome in achieving these changes, and the planning of an effective strategy for accomplishing the desired results. Their part in this process is that of helper, guide, encourager, consultant, and resource—not that of transmitter, disciplinarian, judge, and authority. They recognize that it is less important that their clients know the right answers to the questions they think are important than that the clients know how to ask the important questions and find the answers for themselves. Their ultimate objective is to help people grow in the ability to learn, to help people become mature selves.

I can illustrate at least some of the dimensions in this shift in role from my own career as an adult educator. When I entered the field in 1935 my role as a program administrator was defined as a manager of logistics—one who conducted surveys to determine the needs and interests of individuals, who organized classes for groups of individuals and found instructors for them, who scheduled them into rooms at specified times, who developed brochures and other promotional materials to recruit students for them, who built a budget to assure that income would at least equal expenses, and who evaluated them through easy-to-score questionnaires. And my role as a teacher of adults was defined as one who decided what the students should learn, how and when they would learn it (primarily through my lectures), and if they had learned it. As the years have gone by I have found less and less of my time as a program administrator being spent in managing logistics and more and more of it being spent serving as a consultant to larger social systems—corporations, educational institutions, government agencies, religious denominations, voluntary organizations—helping them build total environments more conducive to human growth and development. And during these same years I have found that in my role as a teacher of adults I have spent less and less of my time deciding what students should learn and then transmitting it to them, and more and more of my time helping them discover for themselves what they need to learn and then helping them find and use the most effective resources (including my resources) for learning those things.

These are entirely new roles, requiring entirely different skills, knowledge, attitudes, and values from those of the traditional educator. But it is now becoming clear that they are required to fulfill the new mission of adult education—to develop a total environment conducive to human growth and self-actualization; to create an educative society.

For Your Continuing Inquiry . . .

Regarding What Is Adult Education

Axford, Roger W. *Adult Education: The Open Door*. Scranton, Pa.: International Textbook Co., 1969.

Bryson, Lyman. *Adult Education*. New York: American Book Co., 1936.

Dobbs, Ralph C. *Adult Education in America*. Cassville, Mo.: Litho Printers, 1971.

Elias, John, and Merriam, Sharan. *Philosophical Foundations of Adult Education*. Huntington, N.Y.: Krieger Publishing Co., 1979.

Grattan, C. Hartley. *In Quest of Knowledge: A Historical Perspective of Adult Education*. New York: Association Press, 1955.

Johnstone, John W. C., and Rivera, William. *Volunteers for Learning: A Study of the Educational Pursuits of American Adults*. Chicago: Aldine Publishing Co., 1965.

Knowles, Malcolm S. *The Adult Education Movement in the United States*. 2nd ed. Huntington, N.Y.: Krieger Publications, 1977.

Smith, Robert, et al. *Handbook of Adult Education in the United States*. New York: Macmillan, 1970.

Regarding the Role and Mission of the Adult Educator

Craig, R. L. (ed.). *Training and Development Handbook*. 2nd ed. New York: McGraw-Hill, 1976.

Cross, K. Patricia. *The Missing Link: Connecting Adult Learners to Learning Resources*. Princeton, N.J.: College Board Publications, 1979.

Cross, K. Patricia, and Valley, John R. (eds.). *Planning Nontraditional Programs*. San Francisco: Jossey-Bass, 1974.

Faure, Edgar, et al. *Learning to Be: The World of Education Today and Tomorrow*. Paris: UNESCO, 1972.

Gould, Samuel, et al. *Diversity by Design.* San Francisco: Jossey-Bass, 1973.

Heffernan, James M., et al. *Educational Brokering: A New Service for Adult Learners.* Syracuse, N.Y.: National Center for Educational Brokering, 1976.

Hesburgh, T. M., et al. *Patterns for Lifelong Learning.* San Francisco: Jossey-Bass, 1973.

Houle, Cyril O. *The External Degree.* San Francisco: Jossey-Bass, 1973.

Jensen, Gale, et al. *Adult Education: Outlines of an Emerging Field of University Study.* Washington, D.C.: Adult Education Association of the U.S.A., 1964.

Keeton, Morris T., and Tate, Pamela J. *A Boom in Experiential Learning.* New Directions for Experiential Learning, No. 1. San Francisco: Jossey-Bass, 1978.

Nadler, Leonard. *Developing Human Resources.* Houston: Gulf Publishing Co., 1970.

Peterson, Richard E., et al. *Lifelong Learning in America.* San Francisco: Jossey-Bass, 1979.

Rust, Val. D. *Alternatives in Education: Historical and Theoretical Perspectives.* Beverly Hills, Cal.: Sage Publications, 1977.

Shaw, Nathan. *Administration of Continuing Education.* Washington, D.C.: National Association for Public and Continuing Education, 1969.

Vermilye, Dyckman W. (ed.). *Lifelong Learners: A New Clientele for Higher Education.* San Francisco: Jossey-Bass, 1974.

Regarding the Adult Educator As Change Agent

Arends, Richard I., and Arends, Jane H. *System Change Strategies in Educational Settings.* New York: Human Sciences Press, 1977.

Argyris, Chris. *Intervention Theory and Method.* Reading, Mass.: Addison-Wesley, 1970.

Bell, Chip R., and Nadler, Leonard. *The Client-Consultant Handbook.* Houston: Gulf Publishing Co., 1979.

Bennis, Warren; Benne, Kenneth; and Chin, Robert. *The Planning of Change.* New York: Holt, Rinehart & Winston, 1968.

Carkhuff, Robert R. *Helping and Human Relations.* New York: Holt, Rinehart & Winston, 1969.

Combs, A. W., et al. *Helping Relationships: Basic Concepts for the Helping Professions.* 2nd ed. Rockleigh, N.J.: Allyn & Bacon, 1978.

Eiben, Ray, and Milliren, Al (eds.). *Educational Change: A Humanistic Approach.* La Jolla, Cal.: University Associates, 1976.

Lippitt, Gordon. *Organization Renewal.* New York: Appleton-Century-Crofts, 1969.

Lippitt, Gordon, and Lippitt, Ronald. *The Consulting Process in Action.* La Jolla, Cal.: University Associates, 1978.

Schein, Edgar. *Process Consultation: Its Role in Organization Development.* Reading, Mass.: Addison-Wesley, 1969.

4
What Is Andragogy?

In the Beginning Was Pedagogy

Until recently there was only one model of assumptions about learning and the characteristics of learners on which educators could base their curricula and teaching practices. It evolved in the monastic schools of Europe between the seventh and twelfth centuries and came to dominate secular schools when they were organized in the twelfth century and universities when they began emerging, first in Bologna and Paris, toward the close of the twelfth century. This was the model of *pedagogy*—a term derived from the Greek words *paid* (meaning "child") and *agogus* (meaning "leading"). So "pedagogy" means, literally, the art and science of teaching children.

The pedagogical assumptions about learning and learners were, therefore, based initially on observations by the monks in teaching very young children relatively simple skills—originally mostly reading and writing. With the spread of elementary schools throughout Europe and North America—and much of the rest of the world, especially by missionaries—in the eighteenth and nineteenth centuries this model was adopted and reinforced. And when educational psychologists started scientifically studying learning around the turn of the twentieth century they further contributed to the enthronement of the pedagogical model by limiting their research mostly to the reactions of children and animals to didactic teaching. In fact, as we shall see later, we didn't get much knowledge about *learning* (in contrast to reactions to teaching) until studies on adult learning began to appear after World War II.

When adult education began to be organized systematically during the 1920s, teachers of adults began experiencing several problems with the pedagogical model.

One problem was that pedagogy was premised on a conception of the purpose of education—namely, the transmittal of knowledge and skills that had stood the test of time—that adult learners seemed to sense was insufficient. Accordingly, their teachers found them to be resistant frequently to the strategies that pedagogy prescribed, including fact-laden lectures, assigned readings, drill, quizzes, rote memorizing, and examinations. Adults appeared to want something more than this, and drop-out rates were high.

Although the teachers were not aware of it, one of the great philosophers of this century, Alfred North Whitehead, was suggesting what was wrong. In an obscure footnote he pointed out that it was appropriate to define education as a process of transmittal of what is known only when the time-span of major cultural change was greater than the life-span of individuals. Under this condition, what people learn in their youth will remain valid and useful for the rest of their lives. But, Whitehead emphasized, "We are living in the first period in human history for which this assumption is false . . . today this time-span is considerably shorter than that of human life, and accordingly our training must prepare individuals to face a novelty of conditions."[1] An attempt is made in Exhibit 3 to portray Whitehead's concept graphically.

Exhibit 3

THE RELATIONSHIP OF THE TIME-SPAN OF SOCIAL CHANGE
TO INDIVIDUAL LIFE-SPAN

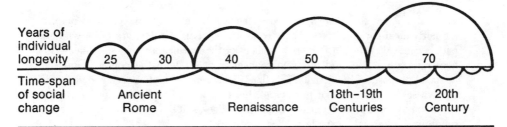

Years of individual longevity	25	30	40	50	70
Time-span of social change	Ancient Rome		Renaissance	18th–19th Centuries	20th Century

Note that up to the early part of the twentieth century the time-span of major cultural change (e.g., massive inputs of new knowledge, technological innovation, vocational displacement, population mobility, change in political and economic systems, etc.) extended over several generations, whereas in the twentieth century several cultural revolutions have already occurred and the pace is accelerating. Under this new condition, knowledge gained at any point of time is largely obsolete within a matter of years; and skills that made people productive in their twenties become out-of-date in their thirties. So it is no longer functional to define education as a process of transmitting what is known; it must now be defined as a lifelong process of continuing inquiry. And so the most important learning of all—for both children and adults—is learning how to learn, the skills of self-directed inquiry.

Another problem the teachers of adults experienced with the pedagogical model was that many of the assumptions about the characteristics of learners did not seem to fit their adult students. And so they began experimenting with different assumptions and found out that they often produced better results.

Then Came Andragogy

Between 1929 and 1948 the *Journal of Adult Education*, published by the American Association for Adult Education, carried articles by successful teachers of adults[2] describing ways in which they were treating adults that deviated from the pedagogical model. Frequently the authors of these articles expressed a sense of guilt for violating academic standards (such as substituting interviews for quizzes). Obviously, they were feeling guilty because they had no theory to support their practices; they were simply being pragmatic and following their intuitions.

During the 1950s there began appearing books which analyzed these teachers' reports and extracted principles that were common to them—my first book, *Informal*

---

[1]Alfred N. Whitehead, "Introduction," Wallace B. Donham, *Business Adrift* (New York: McGraw-Hill Book Co., 1931), pp. viii–xix.

[2]"Successful teachers of adults" is operationally defined as teachers who can retain their students; note that this is not a criterion of success for teachers of children under compulsory attendance.

Adult Education, published in 1950, was just such a listing of principles, but it made no attempt to envelop them in a unifying theory.

Then, in the 1960s, we began getting findings from scientifically designed research that focused on the internal processes of adult learning. The seminal study that launched this direction of movement was Cyril O. Houle's *The Inquiring Mind,* published by the University of Wisconsin Press in 1961. Houle found, through in-depth interviews with twenty-two "continuing learners," that his subjects fell into three subgroups:

> The first, . . . the *goal-oriented,* are those who use education as a means of accomplishing fairly clear-cut objectives. The second, the *activity-oriented,* are those who take part because they find in the circumstances of the learning a meaning which has no necessary connection, and often no connection at all, with the content or the announced purposes of the activity. The third, the *learning-oriented,* seek knowledge for its own sake. These are not pure types; the best way to represent them pictorially would be by three circles which overlap their edges. But the central emphasis of each subgroup is clearly discernible.[3]

One of Houle's students, Allen Tough, extended this line of investigation from his position on the faculty of the Ontario Institute for Studies in Education later in the same decade. Tough's research question was, paraphrased: "How do adults learn naturally—when they are not being taught." His first findings, reported in two reports, *Learning Without a Teacher* (1967) and *The Adult's Learning Projects* (1971), showed that 1) almost all adults engage in from one to twenty major learning projects each year—with the average number being around eight; 2) only about 10 percent of the learning projects were associated with educational institutions; 3) there is a fairly universal "natural" process of learning—adults who undertake to learn something on their own go through a similar sequence of steps; 4) adults almost always turn to somebody for help at one or more points in this sequence; 5) usually they go to "helpers" who have not been trained as teachers, but frequently when they go to teachers the teachers interfere with their learning by substituting their own pedagogical sequence of steps rather than flowing with the learners' natural sequence.

A great deal of other knowledge about adult learning was accumulating during the sixties from related disciplines—clinical psychology, developmental psychology (especially the new group of life-span developmental psychologists), gerontology, sociology, and anthropology—both in North America and Europe. By and large, this research-based knowledge supported the intuitions of the earlier teachers, and theorists began fitting the knowledge drawn from both sources into a comprehensive, coherent theory of adult learning.

Early in this process European adult educators felt the need for a label for this new theoretical model that would enable them to talk about it in parallel with pedagogy. They coined the label "andragogy," which is based on the Greek word *anēr* (with the stem *andr-*), meaning "man, not boy" or adult. I first learned of the new label from a Yugoslavian adult educator in the mid-sixties and used it in an article in *Adult Leadership* in 1968. Since that time it has appeared with increasing frequency in the literature around the world, and presumably will be listed in the standard dictionaries before long.[4]

---

[3]Cyril O. Houle, *The Inquiring Mind* (Madison, Wis.: University of Wisconsin Press, 1961), pp. 15–16.
[4]For a detailed description of the evolution of the term "andragogy," see my *The Adult Learner: A Neglected Species* (Houston: Gulf Publishing Co., 2nd ed., 1978), pp. 48–51; and for further elaboration on the etymology of "andragogy" see the correspondence between the author and the publishers of Merriam-Webster dictionaries in Appendix A.

Originally I defined andragogy as the art and science of helping adults learn, in contrast to pedagogy as the art and science of teaching children. Then an increasing number of teachers in elementary and secondary schools (and a few in colleges) began reporting to me that they were experimenting with applying the concepts of andragogy to the education of youth and finding that in certain situations they were producing superior learning. So I am at the point now of seeing that andragogy is simply another model of assumptions about learners to be used alongside the pedagogical model of assumptions, thereby providing two alternative models for testing out the assumptions as to their "fit" with particular situations. Furthermore, the models are probably most useful when seen not as dichotomous but rather as two ends of a spectrum, with a realistic assumption in a given situation falling in between the two ends. For example, taking the assumption regarding dependency versus self-directedness, a six-year-old may be highly self-directing in learning the rules of a game but quite dependent in learning to use a calculator; on the other hand, a forty-year-old may be very dependent in learning to program a computer but completely self-directing in learning to repair a piece of furniture. As I see it, whenever a pedagogical assumption is the realistic one, then pedagogical strategies are appropriate, regardless of the age of the learner—and vice versa. But I would like to make one caveat: an ideological pedagogue—one who has a deep loyalty and commitment to the pedagogical model—may be tempted to underrate the extent to which an andragogical assumption may be realistic and may, for example, want to keep a learner dependent long after the learner has become able to be self-directing.

Assumptions of Pedagogy and Andragogy

Exhibit 4 portrays how I see the difference in assumptions between the two models:

Exhibit 4

A COMPARISON OF THE ASSUMPTIONS
OF PEDAGOGY AND ANDRAGOGY

Regarding:	Pedagogy	Andragogy
Concept of the learner	The role of the learner is, by definition, a dependent one. The teacher is expected by society to take full responsibility for determining what is to be learned, when it is to be learned, how it is to be learned, and if it has been learned.	It is a normal aspect of the process of maturation for a person to move from dependency toward increasing self-directedness, but at different rates for different people and in different dimensions of life. Teachers have a responsibility to encourage and nurture this movement. Adults have a deep psychological need to be generally self-directing, although they may be dependent in particular temporary situations.

Regarding:	Pedagogy	Andragogy
Role of learners' experience	The experience learners bring to a learning situation is of little worth. It may be used as a starting point, but the experience from which learners will gain the most is that of the teacher, the textbook writer, the audiovisual aid producer, and other experts. Accordingly, the primary techniques in education are transmittal techniques—lecture, assigned reading, AV presentations.	As people grow and develop they accumulate an increasing reservoir of experience that becomes an increasingly rich resource for learning—for themselves and for others. Furthermore, people attach more meaning to learnings they gain from experience than those they acquire passively. Accordingly, the primary techniques in education are experiential techniques—laboratory experiments, discussion, problem-solving cases, simulation exercises, field experience, and the like.
Readiness to learn	People are ready to learn whatever society (especially the school) says they ought to learn, provided the pressures on them (like fear of failure) are great enough. Most people of the same age are ready to learn the same things. Therefore, learning should be organized into a fairly standardized curriculum, with a uniform step-by-step progression for all learners.	People become ready to learn something when they experience a need to learn it in order to cope more satisfyingly with real-life tasks or problems. The educator has a responsibility to create conditions and provide tools and procedures for helping learners discover their "needs to know." And learning programs should be organized around life-application categories and sequenced according to the learners' readiness to learn.
Orientation to learning	Learners see education as a process of acquiring subject-matter content, most of which they understand will be useful only at a later time in life. Accordingly, the curriculum should be organized into subject-matter units (e.g., courses) which follow the logic of the subject (e.g., from ancient to modern history, from simple to complex mathematics or science). People are subject-centered in their orientation to learning.	Learners see education as a process of developing increased competence to achieve their full potential in life. They want to be able to apply whatever knowledge and skill they gain today to living more effectively tomorrow. Accordingly, learning experiences should be organized around competency-development categories. People are performance-centered in their orientation to learning.

To summarize, andragogy is premised on at least these four crucial assumptions about the characteristics of learners that are different from the assumptions on which traditional pedagogy is premised. These assumptions are that as individuals mature: 1) their self-concept moves from one of being a dependent personality toward being a self-directed human being; 2) they accumulate a growing reservoir of experience that becomes an increasingly rich resource for learning; 3) their readiness to learn becomes oriented increasingly to the developmental tasks of their social roles; and 4) their time perspective changes from one of postponed application of knowledge to immediacy of application, and accordingly, their orientation toward learning shifts from one of subject-centeredness to one of performance-centeredness.

Some Implications of the Assumptions for Practice

I would like to explore these assumptions a little more fully and suggest some of their implications for educational practice.

Self-Concepts and Teachers' Concepts of Learners

Children enter this world in a condition of complete dependency. Their needs, except for purely biological functions, must be taken care of by someone else. The first image children get of themselves as separate entities is that of dependent personalities whose lives are managed for them by the adult world. At home, often at play, in church, in the community, and in school, they expect the will of adults to be imposed on them. That is what life is like when you are a kid.

This self-concept of dependency is encouraged and reinforced by the adult world. In fact, society defines the appropriate role of children as that of learners; this is their full-time occupation, the source of their rewards and self-fulfillment. And on the whole, this role is defined as the more or less passive one of receiving and storing up the information adults have decided children should have.

As children's self-identities begin to take shape, they begin to see themselves as having the capacity to start making decisions for themselves, at first experimentally and in small matters that do not impinge on the adult world. But increasingly, as they mature, children's self-concepts move in the direction of greater self-direction, and during adolescence their need to take significant responsibility for managing their own lives becomes so strong that it often puts them in open rebellion against control by the adult world. The tragedy is that in our culture the adult world tends to hold onto its concept of the child as a dependent personality until the last possible moment.

Although this cultural lag between children's capacity to take responsibility and the freedom the adult world allows them to take responsibility applies to almost all aspects of their lives, it is especially evident in regard to their education. Interestingly, in the kindergarten and early primary years our teachers typically involve students in planning and conducting learning activities to a considerable degree. But as children move up the educational ladder, they encounter more and more of the responsibility for their learning being taken by the teachers, the curriculum planner, and their parents. The net effect is to freeze them into self-concepts of dependency.

But something dramatic happens to their self-concepts when people define themselves as adults. They begin to see their normal role in life no longer as being full-time learners. They see themselves increasingly as producers or doers. Their chief sources of self-fulfillment are now their performances as workers, spouses, parents, and citizens. Adults acquire a new status, in their own eyes and in the eyes of others, from these noneducational responsibilities. Their self-concept becomes that of a self-directing personality. They see themselves as being able to make their own decisions and face the consequences, to manage their own lives. In fact, the psychological definition of adulthood is the point at which individuals perceive themselves to be essentially self-directing. And at this point people also develop a deep psychological need to be seen by others as being self-directing.

This fact presents a special problem to teachers of adults. Adults have been so deeply conditioned by their previous schooling (under the pedagogical model) to perceive the appropriate role of learner to be that of a dependent, more or less passive recipient of transmitted content, that even though they may be completely self-directing in all other aspects of their lives, the minute they enter into any activity labeled "education," they sit back, fold their arms, and say, "Teach me." The problem arises when teachers take this stance at face value and start treating adult learners as if they were dependent personalities, for this induces an inner conflict within the adults between this preconditioned intellectual model of the role of learner and the adults' deep psychological need to be self-directing. Hence there is the need to build into our program designs some preparatory experiences that will help adults get a new way of thinking about the role of learner and some new skills in self-directed learning.[5]

Often there is another ingredient in the self-concept of adults that affects their role as learners. They may carry over from their previous experience with schooling the perception that they are not very smart, at least in regard to academic work. This fact about the adult psyche has several consequences for adult education. In the case of some adults the remembrance of the classroom as a place where one is treated with disrespect and may fail is so strong that it serves as a serious barrier to their becoming involved in adult-education activities at all. This barrier can be reduced by interpreting adult learning activities as being different and enjoyable and perhaps by having the meetings in nonacademic locations. In the case of other adults, simply providing them with some early success experiences that will help them build positive self-concepts as learners will be sufficient.

Fortunately, once adults make the discovery that they can take responsibility for their own learning, as they do for other facets of their lives, they experience a sense of release and exhilaration. They then enter into learning with deep ego-involvement, with results that are frequently startling both to themselves and to their teachers. Teachers who have helped their adult students to achieve this breakthrough report repeatedly that it is one of the most rewarding experiences of their lives.

Implications for Practice

Several implications for practice flow from this difference in assumptions about learners.

1. *The learning climate.* The self-concept of being an adult has several consequences regarding the requirements of an environment that will be conducive to adult learning. It suggests that the physical environment should be one in which adults feel at ease. Furnishings and equipment should be adult-sized and comfortable; meeting rooms should be arranged informally and should be decorated according to adult tastes; and acoustics and lighting should take into account declining audiovisual acuity.

---

[5]My *Self-Directed Learning: A Guide for Learners and Teachers* (Chicago: Association Press/Follett, 1975) was written as a resource for this purpose.

Even more importantly, the psychological climate should be one which causes adults to feel accepted, respected, and supported; in which there exists a spirit of mutuality between teachers and students as joint inquirers; in which there is freedom of expression without fear of punishment or ridicule. People tend to feel more "adult" in an atmosphere that is friendly and informal, in which they are known by name and valued as unique individuals, than in the traditional school atmosphere of formality, semianonymity, and status differentiation between teacher and student.

In andragogical practice, care is taken to determine what are the symbols of childishness to particular groups of adults, and to remove them. For some—particularly undereducated adults—it is a school building, in which case social-agency facilities, churches, commercial properties, or living rooms would probably be environments more conducive to learning. For others a podium on a stage makes them feel that they are being talked down to, in which case a small table on the floor would provide a more appropriate work space for the teacher. Many adults associate rooms in which chairs are placed in rows with childhood regimentation and passivity, and find rooms in which participants are seated in small groups in circles or around tables more conducive to adult-type relationships. A few adults report that chalkboards are a symbol of childishness to them, which may help to explain the growing popularity in adult education of newsprint-pads on easels.

The behavior of the teacher probably influences the character of the learning climate more than any other single factor, however. Teachers convey in many ways whether their attitude is one of interest in and respect for the students or whether they see the students essentially as receiving sets for transmissions of wisdom. Teachers who take the time and trouble to get to know their students individually and who call them by name (especially by first name) obviously convey the first set of attitudes. But probably the behavior that most explicitly demonstrates that a teacher really cares about students and respects their contributions is the act of really listening to what the students say.

The notion of a climate of adultness can be extended beyond individual classrooms and applied to total institutions. Indeed, such a climate is likely to be established in classrooms if it pervades the whole institution and is reflected in its architecture, decor, policies, procedures, leadership style, and human relations. One can sense rather quickly on entering an institution, for example, whether it cares more about people or things, whether it is concerned about the feelings and welfare of individuals or herds them through like cattle, and whether it views adults as dependent personalities or self-directing human beings.

2. *Diagnosis of needs.* The adult's self-concept of self-directivity is in direct conflict with the traditional practice of the teacher telling the students what they need to learn. Indeed it is even in conflict with the social philosophy that society has a right to impose its ideas about what they need to learn on them. Of course, adults will learn what others want them to learn if their power to punish them for not learning is strong enough. But they are more deeply motivated to learn those things they see the need to learn.

In andragogy, therefore, great emphasis is placed on the involvement of adult learners in a process of *self-diagnosis* of needs for learning. As will be described in greater detail in Chapter 11, this process consists of three phases: 1) constructing a model of the competencies or characteristics required to achieve a given ideal model of performance, so that the learner has some vision of the "good" supervisor, the "good" public speaker, the "good" parent, and the like—and of the competencies required to become "good." It is in this model-building phase that the values and expectations of the teacher, the institution, and society are amalgamated with those of the learner into a composite picture; 2) providing diagnostic experiences in which the learners can assess their present level of competencies in the light of those portrayed in the model; this is an underdeveloped area of andragogical technology, but one in which there is currently a ferment of invention. Such techniques as critical incident processes, sociodrama, computerized games, laboratory methods, and simulation exercises are being developed to enable learners to perform and then to get feedback that helps them in objectively assessing the strengths and weaknesses of their performance; 3) helping the learners to measure the gaps between their present competencies and those required by the model, so that they experience a feeling of dissatisfaction about the distance between where they are and where they would like to be, and so are able to identify specific directions of desirable growth. This experiencing of self-induced dissatisfaction with present inadequacies, coupled with a clear sense of direction for self-improvement, is in fact a good definition of "motivation to learn."

3. *The planning process.* There seems to be a law (or, at least, a tendency) of human nature that goes like this: human beings tend to feel committed to a decision (or an activity) to the extent that they have participated in making it (or planning it). Teachers of adults who do all the planning for their students, who come into the classroom and impose preplanned activities on them, typically experience apathy, resentment, and probably withdrawal. This imposition of the will of the teacher is incongruent with the adult's self-concept of self-directivity.

Accordingly, a basic element in the technology of andragogy is the involvement of the learners in the process of planning their own learning, with the teacher serving as a procedural guide and content resource. When the number of students is small enough, they can all be involved in the planning directly; when the number gets much over thirty, adult educators make use of representative councils, committees, task forces, teams, or other devices through which the learners feel that they are participating in the planning by proxy.

The function of planning, with which the remainder of this book is largely concerned, consists of translating diagnosed needs into specific educational objectives (or directions of growth), designing and conducting learning experiences to achieve these objectives, and evaluating the extent to which these objectives have been accomplished. In andragogy, responsibility for performing this function is a mutual one between the learners and the teacher.

4. *Conducting learning experiences.* In traditional pedagogical practice (and in contemporary programmed instruction) the function of the teacher is defined as "to teach." The teacher is expected to take full responsibility for what happens in the teaching-learning transaction. The learner's role tends to be that of a fairly passive recipient of the teacher's instruction.

In contrast, in congruence with the adult's self-concept of self-directivity, andragogical practice treats the learning-teaching transaction as the mutual responsibility of learners and teacher. In fact, the teacher's role is redefined as that of a procedural technician, resource person, and coinquirer; more a catalyst than an instructor, more a guide than a wizard. Andragogy assumes that a teacher cannot really "teach" in the sense of "make a person learn," but that one person can only *help* another person learn. (In my own practice, when I succumb to the compulsion to teach my students something I know they ought to know but that they do not yet know they ought to know, which I sometimes do because bad habits take time to break, they report that it gets in the way of their learning. My practice has improved since I adopted the policy of authorizing them to signal me when they sense this happening.)

Later chapters describe procedures by which learners can responsibly share in taking responsibility for their own learning. Suffice it to say at this point that an andragogical learning situation, whether it be a course, an institute, a training program, or a conference, is alive with meetings of small groups—planning committees, learning-teaching teams, consultation groups, project task forces—sharing responsibility for helping one another learn.

5. *Evaluation of learning.* Probably the crowning instance of incongruity between traditional educational practice and the adult's self-concept of self-directivity is the act of a teacher giving a grade to a student. Nothing makes an adult feel more childlike than being judged by another adult; it is the ultimate sign of disrespect and dependency, as the one who is being judged experiences it.

For this reason, andragogical theory prescribes a process of self-evaluation, in which the teacher devotes energy to helping the adults get evidence for themselves about the progress they are making toward their educational goals. In this process, the strengths and weaknesses of the educational program itself must be assessed in terms of how it has facilitated or inhibited the learning of the students. So evaluation is a mutual undertaking, as are all other phases of the adult learning experience.

In fact, what is happening in practice is that precisely the same procedures that are used for the diagnosis of learning needs are being employed to help the learners measure gains in competence. For instance, by comparing their performance in solving a critical incident at the end of a learning experience with their performance in a similar critical incident at the beginning of the experience, learners can quite precisely measure the changes produced by the experience. Because of the similarity of these two processes, I find myself now thinking less and less in terms of the evaluation of learning and more and more in terms of the *rediagnosis* of learning needs. And I find that, when my adult students perceive what they do at the end of a learning experience as rediagnosing rather than evaluating, they enter into the activity with more enthusiasm and see it as being more constructive. Indeed, many of them report that it launches them into a new cycle of learning, reinforcing the notion that learning is a continuing process.

This shift from evaluation to self-evaluation or rediagnosis places a heavy burden on teachers of adults. They must set the example of being open to feedback regarding their performance. They must be skillful in establishing a supportive climate in which hard-to-accept information about one's performance can be looked at objectively. And they must be creative about inventing ways in which students can get comprehensive data about their own performance. Some of the techniques available in carrying this burden are explored in later chapters.

My own feeling is that the single most critical difference between children and adults as learners is the difference in assumptions we make about their self-concepts, and this is why these assumptions and their technological implications have been dealt with in such detail. But there are other important differences.

The Role of Experience

Adults enter into any undertaking with a different background of experience from that of their youth. Having lived longer, they have accumulated a greater *volume* of experience. But they have also had different *kinds* of experience. Children have not had the experience of making their own living, marrying, having children, taking real community responsibility, or being responsible for the welfare of others (although they have observed all these things in their families and on television!).

There is, it seems to me, another subtle difference between children and adults as regards their experience. To children, experience is something that happens *to* them; it is an external event that affects them, not an integral part of them. If you ask children who they are, they are likely to identify themselves in terms of who their parents are, who their older brothers and sisters are, where they live, and what school they attend. Their self-identity is largely derived from external sources.

But adults derive their self-indentity from their experience. They define who they are in terms of the accumulation of their unique sets of experience. So if you ask adults who they are, they are likely to identify themselves by describing what their occupations are, where they have worked, where they have traveled, what their training and experience have equipped them to do, and what their achievements have been. Adults *are* what they have *done*.

Because adults define themselves largely by their experience, they have a deep investment in its value. And so when they find themselves in situations in which their experience is not being used, or its worth is minimized, it is not just their experience that is being rejected—they feel rejected as persons.

These differences in experience between children and adults have at least three consequences for learning: 1) adults have more to contribute to the learning of others; for most kinds of learning they are themselves a rich resource for learning; 2) adults have a richer foundation of experience to which to relate new experiences (and new learnings tend to take on meaning as we are able to relate them to our past experience); 3) adults have acquired a larger number of fixed habits and patterns of thought, and therefore tend to be less open-minded.

Implications for Practice

Several implications for practice flow from these differences in experience.

1. *Emphasis on experiential techniques.* Because adults are themselves richer resources for learning than is true of children, greater emphasis can be placed on techniques that tap the experience of the adult learners, such as group discussion, the case method, the critical-incident process, simulation exercises, role playing, skill-practice exercises, field projects, action projects, laboratory methods, consultative supervision, demonstration, seminars, work conferences, counseling, group therapy, and community development. There is a distinct shift in emphasis in andragogy away from the transmittal techniques so prevalent in youth education—the lecture, assigned readings, and canned audiovisual presentation—toward the more participatory experiential techniques. Indeed, "participation" and "ego-involvement" are boldfaced words in the lexicon of the adult educator, with the assumption often being made that the more active the learner's role in the process, the more they are probably learning.

2. *Emphasis on practical application.* Skillful adult educators have always taken care to see that new concepts or broad generalizations were illustrated by life experiences drawn from the learners. But numerous recent studies on the transfer of learning and the maintenance of behavioral change indicate the desirability of going even further, and actually building into the design of learning experiences provision for the learners to plan—and even rehearse—how they are going to apply their learnings to their day-to-day lives.

3. *Unfreezing and learning to learn from experience.* A growing andragogical practice is to build into the early phases of a course, workshop, conference, institute, or other sequential educational activity an "unfreezing" experience, in which the adults are helped to be able to look at themselves more objectively and free their minds from preconceptions. Many of the diagnostic procedures and structured exercises described in Chapter 11 help to serve this purpose.

Readiness to Learn

It is well accepted in our culture now that children learn best those things that are necessary for them to know in order to advance from one phase of development to the next. These have been dubbed "developmental tasks" by developmental psychologists:

> A developmental task is a task which arises at or about a certain period in the life of the individual, successful achievement of which leads to his happiness and to success with later tasks, while failure leads to unhappiness in the individual, disapproval by the society, and difficulty with later tasks.[6]

Each of these developmental tasks produces a "readiness to learn" which at its peak presents a "teachable moment." For example, parents now generally accept the fact that they cannot teach children to walk until they have mastered the art of crawling, their leg muscles are strong enough, and they have become frustrated at not being able to stand up and walk the way everybody else does. At that point, and only then, are they able to learn to walk; for it has become their developmental task.

Recent research suggests that the same phenomenon is at work during the adult years. Adults, too, have their phases of growth and resulting developmental tasks, readinesses to learn, and teachable moments. But whereas the developmental tasks of youth tend to be the products primarily of physiological and mental maturation, those of the adult years are the products primarily of the evolution of social roles. Robert J. Havighurst, one of the pioneers in this area of research, divides the adult years into three phases—"early adulthood," "middle age," and "later maturity"—and identifies ten social roles of adulthood: worker, mate, parent, homemaker, son or daughter of aging parents, citizen, friend, organization member, religious affiliate, and user of leisure time. The requirements for performing each of these social roles change, according to Havighurst, as we move through the three phases of adult life, thereby setting up changing developmental tasks and, therefore, changing readiness to learn.

For example, in a person's role of worker, the first developmental task is to get a job. At that point individuals are ready to learn anything required to get a job, but they definitely are not ready to study supervision. Having landed a job, they are faced with the task of mastering it so that they will not get fired from it; and at that point they are ready to learn the special skills it requires, the standards that are expected, and how to get along with fellow workers. Having become secure in a basic job, the next task becomes one of working up the occupational ladder. Now they become ready to learn to become a supervisor or executive. Finally, after reaching their ceiling, they face the task of dissolving the role of worker—and to learn about retirement or substitutes for work.

---

[6]Robert J. Havighurst, *Developmental Tasks and Education* (New York: David McKay Co., 1961), p. 2. By permission.

Havighurst illustrates the changes in developmental tasks during the three periods of adult life as follows:

Early Adulthood (ages 18 to 30):
—Selecting a mate
—Learning to live with a marriage partner
—Starting a family
—Rearing children
—Managing a home
—Getting started in an occupation
—Taking on civic responsibility
—Finding a congenial social group

Middle Age (ages 30 to 55):
—Achieving adult civic and social responsibility
—Establishing and maintaining an economic standard of living
—Assisting teenage children to become responsible and happy adults
—Developing adult leisure-time activities
—Relating to one's spouse as a person
—Accepting and adjusting to the physiological changes of middle age
—Adjusting to aging parents

Later Maturity (ages 55 and over):
—Adjusting to decreasing physical strength and health
—Adjusting to retirement and reduced income
—Adjusting to the death of a spouse
—Establishing an explicit affiliation with one's age group
—Meeting social and civic obligations
—Establishing satisfactory physical living arrangements[7]

As Havighurst concludes, "People do not launch themselves into adulthood with the momentum of their childhood and youth and simply coast along to old age. . . . Adulthood has its transition points and its crises. It is a *developmental period* in almost as complete a sense as childhood and adolescence are developmental periods."[8]

Since Havighurst's foundational work on developmental tasks, a number of other investigations of the life stages, transitions, passages, crises, and transformations of the adult years have been published; they are listed in the suggested readings at the end of this chapter. I have included my own list of "Life Tasks of American Adults" in Appendix C. The chief value of these lists for the adult-educational practitioner is to stimulate ideas as to what adults at different stages of development are ready to learn. But one word of caution about them: most of the lists are based on studies of middle-class Americans.

Implications for Practice

At least two sets of implications for practice flow from this difference in readiness to learn:

1. *The timing of learnings.* If the teachable moment for particular adults to acquire a given learning is to be captured, it is obvious that the sequence of the curriculum must be timed so as to be in step with their developmental tasks. This is the appropriate

---

[7]Ibid., pp. 72–98.
[8]Robert J. Havighurst and Betty Orr, *Adult Education and Adult Needs* (Boston: Center for the Study of Liberal Education for Adults, 1956), p. 1.

organizing principle for an adult-education program, rather than the logic of the subject matter or the needs of the sponsoring institution. For instance, an orientation program for new workers would not start with the history and philosophy of the corporation, but rather with real-life concerns of new workers: Where will I be working? With whom will I be working? What will be expected of me? How do people dress in this company? What is the time schedule? To whom can I go for help?

There have been some classic examples of the consequences of violating this organizing principle. One was the introduction of courses on supervision in trade schools, nursing schools, and other preservice vocational programs after World War II, when there was a great shortage of experienced supervisors. The courses were plagued with absenteeism, flunk-outs, and drop-outs—simply because it was not yet a developmental task of people who have not become secure about doing a job themselves to learn how to supervise others in doing the job. Other examples of failure of programs resulting from violation of the readiness-to-learn principle are the several attempts by corporations and at least one national social agency to institute programs on "preparation for retirement" that are geared to people in their forties. Almost universally these programs have resulted in low enrollment, for the simple reason that people whose eyes are still set on going up the occupational ladder are not ready to invest energy in studying how to get off the ladder.

2. *The grouping of learners.* The concept of developmental tasks provides some guidance regarding the grouping of learners. For some kinds of learnings homogeneous groups according to developmental task are more effective. For instance, in a program on child care, young parents would have quite a different set of interests from the parents of adolescent children. For other kinds of learnings, heterogeneous groups would clearly be preferable. For instance, in a program of human-relations training in which the objective is to help people learn to get along better with all kinds of people, it would be important for the groups to cut across occupational, age, status, sex, and perhaps other characteristics that make people different. In my own practice, I have adopted the policy of making provision in the design of any adult-learning activity for a variety of subgroups so as to give the students a flexibility of choice; and I find that they quickly discover colleagues with similar developmental tasks.

Orientation to Learning

Adults enter into education with a different time perspective from children, which in turn produces a difference in the way they view learning. Children tend to have a perspective of postponed application on most of their learning. For example, most of what I learned in elementary school I learned in order to be able to get into high school; and most of what I learned there I learned to prepare me for college; and most of what I learned in college I hoped would prepare me for a happy and productive adult life. To a child, education is essentially a process of the accumulation of a reservoir of subject matter—knowledge and skills—that might be useful later in life. Children tend, therefore, to enter any educational activity in a *subject-centered* frame of mind.

Adults, on the other hand, tend to have a perspective of immediacy of application toward most of their learning. They engage in learning largely in response to pressures they feel from their current life situation. To adults, education is a process of improving their ability to cope with life problems they face now. They tend, therefore, to enter an educational activity in a *problem-centered* or *performance-centered* frame of mind.

Implications for Practice

Several implications for practice flow from this difference in orientation to learning.

1. *The orientation of adult educators.* Just as adults have a different orientation to learning from that of children, so it would seem to follow that a different orientation toward learning is required on the part of educators of adults from the orientation traditionally inculcated in educators of children. Where youth educators can, perhaps appropriately, be primarily concerned with the logical development of subject matter and its articulation from grade to grade according to levels of complexity, adult educators must be primarily attuned to the existential concerns of the individuals and institutions they serve and be able to develop learning experiences that will be articulated with these concerns.

2. *The organization of the curriculum.* The original basis of organization for the curriculum of youth education was the seven subjects—the trivium (grammar, rhetoric, and logic) and quadrivium (arithmetic, music, geometry, and astronomy) of the medieval schools. Although the number of subjects has proliferated since the Middle Ages, the subject-matter concept of curricular organization still remains relatively intact. But with the emergence of the insights of andragogy the curriculum—which, incidentally, in adult education is increasingly referred to as "program"—of adult education is coming to look less and less like the curriculum of youth education.

Because adult learners tend to be problem-centered in their orientation to learning, the appropriate organizing principle for sequences of adult learning is *problem areas,* not *subjects.* For example, instead of offering courses on "Composition I" and "Composition II," with the first focusing on grammar and the second on writing style, andragogical practice would put in their place "Writing Better Business Letters" and "Writing Short Stories." In the adult courses, matters of grammar and style would be treated in the context of the practical concerns of the learners. Even the broad curricular categories used to describe what adults study have departed from the traditional categories of the academic disciplines. In the *Handbook for Adult Education,* for example, such labels were given to the "Program Areas" as "Education for Family Life," "Education for Social and Public Responsibility," and then "Education for Self-Fulfillment."[9]

3. *The design of learning experiences.* The problem-orientation of the learners implies that the most appropriate starting point for every learning experience is the problems and concerns that the adults have on their minds as they enter. Whereas the opening session of a youth-education activity might be titled "What This Course Is All About," in an adult-educational activity it would more appropriately be titled "What Are You Hoping to Get Out of This Course?" Early in the session there would be a problem census or a diagnostic exercise through which the participants would identify the specific problems they want to be able to deal with more adequately. This is not to suggest that a good adult-learning experience ends with the problems the learners are aware of in the beginning, but that is where it starts. There may be other problems that the teacher or institution expects to be dealt with, and these are put into the picture along with the students' problems for negotiation between teacher and students.

---

[9]R. M. Smith, George Aker, and J. R. Kidd, *Handbook of Adult Education* (New York: Macmillan, 1970).

Some Other Assumptions about Learning and Teaching

The critical element in any adult-education program is, of course, what happens when a teacher comes face-to-face with a group of learners. As I see it, the andragogical approach to the learning-teaching transaction is premised on three additional assumptions about learning and teaching:

1. *Adults can learn.* The central proposition on which the entire adult-education movement is based is that adults can learn. One of the great moments in the history of the movement occurred at the annual meeting of the American Association for Adult Education held in Cleveland in 1927, when Edward L. Thorndike reported for the first time his findings that the ability to learn declined only very slowly and very slightly after age twenty. Until that moment adult educators had based their whole work on blind faith, in direct opposition to the prevailing belief that "you can't teach an old dog new tricks." But now their faith had been vindicated; there was scientific proof that adults can learn.

Actually, Thorndike's early studies did seem to indicate a decline in learning capacity of about 1 percent per year after age twenty-five. But later studies, especially those of Thorndike's colleague Irving Lorge, revealed that what declined was the speed of learning, not intellectual power—and that even this decline was likely to be minimized by continued use of the intellect.

The research to date of adult learning clearly indicates that the basic ability to learn remains essentially unimpaired throughout the life span and that therefore, if individuals do not actually perform as well in learning situations as they could, the cause must be sought in such factors as the following:

—Adults who have been away from systematic education for some time may underestimate their ability to learn, and this lack of confidence may prevent them from applying themselves wholly.

—Various physiological changes occur in the process of aging, such as decline in visual acuity, reduction in speed of reaction, and lowering of energy levels, which operate as barriers to learning unless compensated for by such devices as louder sound, larger printing, and slower pace.

—Adults respond less readily to external sanctions for learning (such as grades) than to internal motivation.

2. *Learning is an internal process.* In our inherited folk wisdom there has been a tendency to look upon education as the transmittal of information, to see learning as an almost exclusively intellectual process consisting of the storing of accumulated facts in the filing drawers of the mind. The implicit assumption underlying this view of learning is that it is essentially an external process in the sense that what the student learns is determined primarily by outside forces, such as the excellence of the teacher's presentation, the quality of reading materials, and the effectiveness of school discipline. People holding this view even today insist that teachers' qualifications be judged only by their mastery of subject matter and clamor against their wasting time learning about the psychology of learning. For all practical purposes this view defines the function of the teacher as being to teach subject matter, not students.

A growing body of research into what really happens when learning takes place has put this traditional conception of learning in serious jeopardy. Although there is not yet agreement on the precise nature of the learning process (in fact there are many theories which seem to explain different parts of it), there is agreement that it is an internal process controlled by the learners and engaging their whole being—including intellectual, emotional, and physiological functions. Learning is described psychologically as a process of need-meeting and goal-striving by the learners. This is to say that individuals are motivated to engage in learning to the extent that they feel a need to learn and perceive a personal goal that learning will help to achieve; and they will invest their energy in making use of available resources (including teachers and readings) to the extent that they perceive them as being relevant to their needs and goals.

The central dynamic of the learning process is thus perceived to be the experience of the learners; experience being defined as the interaction between individuals and their environment. The quality and amount of learning is therefore clearly influenced by the quality and amount of interaction between the learners and their environment and by the educative potency of the environment. The art of teaching is essentially the management of these two key variables in the learning process—environment and interaction—which together define the substance of the basic unit of learning, a "learning experience." The critical function of the teacher, therefore, is to create a rich environment from which students can extract learning and then to guide their interaction with it so as to optimize their learning from it.

The important implication for adult-education practice of the fact that learning is an internal process is that those methods and techniques which involve the individual most deeply in self-directed inquiry will produce the greatest learning. This principle of ego-involvement lies at the heart of the adult educator's art. In fact, the main thrust of modern adult-educational technology is in the direction of inventing techniques for involving adults in ever-deeper processes of self-diagnosis of their own needs for continued learning, in formulating their own objectives for learning, in sharing responsibility for designing and carrying out their learning activities, and in evaluating their progress toward their objectives. The truly artistic teachers of adults perceive the locus of responsibility for learning to be in the learner; they conscientiously suppress their own compulsion to teach what they know students ought to learn in favor of helping students learn for themselves what they want to learn. I have described this faith in the ability of individuals to learn for themselves as the "theological foundation" of adult education, and I believe that without this faith a teacher of adults is more likely to hinder than to facilitate learning. This is not to suggest that teachers have less responsibility in the learning-teaching transaction, but only that their responsibility lies less in giving ready-made answers to predetermined questions and more in being ingenious in finding better ways to help students discover the important questions and the answers for themselves.

One of the clearest statements of this insight about adult learning was made in 1926 by the great American pioneer adult-education theorist, Eduard C. Lindeman:

> I am conceiving adult education in terms of a new technique for learning, a technique as essential to the college graduate as to the unlettered manual worker. It represents a process by which the adult learns to become aware of and to evaluate his experience. To do this he cannot begin by studying "subjects" in the hope that some day this information will be useful. On the contrary, he begins by giving attention to situations in which he finds himself, to problems which include obstacles to his self-fulfillment. Facts and information from the differentiated spheres of knowledge are used, not for the purpose of accumulation, but because of need in solving problems. In this process the teacher finds a new function. He is no longer the oracle who speaks from the platform of authority, but rather the guide, the pointer-out who also participates in learning in proportion to the vitality and relevancy of his facts and experiences. In short, my conception of adult education is this: a cooperative venture in nonauthori-

tarian, informal learning, the chief purpose of which is to discover the meaning of experience; a quest of the mind which digs down to the roots of the preconceptions which formulate our conduct; a technique of learning for adults which makes education coterminous with life and hence elevates living itself to the level of adventurous experiment.[10]

3. *There are superior conditions of learning and principles of teaching.* It is becoming increasingly clear from the growing body of knowledge about the processes of adult learning that there are certain conditions of learning that are more conducive to growth and development than others. These superior conditions seem to be produced by practices in the learning-teaching transaction that adhere to certain superior principles of teaching as identified below:

Conditions of Learning	Principles of Teaching
The learners feel a need to learn.	1) The teacher exposes the learners to new possibilities for self-fulfillment.
	2) The teacher helps the learners clarify their own aspirations for improved behavior.
	3) The teacher helps the learners diagnose the gap between their aspirations and their present level of performance.
	4) The teacher helps the learners identify the life problems they experience because of the gaps in their personal equipment.
The learning environment is characterized by physical comfort, mutual trust and respect, mutual helpfulness, freedom of expression, and acceptance of differences.	5) The teacher provides physical conditions that are comfortable (as to seating, smoking, temperature, ventilation, lighting, decoration) and conducive to interaction (preferably, no person sitting behind another person).
	6) The teacher accepts the learners as persons of worth and respects their feelings and ideas.
	7) The teacher seeks to build relationships of mutual trust and helpfulness among the learners by encouraging cooperative activities and refraining from inducing competitiveness and judgmentalness.
	8) The teacher exposes his or her own feelings and contributes resources as a colearner in the spirit of mutual inquiry.
The learners perceive the goals of a learning experience to be their goals.	9) The teacher involves the learners in a mutual process of formulating learning objectives in which the needs of the learners of the institution, of the teacher, of the subject matter, and of the society are taken into account.
The learners accept a share of the responsibility for planning and operating a learning experience, and therefore have a feeling of commitment toward it.	10) The teacher shares his or her thinking about options available in the designing of learning experiences and the selection of materials and methods and involves the learners in deciding among these options jointly.

---

[10]Robert Gessner (ed.), *The Democratic Man: Selected Writings of Eduard C. Lindeman* (Boston: Beacon Press, 1956), p. 160. By permission.

Conditions of Learning	Principles of Teaching
The learners participate actively in the learning process.	11) The teacher helps the learners to organize themselves (project groups, learning-teaching teams, independent study, etc.) to share responsibility in the process of mutual inquiry.
The learning process is related to and makes use of the experience of the learners.	12) The teacher helps the learners exploit their own experiences as resources for learning through the use of such techniques as discussion, role playing, case method, etc.
	13) The teacher gears the presentation of his or her own resources to the levels of experience of particular learners.
	14) The teacher helps the learners to apply new learnings to their experience, and thus to make the learnings more meaningful and integrated.
The learners have a sense of progress toward their goals.	15) The teacher involves the learners in developing mutually acceptable criteria and methods for measuring progress toward the learning objectives.
	16) The teacher helps the learners develop and apply procedures for self-evaluation according to these criteria.

Some Implications for Youth Education

The differences between children and adults are not so much real differences, I believe, as differences in assumptions about them that are made in traditional pedagogy. Actually, in my observation (and retrospection), the children start fairly early to see themselves as being self-directing in broadening areas of their lives; they start accumulating experience that has increasing value for learning; they start preparing for social roles (such as through part-time jobs) and therefore experiencing adultlike readinesses to learn; and they encounter life problems for which they would like some learnings for immediate application. Therefore, many of the principles of andragogy have direct relevance to the education of children and youth.

The fact is that many of the new developments in the curricula of our elementary and secondary schools have some of the flavor of andragogy. The "new math," "new biology," and linguistics programs start with the concerns of the students and engage them in a process of largely self-directed discovery. Some of the products of today's schools who become adults in the 1980s and 1990s will, therefore, presumably be better equipped to continue a process of lifelong learning than are today's adults.

But these developments are quite piecemeal, and the practitioners have lagged far behind the curriculum theorists in helping students learn how to learn rather than just teaching them what they "ought" to know. What is required, if youth education is to produce adults who are capable of engaging in a lifelong process of continuing self-development, is a whole new set of assumptions about the purpose of youth education and a new technology to carry out that purpose. I can foresee that the result would be a more andragogical approach to the education of children and youth. As my contribution toward movement in this direction I am presenting in Appendix D a schema I prepared for UNESCO, "Toward a Model of Lifelong Education."

The Andragogical Process of Program Development

When the principles of andragogy are translated into a process for planning and operating educational programs, that process turns out to be quite different from the curriculum planning and teaching processes traditionally employed in youth education. The rest of this book is concerned with describing this process as it applies to the planning of comprehensive programs of adult education (Chapters 5 through 10) and to the management of specific learning experiences (Chapter 11).

As I see it, this andragogical process involves the following phases consistently in both levels of application (total programs and individual learning activities):

1) The establishment of a climate conducive to adult learning;
2) The creation of an organizational structure for participative planning;
3) The diagnosis of needs for learning;
4) The formulation of directions of learning (objectives);
5) The development of a design of activities;
6) The operation of the activities;
7) The rediagnosis of needs for learning (evaluation).

How Do We Know That It Is Better?

People frequently ask me what research has been done vis-à-vis the andragogical model that supports the proposition that it is superior to the pedagogical model. My automatic-reflex response is, "That is not the question; nobody—at least, not I—is saying that."

This kind of question arises from a curious disease that seems to be endemic in the world of learning theory. It might be called panacea-addiction. Philosophers call it either-or thinking. It is a compulsion for neat, simple, single solutions to complex problems.

As I said in an earlier chapter, I have the impression that many traditional teachers (and learning theorists, for that matter) have an almost ideological attachment to the pedagogical model. It is something they have to be loyal to, enforce with sanctions (like normative grading), and protect from heresy. I don't see andragogy as an ideology at all, but a system of assumptions about learners that needs to be tested out for different learners in different situations. In a sense, it is a system that encompasses the pedagogical model, since it makes legitimate the application of pedagogical strategies in those situations in which the assumptions of the pedagogical model are realistic.

The appropriate question to ask, I think, is "What research has been done to indicate under what conditions the andragogical model is appropriate, in whole or in part?" And to satisfy the curiosity of those of you who are asking that question, I am including in Appendix E a list of the papers, research reports, books, and experiments regarding andragogy that I know about.

For Your Continuing Inquiry . . .

Regarding the Pedagogical Model

Bigge, Morris L. *Learning Theories for Teachers*. New York: Harper & Row, 1971.

Bruner, Jerome S. *Toward a Theory of Instruction*. Cambridge, Mass.: Harvard University Press, 1966.

Crawford, W. R., and DeCecco, John P. *The Psychology of Learning and Instruction*. Englewood Cliffs, N.J.: Prentice-Hall, 1974.

Eble, Kenneth E. *The Craft of Teaching*. San Francisco: Jossey-Bass, 1976.

Farnham-Diggory, Sylvia. *Cognitive Processes in Education*. New York: Harper & Row, 1972.

Gagne, Robert M. *The Conditions of Learning*. New York: Holt, Rinehart & Winston, 1965.

Hyman, Ronald T. (ed.). *Contemporary Thought on Teaching*. Englewood Cliffs, N.J.: Prentice-Hall, 1971.

Joyce, Bruce, and Weil, Marsha. *Models of Teaching*. Englewood Cliffs, N.J.: Prentice-Hall, 1972.

Mueller, Richard J. *Principles of Classroom Learning and Perception*. New York: Praeger Press, 1974.

Postman, Neil, and Weingartner, C. *Teaching as a Subversive Activity*. New York: Delacorte Press, 1969.

Skinner, B. F. *The Technology of Teaching*. New York: Appleton-Century-Crofts, 1968.

Taba, Hilda. *Curriculum Development: Theory and Practice*. New York: Harcourt Brace & World, 1962.

Travers, Robert. *Second Handbook of Research on Teaching*. Chicago: Rand McNally, 1973.

Tyler, Ralph W. *Basic Principles of Curriculum and Instruction*. Chicago: University of Chicago Press, 1957.

Regarding Adult Learning

Bischof, Ledford J. *Adult Psychology*. New York: Harper & Row, 1969.

Howe, Michael J. A. *Adult Learning: Psychological Research and Applications*. New York: John Wiley & Sons, 1977.

Ingalls, John D., and Arceri, J. M. *A Trainer's Guide to Andragogy*. (SRS 72-05301) U.S. Department of Health, Education & Welfare. Washington, D.C.: Government Printing Office, 1972.

Kidd, J. R. *How Adults Learn*. Chicago: Association Press/Follett, 1973.

Knowles, Malcolm S. *The Adult Learner: A Neglected Species*. 2nd ed. Houston, Texas: Gulf Publishing Co., 1978.

Thorndike, Edward L. *Adult Learning*. New York: Macmillan, 1928.

Tough, Allen. *The Adult's Learning Projects*. 2nd ed. Toronto: Ontario Institute for Studies in Education, 1979.

Regarding Self-Concept

Adams-Webber, J.R. *Personal Construct Theory: Concepts and Applications*. New York: Wiley-Interscience, 1979.

Bannister, D. (ed.). *Perspectives in Personal Construct Theory.* New York: Academic Press, 1970.

Erikson, Erik H. *Dimensions of a New Identity.* New York: Norton, 1974.

Felker, Donald W. *Building Positive Self-Concepts.* Minneapolis, Minn.: Burgess, 1974.

Kelly, G. S. *The Psychology of Personal Constructs.* New York: Norton, 1955.

Klapp, Orrin E. *Collective Search for Identity.* New York: Holt, Rinehart & Winston, 1969.

Lefcourt, H. M. *Locus of Control.* Hillsdale, N.J.: Erlbaum, 1976.

Loevinger, Jane. *Ego Development: Conceptions and Theories.* San Francisco: Jossey-Bass, 1976.

Thompson, W. *Correlates of the Self Concept.* Nashville, Tenn.: Dede Wallace Center, 1972.

Tyler, Leona. *Individuality: Human Possibilities and Personal Choice in the Psychological Development of Men and Women.* San Francisco: Jossey-Bass, 1978.

Regarding Self-Directed Learning

Block, J. H. *Mastery Learning: Theory and Practice.* New York: Holt, Rinehart & Winston, 1971.

Dressel, Paul L., and Thompson, Mary M. *Independent Study.* San Francisco: Jossey-Bass, 1973.

Gross, Ronald. *The Lifelong Learner: A Guide to Self-Development.* New York: Simon & Schuster, 1977.

Houle, Cyril O. *Continuing Your Education.* New York: McGraw-Hill, 1964.

Hunkins, Francis P. *Involving Students in Questioning.* Rockleigh, N.J.: Allyn & Bacon, 1975.

Knowles, Malcolm S. *Self-Directed Learning: A Guide for Learners and Teachers.* Chicago: Association Press/Follett, 1975.

Massialas, B. G., and Zevin, J. *Creative Encounters in the Classroom: Teaching and Learning Through Discovery.* New York: John Wiley & Sons, 1967.

Rogers, Carl R. *Freedom to Learn.* Columbus, Ohio: Charles E. Merrill, 1969.

Silberman, M. L.; Allender, J. S.; and Yanoff, J. M. *The Psychology of Open Teaching and Learning: An Inquiry Approach.* Boston: Little, Brown, 1972.

Tough, Allen. *Learning Without a Teacher.* Toronto: Ontario Institute for Studies in Education, 1967.

Regarding Developmental Stages

Baltes, Paul D. (ed.). *Life-Span Development and Behavior.* Vol. 1. New York: Academic Press, 1978.

Bromley, D. B. *The Psychology of Human Aging.* Baltimore: Penguin, 1966.

Bruno, Frank J. *Human Adjustment and Personal Growth: Seven Pathways.* Somerset, N.J.: John Wiley & Sons, 1977.

Coleman, James S., et al. *Youth: Transition to Adulthood.* Chicago: University of Chicago Press, 1974.

Datan, Nancy, and Ginsberg, Leon H. *Normative Life Crises.* New York: Academic Press, 1975.

Erikson, Erik. *Identity and the Life Cycle.* New York: International Universities Press, 1959.

Goulet, L. R., and Baltes, Paul B. *Life-Span Developmental Psychology: Research and Theory.* New York: Academic Press, 1970.

Gubrium, Jaber F., and Buckholdt, David R. *Toward Maturity: The Social Processing of Human Development.* San Francisco: Jossey-Bass, 1977.

Havighurst, Robert. *Developmental Tasks and Education.* 2nd ed. New York: David McKay, 1970.

Kaluger, George, and Kaluger, Meriem. *Human Development: The Span of Life.* St. Louis: C. V. Mosby, 1974.

Kastenbaum, Robert. *Humans Developing: A Lifespan Perspective.* Rockleigh, N.J.: Allyn & Bacon, 1979.

Knox, Alan B. *Adult Development and Learning.* San Francisco: Jossey-Bass, 1977.

Kuhlen, Raymond G. (ed.). *Psychological Studies of Human Development.* New York: Appleton-Century-Crofts, 1963.

Levinson, Daniel J. *The Seasons of a Man's Life.* New York: Alfred A. Knopf, 1978.

Lowenthal, Marjorie F., et al. *Four States of Life: A Comparative Study of Women and Men Facing Transitions.* San Francisco: Jossey-Bass, 1975.

Maas, Henry S., and Kupers, Joseph A. *From Thirty to Seventy: A Forty-Year Longitudinal Study of Adult Life Styles and Personality.* San Francisco: Jossey-Bass, 1975.

Neugarten, Bernice L. (ed.). *Middle Age and Aging.* Chicago: University of Chicago Press, 1968.

Newman, B. M., and Newman, P. R. *Development Through Life.* Homewood, Ill.: Dorsey Press, 1975.

Pressey, Sidney L., and Kuhlen, Raymond G. *Psychological Development Through the Life Span.* New York: Harper, 1957.

Sheehy, Gail. *Passages: Predictable Crises of Adult Life.* New York: E. P. Dutton, 1974.

Stevens-Long, Judith. *Adult Life: Developmental Processes.* Palo Alto, Cal.: Mayfield Publishing Co., 1979.

Troll, Lillian E. *Early and Middle Adulthood.* Monterey, Cal.: Brooks/Cole, 1975.

Organizing and Administering Comprehensive Programs of Adult Education

Part II

5
Establishing an Organizational Climate and Structure

The Purpose of Organizations

Providing an Educative Environment

One of the misconceptions in our cultural heritage is the notion that organizations exist purely to get things done. This is only one of their purposes; it is their *work* purpose. But every organization is also a social system that serves as an instrumentality for helping people meet human needs and achieve human goals. In fact, this is the primary purpose for which people take part in organizations—to meet their needs and achieve their goals—and when an organization does not serve this purpose for them they tend to withdraw from it. So organizations also have a human purpose.

Adult education is a means available to organizations for furthering both purposes. Their work purpose is furthered to the extent that they use adult education to develop the competencies of their personnel to do the work required to accomplish the goals of the organizations. Their human purpose is furthered to the extent that they use adult education to help their personnel develop the competencies that will enable them to work up the ladder of Maslow's hierarchy of needs from survival through safety, affection, and esteem to self-actualization.

As if by some law of reciprocity, therefore, an organization provides an environment for adult education. In the spirit of Marshall McLuhan's *The Medium Is the Message*, the quality of learning that takes place in an organization is affected by the kind of organization it is. This is to say that an organization is not simply an instrumentality for providing organized learning activities to adults; it also provides an environment that either facilitates or inhibits learning.

For example, if young executives are being taught in the corporation's management-development program to involve their subordinates in decision-making within their departments, but their own superiors never involve them in making decisions, which management practice are they likely to adopt? Or if an adult church member is being taught to "love thy neighbor," but the total church life is characterized by discrimination, jealousy, and intolerance, which value is more likely to be learned? Or if an adult student in a course on "The Meaning of Democratic Behavior" is taught that the clearest point of differentiation between democracy and other forms of government is the citizen's sharing in the process of public policy formulation, but the teacher has never given the students a chance to share responsibility for conducting the course and the institution has never asked their advice on what courses should be offered, what is likely to be learned about the meaning of democracy?

No educational institution teaches just through its courses, workshops, and institutes; no corporation teaches just through its inservice education programs; and no voluntary organization teaches just through its meetings and study groups. They all teach by everything they do, and often they teach opposite lessons in their organizational operation from what they teach in their educational program.

With this deepened insight that it is the total environment that educates, we are having to rethink the meaning of an organization as an environment for learning. We are having to conceptualize an organization as not only a provider of organized educational activities, but as a *system of learning resources*. In assessing the educative quality of an organization we have to ask, what are the resources for learning that exist in the environment, and how effectively are these being made available to all the people in the organization?

Among the resources for learning that typically exist in an organization are at least the following:

All supervisors and managers
Libraries and media centers
Peer groups
Individuals' daily experience
Personnel appraisal systems
Seminars, workshops, institutes operated by the training division
Linkage with community resources—schools, colleges, commercial vendors of
    educational programs, consultants
Supportive policies—flextime, tuition reimbursement, rewards for improvement
    of performance

One of the principal tasks of the people responsible for human resources development, then, is to devise ways to help employees make use of these resources for continuous, systematic self-development. Some strategies, such as contract learning, for accomplishing this task are suggested in Chapter 11.

This line of reasoning has led modern adult-education theorists to place increasing emphasis on the importance of building an educative environment in all institutions and organizations that undertake to help people learn. What are the characteristics of an educative environment? They are essentially the manifestations of the conditions of learning listed at the end of the last chapter. But they can probably be boiled down to four basic characteristics: 1) respect for personality; 2) participation in decision making; 3) freedom of expression and availability of information; 4) mutuality of responsibility in defining goals, planning and conducting activities, and evaluating.

In effect, an educative environment—at least in a democratic culture—is one that exemplifies democratic values, that practices a democratic philosophy.

Practicing a Democratic Philosophy

A democratic philosophy is characterized by a concern for the development of persons, a deep conviction as to the worth of every individual, and faith that people will make the right decisions for themselves if given the necessary information and support. It gives precedence to the growth of *people* over the accomplishment of *things* when these two values are in conflict. It emphasizes the release of human potential over the control of human behavior. In a truly democratic organization there is a spirit of mutual trust, an openness of communications, a general attitude of helpfulness and cooperation, and a willingness to accept responsibility, in contrast to paternalism, regimentation, restriction of information, suspicion, and enforced dependency on authority.

When applied to the organization of adult education, a democratic philosophy means that the learning activities will be based on the real needs and interests of the participants; that the policies will be determined by a group that is representative of all participants; and that there will be a maximum of participation by all members of the organization in sharing responsibility for making and carrying out decisions. The intimate relationship between democratic philosophy and adult education is eloquently expressed in these words of Eduard Lindeman:

> One of the chief distinctions between conventional and adult education is to be found in the learning process itself. None but the humble become good teachers of adults. In an adult class the student's experience counts for as much as the teacher's knowledge. Both are exchangeable at par. Indeed, in some of the best adult classes it is sometimes difficult to discover who is learning most, the teacher or the students. This two-way learning is also reflected in the management of adult-education enterprises. Shared learning is duplicated by shared authority. In conventional education the pupils adapt themselves to the curriculum offered, but in adult education the pupils aid in formulating the curricula. . . . Under democratic conditions authority is of the group. This is not an easy lesson to learn, but until it is learned democracy cannot succeed.[1]

Exemplifying Change and Growth

I have a suspicion that for an organization to foster adult learning to the fullest possible degree it must go even further than merely practicing a democratic philosophy, that it will really stimulate individual self-renewal to the extent that it consciously engages in continuous self-renewal for itself. Just as a teacher's most potent tool is the example of his or her own behavior, so I believe an organization's most effective instrument of influence is its own behavior.

This proposition is based on the premise that an organization tends to serve as a role model for those it influences. So if its purpose is to encourage its personnel, members, or constituents to engage in a process of continuous change and growth, it is likely to succeed to the extent that it models the role of organizational change and growth. This proposition suggests, therefore, that an organization must be innovative as well as democratic if it is to provide an environment conducive to learning. Exhibit 5 provides some illustrative characteristics that seem to distinguish innovative from static organizations, as I interpret the insights from recent research on this fascinating subject. The right-hand column might well serve as a beginning checklist of desirable organizational goals in the dimensions of structure, atmosphere, management philosophy, decision making, and communication.

The Organizational Setting of Adult Education

Very few of the adult-education enterprises in this country are independent organizations. There are a small number of citizen-supported adult-education centers, proprietary schools, adult-education councils, educational television stations, and voluntary associations that were founded exclusively for the education of adults and that are autonomous. But most adult education takes place in settings that were established for purposes other than the education of adults—such as the education of children and

---

[1]Robert Gessner (ed.), *The Democratic Man: Selected Writings of Eduard C. Lindeman* (Boston: Beacon Press, 1956), p. 166. By permission.

Exhibit 5

SOME CHARACTERISTICS OF
STATIC VS. INNOVATIVE ORGANIZATIONS

Dimensions	Characteristics	
	Static Organizations	Innovative Organizations
Structure	Rigid—much energy given to maintaining permanent departments, committees; reverence for tradition, constitution, and by-laws. Hierarchical—adherence to chain of command. Roles defined narrowly. Property-bound.	Flexible—much use of temporary task forces; easy shifting of departmental lines; readiness to change constitution, depart from tradition. Multiple linkages based on functional collaboration. Roles defined broadly. Property-mobile.
Atmosphere	Task-centered, impersonal. Cold, formal, reserved. Suspicious.	People-centered, caring. Warm, informal, intimate. Trusting.
Management Philosophy and Attitudes	Function of management is to control personnel through coercive power. Cautious—low risk-taking. Attitude toward errors: to be avoided. Emphasis on personnel selection. Self-sufficiency—closed system regarding sharing resources. Emphasis on conserving resources. Low tolerance for ambiguity.	Function of management is to release the energy of personnel; power is used supportively. Experimental—high risk-taking. Attitude toward errors: to be learned from. Emphasis on personnel development. Interdependency—open system regarding sharing resources. Emphasis on developing and using resources. High tolerance for ambiguity.
Decision Making and Policymaking	High participation at top, low at bottom. Clear distinction between policymaking and policy execution. Decision making by legal mechanisms. Decisions treated as final.	Relevant participation by all those affected. Collaborative policymaking and policy execution. Decision making by problem-solving. Decisions treated as hypotheses to be tested.
Communication	Restricted flow—constipated. One-way—downward. Feelings repressed or hidden.	Open flow—easy access. Multidirectional—up, down, sideways. Feelings expressed.

youth, the production of goods, or the provision of services other than educational. Consequently, the adult-education enterprise is usually a part of and subordinate to some larger enterprise.

And this fact of life presents special problems to adult educators in developing organizational structures that are congruent with principles of andragogy. If their institutional setting is a public school, general policies are made by a school committee or board of education; administrative policies are made by a superintendent; and academic policies are made by a faculty—most of whom are oriented to the education of children. If the setting is a university, similar functions are performed by a board of trustees, president, and faculty whose orientation is youth education. If the setting is industry, these functions are usually performed by a board of directors and a chief executive whose orientation is primarily toward work productivity. If the setting is a government agency, a labor union, a library, a museum, a religious institution, a social agency, or a voluntary organization, the policy-making machinery is likely to be managed by people who do not have a primary orientation to the education of adults. Only in religious institutions and some social agencies, such as the YMCA, has there been a tradition of participant involvement in policy making that comes close to the requirements of andragogy. But even in these institutions, there is often a strong flavor of doing things *for* people that conflicts with the andragogical principle of mutual self-direction.

So adult educators are confronted with a choice of strategies for achieving an environment that is conducive to adult learning: 1) they can seek to change the larger organization so that its philosophy and practice will be more congruent with andragogical concepts; 2) they can develop a semi-independent structure for the adult-education operation within the larger structure; or 3) they can negotiate gradual modifications in policy (for example, as regards certification of teachers) and areas of freedom to experiment with organizational mechanisms (such as advisory councils) that would enable the adult educational operation to develop as a subenvironment within but not abrasive to the total organizational environment. My observation is that the adult-educational administrators, especially in schools, colleges, and industry, who have succeeded in developing the best educative environments, have started with the third strategy and then found that many of the changes they made in the adult-education program were picked up and adopted by the larger organization—which is, in effect, the intended result of the first strategy.

Providing a Policy Base

One of the visible trends in institutions of all sorts in recent years has been the increasing delineation of the adult-educational function. For example:

In Industry—

At first, the educational function was merely a secondary aspect of the line operations—an extra duty of the master craftsmen, foremen, supervisors, department heads, and executives. Then as personnel management became differentiated as a function, responsibility for training tended to become subsumed under it. Later there was a tendency for departments of training, personnel development, or employees' education to become separated out as independent units responsible to top management.[2]

---

[2]Malcolm S. Knowles, *The Adult Education Movement in the United States* (Huntington, N.Y.: Krieger Publishing Co., 1977), p. 80.

In Universities—

In spite of opposition at times from other departments, extension divisions or evening colleges were established in an increasing number of universities to coordinate all work with adults by these institutions.[3]

In Health and Welfare Agencies—

In the earlier HANDBOOKS (1934, 1936, 1948) only one agency (the YMCA) was identified as having an officer specifically responsible for adult education; but in 1960 almost every agency specified an office carrying a title such as "Director of Public Education," "Director, Health Education Department," "National Training Director," or "Director, Adult Program Services Department."[4]

In Public Schools—

It is not known how many full-time directors of adult education (or evening schools) had been appointed by city or county school systems by the end of World War I, but . . . in 1961 the National Association of Public School Adult Educators estimated that there existed about 500 full-time city directors of adult education and about 3,500 part-time directors or supervisors.[5]

It is clear to anyone who has observed this evolutionary phenomenon over the years that as institutions recognized the unique requirements of serving the educational needs of adults by establishing differentiated administrative units for this purpose, the volume and quality of these services rose dramatically. On the other hand, in those institutions in which the adult-educational function has remained as a secondary responsibility attached to other functions, the programs are often marginal and ineffective.

My observation of adult-education programs in all kinds of institutions across the country supports the generalization that there is a direct correlation between the strength of a program (as measured by size, vitality, quality of output, and support from the system) and its status in the policy-making structure. Thus, the strongest public-school programs are found in those systems in which the adult-education unit is parallel with elementary and secondary, and its chief executive officer is an associate superintendent; the strongest programs in industry are in those firms in which the employee-development function is parallel to personnel, production, sales, and other equivalent functions, and the chief executive officer is a vice-president; and the strongest programs in universities are in those institutions in which the adult-education unit is parallel to academic affairs, student personnel, and equivalent functions, and the chief executive officer is a vice-president for continuing education. The increased power and prestige that come with high organizational status do not in themselves entirely account for the improvement in performance, I believe; the more important consideration is that with autonomy and status the adult-education unit is able to concentrate on processes uniquely effective for the education of adults. And it is better able to attract specialists in andragogy to manage the program.

Criteria for a Policy Statement

Even with relatively autonomous administrative status, however, the adult-education unit is likely to be unable to come up to its full potential for service unless it is undergirded by a firm statement of institutional policy. From an analysis of policy

---

[3]Ibid., p. 85.
[4]Ibid., p. 105.
[5]Ibid., pp. 141-142.

statements of various institutions I have arrived at the conclusion that those in which adult education is the strongest applied such criteria as the following:

1. The part that adult education is uniquely to have in contributing to the accomplishment of the institution's mission is described clearly and with conviction.

2. A philosophical commitment to the absolute value of human growth and development and individual self-fulfillment is explicitly stated.

3. The specific purposes (in terms of individual and organizational outcomes) for which the adult-education program is established are described, but with latitude for the dynamic exploration of new possibilities for service.

4. The nature of the commitment of resources (in terms of priority order in relation to other purposes) of the policy makers to the furtherance of the adult-educational purposes is made clear, and is substantial.

5. The relationship of the adult-education component with other components of the institution is specified, preferably with emphasis on their processes of collaboration rather than on their divisions of authority and responsibility.

6. The target populations to be served by the program are specified.

7. Any limitations placed by the policy makers on the authorized scope of activities are clearly stated.

8. Any special conditions governing the employment, training, supervision, and compensation of personnel for the adult-education unit are stated.

9. Any special provisions for financial management and budgetary practices are specified.

10. The authorized bases of relationship with other institutions (such as in regard to services to be given or received, cosponsorship, financial arrangements, and sharing of facilities) are made clear.

Examples of Policy Statements

Some examples of policy statements for adult-education units in different institutions are given in Appendix F: for corporations (F–1), for a community college (F–2), for federal agencies (F–3 and 4), for health agencies (F–5), and for a university (F–6).

Building a Committee Structure

Types of Committees

Since most adult-education programs are attached to institutions or are aspects of organizations that also serve other purposes, there is usually a general policy-making board that has overall responsibility for the operation of the total agency. For example, in the case of a public school it is the school committee or board of education; in a university it is the trustees; in a church it is some equivalent by any of a number of names; in most social agencies and voluntary organizations it is a board of directors. These boards usually make the original decision to create an adult-education program and usually retain ultimate jurisdiction over its operation.

In many instances, especially in schools and universities, these general policy boards also attempt to maintain direct policy control over the adult-education program, delegating authority only to employed staff. This practice is likely to have several negative consequences. It often results in poor representation of the unique clientele served by the adult-education program, since the general board has to be representative of a broader clientele. It often results in overly rigid policy structures, since the general board cannot take time away from broad institutional problems to give attention to the day-to-day policy adjustments that make for vitality in an adult-education program. And it is bound to result in a low degree of ego-involvement on the part of the participants of the adult-education program in the life of the institution.

Higher-quality programs seem consistently to have resulted in those institutions in which the general board has created a committee structure with specific delegations of responsibility and authority for overseeing the operation of the adult-education program. In a social agency or voluntary organization there is usually a program committee or an adult-education committee with broad authority to establish operating policies within the framework of institutional policies. In a school system or university the more usual form is a citizens' advisory committee with more limited recommendatory authority. In a corporation or government agency the typical structure is an inservice-education committee, with the delegated authority being fairly specifically spelled out.

Just as the general board of an organization has too many responsibilities to be able to give the full attention required for the operation of an adult-education program, so an adult-education committee usually finds that it can be more effective if it delegates some of its responsibilities to subcommittees. Some of the subcommittees frequently found in effective adult-education programs are the following:

Budget and Finance
Program
Leadership Selection and Training
Physical Facilities and Equipment
Special Events
Promotion and Public Relations
Library, Visual Aids, and Curriculum Materials
Social Affairs and Entertainment
Counseling and Registration

Another device that has proved especially useful in large institutions is a substructure of specific program-area committees. Under this system a separate advisory committee is established for each program area—such as academic subjects, business subjects, arts and crafts, community service, literacy education, health education, home and family-life education, public-affairs education, science education, and the like. These subcommittees are delegated responsibility for assessing needs for new offerings in their respective subject areas, recruiting resource specialists, and in other ways helping to maintain high-quality learning. A good case can be made for populating these program subcommittees with representatives of the program participants, faculty members, subject specialists, and—where relevant—practitioners from the community. The chairmen of the subcommittees might well make up the overall program committee.

I cannot emphasize too strongly the importance of this kind of organizational structure in adult education. I have observed many adult-education programs across the country in schools, corporations, government agencies, universities, and social agencies, and the one characteristic that most clearly differentiates the weak programs from the strong programs is that the strong programs almost always have representative committee structures with a high delegation of authority to operate the programs, while the weak programs almost never do.

Of special utility in large adult-education programs is a modification of the familiar student council found in high schools and colleges. It might be called a participants' council or a program-advisory council. This device has been developed to the highest degree at Chicago's Central YMCA, where it works as follows: toward the end of each program year each activity unit (class or special-interest club) selects one person, through a process that combines volunteering and electing, to serve on the council for the succeeding year. At the first meeting of each new council, which is usually held in May, the members do three things: 1) they evaluate the program of the past year and make suggestions for improvements and additions for the following year; 2) they organize themselves into subcommittees of the types listed above; and 3) they nominate a small delegation of representatives to serve on the directing committee of the agency.

In September, members of the council are recruited to help the staff in the registration process, to serve as hosts and hostesses to greet new students and make them feel at home, to arrange exhibits interpreting the scope and content of the various activities of the program, to serve refreshments, and in other ways to enrich the educative environment. Members of the council are then assigned to serve as student hosts in the informal courses (for which they get their tuition free), in which capacity they introduce the students to one another, make administrative announcements, take care of administrative details (such as collecting registration cards, taking attendance, etc.), and generally assist the instructors. It has been the experience of this agency that such a council adds a great deal to the informal atmosphere for which the institution is well known in Chicago, that it greatly relieves the staff load in regard to certain administrative details, and that it gives the students a sense of direct participation in the management of their own affairs.

Functions of a Committee

Committees can be used for a variety of purposes, ranging from merely giving advisory opinions to the administrator or policy boards to taking full responsibility for operating policies under delegation from the board. In general, the more responsibility a committee is given, the more responsible it will be, the more deeply its members will become involved, and the more congruent the organization will be with principles of andragogy. Committees that are only asked for advice that can be accepted or rejected usually are not motivated to invest much energy in the welfare of the enterprise.

Among the functions that can be performed effectively by committees are the following:

1. Helping in the development of plans for surveys of the needs and interests of organizational members or the total community and perhaps sharing in the specific tasks involved in executing these plans;

2. Identifying current community and societal problems with which an adult-education program should be concerned;

3. Helping in the establishment of priorities among the various needs, interests, and problems;

4. Establishing policies governing the operation of the adult-education program within the limits of their delegated authority;

5. Formulating short-run goals or directions of movement for the program, subject to review by the policy board;

6. Interpreting the past achievements and future needs of the program to the policy board and exerting more potent influence on policy makers than is usually available to staff;

7. Contributing fresh and creative ideas to program planning;

8. Serving as talent scouts for new instructors, leaders, and resource people;

9. Providing linkages with target populations, institutions, and community agencies;

10. Lending volunteer help in registering students, conducting orientation sessions, checking physical facilities, and other administrative services during crisis periods;

11. Helping in the periodic evaluation of the total program;

12. Helping in the interpretation of the adult-education program to the general public.

If a committee is to be effective, however, it is crucial that its purpose, functions, and authority be clearly understood by everyone concerned. A written job description (or commission) should be approved by the appointing body and given to committee members as they are appointed. Exhibit 6 illustrates a commission to a committee that has been delegated a high degree of operating responsibility.

Composition of a Committee

Most membership organizations, such as church groups, men's and women's organizations, labor unions, and business firms, constitute their committees entirely from the membership of the organization. Committee members may be appointed by the president of the organization or by the chairman of the committee, or they may be elected by ballot, preferably for limited terms of office. In any case, the committee will be most effective if it includes representatives of the various points of view, special interests, and friendship circles (or cliques) within the membership. Members of any organization tend to accept and support programs to the extent that they perceive their special interests to have been adequately represented in the planning of them.

Institutional committees, on the other hand, such as those found in the schools, social agencies, and governmental organizations, usually attempt to include representation from a broad scope of community interests. In general, it is wise for such committees to include the following three types of representation:

1. The various points of view and interests within the participating membership of the organization itself;

2. The points of view, interests, geographic location, and types of experience in the community at large that are significant in relation to a particular program or institution (such as business, labor, racial and nationality groups, churches, etc.);

3. Experts with specialized skills or knowledge that are needed in program planning (such as librarians, physicians, artists, scientists, audiovisual experts, professional educators, public-relations specialists, etc.).

There is a danger, of course, that a committee that is truly representative of a wide variety of community interests would be too large and unwieldy. Cyril Houle has developed a simple system for selecting individuals who represent several categories. It is a two-way grid, portrayed in Exhibit 7, in which the criteria of representation are listed vertically and the board members are listed horizontally. In this example, three new board members are to be selected. Houle points out that, given the categories represented by the nine present board members, two of the new members should be under 35 years of age and one should be in the 35 to 50 bracket; two or three should be from the south side; probably all should be men; one should be a lawyer; and one should be an expert on building operation.

It would be a mistake, however, to form a committee purely on the basis of representation. Care must be taken to select individuals who not only represent some-

---

Exhibit 6

COMMISSION TO THE ADULT-EDUCATION COMMITTEE OF THE XYZ COMMUNITY CENTER

I. *Purpose.* The Adult Education Committee is created as a standing committee of the Board of Directors with responsibility to the Board for the development and operation of a program of services and activities, such as informal classes, clubs, forums, institutes, exhibits, and publications, for the adult residents of XYZ.

II. *Functions.* The Adult Education Committee is responsible to the Board for the establishment of policies governing the adult education program, and for reviewing and evaluating the execution of those policies. Through its chairperson it will report at each regular meeting of the Board concerning the work for which it is responsible.

III. *Membership.* The Adult Education Committee shall consist of a chairperson who is a member of the Board of Directors and who is appointed by the chairperson of the Board, and not more than twenty-five other members, to be appointed by the chairperson of the Adult Education Committee in consultation with the staff. In general, members of the Committee will be drawn from such representative groups, fields of experience, and points of view as the following:

Participants in the program	Racial and nationality groups
Public relations	International affairs
Libraries and museums	Science
Psychology and medicine	Audiovisual aids
Civic organizations	Press and radio
Industrial training	Religious institutions
Business and industry	Law
Labor	Literature
The arts	Recreation
Education	Government
Social service	Service clubs

IV. *Staff Relationships and Functions.* The Director of Adult Education is responsible for the execution of policies and the administration of the Adult Education Department. He or she exercises direct supervision over other employed and volunteer members of the staff, which is responsible for the following functions, within the policies established by the Committee and subject to review by it:

The establishment and supervision of class and group programs
Budgeting and financial control
Employment, training, supervision, and discharge of instructors and leaders
Planning and execution of promotion campaigns
Office management and administrative procedures
Staff work for the Committee

thing, but who will be effective, and such personal qualities must be kept in mind in selecting committee members as the following:

1) Interest in the program and its objectives;
2) Willingness to serve;
3) Competence or educability for the work of the committee;
4) Availability for the work, in terms of time, health, strength, and convenience of location;
5) Ability to work with other members of the committee;
6) Position of influence with significant elements of the community.

Some Guidelines for Effective Committee Operation

Getting committees to work effectively is dependent not only upon their having clear responsibilities and authority and having the right people on them, but also upon their having proper leadership. Probably the most vital element in proper leadership is the underlying attitude of the leaders—and through them, of the group—toward the locus of responsibility. When leaders feel that they, personally, are responsible for the success of the committee—that in effect it is their committee—the inevitable result is to reduce the feeling of responsibility of the other members of the group. Good group leaders will consistently throw back to the group all responsibilities that properly belong to the group as a whole. They will avoid making decisions that are the group's

Exhibit 7

GRID FOR SELECTING BOARD MEMBERS[6]

Criteria	Present Board Members									Potential Board Members		
	A	B	C	D	E	F	G	H	I	X	Y	Z
AGE under 35 years of age	X											
from 35 to 50 years of age		X		X		X						
over 50 years of age			X	X		X		X	X			
RESIDENCE north side of city	X	X			X	X		X				
west side of city			X				X		X			
south side of city				X								
SEX men			X		X		X					
women	X	X		X		X		X	X			
RESPONSIBILITIES personnel	X	X				X						
investment			X				X	X				
benefit		X			X			X				
contributions	X				X	X	X					
legal												
building			X				X					

[6]Cyril O. Houle, *The Effective Board* (New York: Association Press, 1960), p. 30.

to make, or doing their thinking for them. Those committees that have developed a high sense of group responsibility—of feeling that it is *our* committee, not *his* or *her* (the chairperson's) committee, or even *their* (the institution's) committee—are likely to be the most productive.

Several guiding principles apply specifically to committee operation:

1. A committee should understand clearly what it is to do and what its powers are. It isn't enough that it be given a written commission stating its objectives, functions, and authority; at least once each year it should review and test the meaning of such a commission in open discussion.

2. The committee should concern itself with real problems. It should not be put in the position of merely giving rubber-stamp approval to policies that have already been put into effect.

3. The agenda for each meeting should be based on problems and concerns the committee members consider important. An agenda that is developed from a problem census of the members of the committee will receive more responsible consideration than one that is prepared in advance by the chairman or staff member. (The problems that are of concern to the chair and the staff will, of course, be included in the problem census.)

4. The outcome of the committee's work should be continually interpreted to it. Activity leaders may be invited to committee meetings to describe outstanding achievements, exhibits may be arranged, and reports may be presented. It is important for the committee to have visual evidence of the significance of its work.

5. Committee members should be given first-hand experiences with the program, by appearing at ceremonial events, inspecting activities, serving as resource people in programs, and otherwise taking an active part.

6. The administrative work involved in efficient committee operation should be handled smoothly. Notices of meetings should be sent well in advance, materials of value in preparing for discussion should be distributed in time to be read, minutes of meetings should be duplicated and distributed, and appropriate action should be taken and reported on decisions made by the committee.

7. The committee should evaluate its work periodically by appropriate procedures as suggested in Chapter 10.

8. Responsibilities accepted by committee members should be clear, specific, and definite. Provision should be made by the committee for some method of following up on committee assignments, preferably by one of their own number rather than by the staff.

Providing Staff Services

There is such a diversity of management patterns in the wide range of institutions that are in the business of adult education that it is hazardous to become too prescriptive about a model staff structure. But the principles of andragogy suggest some guidelines that may help to strengthen the quality of administrative services in the adult-education units of institutions of all sorts:

1. *Differentiation of role.* The increasing insight that the adult-education process is different from other organizational processes requires that the personnel managing these processes be perceived as performing specialized roles that require specialized training. The time is past when any good teacher or principal has the equipment necessary to manage a public school adult-education program, or any good professor or dean can administer a university division of continuing education, or any good personnel manager can direct a training program in industry. These positions are no longer merely administrative jobs just like other administrative jobs; they are professional roles requiring specialized professional attitudes and competencies. This is not to say that people already in these positions cannot acquire these attitudes and competencies; they can, through self-study, attendance at workshops, and participation in graduate programs in adult education in some eighty universities. But this is likely to happen to the extent that the organizational structure acknowledges the professional nature of the role and provides for career development in it.

2. *Job description.* The unique nature of the adult-education process requires a more complex job description for the adult-education staff than is required by most other organizational positions. For one thing, if the talents of well-trained adult educators are to be used optimally by an organization, they must function both as line officers—managing the adult-education activities for which they are directly responsible—and as staff officers—influencing policies that affect the educative quality of the total organizational environment and providing consultative and training services to all personnel in the organization regarding their part in the educative process. For another thing, the very fluid nature of adult interests and needs dictates that a staff which has responsibility for keeping programs in tune with changing needs and interests have a greater degree of freedom to change plans quickly than is required in most other staff operations. The practice of requiring detailed program projections two years in advance has caused adult-education programs in some organizations to become irrelevant quickly. Job descriptions for adult-education staffs, therefore, tend to be broader, more general, more complicated, and more flexible than those for their organizational counterparts.

3. *Criteria for selection.* I frequently make an observation about the students attracted to graduate programs in adult education that I think has something to say about the peculiar character of andragogy and has some implications for criteria of selection of personnel for adult-education positions. My observation is that the people in graduate programs in adult education tend to be different from those attracted to other departments, such as secondary school teaching or the principalship or the superintendency. They tend to be less conformist, less inhibited, more adventuresome, more sensitive, and more active in community causes on the whole. They have a generalized attitude of experimentalism about themselves and their work, and take pride in the fact that they are pioneers in a new field. They tend to be impatient with the rituals and constraints of bureaucracy and to have a high tolerance for ambiguity. A person with a deep need for certainty, prescribed direction, and order often finds it difficult to tolerate the degree of personal flexibility that seems to be required to be an effective adult educator.

It is my observation that the administrators of the really effective adult-education programs in institutions of all sorts across the country stand out as being different from the general run of administrative personnel, too. These observations lead me to hypothesize that, owing to the unique requirements of the andragogical process, the effective adult-education administrators possess these characteristics:

1. They have a genuine respect for the intrinsic capacity of adults to be self-directing.

2. They derive their greatest satisfactions as administrators and educators from accomplishment through others.

3. They value the experience of others as a resource for accomplishing both work and learning by themselves and others.

4. They are willing to take risks that are involved in experimenting with new ideas and new approaches, and view failures as things to be learned from rather than defensive about.

5. They have a deep commitment to and skill in the involvement of people in organizational and educational processes.

6. They have a deep faith in the potency of educational processes for contributing to the solution of organizational and societal problems.

7. They are able to establish warm, empathic relationships with people of all sorts; to see the world through their eyes; to be a good listener.

8. They engage in a process of continuing education for themselves.

For Your Continuing Inquiry . . .

Regarding Organizational Philosophy and Structure

Baldrige, Victor, et al. *Policy Making and Effective Leadership: A National Study of Academic Management.* San Francisco: Jossey-Bass, 1978.

Basking, Samuel (ed.). *Organizing Nontraditional Study.* New Directions for Institutional Research, No. 4. San Francisco: Jossey-Bass, 1974.

Bennis, Warren G. *Changing Organizations.* New York: McGraw-Hill, 1966.

Carnegie Commission on Higher Education. *The Open Door Colleges: Policies for the Community College.* New York: McGraw-Hill, 1970.

Cohen, Arthur M., et al. *College Responses to Community Demands: The Community College in Changing Times.* San Francisco: Jossey-Bass, 1975.

Cross, K. Patricia, and Valley, John R. (eds.). *Planning Nontraditional Programs.* San Francisco: Jossey-Bass, 1974.

Eble, Kenneth E. *The Art of Administration: A Guide for Academic Administrators.* San Francisco: Jossey-Bass, 1978.

Evans, N. D., and Neagley, P. L. *Planning and Developing Innovative Community Colleges.* Englewood Cliffs, N.J.: Prentice-Hall, 1973.

Goodman, Paul S., et al. *New Perspectives on Organizational Effectiveness.* San Francisco: Jossey-Bass, 1977.

Gould, Samuel, et al. *Diversity by Design.* San Francisco: Jossey-Bass, 1973.

Hall, Laurence, et al. *New Colleges for New Students.* San Francisco: Jossey-Bass, 1974.

Harlacher, Ervin L., and Gollattscheck, James F. (eds.). *Implementing Community-Based Education.* New Directions for Community Colleges, No. 21. San Francisco: Jossey-Bass, 1978.

Hoppe, William A. (ed.). *Policies and Practices in Evening Colleges, 1971.* Metuchen, N.J.: Scarecrow Press, 1972.

Houle, Cyril O. *The External Degree.* San Francisco: Jossey-Bass, 1973.

Ingalls, John D. *Human Energy: The Critical Factor for Individuals and Organizations.* Reading, Mass.: Addison-Wesley, 1976.

Knowles, Malcolm S. *Higher Adult Education in the United States.* Washington, D.C.: American Council on Education, 1969.

Likert, Rensis. *The Human Organization: Its Management and Value*. New York: McGraw-Hill, 1967.

Lippitt, Gordon. *Organizational Renewal*. New York: Appleton-Century-Crofts, 1969.

Marty, Myron (ed.). *Responding to New Missions*. New Directions for Community Colleges, No. 24. San Francisco: Jossey-Bass, 1978.

McGregor, Douglas. *Leadership and Motivation*. Cambridge, Mass.: The Massachusetts Institute of Technology Press, 1967.

Richardson, Richard C., et al. *Governance for the Two-Year College*. Englewood Cliffs, N.J.: Prentice-Hall, 1972.

Rourke, Francis. *The Managerial Revolution in Higher Education*. Baltimore: Johns Hopkins Press, 1969.

Shaw, Nathan. *Administration of Continuing Education*. Washington, D.C.: National Association for Public Continuing and Adult Education, 1969.

Turk, Herman. *Organizations in Modern Life*. San Francisco: Jossey-Bass, 1977.

Vermilye, Dyckman W. (ed.). *Learner-Centered Reform*. San Francisco: Jossey-Bass, 1975.

Regarding Committee Operation

Houle, Cyril O. *The Effective Board*. Chicago: Association Press/Follett Publishing Co., 1960.

Trecker, Harleigh B. *Citizen Boards at Work*. Chicago: Association Press/Follett Publishing Co., 1970.

Regarding Staff Services

Chaddock, Paul H. "Selection and Development of the Training Staff," in Robert L. Craig (ed.)., *Training and Development Handbook*. Second edition. New York: McGraw-Hill, 1976, 3:1–19.

Human Development Library. *The Critical Requirements for Training Directors*. Cincinnati: Devine Garner and Associates, 1972.

Johnson, Richard B. "Organization and Management of Training," in Robert L. Craig (ed.)., op. cit., 2:1–17.

Leslie, David W. (ed.). *Employing Part-Time Faculty*. New Directions for Institutional Research, No. 18. San Francisco: Jossey-Bass, 1978.

Nadler, Leonard. *Developing Human Resources*. Houston: Gulf Publishing Co., 1970.

O'Banion, Terry (ed.). *Developing Staff Potential*. New Directions for Community Colleges, No. 19. San Francisco: Jossey-Bass, 1977.

Pinto, Patrick R., and Walker, James W. *A Study of Professional Training and Development Roles and Competencies*. Madison, Wis.: American Society for Training and Development, 1978.

Yarrington, Roger (ed.). *Educational Opportunity for All: New Staff for New Students*. Washington, D.C.: American Association of Junior and Community Colleges, 1973.

6
Assessing Needs
and Interests
in Program Planning

The Crucial Importance of This Step

In my several decades of visiting adult-education programs of all kinds around the continent, I have evolved a kind of divining rod for predicting before my visit where the program will fit along a spectrum ranging from one that is limping along from year to year at one end, to one that is vibrant with activity and flourishing at the other end. I simply ask on what bases the decisions are made as to what will be offered in the program.

If the answer is that the program is entirely planned by the staff on the basis of what the staff thinks people *ought* to be interested in, I can fairly confidently predict that participation in the program will be rather apathetic. On the other hand, if the answer is that the program is planned with the assistance of a planning committee (or advisory council) which conducts periodic surveys of the needs and interests of the clientele the program seeks to serve, then I predict that I will find a thriving program.

Educators who are oriented only to the pedagogical model, in which the educator is assigned the responsibility for determining what should be learned, have a difficult time understanding this fact of adult life. For there *are* things adults *ought* to learn in order to survive, to be employable, to stay healthy, to be happy, and to be good citizens. And if they were children we would make sure that they did learn these things—or else. But this is one of the central differences between pedagogy and andragogy. Children are essentially compulsory learners, in the sense that society administers punishments if they don't learn what they ought to, whereas adults are mostly volunteers in learning, in the sense that society does not punish them (at least directly) if they don't learn what they ought to; for them the "or else" is absent or, at most, weak.

So in andragogy the starting point in program planning is always the adults' interests, even though the end objective may be to meet their (and an institution's and society's) "real" needs. In fact, perhaps the highest expression of the art of the adult educator is skill in helping adults to discover and become interested in meeting their real needs. But in order for adult educators to have a chance to practice this art, they have first to reach their learners through their "felt needs" or interests.

The Nature of Needs

There is a good deal of confusion and controversy in the psychological literature regarding the nature of needs and interests, and the differences between them. It is not relevant to the purpose of this book to explore these issues, but the reader who is intrigued by the problem can engage in further inquiry through the references given at the end of this chapter. What is relevant to this book is the operational definition of needs and interests in a way that is useful for program development (the concern of this chapter) and the teaching-learning transaction (the concern of Chapter 11).

As I see it, two kinds of needs have meaning for adult educators in program development: 1) basic or organismic needs, and 2) educational needs.

Basic Human Needs

Although most psychologists agree that there are certain fundamental biological and psychological requirements common to all human beings, there is no agreement as yet on what they are—or, at least, on what to call them. Let me illustrate this point with a few examples from contemporary psychological literature. One formulation, the "Hierarchy of Needs" by Abraham Maslow, has already been described in Chapter 3. Gardner Murphy describes our "inborn needs" in terms of these quite different categories:

1. Visceral needs—that is, needs directly related to the vital organs. These include, among others, needs for food, water, air, etc., needs related to the reproductive system; needs related to protection of the body from extremes of cold and heat.

2. Activity needs. These include the need to explore and manipulate and the urge to "keep going" which differentiates a healthy child from a very tired or sick one, and a normal adult from an isolated psychotic adult.

3. Sensory needs. These include needs for color, tone, rhythm; the need to orient ourselves to the environment; the need to escape confusion; the "urge to perceptual clarity."

4. The need to avoid or escape attack, injury, threat, shock, or unbearable disturbance, as exemplified by fear, disgust, rage, and many other "emergency responses."[1]

Erich Fromm identified "man's needs as they stem from the conditions of his existence" as five in number: 1) relatedness vs. narcissism; 2) transcendence—creativeness vs. destructiveness; 3) rootedness—brotherliness vs. incest; 4) sense of identity—individuality vs. herd conformity; and 5) the need for a frame for orientation and devotion—reason vs. irrationality.[2] He then gives these concepts meaning in the context of mental health in these words:

Summing up, it can be said that the concept of mental health follows from the very conditions of human existence, and it is the same for man in all ages and all cultures. Mental health is characterized by the ability to love and to create, by the emergence from incestuous ties to clan and soil, by a sense of identity based on one's experience of self as the subject and agent of one's powers, by the grasp of reality inside and outside ourselves, that is, by the development of objectivity and reason.[3]

Fromm goes on to picture what a sane society, in which these needs would be fully satisfied, would be like.[4]

I have attempted to synthesize the insights regarding basic human needs that I have been able to cull from the psychological literature into a conceptual scheme that

---

[1]Gardner Murphy, *Human Potentialities* (New York: Basic Books, 1958), pp. 60–61.
[2]Erich Fromm, *The Sane Society* (New York: Rinehart, 1955), pp. 27–66.
[3]Ibid., p. 69.
[4]Ibid., p. 276.

I hoped would enable me better to understand human behavior—and particularly, the motivation of behavior. For what it may be worth to others, the result is reproduced in Exhibit 8.

Exhibit 8

ANTECEDENTS TO AN ACT OF BEHAVIOR

Needs (Motivating Forces) + Psychological Field = Behavior

Physical Growth Security New Experience Affection Recognition	+ Situational Forces and Personal Equipment	= AN ACTION

According to this formula, the starting point—the source of energy—for a human act is the pressure being exerted on individuals from their basic needs at a given moment. Usually several alternative courses of action to satisfy these needs and relieve the pressure will be open to us. Which of the alternatives we will choose will be determined (or at least influenced) by cultural forces (such as laws, mores, and economic conditions) and by the character of our personal equipment, including our abilities, goals, values, attitudes, and interests.

I have found several rather simple and practical implications of this conception of basic human needs for my own practice as an adult educator, including the following:

1. *Physical needs.* These are the most easily observed and usually the most consciously experienced needs, since they have to do with maintaining our body—and our body is notoriously gifted in providing symptoms when its needs are not being satisfied. In regard to adult education, people have the need to see, the need to hear, the need to be comfortable, and the need for rest, at the minimum. If writing is too small, if voices are too soft, if chairs are too hard, and if the time between breaks is too long, people tend to become so preoccupied with the symptoms of their unsatisfied physical needs that they cannot concentrate on learning. Notice, for example, how fidgety people become if a meeting drags on after the normal lunch hour, or how drowsy they become during a lecture immediately following lunch or late in the evening, or how irritable they become when they are tired. On the positive side, human beings have a driving need to be healthy, with the result that they are strongly motivated to invest millions of dollars in vitamin pills, patent medicines, and courses in recreational skills and physical fitness. Physical needs are a compelling source of motivation for a large share of people's actions.

2. *Growth needs.* Psychologists and psychiatrists are coming to see the need to grow as perhaps the most basic and universal drive of all. Rogers speculates that "rather than many needs and motives, it seems entirely possible that all organic and psychological needs may be described as partial aspects of this one fundamental need."[5] The term "self-actualization" is used by Goldstein to describe this one basic striving.[6] Sullivan points out that "the basic direction of the organism is forward."[7] According to Horney,

---

[5]Carl R. Rogers, *Client-Centered Therapy* (Boston: Houghton Mifflin Co., 1951), pp. 487–488.

[6]Kurt Goldstein, *Human Nature in the Light of Psychotherapy* (Cambridge, Mass.: Harvard University Press, 1940).

[7]Harry Stack Sullivan, *Conceptions of Modern Psychiatry* (Washington, D.C.: W. A. White Foundation, 1945), p.48.

"The ultimate driving force is the person's unrelenting will to come to grips with himself, a wish to grow and to leave nothing untouched that prevents growth."[8]

The growth urge explains many of the things people do. It is noticeable in children, for example, that the urge to learn to talk, crawl, walk, and to grow in many other ways is so strong that it cannot be diverted. Adolescents feel a driving need to break away from parental control, even in the most permissive and loving homes. There can be no doubt that children are motivated by a powerful urge to grow up.

There is convincing evidence that this urge continues to operate throughout normal life. The mature adult who can see no future for himself is a familiar—and pitiful—figure in psychological clinics. Without some future to grow to, life becomes less worthwhile. Even in old age there is apparently a need to keep growing. Studies of retired persons reveal that those who have found a new purpose in life toward which they can continue to strive tend to make a better adjustment than those who have not mapped out new directions to explore.[9]

The urge for growth is an especially strong motivation for learning, since education is, by definition, growth—in knowledge, understanding, skills, attitudes, interests, and appreciation. The mere act of learning something new gives one a sense of growth.

3. *The need for security.* It has long been recognized that all animal life is dominated by a strong instinct for self-preservation. The need for security includes the need for physical safety but goes beyond this into the requirement of psychological safety—protection against threat to our self-respect and our self-image. It is this need that motivates people to be cautious and reserved in a strange setting. Because of this need we are likely to feel most comfortable in work that is systematic and in surroundings that are orderly. We like to know where to find things, what is going to happen next, and where we are going. We tend to resist giving up old familiar ways of doing things for new ways, even if they seem better, because we are more secure in the old ways.

When the need for security is not satisfied or is violated, various behavioral symptoms are likely to result. Some people in some situations will respond to feelings of insecurity by pulling into their shell—withdrawing from participation, playing it safe until they get their bearings. Others respond to the same feelings in exactly the opposite way: they seek to protect themselves by taking over, controlling, dominating.

4. *The need for new experience.* While human beings seek security, they also crave its opposite—adventure, excitement, and risk. People tend to become bored with too much routine, too much security. When their need for new experience is frustrated, they tend to develop such behavioral symptoms as restlessness, irritability, impulsiveness, or indifference. Because of the need for new experience, people are motivated to seek new friends, new interests, new ways of doing things, and new ideas.

5. *The need for affection.* All people want to be liked, even though the ways they go about achieving it sometimes seem to indicate the opposite desire. This is the most social of the needs, the one that causes people to be willing to do things to please others even at personal sacrifice, that causes them to seek out certain individuals with whom they can share interests, experiences, joys, and sorrows. When people feel they are not liked—when their need for affection is frustrated—they may respond at either of two extremes, either by withdrawing and pouting or by lashing out with aggressive

---

[8]Karen Horney, *Self Analysis* (New York: W. W. Norton, 1946), p. 175.

[9]See Samuel Granick and Robert D. Patterson (eds.), *Human Aging II: An Eleven-Year Follow-up Biomedical and Behavioral Study.* DHEW Publication No. (HSM) 71-9037 (Washington, D.C.: Government Printing Office, 1971).

hostility. Or they may choose the middle route of apple-polishing, pseudodeferential behavior.

6. *The need for recognition.* All human beings need to feel that they have worth, that they are admired and respected by somebody for something. This desire motivates people to strive for position in their social groups, institutions, and communities. It causes them to seek status and attention. People who find themselves denied the satisfaction of this need are likely to develop such symptoms on the one hand as self-deprecation and retreat or on the other hand as showing off, boisterousness, monopolizing conversations, wearing conspicuous clothing, or in other ways seeking attention.

It is sometimes difficult for people to accept these deep personality needs as being normal and natural—much less, as healthy and helpful—because their behavioral symptoms can be so irritating and even destructive. But anyone who wants to help people learn must accept personality needs as inherent in the nature of man and as the most powerful sources of motivation for learning.

Adult educators who understand these needs will take them into account in many ways. They will provide for physical comfort and will seek to develop physical well-being. They will assure individuals a learning experience that will give them a sense of growth. They will offer programs designed to increase the economic, social, psychological, and spiritual security of adults, and will provide an environment in which they will feel secure while learning. They will expose adults to the adventure of new interests, new ideas, new friends, and new ways of doing things, and will make certain that the program never becomes dull and routine. They will provide opportunity for the development of warm relationships between students and teachers and among students, and will try to assure that there is always an atmosphere of friendliness in the activities for which they are responsible. They will accept the fact that all people need recognition and they will be ingenious in creating numerous opportunities for adults to obtain recognition constructively.

Wise leaders of adults will do more. They will develop in themselves the habit of looking beyond the surface symptoms of behavior to their causes. They will refrain from making snap judgments about the goodness or badness of any act, but will always ask, "Why?" They will help adults to become aware of their needs and to enlarge their experience and improve their ability so as to be able to satisfy these needs through more effective behavior. They will see that one of the objectives of all education is to help people gain a more objective understanding of the causes of their own behavior and to become more skillful in diagnosing their own needs for further self-development in order better to satisfy their basic physical and psychological needs.

One other aspect of this notion of basic human needs requires some attention before we leave it, and that is the time dimension. The developmental psychologists emphasize that these basic needs must be understood in the perspective of time—that they change in intensity and quality over the life span. Kuhlen puts it this way:

> We have seen that as years pass there are in adults' lives two contrasting needs: a positive force toward the achievement of positive goals, an expansion, a progressing of the individual; and a negative force, an increasing need to conserve and to protect against losses, often shown in a defensiveness that results in self-limitation and handicapping. The first of these, the positive need, is probably strongest up to middle age; the second, the negative need, becomes increasingly important with increased adult age.[10]

---

[10]Raymond G. Kuhlen, "Patterns of Adult Development," in Gardner Murphy and Raymond Kuhlen, *Psychological Needs of Adults* (Chicago: Center for the Study of Liberal Education for Adults, 1955), pp. 23–24. (Available from Syracuse University Library of Continuing Education.)

There can be no doubt that age does affect basic needs. For example, the need for recognition or achievement may decline with increasing age as a result of satisfaction, and be surpassed by other needs—unless there should occur some threat to this satisfaction (such as loss of job or a family scandal that threatens status) which produces a resurgence of these needs.

But it is dangerous to overgeneralize these effects of aging, as some gerontologists have done, into a "disengagement theory" which in effect postulates that it is a universal human need to disengage from life activities as one grows older. The disengagement theory is stated by its authors, Elaine Cumming and William Henry, as follows:

> Starting from the common-sense observation that the old person is less involved in the life around him than he was when he was younger, we can describe the process by which he becomes so, and we can do this without making assumptions about its desirability. In our theory, aging is an *inevitable* mutual withdrawal or disengagement, resulting in decreased interaction between the aging person and others in the social system he belongs to. [Italics by MSK.][11]

This theory was evolved from and tested by data obtained through interviews with a sample of healthy adults fifty years of age and over in Kansas City, Missouri. It was a cross-sectional study in that it compared characteristics between age groups, rather than a longitudinal study describing changes in individuals over time. And this is a great weakness, considering the difference in the styles of living during the formative years of youth between those born in 1885 (the seventy-year-olds in 1960) and those born in 1910 (the fifty-year-olds in 1960). Cumming and Henry themselves acknowledge, "There is always the possibility that we are getting generational effects where we say we are getting aging effects. Only the testing of the theory put forward here will determine this."[12]

But there are other difficulties with the theory. To what extent do some people pull in their sails as they get older because they think that is what is expected of them? Indeed, to what extent do our social institutions (such as compulsory retirement) force withdrawal of older people from normal life activity? And how are we to interpret the enormous difference among individual older people; what are we to make of the fact that some people really blossom out after retirement and do all the things they have wanted to do all their lives?

Clearly, the disengagement theory is on too shaky ground at this point to stand as an indication of another basic human need. As its authors suggest, its greatest utility lies in the suggestion of lines of further research, especially longitudinal studies. As a guide for action its effect would be curiously negative, for it would result in the curtailment of activities for older people—providing thereby a perfect example of a self-fulfilling prophecy. It seems to me that adult educators, almost as an article of their faith, have a responsibility to pursue the opposite line of action—to provide the richest possible opportunities for continuing growth and self-fulfillment, and to let the older adults choose, individually, which route to follow for themselves. My hunch is that those whose style of life has been one of high involvement will continue to be involved, and that those who have never been deeply involved will continue to be uninvolved. But I think we have to leave them the option.

I believe that I'll have to go along with Abraham Maslow in assuming that the highest human need is for self-actualization, and that we work at it until we die; and with Harry Stack Sullivan, that the deepest human need is for self-esteem, and that each of us has an obligation to help one another achieve and maintain it.

---

[11]Elaine Cumming and William E. Henry, *Growing Old* (New York: Basic Books, 1961), p. 14.
[12]Ibid., p. 35.

Educational Needs

Up to this point we have used the term "needs" in the broad general sense of universal human biological and psychological requirements. These basic needs have relevance to education in that they provide the deep motivating springs for learning, and in that they prescribe certain conditions that the educators must take into account if they are to help people learn.

An educational need, on the other hand, is something people ought to learn for their own good, for the good of an organization, or for the good of society. It is the gap between their present level of competencies and a higher level required for effective performance as defined by themselves, their organization, or society. This definition is portrayed graphically in Exhibit 9.

Exhibit 9

DEFINITION OF EDUCATIONAL NEED

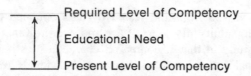

Required Level of Competency

Educational Need

Present Level of Competency

An educational need, therefore, is the discrepancy between what individuals (or organizations or society) want themselves to be and what they are; the distance between an aspiration and a reality. And an educational need can be defined broadly or narrowly. Thus, if I aspire to be a broadly cultured human being who is knowledgeable about the great works and ideas of literature, philosophy, science, and the arts, I have defined an educational need for myself that encompasses most of a liberal education, especially if I am starting from a base of narrow technical training. On the other hand, if I am about to lose my job because the installation of a new system requires that I be able to operate a computer, my educational need is rather narrow and specific.

The more concretely individuals can identify their aspirations and assess their present level of competencies in relation to them—the more exactly they can define their educational needs—the more intensely will they be motivated to learn. And the more congruent the needs of individuals are with the aspirations their organizations and society have for them (or the other way around—the more congruent the aspirations organizations and society are with the educational needs of individuals), the more likely will effective learning take place.

A crucial element in the art of the adult educator is skill and sensitivity in helping the relevant parties to assess the educational needs of individuals, organizations, and society; to negotiate some congruence among them; and then to stimulate the translation of needs into interests. Techniques available in this undertaking are described later in this and succeeding chapters.

The Nature of Interests

In the *Encyclopedia of Psychology*, interests are defined as "factors within an individual which attract him to or repel him from various objects, persons, and activities within his environment."[13] But in the context of our previous discussion perhaps

---

[13]Ralph Berdie, "Interests," *Encyclopedia of Psychology* (New York: Philosophical Library, 1946).

"educational interest" could be more specifically defined as the expressed preference among possible activities perceived as potentially satisfying educational needs. If a need is expressed behaviorally as a "want" or a "desire," then an interest can be said to be expressed as a "liking" or a "preference."

General Interests

Interests are by their nature highly personal and therefore vary widely among individuals and even vary within an individual from time to time. But several attempts have been made to develop generalized categories of interests that serve as useful guidelines in discovering the specific interests of particular people. For example, Lorge has contributed the very practical set of categories of general interests given in Exhibit 10 under the heading "Incentives for Adult Learning."

Exhibit 10

INCENTIVES FOR ADULT LEARNING[14]

People Want to Gain

1. Health
2. Time
3. Money
4. Popularity
5. Improved appearance
6. Security in old age
7. Praise from others
8. Comfort
9. Leisure
10. Pride of accomplishment
11. Advancement: business, social
12. Increased enjoyment
13. Self-confidence
14. Personal prestige

They Want to Be

1. Good parents
2. Social, hospitable
3. Up to date
4. Creative
5. Proud of their possessions
6. Influential over others
7. Gregarious
8. Efficient
9. "First" in things
10. Recognized as authorities

They Want to Do

1. Express their personalities
2. Resist domination by others
3. Satisfy their curiosity
4. Emulate the admirable
5. Appreciate beauty
6. Acquire or collect things
7. Win others' affection
8. Improve themselves generally

They Want to Save

1. Time
2. Money
3. Work
4. Discomfort
5. Worry
6. Doubts
7. Risks
8. Personal embarrassment

Factors That Affect Interest

Lorge's list of interests seems to have a highly middle-class flavor, and one of the strong and much-researched presumptions among adult educators is that interests vary greatly according to socioeconomic level. It is well established, for example, that the

---

[14]Irving Lorge, "Effective Methods in Adult Education," *Report of the Southern Regional Workshop for Agricultural Extension Specialists* (Raleigh: North Carolina State College, June, 1947), p. 25.

proportion of participants over nonparticipants in all forms of adult education rises as such indicators of socioeconomic level as occupation, income, and education rise. The relationship between occupation and participation is graphically illustrated in Exhibit 11.

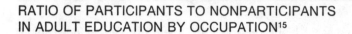

Exhibit 11

RATIO OF PARTICIPANTS TO NONPARTICIPANTS
IN ADULT EDUCATION BY OCCUPATION[15]

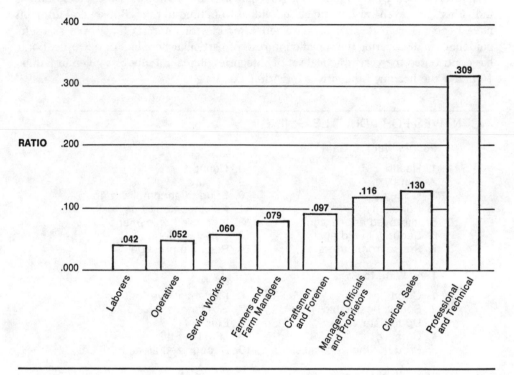

The effect of previous formal education on participation in adult education has been documented by many studies, but most authoritatively in Johnstone's national survey, which showed that the annual rate of participation was 6 percent among those with only a grade-school education, 20 percent for those who had completed high school, and 38 percent among those who had been to college.[16] The following additional generalizations about the influence of socioeconomic factors are made in the Johnstone study:

1. The lower classes place less emphasis on the importance of high educational attainment. . . .

2. The average deprived person is interested in education in terms of how useful and practical it can be to him. . . .

[15]Alan Booth, "A Demographic Consideration of Non-Participation," *Adult Education* XI (Summer, 1961), p. 225. Based on data from Marie Wann and Marthine Woodward, *Participation in Adult Education*, Office of Education Circular No. 539 (Washington: D.C.: Government Printing Office, 1959).
[16]John W. C. Johnstone and Ramon J. Rivera, *Volunteers for Learning* (Chicago: Aldine Publishing Co., 1965), pp. 95–97; copyright ©1965 by National Opinion Research Center.

3. Although education is widely recognized as an appropriate channel for social mobility, the average lower-class person is less ready than the average middle-class person to engage in continuing education even if tangible economic rewards are at stake. . . .

4. The average lower-class person does not perceive education in terms of personal growth or self-realization, and this may explain why the lower classes are much less ready to turn to adult education for recreational purposes than they are for purposes of vocational advancement.[17]

It is well known, too, that interest both in continuing one's education in general and in studying particular subjects varies with such other factors as sex, regional location, urban or rural residence, race, and size and type of community.[18]

Changes in Interest During the Life Cycle

One of the most significant factors for program planning is the changing pattern of interest as a person moves through the life cycle. Although the number of interests a person has through his or her adult life span may remain relatively constant, the content and time-energy investment in them tend to change.

Vocational and family life interests tend to dominate the pattern of concerns of young adults (age eighteen to thirty-five) as they seek to establish themselves in work and home. In middle adulthood (age thirty-five to fifty-five) these concerns decrease in favor of interests in civic and social activities and in health. As individuals near the age of retirement, their area of interest comes to be occupied largely by concerns for cultural and interpretive (including religious) aspects of life and with health problems connected with advancing age.[19]

The following useful word-picture has been developed by Alan Knox to illustrate with three typical subpopulations some of the changing interests of adults during the adult life cycle, how they differ for people who have taken different experiential routes through life, and how adult interests relate to adult-education programs.

> The *middle class homemaker* typically prepares for a career in college and then works for several years, including the first year or two of marriage. Occupational interests then drop abruptly, however, as she spends about ten years of her life with pre-school children in the home. Until about 35 years of age the rate of participation in adult education programs for mothers is substantially lower than for men, or for women who are not mothers, or for mothers after 35—reflecting the incarceration of this period of motherhood. Hendrickson reported that the adult education interests of young married women stress home decoration, improving the personality, first aid, psychology, understanding children, use of income, and moving to new neighborhoods.[20] In Berry's study, three-quarters of the mothers under 35 said that arrangements for child care would make a difference regarding adult education participation.[21] Reasons given for attending adult education programs emphasize meeting new people and escaping dull routine. . . . The period around the time when the youngest

---

[17]Ibid., pp. 236–63.

[18]For a statistical description of these variations, see ibid., pp. 88–115.

[19]For a detailed report of research on changing patterns of interest, see Sidney L. Pressey and R. G. Kuhlen, *Psychological Development through the Life Span* (New York: Harper, 1957).

[20]Andrew Hendrickson and Elizabeth Foster, *Educational Needs of Out-of-School Youth* (Columbus, Ohio: Ohio State University, 1960).

[21]Jane Berry and Sandra Epstein, *Continuing Education of Women: Needs, Aspirations, and Plans* (Kansas City: University of Kansas City, 1963).

child starts to school provides a break in continuity, and is often a turning point. . . . What they do during this young adult period, including adult education, is influenced by their husbands' attitudes. Many enter the labor force with "a job," some return to or launch "a career," and some become heavily involved in community projects such as the League of Women Voters. . . .

The interests of the *middle class man* are dominated by his career. . . . In his twenties, dominant concerns are clarifying his self-concept and focusing his life largely through his career. In his thirties, a primary concern is in collecting his energies for a major drive towards his highest career goal. It is during this period that the rate of participation in adult education is highest, with much emphasis on education in anticipation of assumption of more major responsibility. . . . During middle age, middle class men shift from exerting and asserting themselves to maintaining their position and changing roles. . . . The increase of men in liberal education programs or the arts or political affairs is evident in adult education enrollment figures. As their wives' interests have become more aggressive and egocentric, theirs have become more social and emotional. Adult education programs for this period in the life cycle, and for the next, in which they decide whether to disengage from their career and how, are so infrequent that it is difficult to predict what the responses might be.

The interests of the *man with less education* follow a very different pattern. He started his career earlier, not having to spend four to eight years in college, and hit the peak in terms of job satisfaction, pay, and responsibility in his early thirties. His participation in adult education is far less frequent than his white collar counterpart and it tends to be adaptive, occurring after terminating a job rather than before. The friendship group is far more influential in determining if he will enroll in adult education, as compared with the white collar worker. While the middle class man learns about available adult education programs from the impersonal mass media, the man with less education depends on personal contact and his friends are not likely to have any useful information. Myths about education being "only for children" are far more prevalent in blue collar culture. . . . In addition, the leisure style of the blue collar worker tends not to include participation in formal voluntary associations. The formal organization of most adult education programs creates another barrier. Adult education programs designed to reach large numbers of blue collar workers, and their wives, will need to take into account the major ways in which their interests differ substantially from those of the middle class adults who administer, teach in, and enroll in adult education. To do so will probably require working with and through organizations and informal groups with which the blue collar worker is connected. . . .[22]

General Subject Interests

In spite of variations in interest according to a variety of factors, the fact remains that, taking all the adult-education activities in the country as a whole, certain subjects are more popular than others. In a study commissioned by the Commission on Non-Traditional Study and conducted by the Response Analysis Corporation of Princeton, New Jersey, a representative sample of American adults were asked: 1) "Is there anything in particular that you'd like to know more about, or would like to learn how to do better"; and 2) if you have received instruction within the past twelve months in "evening classes, extension courses, correspondence courses, on-the-job training, private lessons, independent study, TV courses or anything like that." The "would-be learners"—those desiring more education—represented 79.8 million people, and the

---

[22]Alan B. Knox, "Interests and Adult Education," *Journal of Learning Disabilities*, Vol. I, No. 2 (February, 1968). By permission.

"learners"—people actually engaged in part-time education—represented 32.1 million. Their first choices of subjects for study are presented in Exhibit 12.

Exhibit 12

AREAS OF LEARNING INDICATED AS THE FIRST CHOICE OF
WOULD-BE LEARNERS AND STUDIED BY LEARNERS[23]

Areas of Learning	Would-Be Learners Number (in millions)	Percent	Learners Number (in millions)	Percent
Vocational subjects (excluding agriculture)	34.3	43.0	11.2	35.0
Hobbies and recreation	10.7	13.4	13.4	41.8
General education	10.1	12.6	8.1	25.2
Home and family life	9.6	12.0	4.3	13.3
Personal development	5.4	6.8	3.7	11.4
Public affairs	3.6	4.5	2.1	6.4
Religious studies	2.4	3.0	4.4	13.8
Agriculture	2.3	2.9	1.1	3.4

Assessing Needs and Interests

Although it is useful for adult educators to have a broad understanding of the general framework and national patterns of needs and interests presented above, they would be risking their art (if not their jobs) if they presumed that these patterns would apply automatically to particular individuals or constituencies. The chief value of these generalizations is to provide some clues for assessing the specific needs and interests of the individuals, organizations, and communities with which they are dealing directly. There is no shortcut to the crucial but sometimes arduous task of getting the facts about each situation.

There are three sources of needs and interests that must be considered in adult-education program planning: 1) those of the individuals to be served, 2) those of the sponsoring organization or institutions, and 3) those of the community or society at large. Techniques for assessing these three types of needs and interests will be considered in turn.

Needs and Interests of Individuals

Educational Needs

Clues as to what people ought to be learning for their own good can be obtained from several sources:

1. *From the individuals themselves.* Most individuals are aware of some of their needs for further development, whether or not these have yet risen to the point of becoming

---

[23]Samuel B. Gould, et al., *Diversity by Design* (San Francisco: Jossey-Bass, 1973), p. 17. For a more detailed listing of subject interests, see J.W.C. Johnstone and Ramon J. Rivera, *Volunteers for Learning* (Chicago: Aldine Publishing Company, 1965,) pp.49–50.

interests (in the sense that they want to do something about them now). So if you ask people through interviews, group discussion, or questionnaire, "What do you need to learn in order to have a better life?" you will get some answers. The chances are, though, that these will be fairly superficial answers that the respondents feel are safe to give publicly.

But you are likely to get deeper and more reliable clues as to what the individual's real needs are if you don't ask the question that directly. Two alternative techniques available are the projective and the sentence-completion questionnaires.

The projective questionnaire asks respondents to project themselves into some situation and tell how they feel or would behave. For example, a group of young homemakers might be asked questions like the following:

As you are taking your morning shower, getting dressed, and preparing breakfast, what worries about the day ahead typically come into your mind?

When you read your daily newspaper, what topics do you wish you understood better?

What problems do your children present that you feel least adequate to deal with?

When you are shopping in the supermarket and department store, at what points do you wonder if you are making the right choices?

When you are visiting with friends, what subjects of conversation do you find you feel dumb about?

When you think about what you should be doing ten years from now, what insecurities about yourself do you feel?

If you should have to go to work tomorrow, what difficulties would you anticipate?

If your husband should ask you, "How can we make our marriage happier?" what would you say?

It is important, of course, that questionnaires of this type be anonymous and that individual responses be treated confidentially. The contents of the responses can be coded according to categories of needs and can yield rich insights into the range and depth of the gaps a given population feels between their aspirations and their performance.

Two intriguing variations in this technique were developed by two of my former graduate students, both of whom were concerned with inservice education for nurses. One developed a *card sort,* in which she typed on three-by-five cards, one to a card, fifty-two problem situations nurses typically confront in the course of a week's work in a hospital. Then she asked each nurse in her hospital to place these cards in three piles: in the pile on the left, all those situations in which she would feel perfectly secure and competent; in the pile on the right, those situations in which she would feel very insecure; and in the pile in the middle, those situations in which she feels she would perform only moderately well. By tabulating the frequency with which problem situations showed up in the right-hand pile, the director of inservice education was able to identify several training needs that had not previously been identified. The other graduate student developed a *picture sort,* in which she used the same three-pile technique, but with photographs of problem situations which she had actually taken in her hospital. They felt that better data were obtained from the picture sort.

The sentence-completion questionnaire gets much the same quality of information by asking the respondent to complete sentences with such beginnings as the following:

When I get up in the morning and think about the day ahead, I . . .

As a mother, I wish I . . .

As a wife, I would like . . .

When I think about the possibility of having to get a job, I . . .
When participating in serious discussions with friends, I . . .
When I think about the future, I . . .

The content of the completed sentences can be coded according to categories of needs in the same way as the projective questionnaires.

Diagnosis of competency-development needs by use of a competency model is the newest approach to helping individuals assess their needs for learning. The model presented in Appendix B is an example of   preconstructed model of competencies for performing the role of adult educator. Similar models have been developed for roles in the health professions, the ministry, the armed services, elementary and secondary education, counseling, teaching in adult basic education, and industrial management and training. But a number of adult educators have found that it is almost as effective to have the learners develop their own models, usually in teams, and then help one another check out the objectivity of their self-assessments. This procedure is described in greater detail in Chapter 11.

2. *From people in "helping roles" with individuals.* Through interviews or direct questionnaires much useful information regarding the needs of individuals can often be obtained from the people to whom they bring their problems: family-service counselors, ministers, priests, rabbis, social workers, visiting nurses, physicians, State Employment Service interviewers, political ward leaders, and labor-union business agents, for example.

3. *From the mass media.* Editors of newspapers and popular magazines and producers of television programs have been more or less professionally trained to be sensitive to pressure points in the personal lives of the populations they serve. Clues regarding trends in the changing patterns of individual needs can therefore frequently be picked up from an analysis of the themes being given prominence in the mass media. At the time of the writing of this book, for example, the need for individuals better to understand the effects of smoking and drugs is clearly evidenced in all the mass media.

4. *From professional literature.* Professional journals in the fields of adult education, psychology, sociology, anthropology, political science, religion, economics, psychiatry, science, the humanities, and social work carry articles that yield insights into the deeper needs of adults for continuing self-development. Trade books and textbooks in these fields are also rich mines of information.

A strong theme in much of the professional literature of the social sciences in recent times, for instance, has been the growing need for individuals to learn how to adapt to—and participate in—change. It is pointed out that most of the adults living today have been equipped by their education and experience with the attitudes and skills required to maintain stability, and that this equipment is dysfunctional in a society characterized by rapid change. Presumably, as was suggested in Chapter 3, a part of the adult educator's mission is to help adults to learn to cope with change.

5. *From organizational and community surveys.* The techniques that are suggested later in this chapter for assessing the needs of organizations and communities will also produce findings that have implications for the needs of individuals. To the extent that an individual wants to function effectively in an organization and a community, their needs become his or her needs.

Educational Interests

Since interests are expressions of preference among alternative activities, the only valid source of information about the interests of adults is the individuals themselves.

This may seem to be a simple and self-evident truth that is trite to state, but it is surprising how many of us—adult educators and others—in actual practice act on assumptions about what people would be interested in rather than finding out from them.

A simple exercise brings home to my students the danger of prejudging the interests of people; perhaps you would find it interesting to try: 1) think of three people you feel you know best (my students typically pick sweethearts, mothers or fathers, husbands or wives, brothers and sisters, classmates, colleagues at work, or close friends); 2) for each person, take a sheet of paper and write on it a list of the things you think he or she would answer if you asked, "If time and money were no barrier, what new things would you like to know or be able to do, in order of preference?"; 3) then arrange to interview each person, ask that question, and on a separate sheet of paper record the answers; 4) now compare the two lists for each person and see how far off you were in your prediction, both as to content of the items and their priority order. In years of experimenting with this exercise not one of my students has come up with a 100 percent correlation, and most of them are astounded at how far off the mark their predictions were.

From the point of view of getting reliable information, therefore, the time and energy it takes to make periodic surveys of the interests of a program's clientele can be justified. But there is an even more compelling justification which is explained by the theory of andragogy. And this is that the very act of asking individuals to state their preferences involves them in the program-planning process, gives them a sense of influencing decisions that affect them, and makes them feel a part of a mutual undertaking. From this point of view, one might say that good program promotion starts with involving potential participants in interest assessment.

Evidence concerning the interests of individuals can be obtained from two sources:

1. *From the individuals themselves.* As in the case of getting clues about needs, you can ask people directly, through interviews, group discussion, or questionnaires, "What are you interested in learning?"

Interviews can be informal and casual as the program director and committee members meet people under the wide variety of circumstances of their daily activities. Or they can be highly formalized according to the best procedures of survey research, with either random or stratified samples of the population and highly structured interview schedules.[24] Or they can be somewhere in between—say, as a semiformal aspect of the registration process.

Group discussion as a device for interest finding can also range from formal to informal. In organizations or communities in which a number of groups meet regularly for various purposes (boards, committees, recreational groups, religious groups, civic groups, etc.), arrangements can be made for them to set aside a part of a regular meeting to pool their thoughts about new educational activities they would like to have made available to them. Or a systematic series of open hearings, of the sort used frequently in rural communities by the agricultural extension service and in cities by urban-renewal agencies, can be conducted under more or less formal procedures (although even under these conditions, the use of such techniques as buzz groups and brainstorming, described in Chapter 11, may yield enlightening results).

---

[24]For guidance in conducting scientific interview surveys, see Robert Kahn and Charles Cannell, *The Dynamics of Interviewing* (New York: Wiley, 1957).

Questionnaires, as in the case of need assessment, can be either direct or projective. The *direct questionnaire* simply asks respondents to indicate their preferences among a variety of activities, as illustrated in Exhibit 13. Two quick suggestions can greatly increase the usefulness of such a questionnaire: 1) try it out with a small sample of people before distributing it en masse to be sure that it is clear, discriminating, and capable of simple tabulation; and 2) provide for indication of degrees of interest from lukewarm to hot (otherwise you are likely to get mostly what your respondents think would be good for other people). The *projective questionnaire* attempts to tease out more subtle clues as to respondents' interests by asking them to project themselves into situations and reveal their feelings about them. For illustration, a group of young homemakers might be asked questions like these:

When you pick up your daily paper tomorrow morning, what headline would you most like to see at the top of the first page?

What world news event would you like most to see reported?

What national news event would you like most to see reported?

What local news event would you like most to see reported?

When you turn to the woman's page, what topics would you like most to read about?

When you turn to the sports page, what topics would you like most to read about?

(And similar questions could be asked about the financial, travel, real-estate, feature, and other sections of the paper.)

2. *From sources of behavioral evidence of interests.* People give evidence of their interests through their actual behavior in a number of ways. For example, librarians can tell you what type of books are currently most popular. Directors of adult education in other agencies can give you the comparative enrollment figures in their various activities. The United States Census can give you trends in recreational choices. And the various local and state governmental agencies can provide at least impressions of the kinds of things people are asking about or requesting services in.

Needs of Organizations

An organization or institution is a living organism that has needs, too. In terms of Maslow's hierarchy, it has needs for survival, for safety, for belonging, for esteem, and for self-actualization. It is dependent upon its personnel to satisfy these needs and has a vested interest in their possessing the competencies to do so. Institutional management typically thinks of training needs, therefore, as "those changes that *should* be made in employees, by educational techniques, to further efficient operation and mission accomplishment."[25]

In every organization situations occur repeatedly which produce obvious training needs:

—A new employee comes to work or a new member joins;

—An employee or lay leader is assigned to a new job which requires new skills;

—The methods of doing an old job are changed;

—New equipment is installed;

—The mission, the organization, or the working relationships within the organization are substantially changed.

---

[25]United States Civil Service Commission, *Assessing and Reporting Training Needs and Progress,* Personnel Methods Series No. 3 (Washington, D.C.: Government Printing Office, 1956), p. 3. By permission.

Exhibit 13

INTEREST QUESTIONNAIRE

We need your help. The Community Center has decided that one of the important new services it can offer its neighbors is a program of continuing education for adults. We want to provide the courses, clubs, and other kinds of activities that *you* want. Will you let us know your desires by checking the column that most nearly reflects the way you feel? Then please place this form in the postage-paid envelope enclosed and mail it right back to our program committee. Thanks.

SHORT COURSES
(10 weeks)

	Good Idea	Inter-ested	Will Enroll		Good Idea	Inter-ested	Will Enroll
Your Career				*Keep Fit*			
Fashion Design	___	___	___				
Drafting	___	___	___	Fencing	___	___	___
Starting Your Own Business	___	___	___	Golf	___	___	___
				Bowling	___	___	___
Writing for Profit	___	___	___	Skiing	___	___	___
How to Enjoy Retirement	___	___	___	Yoga	___	___	___
				Exercising at Home & Office	___	___	___
Your Home				*Keep Current*			
Making Home Repairs	___	___	___	Practical Politics	___	___	___
Buying & Selling a Home	___	___	___	The Law & You	___	___	___
Landscaping	___	___	___	What It's Like to Be Black	___	___	___
Creative Cooking	___	___	___	Negro History	___	___	___
Antiquing	___	___	___	The New Math	___	___	___
				The Youth Scene	___	___	___
Know Thyself				*Enjoy Leisure*			
Discovering Your Aptitudes	___	___	___	Understanding Art	___	___	___
Logical Thinking	___	___	___	Enjoying Music	___	___	___
Understanding Your Emotions	___	___	___	Acting & Drama	___	___	___
Better Human Relations	___	___	___	Playing String Instruments	___	___	___
Creative Problem Solving	___	___	___	Improving Your Dancing	___	___	___
Preparation for Marriage	___	___	___	Fun with Chess	___	___	___
				Arts & Crafts	___	___	___
Learn More				Painting for Fun	___	___	___
Rapid Reading	___	___	___	Other:			
Public Speaking	___	___	___				
Vocabulary	___	___	___				

CLUBS (Check those you would be most interested in joining):

Hikers	___	Painting	___	Writing	___	French	___
Dance	___	Bridge	___	Dramatics	___	Spanish	___
Discussion	___	Riding	___	Bowling	___	Russian	___
Couples	___	Camping	___	Glee Club	___	German	___
Speakers	___	Music	___	Ceramics	___	Swedish	___
Camera	___	Travel	___	Golf	___	Italian	___

Other:

GENERAL INFORMATION

1. What would be the best time of day for course or club meetings for you:

5:00 P.M. _____	6:30 P.M. _____	8:00 P.M. _____
5:30 P.M. _____	7:00 P.M. _____	8:30 P.M. _____
6:00 P.M. _____	7:30 P.M. _____	Other: _____

2. What would be the best day of the week for course or club meetings for you:

Sunday _____	Tuesday _____	Thursday _____	Saturday _____
Monday _____	Wednesday _____	Friday _____	

3. What is your occupation? _____

4. Where do you work:

Downtown _____	East Side _____	South Side _____
West Side _____	North Side _____	Other: _____

Please give your name and address if you want further information:

Name: _____

Home address: _____

_____ Zip _____

Telephone: Home _____ Business _____

But other training needs are not so obvious. They must be arrived at through careful analysis, based on problems existing or foreseeable in the organization's operation. The techniques available for engaging in a comprehensive and continuing organizational analysis have been described most clearly, concisely, and practically in a pamphlet prepared by the U.S. Civil Service Commission to assist federal agencies in carrying out the presidential directive on training of January 11, 1955. The material in the remainder of this section is taken, with some adaptations, from this pamphlet, *Assessing and Reporting Training Needs and Progress.*[26] The techniques are adaptable to any organization.

Gathering Data

How does one get the information necessary to make a needs analysis? This is simple—in its basic aspects. *Ask* line officials, staff officials, employees. *Observe* employees and their work. *Study* production and other management data.

Specific methods of asking, observing, and studying are many and varied. Exhibit 14 lists advantages and limitations of each of these methods, with suggested "dos and don'ts" for using them. Each of the methods is then discussed in more detail, with samples. This material is intended not to prescribe or instruct but to illustrate; to describe a variety of methods that might be useful; and to stimulate your thinking about what would be most likely to succeed in your own situation. You are urged to accept, reject, or adapt any of it as necessary to meet your own unique requirements.

---

[26]Ibid. By permission.

Exhibit 14

GENERAL METHODS OF NEED DETERMINATION

Method	Advantages	Limitations	Dos and Don'ts
Interview	Reveals feelings, causes, and possible solutions of problems as well as facts. Affords maximum opportunity for free expression of opinion, giving of suggestions.	Is time-consuming, so can reach relatively few people. Results may be difficult to quantify. Can make subject feel he is "on the spot."	Pretest and revise interview questions as needed. Be sure interviewer can and does listen, doesn't judge responses. Do not use to interpret, sell, or educate.
Questionnaire	Can reach many people in short time. Is relatively inexpensive. Gives opportunity of expression without fear or embarrassment. Yields data easily summarized and reported.	Little provision for free expression of unanticipated responses. May be difficult to construct. Has limited effectiveness in getting at causes of problems and possible solutions.	Pretest and revise questions and form as needed. Offer and safeguard anonymity. Use only if prepared to— report findings, both favorable and unfavorable. do something about them.
Tests	Are useful as diagnostic tools to identify specific areas of deficiencies. Helpful in selecting from among potential trainees those who can most profitably be trained. Results are easy to compare and report.	Tests validated for many specific situations often not available. Tests validated elsewhere may prove invalid in new situations. Results give clues, are not conclusive. Tests are second-best evidence in relation to job performance.	Know what test measures. Be sure it is worth measuring here. Apply results only to factors for which test is good. Don't use tests to take blame for difficult or unpopular decisions which management should make.
Group Problem Analysis	Same as for interview *plus:* Permits synthesis of different viewpoints. Promotes general understanding and agreement. Builds support for needed training. Is in itself good training.	Is time-consuming and initially expensive. Supervisors and executives may feel too busy to participate, want work done for them. Results may be difficult to quantify.	Do not promise or expect quick results. Start with problem *known* to be of concern to group. Identify *all* problems of significant concern to group. Let group make own analysis, set own priorities.
Records and Reports Study	Provide excellent clues to trouble spots. Provide best objective evidence of results of problems. Are usually of concern to and easily understood by operating officials.	Do not show causes of problems, or possible solutions. May not provide enough cases (e.g., grievances) to be meaningful. May not reflect *current* situation, recent changes.	Use as *checks* and *clues,* in combination with other methods.

Job Analysis and Performance Review	Produces specific and precise information about jobs, performance. Is directly tied to actual jobs and to on-job performance. Breaks job into segments manageable both for training and for appraisal purposes.	Time-consuming. Difficult for people not specifically trained in job analysis techniques. Supervisors often dislike reviewing employees' inadequacies with them personally. Reveals training needs of individuals but not those based on needs of organization.	Brush up on job-analysis techniques, arrange special training for those who are to do it. Be sure analysis is of *current* job, and *current* performance. Review with employee both— analysis of job, and appraisal of performance.

The kinds of things to be asked about, observed, and studied as clues to possible training needs are also suggested by the discussion of methods and by the examples given in that discussion. These "need indicators" are summarized, for convenience, in the excerpts from *Training the Supervisor,* a publication of the U.S. Civil Service Commission, reproduced in Exhibit 15.

Methods

Interviews of some kind are a must for training officers who would keep a finger on the pulse of their agency. Better than any other device, they help them understand *how* people feel and *why*—understanding crucial to any effort to bring about change. They also demonstrate, in a personalized way, sincere interest in what people in the organization think.

Open-ended, nondirective interviews are more valuable than other kinds for getting at feelings and attitudes and at the causes of problems. But they yield less uniform and less readily quantifiable data than do controlled interviews. Results of the latter are easier to process but may not be as valid, for their very structure tends to restrict and to influence the responses given.

Naturally, the more skilled the interviewer, both in asking and interpreting responses, the more valuable the data will be. So try out your questions in advance and revise them if necessary to get them clearly understood; allow your subjects ample opportunity to talk unhurriedly; concentrate on listening to what they are really saying; do not make "value judgments" on their responses; and do not use the interview to interpret, sell, or educate. In case you feel dubious about your interviewing skill: any information you get will be better than none, you will learn a lot in the process, and your interviewees will have an opportunity to contribute to the solution of mutual problems.

You may get more accurate and more useful information if you ask your subjects about their *problems,* rather than what training they need. On the basis of what you learn, you can then determine with them whether training is needed—and if so, what kind.

Written questionnaires are also useful tools for gathering information from which training needs may be derived.

Questionnaires can reach many people in a short time, usually at reasonable expense. Like interviews, they give people an opportunity to express their feelings—in this case anonymously, without any of the embarrassment or anxiety that can accompany the more personal techniques. If well designed, they yield data that can be processed quickly and used statistically. (Early consultation with statistical services or other machine processing facilities is necessary for best results.)

A limitation of questionnaires is that they get answers only to the questions that are asked, affording less opportunity for free expression of unanticipated kinds of responses. This puts a premium on knowing what to ask and how to ask it. For this reason, questionnaires are best constructed after a few intensive interviews have been made to provide a framework of content.

Questionnaires also have limited effectiveness in getting at causes of problems and the best courses of action to solve the problems. For this reason, they should usually be followed by a few intensive interviews.

Exhibit 15

SOME NEED INDICATORS[27]

Study

Organization Plans
- projected changes in mission, structure, personnel, or procedures.

Employee Records
- high turnover.
- absenteeism.
- sick leave rates.
- accident severity and frequency ratios.
- tardiness.
- grievances.
- merit ratings.
- composition of supervisory force.

Official Inspections Reports
- by own organization.
- classification surveys.

Work and Work-flow
- production bottlenecks.
- fluctuations in production.
- reports on public or customer satisfaction with product or service.
- backlogs and where located.
- records of high cost, waste, excessive errors.

Supervisory Selection Policy
- qualification requirements.
- experience and training background of present supervisors.

Management Audits
- by controlling department or bureau.
- special surveys.

Observe

Morale Factors
- personal friction.
- buckpassing.
- complaints.
- inattention to work.
- leadership not held by appointed leader (the supervisor).
- supervisory ineffectiveness in providing subordinates with sense of worth, belonging, and security.
- lack of supervisory support of subordinates.
- authoritarian leadership.
- absence of sense of purpose and accomplishment.
- etc.

Job Knowledge
- technical phases.
- administrative phases.
- supervisory phases.

Communication Failures
- written and oral instructions misunderstood.
- failure of information to flow up, down, and across.
- inability to express, orally or in writing.
- semantic difficulties.

Poor Supervision
- assignment of work.
- planning and scheduling.
- instructing subordinates.
- handling grievances.
- lack job pride.
- lack job interest.
- poor coordination.
- inadequate recognition.
- failure to motivate.

Job Application
- putting knowledge and skill to work.
- will to improve, self-development.

[27]U.S. Civil Service Commission, *Training the Supervisor*, Personnel Methods Series No. 4 (Washington, D.C.: Government Printing Office, 1956).

Any questionnaire, like any interview, should be pretested and revised as necessary for clarity, adequacy of coverage, etc.

Anonymity must be safeguarded—and participants must be confident that it will be safeguarded.

One Caution. Questionnaires are mass-communications media. They reach many people in a formal way, and these many people who check or write down their answers to your questions will want to know what you find out and what you do about it. *Use this technique only if you're prepared: a) to report your general findings to those who participate, and b) to do something about your findings.*

Management records and reports can also provide valuable clues to training needs. It is desirable, for example, to study audit and inspection reports, personnel records (grievances, turnover, absenteeism, accident frequency and severity, tardiness, suggestions and awards, etc.), cost and production records, etc. Since such records seldom reveal causes of problems, however, they are best used as supplements to and checks on other kinds of need determination. They are, in other words, clues to be followed up.

Tests of various kinds may also be used in determining training needs—and, once an area of need has been found, in selecting the employees to be trained. They can be especially helpful in determining whether the *cause* of a recognized problem is a deficiency in knowledge, or skill, or attitude and, therefore, what kind of action should be taken.

Performance or achievement tests are essentially means of sampling what employees know or can do, and can therefore help to locate areas in which more information or more skill training is needed. Aptitude tests indicate potential to learn or acquire information or skills in a particular area, and so are useful in selecting from among a group of employees those who can most profitably be trained.

Practical tests in typing and stenography can quickly establish an employee's need or lack of need for training in those skills. Similarly, trade information tests are used to determine levels of knowledge and skill in a variety of occupations.

It is true that tests sample *learned* ideas or facts or attitudes which may or may not be carried over into practice on the job. This does not, however, invalidate their usefulness as diagnostic tools. Unless the necessary knowledge, skills, and attitudes have been learned, they can hardly be applied on the job. And if they have been learned but still are not applied, additional training in what has already been learned but is not being applied is not a suitable remedy.

Special suggestions to those who would use tests as aids in diagnosing training needs:

—Be sure that you know what the test actually measures, i.e., knowledge, or skills, or attitudes, and in what area.
—Be sure that what it measures is relevant and important in the particular situation in which it is to be used.
—Be sure that the results of the test are not generalized to apply to areas to which it is not relevant.
—Try to cross-check the results (as with other methods).

Group problem analysis, in which supervisors or executives analyze together the problems of their organizations, is an excellent means of determining training needs.

Groups of supervisors in a given division or bureau, for example, might get together—with or without a training officer—to discuss their problems, to analyze the causes of these problems, and to decide what changes are necessary to solve the problem. Some of these changes may be accomplished through training, others through other management action.

This process not only identifies training needs, but also builds a solid foundation of support for training decided on. (For it permits those immediately concerned both to establish the need for and to help decide what training should be given.) In addition, the process itself is training that helps participants become more analytical in their study of problems, gives them an opportunity to raise problems, make suggestions, hear other participants' viewpoints and suggestions, and help each other.

Any staff person who participates in meetings like these can facilitate discussion, help members clarify their thinking, and advise on what training can and cannot do. But, again, the staff member shouldn't make value judgments, and should be very careful not to direct members' conclusions.

Job analysis combined with performance appraisal is an excellent method of determining training needs of individuals. The process, briefly, is to determine the specific duties of the job, evaluate the adequacy with which the employee performs each of these duties, and locate significant improvements that can be made by training.

The list of duties can be obtained in a number of ways: asking the employee, asking the supervisor, observing the employee, etc. Adequacy of performance can be estimated by the employee, but the supervisor's evaluation must also be obtained. This evaluation will usually be based on observation.

What does the supervisor observe? The employees, while they are working; the work produced; the employees' work relationships. The ease, the speed, the sureness, the safety of the employees' actions, and the way they apply themselves to the job. The accuracy and amount of completed work, its conformity with established procedures and standards, its appearance, and the soundness of judgment it shows. Any signs of good or poor communication, understanding, and cooperation among employees.

Such observation is a normal and inseparable part of the everyday job of supervision. Systematically recorded, evaluated, and summarized, it highlights both general and individual training needs.

A recent refinement of the performance review procedure that is especially consistent with the spirit of andragogy and has proved to be effective in need assessment is the *management by objectives* process. In its simplest form, this is a process by which employees develop a plan detailing short-run and long-run objectives for the operation of their jobs and for their personal development in collaboration with their supervisors. At stated intervals (usually from three months to a year) they assess progress toward each objective with the help of their supervisors, identify obstacles that prevented their full achievement, and prescribe corrective action, including further training.[28]

The critical-incident technique is a job analysis and performance evaluation device that places special emphasis on *kinds of behavior that distinguish effective from ineffective performance*. Only the major requirements of the job—those that make the difference between success and failure—are listed. Under each of these are brief descriptions, usually in checklist form, of observable on-the-job behavior. The supervisors check the forms to record their observations of each employee's behavior, adding whatever explanatory note they feel necessary.

The appraisal panel method is being used increasingly by business and government to identify training needs of executives. It is essentially a process of supervisory

---

[28]For a full description of this process, see George S. Odiorne, *Management by Objectives* (New York: Pitman, 1965).

observation and evaluation, supplemented by the observations and evaluations of others who personally know the appraisees and their work. The basic steps are as follows:

1. *Appraisal.* Appraisal is the process of evaluating an individual's capacity: a) to perform in the present position, and b) for handling more responsible assignments in the future. In this system, appraisal is carried out by a panel composed of the supervisors and two or three others who are at their level in the organization. These other panelists are selected especially because of their knowledge of the appraisee.

2. *Review.* Review is the step in which the supervisors report the findings of their panels to higher management authority. This step gives higher-grade executives an opportunity to:

a) Check on the adequacy of proposed developmental plans for individual appraisees.

b) Assess the total human resources for running the organization now and in the future.

c) Identify individuals with potential for more responsible positions.

3. *Discussion.* Discussion is the step in which the supervisors counsel privately with the appraisees on their strengths and weaknesses and try to motivate the appraisees to accept a development plan.

4. *Development.* Development is the step in which the agreed-upon plan for fostering the appraisees' growth is put into effect. It is compounded of self-help, organizational support and guidance, planned work experiences, and formal education and training.

Analysis of Data

Regardless of the method by which information is obtained, it must be analyzed for training (and other) needs. This is a matter of reviewing, classifying, interpreting, and evaluating the data gathered and of judging what action will best solve the problems found.

In making this judgment, it is important to consider all the alternatives (including their costs, practicality, acceptability, and administrative feasibility) that might accomplish the desired result. Among the alternatives that should usually be considered are reassignment, separation, or training of employees; selection of different kinds or levels of talent; revision of work assignments, methods, equipment, or relationships; and clarification or simplification of agency policy, structure, or instructions.

If the decision is to train employees, it is important to determine as accurately as possible whether the changes needed are changes in knowledge, or skills, or attitudes—and *whose* knowledge, skills, or attitudes. If employees *do not know* (lack of knowledge), *cannot do* (lack of skill), or *do not care* (lack of motivation), they are obviously unlikely to behave as management desires them to behave. But it is necessary to know *which* of these is the problem in order to train effectively.

For example: If the trouble is that employees don't know what they are to do, they need information, not attitude training; pep talks on the importance of the agency's mission are not likely to help much in this case. If they know but can't do, skill practice (or reassignment or other action) rather than information is probably indicated. If they have the necessary job knowledge and skills but simply do not care, additional training in job knowledge and skills isn't likely to improve either their performance or their morale.

If all of these requirements are met—if employees know, can do, and are interested in their work, but still do not behave as management desires them to—we have a problem that cannot be solved by training these employees who aren't behaving as desired. It is then necessary to consider such questions as these: Are management's expectations reasonable? Do such practical limitations as lack of time, inadequate supplies and equipment, too many distractions and interruptions make the desired behavior impossible? Has management created an environment or situation in which the desired behavior would be rewarding?

These are things about which management—line management—must do something. And the focus of its action should most probably be the situation or the group in which the employee works rather than the employee whose behavior was the object of original concern.

This thinking process should be a cooperative line-staff activity. The Michigan Survey Research Center's "feedback" technique of handling survey data can help make it so. The center's surveyors make oral reports of their findings, with some tentative interpretations and suggestions about possible causes, to groups of responsible management officials. These officials discuss and evaluate the findings, check the interpretations, and make their own judgments and decisions about the action to be taken. Advantages of this technique will be obvious to any staff official.

Whether or not you use a Michigan-style feedback, remember that the more responsible and representative the people who help analyze, interpret, and evaluate data, the sounder and more useful the results and conclusions are likely to be. If line officials and others importantly concerned do not actively participate in the analysis, you should at least get a few of them to review the process (not just the conclusions) step by step, to check the interpretations, evaluations, and other judgments made. While this process of cooperative analysis admittedly requires time and attention, it is your best safeguard against unjustifiable expenditures and preventable failures.

Needs of Communities

The meaning of "community" will vary from adult educator to adult educator. For one in an international agency it will mean the whole world. For one in a national agency it will mean the United States. For one in a professional association it will mean that particular professional community. For one in an ethnic organization it may mean the black community or the Jewish community. Or it may mean the community of a neighborhood or town or city or metropolitan area or entire state or region. Adult educators have to define for themselves the communities they intend to serve and then undertake to assess their educational needs.

The Community Survey

The technique that is used to discover the educational needs of a community has been given the label "community survey," but this label can cover everything from a simple studying of documents to an elaborate canvass of organizations and citizens by interviewers and questionnaires. One of the most comprehensive and practical guides for making a community survey is *Studying the Community*, a pamphlet published by the American Library Association to assist local libraries in planning library adult-education services.[29] The material in the remainder of this section is largely adapted from this pamphlet. Although the illustrations are in the context of a library, the

---

[29]*Studying the Community* (Chicago: American Library Association, 1960). By permission.

principles and techniques are applicable to other organizations; and although the community reference is a geographical community, the ideas can be applied to other types of communities with little change. The recommended steps for a community survey follow:

1. *Define the purpose.* Every group concerned with a survey of this sort will want to know why it is important to study the community and what such a study involves. It is desirable, therefore, for a preliminary statement of purpose to be developed by the policy-making group of an adult-education unit. Such a model statement of purpose suggested for libraries is illustrated in Exhibit 16.

Exhibit 16

STATEMENT OF PURPOSE—A LIBRARY COMMUNITY SURVEY[30]

Community Study

Why study the community?
A library fulfills its educational function by meeting the needs of the people it serves. These needs must be discovered before they can be met. One way of discovering these needs is to gather various kinds of information about the community. But first it is necessary to understand how this information can be useful.

Why do we need the information?
   to be able to know what books and other materials we need to buy
   to enable us to set goals for planning our services
   to help us to plan special activities
   to enable us to develop an effective public relations program
   to establish working relationships with other agencies and organizations
   to give the staff insight and understanding about the community based on concrete
      knowledge
   to determine the library's educational role in the community

What do we look for?
   the racial and national backgrounds of the people
   the kinds of jobs they hold
   how much money they are earning, spending, saving
   the organizations and churches they belong to or do not belong to
   the kinds of houses they live in
   the recreation they enjoy
   how old they are
   how much formal education they have had
   the opportunities they have for further learning

Where do we go to find out?
   to newspapers
   to census reports
   to town, city, county records
   to individuals
   to private and governmental agencies
   to organizations

---

[30]Ibid., p. 12.

2. *Create a study organization.* Although a very limited study, involving only some analysis of documents and interviews with a few key organizational leaders, might be managed by an adult-education director alone with the advice and assistance of a policy committee, many advantages can be gained by creating a separate committee and staff to plan and carry out the survey. It is strongly recommended that such a study committee be representative of the major elements of the community from which data will be obtained.

3. *Decide upon the scope of the survey.* No individual or group can hope to make a complete study of a community. Even a very small community is too complex and changing to find out everything about it. So priorities have to be set in terms of such questions as these:

What questions do you want answered? A study is, after all, for the purpose of answering questions. One of the first steps in planning a survey, therefore, is to have the study committee think of all the questions they think might be useful to have answers to and then arrange them in priority order. Questions such as these might appear on an initial list:

What are the outstanding characteristics of the population of our community and its neighborhoods by age, sex, race, occupation, income level, type of housing, and education?

What are their main problems and concerns?

What are the existing resources for adult education?

What segments of the population are using them?

What segments are not using them? Why not?

What additional resources and programs are needed?

What are the unmet needs of the community in general, and of special subpopulations in particular?

What are the characteristics of the people who do not use the services of educational agencies? What are their special needs?

What are the unmet needs peculiarly appropriate for this particular agency to serve?

What drastic changes in the community are expected in the next decade that will produce new educational needs?

What sources of information will you use? You might limit yourself to published information, or you may seek information from selected civic and organizational leaders, or from a sample of the total population—depending on the nature of the questions to be answered and the resources at your disposal.

What portion of your community will you study? The larger the community, the harder it is to study. Because of the size of the community, the limitations of your resources, or a particularly urgent need, it may be necessary to study only one segment of it. Such a limited study can be the beginning of a larger study.

4. *Recruit and train a citizen work force.* Depending upon the scope of the study you have decided on, you may need the help of citizen volunteers. In fact, there is probably a direct correlation between the number of citizens involved in a community survey and the value of its results. Among the roles that can be performed by volunteers are the following:

The planners—those invaluable persons who help both to formulate the questions your study will be designed to answer and to plan the procedures for getting the answers. You may need people with:

a) knowledge of the whole community—a newspaper editor, an elder statesman, the teacher who knows everyone;

b) knowledge of special segments of the community—people who belong to business, labor, farm, religious, racial, national, senior citizens, young adults, or newcomers groups and are likely to know their needs and interests;

c) organizational ability—people who have conducted drives, planned civic improvements;

d) academic training—a college professor, a high school principal, a lawyer;

e) technical skills and knowledge—a sociologist, a statistician, a community planner.

The formulators—those who devise such tools as interview schedules, questionnaires, data-report forms. You may need people with:

a) special knowledge of the subject of investigation, e.g., to develop a questionnaire for senior citizens—a social security officer, a staff member from the Family Service Agency, a minister trained in counseling older people;

b) knowledge of segments of the community with which the tool will be used;

c) technical skills and knowledge of survey methods—a researcher, a social scientist, a statistician;

d) ability to organize ideas—a writer, a secretary, an advertising-agency representative;

e) accuracy and care for detail—a printer, a stenographer, a lawyer, a librarian from a library other than your own.

The field people—those who interview others, meet with groups, administer questionnaires, publicize the project, and generally represent the library and the study personnel in face-to-face contacts. You may need people with:

a) community status (to open doors readily)—elder statesmen, civic leaders, old residents, public figures, elected or appointed officials;

b) experience in meeting people—organization workers, salespeople, public-relations workers, personnel officers, public speakers, trained discussion leaders;

c) ability to follow directions—those valuable people who will work well in many capacities;

d) courage to try—the people who do a good job if they have a chance.

The reporters—those who organize the data and put it into shape for use with groups and for reports to the community. You may need people with:

a) ability to organize information—editors (newspaper, radio, TV), educators (teachers of all grade levels), agricultural extension staff, other administrators;

b) skill in visual presentation—artists, advertising personnel, teachers, window display artists;

c) skill in writing—newspaper writers, copywriters, authors (professional and amateur).

The interpreters—those who are able to see relationships between various categories of data and what the information means in terms of the community's educational needs. You may need people with:

a) analytical ability—persons with training in any professional field with marked common sense, whatever their role;

b) vision—workers for good government, volunteers for activities to improve the community, library patrons whose reading shows open inquiring minds, participants in American Heritage or Great Books groups;

c) special knowledge—sociologists, educators, community planners.

5. *Identify the sources of information required.* The listing of sources of information in the ALA's *Studying the Community* is so concise and comprehensive that it is reproduced below in full:

Published Materials

Here is a list of some kinds of materials that can be helpful. You will think of others:

If you want to know about	Use
the nature of the population— age, sex, mobility or stability, economic and educational levels	census reports government and agency reports surveys
the organization of the community— governmental, social, religious, educational, cultural	government and agency reports organization files, reports, and yearbooks, handbooks, maps, guides, directories histories surveys
educational and cultural life— educational institutions, communication agencies, recreational facilities, churches	government and agency reports organization files and yearbooks
business and economic life— income, occupational groupings, type of work, family income	census reports government and agency reports surveys handbooks, maps, guides, directories

What kind of information is each category under "Use" in the list preceding most likely to supply that will be of value to library-community study? Here are some suggestions:

Census reports—including *County and City Data Book;* U.S. censuses, especially Population, Housing, Business, Manufacturers, and Agriculture; local school, church, chamber of commerce, public health, and other agency census reports. Supplementing these, and bringing them up to date, are the estimates and projections often available from state and local agencies.

What to look for:

    evidence of change, i.e., by comparing data from different years and periods, e.g., 1940 data with 1950 data

    highs and lows

    variations from state and national averages or medians

Local government and other agency reports—as a government department itself, the library should receive most of these but may have to seek out reports of volunteer and private agencies.

What to look for:

    purpose of the agency and of the report

    size of staff

    description of activities

    requirements for participation

    analysis of participants (age, sex, education, income group, affiliations)

    materials used and their source

    resources needed or desirable for conducting activities

Surveys—already made by individuals, agencies, organizations, businesses. The library, or almost any other agency or organization, may already have made a survey that needs only expansion and bringing up to date. Utility companies and department stores often conduct regular, periodic surveys of the community or section of the community which they serve. Traffic and health surveys are sometimes made by local and state government departments. A military reservation may have made a survey of the larger community of which it is a part. Churches frequently survey their membership.

What to look for:

reasons for *status quo*, change, and community characteristics
effects of change, such as development of new industries
pressing problems
recommendations for action
projections into the future

Organization files, reports, and yearbooks—although the library may have an organization file, it is not so likely to receive reports regularly from community organizations, and a special effort will probably have to be made to acquire these.

What to look for:

purpose of the organization and of the report
requirements for membership
size and analysis of membership
description of activities
materials used and their source
methods used
sources of resource personnel
recognized blocks in meeting goals
resources needed or desirable for conducting activities and programs at
    meetings
importance to special segments of the community

Handbooks, maps, guides, directories—government departments are most likely to have produced maps, but historical and other maps may have been prepared by societies and businesses interested in publicizing the area. Almost any group may have put out a guide, or handbook, or directory.

What to look for:

physical and economic characteristics
relationships to surrounding area
place and personal names

Histories—of the community, the library, other agencies, institutions, organizations, and businesses in the community or including the community. There may be area or neighborhood histories, perhaps in manuscript form, done by club members for programs or by individuals as hobbies. A teacher or student may have written a history of local education as a term paper or dissertation. A business or businessmen's club may have published a history as a public-relations device. A department store or factory, planning a branch or expansion, may have contracted for a history of the community. A history may have appeared at one time in the local paper or in a regional publication of some sort. Special histories may have appeared in house organs or association publications, or may be filed in the offices of the agencies or organizations concerned.

What to look for:

patterns of cultural change, i.e., coming of new stock, opening of transportation
    to other communities

development of tradition, enriching or limiting community progress

stability or instability of the community development of institutions and
    activities

Newspapers—daily and weekly, city, county, or neighborhood. The newspaper is an essential source of community information. A poor one is better than none at all. What to look for:

matters of community concern—reflected in editor's choice of news, in
    editorials, in letters to editor

community attitudes—in reports of speeches, interviews, choice of pictures and
    news; reports of local political and social activity

public interests—in reports of organizational activity; response to special events

educational resources—in news of agencies and special events; advertisements
    of bookstores, adult courses

Most of these materials, except for histories and special surveys, are serial in nature. Appearing annually or more often, they form a basis for the continuing study of the community. The original intensive examination of these documents, as you start your community study, will provide a groundwork for quick appraisal of future issues.

6. *Establish community contacts.*

Agency personnel. In every community there are people who are paid to direct the activities of an agency, public or private. They are especially useful to the study. First of all, agency employees' jobs require a certain knowledge of the community in general and a detailed knowledge of the agency they serve. They may have special background and training in analysis, interpretation, and planning. They are usually intensely interested in community study since the results may be of significance to their agencies. They are almost always helpful and cooperative.

Agencies fall in several general categories:°

a) Governmental—publicly supported, usually with specially trained staff and politically defined areas of service. They include among others: public schools, some colleges and universities; departments of municipal government such as health, welfare, recreation; departments of county government such as agriculture; units of state or national government such as child guidance clinics, social security offices, departments of education, library extension agencies.

b) Volunteer—supported by endowment or subscription, often with trained staff working with large numbers of volunteers, frequently crossing political boundaries in their service areas. They include: Red Cross, YMCA, Urban League, Volunteer Service Bureau, Association for the Blind, Scouts, private colleges and universities, and many others.

c) Mass media—commercially supported, with trained staff and service boundaries determined by demand or equipment. They include newspapers, radio, and TV.

Representatives of agencies may serve on study committees or undertake particular study activities and may be regarded as key people. We are considering them here, however, as sources of information concerning their own agencies. They can tell you about their agencies as educational resources. From them you can learn of special opportunities provided for certain groups of people, of materials and services available

---

*An excellent example of the difficulties in exact categorizing for purposes of community study is the U.S. Cooperative Agricultural and Home Economics Extension Service, a governmental agency on the national, state, and local levels, working extensively with volunteers. Other agencies are also hard to fit into patterns. It is important to remember that any system of categories is set up for convenient reference only and should never limit study activities for the sake of consistency alone.

to the public at large, of training opportunities (in leadership, for instance) from which other agency and organizational personnel can benefit. Agency representatives can also tell you about the agency's clientele—their special characteristics, their needs (those filled by the agency and those the agency cannot meet), their interests, and their attitudes. Often the agency staff member has information about the people he or she does not reach, just as librarians frequently know a great deal about nonusers of the library. It is difficult to imagine a community study question to which agencies could not contribute some significant answers.

Officers and members of organizations. The American community is distinguished by the tendency of many of its citizens to form organizations. These organizations—social, civic, professional, vocational, patriotic, hobby or special interest, religious, and other—contribute in varying degrees to the educational life of the community and are a source of information about the people who form their memberships.

Few organizations have paid trained staff at the local level. Elected officers are their agents of communication, and it is to them that you will go for information. Their ability to help will vary greatly, since they have come to their positions not as a result of training or background, but as a result of a wide range of personal, social, economic, and interest factors. The officers can describe the purposes of their organizations, the size and nature of the membership, the activities, the program methods and materials used, the problems the organizations face, and the contributions they can make to the education of the community at large.

Membership in an organization implies certain similarities among the members. Therefore, if you go to the membership for information, you must recognize how wide or how narrow a cross section of the community you are reaching. The members can tell you specifically their reactions to the experiences the organization provides. Beyond that they can tell you, as individuals, about their attitudes, aspirations, interests, and observations. Although the organization is too important a part of American life to be omitted from a community study, it is necessary to remember that many people—often the majority of the people—in the community do not belong to organizations. Therefore, as sources of information, organizations are important but limited.

Key people. By the nature of their work, their opportunities to take part in certain activities, or their personalities, some people in every community are especially well informed about the community as a whole or about certain segments or aspects of it. Many of the people who are selected to help with the community study will be in this group, but there will be others who are equally valuable sources of information. You will know, or know about, many of the key people, but you might check a list like the following, making your own additions, to be sure that you are not missing some who can be especially helpful:

a) Community leaders—they hold chairmanships in fund drives, are representatives to councils, sometimes lobby for public causes, organize committees for special purposes, and make themselves generally useful for the welfare of the community as they see it. Do not underestimate their knowledge of people, forces, and methods because their public objectives are not always the same as yours.

b) Public employees—the agency staff we have mentioned and other elected or appointed government officials. Some of these are specialists, such as the fireman or the game warden; others are generalists, such as the county or city commissioner. They have information and access to information on the nature and structure of the community and may know a great deal about the people.

c) Educators—they may or may not be public employees. They may be employed by labor or industry or work in private or religious educational institutions. They know about educational resources, and their work brings them into relationships with many kinds of people.

d) Operators of small businesses—the druggist, the gas station owner, the lunch room operator may be the best source of information on certain aspects of a neighborhood or a small community. Some of them are confidants of groups about whom no one else knows very much.

e) Newspaper editors and other employees—it is their business to know what is happening, what is needed in a community, how people act and feel.

A word of warning here. Information obtained from key people may be accurate and documented. It may be accurate but not subject to proof. It may be inaccurate, prejudiced, misleading. It is necessary to get information and opinions from a number of such people and to consider it in relation to data from other sources. Key people, however, can provide a picture of the community's aspirations, potential, limitations, and self-image that tabulated data will not give you.

Whenever key people are mentioned, someone nods knowingly and says, "Oh, yes! The power structure." It is important to differentiate between the two. Key people, as the term is used here, are sources of information. The people in the power structure are factors in community action. Some people may fill both roles; others do not. You go to key people when you want to know something, to people in the power structure when you want to change something. Since the power figures will be important to the success of any civic action that the study may stimulate, it is well to know who they are and how to work effectively with them. Do not, however, expect them necessarily to serve as sources of information.

The general public. To know the complete answer to many community study questions, you would have to talk to every single adult in the community. Since this is obviously impossible, a number of devices have been invented for sampling a community. By using these devices you can learn from the public at large the geographical or organizational distribution of people by such categories as age, vocation, education, national background, race, or religion. People can identify for you certain of their concerns and interests. They can indicate the extent of their knowledge of the services of the community and the impressions they have of the community and their relationships to it.

The sources of information listed previously will not substitute for a population sample. On the other hand, the population sample will not provide all the information you need. The people who contribute to this part of the study are not motivated by your purposes, as many of the people in the other categories are. They have little opportunity to think about the questions they are asked, and they may in good faith give erroneous information. Be sure that you seek from them information that they are able to give and that you interpret it carefully in relation to other information.

7. *Collect the information.* Probably the most efficient procedure for collecting the required information is to organize specialized study teams to accomplish as many of the following tasks as are relevant to the scope of the survey you have decided on:

a) a documentary-analysis team—to assemble the relevant published materials as suggested in the list above and to extract from them the answers to the questions posed by the survey;

b) an agency-survey team—to identify which governmental, volunteer, and mass-media agencies are relevant sources of information; to develop a list of the persons in the agencies who can provide the information; to construct interview schedules or questionnaires designed to obtain the information; to conduct the interviews or distribute the questionnaires; and to tabulate, analyze, and report the data;

c) an organization-survey team—to perform the above functions as regards relevant social, civic, professional, vocational, patriotic, cultural, ethnic, religious, and avocational organizations;

d) a key-people-survey team—to perform the above functions as regards selected community leaders, public employees, educators, operators of small businesses, newspapermen, and grass-roots spokesmen;

e) a population-sample-survey team—to perform the above functions as regards a sample (random or stratified) of the general population.

The devising of questionnaires, training of interviewers, and construction of population samples are highly technical undertakings in which it is wise to involve a specialist from a university or commercial marketing company.

8. *Organize the information.* The following helpful suggestions are made in the ALA pamphlet concerning the organization of the data that have been collected.

All of the information collected in a study must be organized for interpretation. Since interpretation is usually done by a group, the data must be put together for quick reference and visual clarity. Forethought can make the organization task much easier. Before interviews are undertaken, questionnaires reproduced, or records analyzed, plan the ultimate arrangement of the answers. It may be necessary to change the plan or to organize the same data in different ways for different purposes, but a basic scheme of action will facilitate the entire process. Good sense, visual imagination, reference to other data presentations, and the advice of a specialist will all be helpful. Here are some suggestions to get you started.

Tables
Information should be arranged in a list or table; its significance will be increased by its organization to show relationships.

For example, the agencies with educational purposes can be listed alphabetically—a practical organization for some purposes. A more significant organization is by such factors as types of clientele served, services provided, materials available. One table, carefully constructed, can show the overall agency picture and provide a guide to the full material on each agency.

	Adult Clientele	Services	Materials
YMCA	Principally men (women take part in some activities)	Swimming and other sports Classes Counseling Special interest clubs Welfare—support of a day camp	Films on sports training, character building Camping handbook Discussion outlines

Narrative Summaries
The material from group and individual interviews requires another kind of organization. It may be by questions and topical answers:

What, in your opinion, is the most serious problem this community faces?
Citizen apathy (5 times)
Lack of recreational facilities for young people (3)
Lack of parking space (2)
Outmoded form of government (2)

It may be by selection of especially pertinent comments from certain people:

Newspaper editor—"This is a booming town, with all the problems of too little service, too much crime, and fly-by-night business that come with a boom."

City councilman—"The people do not understand that if we are to attract industry, we must spruce up the town, and appropriate some money to make coming here financially attractive."

Or it may be a set of telegraphic-style paragraphs:

Laketon area—old, stable neighborhood; people farm, fish, cater to tourists in summer; young people leave to work elsewhere; since 1951 no high school here—students go to Brownville; three churches centers of organizational life.

A surprising amount of narrative information can be compressed into a page or two for purposes of examination and discussion.

Maps

The kinds of information that can be shown on a map are well known. Overlays to show relationships are valuable. A map dotted to indicate residence locations of library borrowers or of adults in public-school adult-education classes becomes doubly significant with an overlay indicating areas delineated by such factors as average property values, density of population, or predominating national backgrounds. Overlays are expensive unless you can find people skilled in this kind of work to volunteer their services. Amateurs can make simple tissue overlays, but they are not likely to be too satisfactory. Use several separate maps instead, or a combination of colors and dots or pins.

Charts

For use with fairly large groups, charts have the advantage of good visibility, as well as dramatic presentation of relationships. "Pie," bar, and line charts are relatively easy to prepare. Use colored paper and tape to avoid hand drawing. Consider photographing and blowing up charts to achieve the size you want.

Photographs

Pictures of educational facilities, adequate or inadequate, of new areas of development, of problem situations (overcrowded areas, inadequate parking, poor traffic control) can illustrate your data effectively. They do not serve as a data organization device in the strictest sense but are useful for graphic presentation.

The Package

When you have the separate kinds of data tabulated, summarized, mapped, and charted, you will have to consider putting all of your pieces together. Your purpose may be to provide the study committee with a basis for interpretation; to report to the entire community or to the citizens who worked on the study; to provide a presentation of the data for discussion by representatives of agencies or of government, or by other groups. You will select your package in relationship to your need and your budget. Consider these:

Mimeographed, multilithed, or printed pages in: looseleaf notebooks, pocket folders, stapled booklets, or continuous folded strip

Posters

Flip charts

Slides

Filmstrips

Recorded tapes

The material prepared for public presentation will probably be briefer than that prepared for the study committee. Try out patterns of organization and presentation of the data with the study committee, and use that experience to develop effective devices for more general use of your study information.

9. *Interpret the information.* As you gather information and organize it, you will be aware that the information itself does not define community needs. A process of interpretation is required—an undertaking in which a strong citizen committee is especially valuable and which involves these steps:

—Take each question the survey raised and see what answers the data give or suggest.

—Now take another look at the data across questions, and see what community problems, concerns, or deficiencies the data reveal or suggest.

—Draw up a tentative list of problems, concerns, and deficiencies, with supporting data for each one.

—Discuss the tentative list with specialists, community groups, agency leaders, and government officials; check it and refine it.

—Ask about every concern, "Who needs to know what about this?" and make specific lists of *educational* needs.

These educational needs can be of several kinds:

—the direct need for educational opportunities, such as:

a) high school classes for adults (revealed by low educational level, no existing classes, or classes inadequate in number or location, or high in cost);

b) orientation classes (revealed by large number of noncitizens or new residents from other areas—resettled American Indians, Puerto Ricans—no existing training program);

c) vocational training (revealed by industrial change, shifting labor patterns, older population, no training program);

—the need for education in understanding public problems, such as:

a) lack of adequate public transportation (revealed by interviews, questionnaires, newspapers);

b) impact of new population on a community (revealed by population breakdowns, interviews);

c) national and state decisions (revealed by lack of resources for information and discussion);

d) lag in the development of good intercultural relations (revealed by population breakdowns, interviews, newspapers);

e) the lack of any training opportunities such as those listed under "the direct need for educational opportunities" above;

—the need for education in good citizenship practices, such as:

a) observance of safety rules (revealed by accident death rate);

b) intelligent voting (revealed by low voting rate, votes for a service and against the bond issue to support it);

c) civic neatness (revealed by observation, other agency concern, newspapers);

—the need for education to meet personal problems resulting from community situations, such as:

a) low income level—may suggest education on other job opportunities, vocational retraining, building and repair skills, low-cost menu planning, money management;

b) crowded schools—may suggest parent education on giving children background experience, encouraging home reading, training in human relations.

The process by which the needs and interests of individuals, the needs of organizations, and the needs of communities get translated into program objectives is the subject of the next chapter.

For Your Continuing Inquiry . . .

Regarding Basic Human Needs

Allport, Gordon W. *Becoming*. New Haven, Conn.: Yale University Press, 1955.
Boshear, Walton C., and Albrecht, Karl G. *Understanding People: Models and Concepts*. La Jolla, Cal.: University Associates, 1977.
Combs, Arthur W., and Snygg, D. *Individual Behavior*. New York: Harper & Row, 1959.
Erikson, Erik H. *Childhood and Society*. New York: W. W. Norton, 1963.
Fromm, Erich. *The Sane Society*. New York: Rinehart, 1955.
Goble, Frank. *The Third Force: The Psychology of Abraham Maslow*. New York: Grossman, 1970.
Loevinger, Jane. *Ego Development: Concepts and Theories*. San Francisco: Jossey-Bass, 1976.
Maslow, Abraham. *Motivation and Personality*. New York: Harper & Row, 1970.
Murphy, Gardner. *Human Potentialities*. New York: Basic Books, 1970.
Rogers, Carl. *On Becoming a Person*. Boston: Houghton Mifflin, 1961.

Regarding Educational Needs and Interests of Individuals

Baltes, Paul D. (ed.). *Life-Span Development and Behavior*. Volume 1. New York: Academic Press, 1978.
Fuller, Edward, et al. *A Competency Based Training Program for Manpower Counselors*. Portland, Ore.: Northwest Regional Educational Laboratory, 1973.
Grant, Gerald, et al. *On Competence: A Critical Analysis of Competence-Based Reforms in Higher Education*. San Francisco: Jossey-Bass, 1979.
Gubrium, Jaber F., and Buckholdt, David R. *Toward Maturity: The Social Processing of Human Development*. San Francisco: Jossey-Bass, 1977.
Havighurst, Robert. *Developmental Tasks and Education*. 2nd ed. New York: David McKay, 1970.
Kidd, J. R. *How Adults Learn*. Chicago: Association Press/Follett Publishing Co., 1973.
Knox, Alan B. *Adult Development and Learning*. San Francisco: Jossey-Bass, 1977.
Leagans, Paul; Copeland, Harlan; and Kaiser, Gertrude. *Selected Concepts from Educational Psychology and Adult Education for Extension and Continuing Educators*. Syracuse, N.Y.: Syracuse University Publications in Continuing Education, 1971.
McKenzie, Leon, and McKinley, John (eds.). *Adult Education: The Diagnostic Procedure*. Bulletin of the School of Education, Vol. 49, No. 5, Bloomington, Ind.: Indiana University, 1973.
Pikunas, Justin. *Human Development: A Science of Growth*. New York: McGraw-Hill, 1969.
Pinto, Patrick R., and Walker, James W. *A Study of Professional Training and Development Roles and Competencies*. Madison, Wis.: American Society for Training and Development, 1978.

Pressey, Sydney L., and Kuhlen, Raymond G. *Psychological Development Through the Life Span.* New York: Harper, 1957.

Stevens-Long, Judith. *Adult Life: Developmental Processes.* Palo Alto, Cal.: Mayfield Publishing Co., 1979.

Torshen, Kay P. *The Mastery Approach to Competency-Based Education.* New York: Academic Press, 1977.

Tough, Allen. *The Adult's Learning Projects.* Toronto: Ontario Institute for Studies in Education, 1971.

Regarding Organizational Needs

Argyris, Chris. *Integrating the Individual and the Organization.* New York: John Wiley & Sons, 1964.

Barrett, Jon H. *Individual Goals and Organizational Objectives.* Ann Arbor, Mich.: Institute for Social Research, University of Michigan, 1970.

Brown, F. Gerald, and Wedel, Kenneth R. *Assessing Training Needs.* Washington, D.C.: National Training and Development Service Press, 1974.

Craig, R. L. (ed.). *Training and Development Handbook.* 2nd ed. New York: McGraw-Hill, 1976.

Dalton, Gene W. *Motivation and Control in Organizations.* Homewood, Ill.: Richard D. Irwin, Inc., 1971.

Herzberg, Frederick. *Work and the Nature of Man.* Cleveland: The World Publishing Co., 1966.

Hospital Continuing Education Project. *Training and Continuing Education: A Handbook for Health Care Institutions.* Chicago: Hospital Research and Educational Trust, American Hospital Association, 1970.

Lefton, Robert E., et al. *Effective Motivation through Performance Appraisal: Dimensional Appraisal Strategies.* New York: Wiley-Interscience, 1977.

Schein, Edgar. *Organizational Psychology.* Englewood Cliffs, N.J.: Prentice-Hall, 1965.

Regarding Community Needs

Berridge, Robert I. *Community Education Handbook.* Midland, Mich.: Pendell, 1973.

Fessler, Donald R. *Facilitating Community Change: A Basic Guide.* La Jolla, Cal.: University Associates, 1976.

Franklin, Richard. *Patterns of Community Development.* New York: Public Affairs Press, 1966.

Klein, Donald D. *Community Dynamics and Mental Health.* New York: John Wiley & Sons, 1968.

Kochan, Manfred, and Donahue, Joseph D. *Information for the Community.* Chicago: American Library Association, 1976.

McMahon, Ernest E. *Needs: of People and their Communities—and the Adult Educator.* Washington, D.C.: Adult Education Association of the U.S.A., 1970.

Sarason, Seymour B. *The Psychological Sense of Community.* San Francisco: Jossey-Bass, 1974.

Studying the Community. Chicago: American Library Association, 1959.

Warren, Roland. *Studying Your Community.* New York: Russell Sage Foundation, 1955.

7
Defining Purposes and Objectives

The Nature and Function of Purposes and Objectives

"Aims," "purposes," "objectives," "goals," and "targets" seem to be used among the practitioners of adult education—and, indeed, in the dictionaries—almost interchangeably to convey the broad meaning "ends toward which effort is directed." As I examine the program-planning documents in our field, it seems to me that this confusion of terminology has resulted in some confusion about the program-planning process. I should like to propose a terminology, therefore, that I hope might help to clarify the discrete character of the direction-setting function at three different levels of the program-development process.

I propose that "general purposes" be used when referring to the broad social and institutional goals the adult-education operation was established to achieve; and I find that "aims" is an acceptable synonym in this context.

I propose that "program objectives" be used when referring to the educational and operational outcomes toward which a total program will be directed for a prescribed period of time (such as "the next year"); and I could use either "targets" or "priorities" in this sense.

And I propose that "learning objectives" be used when referring to the specific behavioral outcomes that an identifiable group of individuals will be helped to seek in a particular learning activity (such as a course, a meeting, a workshop); and so far as I am concerned, "activity objectives" would convey the same meaning.

In this chapter we shall be concerned only with the first two levels, general purposes and program objectives, since they are the ones that are relevant to organizing and administering total programs; learning objectives will be treated in Chapter 11, which deals with planning particular learning activities.

Defining General Purposes

The general purposes of a program are typically found in the charter or policy statement (as described in Chapter 5) promulgated at the time an adult-education unit is established in an institution. A statement of general purposes defines the part adult education is expected to play in helping the institution to accomplish its total mission; it delineates the social and institutional goals the program is authorized to serve; it provides both a sense of direction and specification of limits for a program; and it conveys the educational philosophy or system of values that should govern choices among alternative lines of action and according to which the worth of the program will be judged by the institution.

Turn to Appendix G and compare the statements of purpose and objectives for public school programs (Exhibit G–1), community college and technical institute programs (Exhibit G–2), college and university programs (Exhibit G–3), and programs in business and industry (Exhibit G–4), along with the goal statements found in Appendix F. Notice the wide variation among them in the clarity and levels of specificity with which goals, values, target populations, and types of service are stated. Presumably a certain amount of vagueness allows greater flexibility; but it also renders the evaluation of results more difficult. Statements of general purpose can be made congruent with the spirit of andragogy by describing what an institution will help people to do, rather than what it will do to people.

Since general purposes are usually set at the time an adult-education operation is launched, and their function is to give long-run direction, there is a tendency to regard them as being more or less permanent. This tendency has led, in my observation, to some rather deplorable cultural lags. I know of at least one county agricultural extension service, for example, that continued to focus its energies on helping farmers improve their efficiency in growing crops, as provided in its statement of purposes, long after almost all of the land of the county had become occupied by suburban homes. (I must hastily add that I know of no agency in which this cultural lag is less likely to occur than the Cooperative Extension Service, because of the elaborate machinery it has established for continuous program review.) I know of a YMCA that continued to operate a health club for business executives, as provided in its by-laws, long after its neighborhood had become a depressed area and few businessmen came near it. Examples of this sort could be multiplied from the experiences of schools, universities, churches, business firms, and every other kind of institution.

It is urgent, therefore, especially in an era of accelerating social change, that an institution's general purposes as regards adult education be continuously tested against changing needs as an integral part of the ongoing program-development process.

Defining Program Objectives

Whereas a statement of purposes provides a broad sense of direction for a program that differentiates it from other programs in a community, a list of program objectives provides a platform of specific goals toward which a program should be directed in the period immediately ahead. It is on the basis of the program objectives that decisions will be made as to what particular activities will be scheduled for what groups of participants; they are the concrete guidelines for program development.

Program objectives also provide guidelines and focus for the varied activities that make up a comprehensive adult-education program. Teachers and activity leaders can refer to the program objectives to identify common areas of concern toward which they should be gearing their learning objectives. For example, I can well remember how, when I was the adult-education director at the Chicago Central YMCA, the promulgation of the program priority "to help our participants gain a better understanding of the feelings and problems of minority-group members" caused teachers of such diverse courses as social dancing, public speaking, and operating a small business to work out learning experiences with their students that would further this objective.

Finally, program objectives provide the benchmarks by which the program can be evaluated. The procedures for accomplishing this are the subject of Chapter 10.

Translating Needs into Program Objectives

The starting point for developing program objectives is the pool of needs that have been evolved through the procedures described in Chapter 6. The process for translating these needs into objectives involves, it seems to me, the following steps:

1. *Organize the needs into a priority system.* The processes by which you assess the needs of the individuals in your constituency, of your organization, and of your community, will presumably produce three more or less extensive sets of needs. The problem now becomes one of organizing these needs into categories and priorities. It is probably useful to make an initial division into operational needs and educational needs.

Operational needs have to do with providing the institutional resources for meeting the educational needs. They include such things as:

Broadening and deepening the quality of involvement of citizens, participants, and faculty in planning and operating the program;

Providing more adequate physical facilities for the program;

Enlarging the financial base of the program;

Enlarging and improving the quality of the faculty;

Improving the efficiency of the administrative procedures;

Expanding the interpretation of the program to the public;

Establishing closer working relationships with other institutions in the community;

Improving the quality of the materials and equipment available for the program;

And so on.

Operational needs may not appear directly in the list resulting from a need assessment (they are more likely to be revealed starkly through the evaluation procedures described in Chapter 10); but they can often be inferred from an analysis of individual, organizational, and community needs. For example, if a need assessment indicates that the parents in a particular section of a city have a strong need to learn how better to take care of their children's nutrition, this might suggest such operational needs for a given institution as improving their communication with the subpopulation, establishing outpost centers in that part of the city, and recruiting nutrition experts to the faculty.

After a list of operational needs has been developed, some judgment has to be applied in arranging them in a priority order—which is where a strong advisory committee can be especially helpful.

Educational needs are the things people "ought" to learn for their own good, for the good of the organization, and for the good of the community. The need assessment procedures described in Chapter 6 presumably will have produced three lists of such needs derived from individuals, the organization, and the community. The problem now becomes one of amalgamating the needs from these three sources into a composite set of needs and arranging them in a priority order. Presumably some day all of us will have computer time available for accomplishing this task in a simple and systematic way. But for most of us now this is an artistic, not a mechanical process. I know of no other way of doing this at this point than to put the three lists in front of you and feel out the agreements and contradictions among them and then think through their probable meanings.

But it will probably be helpful in going through this process if you have a system of categories in mind into which to organize a composite list. I can think of three possible systems of categories, and there may well be others:

1) Program areas to which needs are related, such as:
—job-related subjects and skills
—hobbies and recreation
—religion, morals, and ethics
—general education
—home and family life
—personal development
—current events, public affairs, and citizenship
—agriculture
—miscellaneous

2) Social roles—that is, the needs related to the adequate performance of such roles as:
—worker
—parent
—husband and wife
—homemaker or home member
—son or daughter of aging parents
—citizen
—friend
—club or association member or leader
—member of a religious group
—user of leisure time

3) Types of behavioral changes involved, such as:
—knowledge
—understanding
—skills
—attitudes
—interests
—values

Regardless of which system of categories you use (and it may produce some worthwhile insights to try to organize the same set of needs into two or three systems of categories), you should end up with many more needs than any single program could attempt to meet; hence, the necessity of the next step.

2. *Screen the needs through appropriate filters.* In order for a given need to end up being translated into a program objective, it should be able to pass through the following figurative filters:

a) Institutional purposes and philosophy of education. Taking the example of the Midway Adult High School in Exhibit G-1, a need for advanced knowledge of atomic medicine by San Diego physicians would be screened out, since it does not fit into the general purposes of the high school program. The director of adult education in this case would, it is hoped, alert the school of medicine of an appropriate university as to the existence of this need.

One particularly troublesome problem to many adult educators regarding this phase is that of the relationship of their program to other programs in the community. Most of them wish to avoid competing with or duplicating the programs of other agencies, and yet it is frequently difficult to know when duplication exists. I suggest that duplication should not be considered to exist if any of the following conditions obtain:

—If the programs serve essentially different clienteles, as determined by membership requirements, convenience of location, educational prerequisites, etc.;

—If there is a substantial difference in the costs to the participants;

—If there is a significant difference in the objectives of the "competing" programs (for instance, those programs whose purpose is primarily degree-granting or technical training do not, for the most part, serve the same needs as informal programs);

—If there are radically different methods of instruction (for instance, a series of lectures to two hundred people does not serve the same needs as a seminar group of twenty);

—If there is a difference in the subject matter treated (many courses are concerned with specialized parts of larger subjects, and may not therefore be duplicating even though the overall title is the same);

—If existing programs are filled to capacity and cannot take additional students;

—If other programs are offered at a different time of day or year.

My own impression is that the needs of adults are so much greater than present resources are meeting that the problem of duplication can easily be overemphasized.

b) Feasibility. Some needs will be screened out simply because it is not feasible for a given institution to try to meet them at a given time. Needs that require enormously expensive equipment, such as a cyclotron or an elaborate computer system or an ocean-research ship, are appropriate for only a few highly specialized institutions to consider. Other needs may be screened out because of the psychology of learning— certain things just can't be learned in the time or under the conditions prevailing, or are not within the range of possibility of the potential clientele.

c) The interests of individuals. This is where the interest assessment described in Chapter 6 comes into the picture. Which of the needs do not fall within the scope of the interests expressed by the potential participants? And should these then be automatically screened out? Not necessarily, in my opinion. Perhaps the development of interest in these needs should become an educational objective. Or perhaps some of these needs can be worked on by attaching them to existing interests.

3. *Translate the surviving needs into program objectives.* The needs that have survived the screening through these three sets of filters provide the raw material out of which program objectives are manufactured. The form in which the objectives are stated will affect their usefulness as guides to program development and evaluation. The more specifically they define the desired outcomes, the more useful they will be. And just as a distinction was made above between operational needs and educational needs, so I suggest the utility of distinguishing between operational objectives and educational objectives.

Operational objectives identify the things that will be done to improve the quality of the institutional resources for meeting the educational needs. Taking the list of illustrative operational needs on page 122, these might be translated into operational objectives something like this:

—To institute procedures for the election of five representatives from the student body and five representatives from the faculty to serve with ten representatives of the community appointed by the board as a program advisory council, the responsibilities of which are to be defined by the board;

—To locate and arrange for fifteen additional informal meeting rooms in nearby facilities;

—To increase funds available for program subsidy by $35,000 through the solicitation of industrial and individual contributions;

—To institute a program of inservice education for faculty members on the technology of adult education, including a one-day orientation workshop and three follow-up clinical meetings each quarter;

—And so on.

Educational objectives define the kinds of behavioral outcomes that participants are to be invited to seek in specific areas of content. These objectives might be organized according to any of the three systems of categories described on page 123 or any other system that fits better with the reality of a particular situation. An attempt is made in Exhibit 17 to reduce the process of translating educational needs into objectives to graphic form.

Exhibit 17

THE PROCESS OF TRANSLATING NEEDS INTO OBJECTIVES

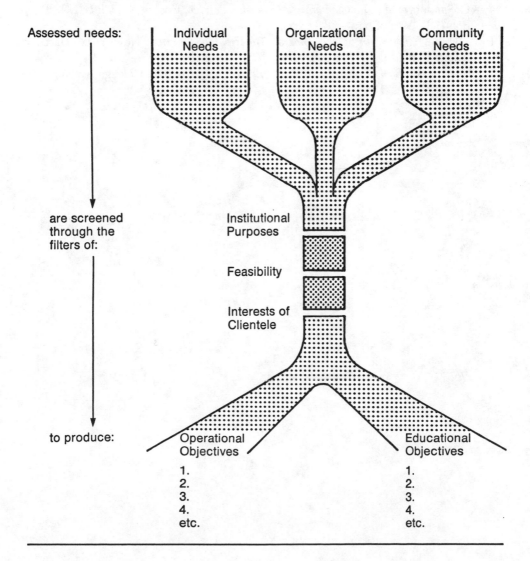

For Your Continuing Inquiry . . .

Bloom, Benjamin S. (ed.). *Taxonomy of Educational Objectives, Handbook I: Cognitive Domain.* New York: David McKay, 1956.

Boyle, Patrick G., and Jahns, Irwin R. "Program Development and Evaluation," in Robert Smith et al., *Handbook of Adult Education.* New York: Macmillan, 1970.

French, Will, et al. *Behavioral Goals of General Education in High School.* New York: Russell Sage Foundation, 1957.

Haas, G.; Wiles, K.; and Bondi, J. *Curriculum Planning: A New Approach.* Boston: Allyn & Bacon, 1974.

Houle, Cyril O. *The Design of Education.* San Francisco: Jossey-Bass, 1972.

Krathwohl, David R., et al. *Taxonomy of Educational Objectives, Handbook II: Affective Domain.* New York: David McKay, 1964.

Mager, Robert. *Goal Analysis.* Belmont, Cal.: Fearon Publishers, 1972.

Pesson, Lynn L., "Extension Program Planning with Participation of Clientele," in H. C. Sanders et al., *The Cooperative Extension Service.* Englewood Cliffs, N.J.: Prentice-Hall, 1966, Chapter 8.

Taba, Hilda. *Curriculum Development: Theory and Practice.* New York: Harcourt Brace & World, 1962.

Tyler, Ralph W. *Basic Principles of Curriculum and Instruction.* Chicago: University of Chicago Press, 1957.

8
Designing
a Comprehensive
Program

Here we come to the truly artistic phase of the program-development process—the transformation of program objectives into a pattern of activities. Some writers refer to this phase as "engineering"; but to me this analogy implies too mechanical an interpretation of what I think is involved. Perhaps it comes closer to call this the "architectural" phase of program development, since it is in essence a process of building an edifice of activities out of certain types of structural materials according to the specifications of program objectives. But I discovered a few years ago that something happened in my own practice—my programs took on an entirely different quality—when I went even further than this kind of analogizing and started thinking of the design of adult-education programs as being itself a discrete art form.

The Far-Out Notion of Adult Education as an Art Form

I use the concept "art form" broadly here, of course. Adult-education programs cannot be an art form in the sense that poems, paintings, sculptures, cathedrals, plays, symphonies, and the dance are art forms. They cannot be free, creative expressions of human feeling that are ends in themselves. But adult-education programs can possess many of the same qualities that cause the true art forms to be aesthetic experiences. They can be experienced as beautiful, plain, or ugly. And the proposition I am hypothesizing is that the aesthetic quality of an adult-education program directly affects its educative quality.

What are the qualities, then, that make an art form an aesthetic experience? And how can they be applied to the designing of adult-education programs?

A set of guidelines I have found to be clear and practical are in Henry N. Rasmusen's *Art Structure: A Textbook of Creative Design.*[1] In this book the author is concerned mainly with the plastic and graphic arts, but many of his principles have application to all art forms.

Rasmusen sets up as an initial condition for the creation of an aesthetic experience the existence of "the creative attitude," on which he elaborates as follows:

> To create is to select or invent elements significant to a given purpose and organize them into a new and unique form. It means originality. It means individuality. It means freedom of action. The opposites of creation in art are imitation, academicism,

---

[1]Henry N. Rasmusen, *Art Structure: A Textbook of Creative Design* (New York: McGraw-Hill, 1950). By permission.

intellectual and emotional slavery. Creativeness depends on a certain attitude of mind. It is democracy in practice—an invitation to free thinking, exploration, and progression. Its opposite, imitation, spells conformity, reaction, and decadence.[2]

As I sat at my typewriter transcribing that paragraph, I couldn't help glancing at the dozen or so announcements of adult-education programs from across the country that are spread out on the table to my side. How like one another most of them are— the same layout, the same academic-type courses, the same drab language describing the courses, the same stereotypic time schedule, and so on. But two of the dozen jump out at me: the University of California Riverside's Lifelong Learning program and the Oklahoma City Libraries' Community Workshop program (these two just happened to be in this particular set; others will no doubt appear in future dozens I shall lay out before me). Each one has an imaginative layout, a wide variety of different kinds of activities, a functional system of categories for grouping the activities, lively descriptive language, a sense of unique personality.

This requirement of a creative attitude poses what may appear to be a paradox. Previous chapters have emphasized the importance of involving many people in the planning process and of anchoring the program to the needs of individuals, organizations, and the community. Don't these requirements inhibit the freedom of the adult-education director to be creative in the final act of designing a program? Not necessarily. Truly creative adult educators are able to excite committees and councils and colleagues on the staff into joining in the creative attitude, with the result that creative ideas flow from many sources. A climate pervaded by this attitude will also produce a sense of trust that will encourage program directors to exercise their individual creativity in the final decisions about program design. Under these conditions, the data about needs are taken as challenges to experiment with more effective ways of meeting needs rather than as rigid boundaries within which the program must be contained.

Given a creative attitude, the task of the designers of aesthetic experiences is to create a sense of order—a satisfying composition—out of the elements they have to work with. Rasmusen summarizes these elements succinctly in the following excerpts:

> In a first consideration of a work of art we find that there are three main divisions: form, theme, and technique. In its biggest meaning form might be called the plastic structure, the inner and outer shape of an existing object. This would apply to any single part as well as to a combination or group of units which go to make up the whole. In a painting, form is the resulting appearance of a combination of the quantities line, tone, space, and color.
>
> Theme is the psychological aspect of the structure. It is the subject matter involved and the general idea, mood, or meaning to be communicated or expressed.
>
> Technique is the physical structure—the craftsmanship or handling of materials for quality, permanency, and fitness to purpose. . . .
>
> The essential quantities or means of form are, as noted before, line, tone, space, and color. We might add to these the secondary quantity, texture. Considering the quality of a form, we can say that a good work of art is one that has unity. A bad work of art is one that has disunity. . . .
>
> The true artist is a builder with a plan. His materials or quantities are lines and spaces, tones, colors, and textures. His binding elements or qualities are the principles of design—opposition and transition. The end result is balance and cohesion. Added results, which are refinements rather than basic principles, are variation and dominance. All of these together, depending on the success of the plan and its execution, equal unity.[3]

---

[2]Ibid., p. 1.
[3]Ibid., pp. 6–7. By permission.

Let us now examine the application of each of these elements to the designing of adult-education programs and begin a process of brainstorming some of their implications.

Art Principles Applied to Adult Education

Line is the sense of direction, continuity, and movement in a design. Some of the ways "line" can be expressed in an adult-education program are as follows:

—By a dynamic integrating theme; e.g., "Learning for Living" conveys a feeling of motion, whereas "Evening Classes" seems static;

—By indicating progressive sequences of activities participants might choose to follow; e.g., students interested primarily in enriching their leisure time might start with "Exploring the Arts," and move from there into a series of broadening and deepening activities in handicrafts, the fine arts, literature, music, drama, etc.;

—By scheduling activities so that participants can engage in a primary interest in an early period (e.g., 7:00–8:30 P.M.) and then move into a secondary interest in a later period (e.g., 8:30–10:00 P.M.).

Space is the shape of a program in terms of its length, width, and depth; and *space patterns* are the relationship of the various units of a program within the limits of that shape. Some of the ways "shape" can be expressed in an adult-education program are as follows:

—By clear definition of the limits of the program in terms of purposes, clientele, content, and methodology (how the "shape" of this program differs from the "shape" of other programs in the community);

—By manipulating the length of time of individual meetings (short to long) and terms (ten-week, quarter, semester) and by making them uniform or varied;

—By varying the depth of the activities (e.g., from light to heavy, elementary to advanced, exploratory to intense);

—By specifying the limits in size of the various activities;

—By manipulating the costs of fees and materials;

—By manipulating the physical settings; e.g., type and size of meeting rooms, library space, lounging areas, and location (in-plant vs. out-in-the-community).

Tone is the shading or relative emphases in a program. Some of the ways "tone" can be expressed in an adult-education program are:

—By conveying a primary concern for people and their wants vs. for subjects and their requirements;

—By varying the emphasis given to the various program areas (e.g., emphasis in the fall on self-improvement, in the spring on leisure-time activities) or client groupings (e.g., emphasis in morning activities on homemakers, afternoon activities on the older adults, and evening activities on young adults);

—By manipulating the relative emphasis given in the catalog to the subject and the teacher (e.g., some catalogs merely give the name of the teacher for each subject, whereas others provide informative descriptions of the teachers and their qualifications).

Color is the hue and intensity of a program which enables one to apply such descriptive adjectives to it as bright or dull, warm or cool, informal or formal, lively or dead, inspiring or depressing, and friendly or aloof. Some of the ways "color" can be expressed in an adult-education program are as follows:

—By portraying the program in announcements, publicity, and catalogs in bright, warm, informal, lively, inspiring, and friendly terms;

—By providing comfortable, warmly decorated, informal physical facilities;

—By maintaining an atmosphere of warmth and friendliness through the use of hosts and hostesses, personal introductions to faculty and fellow students, personalizing enrollment procedures, etc.;

—By selecting faculty who are colorful, person-centered, and inspiring, and supporting them in expressing their individuality and creativity.

Texture is the tactile feel of a program—how it feels to the touch; a program might "feel" rough or smooth, soft or hard, broken or connected, spotty or even. As Rasmusen pointed out, "Texture is not a basic means of form in itself but rather a result of the other means."[4] So the texture of a program will be determined by how well the quantities of line, space, tone, and color have been handled. But it provides another criterion by which to test the quality of a program.

Rasmusen stresses that the ultimate test of quality in a work of art is its sense of unity—the harmony and mutual reinforcement among the quantities of line, space, tone, color, and texture:

> Whatever the form might be, the measuring gauges for quality are creativeness and unity. A work will have quality if there is consistency in style and technique, form and theme, spirit and function. Such a new creative organism exists in its own right as any other creation in nature exists—bound into a living oneness by the principles of unity.[5]

No wonder so many adult-education programs are experienced by their participants as hodgepodges of à-la-carte offerings of disconnected stereotypic academic crumbs rather than as aesthetic experiences. But perhaps as we come to understand more clearly the insight that adult education can be an art form, adult-education programs will become more beautiful to behold.

Selecting the Formats for Learning

The architectural function in the designing of comprehensive programs of adult education consists of selecting that combination of learning units or formats that will most effectively accomplish the objectives of the program and arranging them into a pattern according to the above art principles. A wider variety of formats is available to program designers than is reflected in most programs—a fact which is to be deplored, since a wider range of individual needs for learning, styles of learning, and conditions for learning can be met when there is a wide choice of formats. Besides, a variety of formats adds to the aesthetic quality of a program by giving it a sense of liveliness and rhythm, and a richer texture.

What is meant by "format for learning"?

The technology of adult education is still in such an early formative stage that a standardized lexicon of its terminology has not yet emerged. As a result, writers in the field—and practitioners as well—use a variety of labels to describe the same phenomena. A start has been made to bring order out of this chaos by Dr. Coolie Verner of the University of British Columbia. Verner distinguishes three elements in the notion of processes for adult education, each of which describes a separate function:

> The first element is the method: the organization of the prospective participants for purposes of education. The second element involves techniques: the variety of ways

---

[4]Ibid., pp. 11–12.

[5]Ibid., p. 82.

in which the learning task is managed so as to facilitate learning. The third and final element involves devices: all those particular things or conditions which are utilized to augment the techniques and make learning more certain.[6]

Verner elaborates on his concept of method as follows:

> The method of education identifies the ways in which people are organized in order to conduct an educational activity. A method establishes a relationship between the learner and the institution or agency through which the educational task is accomplished. Formal educational institutions establish such a relationship for learning by having the participants come to the institution and organizing them into groups according to age, ability, subject matter, or some other criterion. These groups are referred to as classes. Since pre-adult education is almost exclusively institutionalized through the school, the principal method employed is the class. Adult education, on the other hand, is not exclusively institutionalized; therefore, it employs the class method as only one in a variety of methods.
>
> Because the method describes a way of organizing participants, the methods of adult education tend to fall into a classification scheme that is predetermined by the ways in which people are naturally organized in the society. People may be found as isolated individuals, as small or large aggregations, or collected into communities. Thus, the methods of adult education can be classified as individual, group, or community methods.[7]

I am using "format" with precisely the same meaning Verner gives "method." I prefer "format" because it seems to me to convey more the sense of a structural element and because it is more clearly separated from "technique" than is "method."

Cyril O. Houle, in his *The Design of Education*, describes what he labels "the fundamental system" of educational design consisting of two complementary actions: 1) "the examination of the situation in which the learning activity occurs to determine the basic category to which it belongs" (Exhibit 18); 2) "and the application to that situation, in ways which are profoundly influenced by its category, of a basic framework or model in order to produce a design or program" (Exhibit 19).[8] Houle's fundamental system is far too elaborate to be explained adequately here, but I hope that exposure to these two exhibits will whet your appetite for the full-course dinner in Houle's book.

For the purposes of the kinds of comprehensive programs with which this book is concerned, I prefer to use three simple categories of format: 1) formats for individual learning, 2) formats for group learning, and 3) the format of community development or community education.

Formats for Individual Learning

Several formats are available for helping individuals learn separately, often more or less in terms of their own unique objectives and at their own pace. Some of these formats do not require the physical presence of the individual in an institution, and so are particularly appropriate for disabled, elderly, incarcerated, or geographically isolated students.

---

[6]Coolie Verner, *A Conceptual Scheme for the Identification and Classification of Processes for Adult Education* (Washington, D.C.: Adult Education Association, 1962), pp. 9–10.

[7]Coolie Verner and Alan Booth, *Adult Education* (New York: Center for Applied Research in Education, 1964), pp. 68–69.

[8]Cyril O. Houle, *The Design of Education* (San Francisco: Jossey-Bass, 1973), p. 40.

Exhibit 18

HOULE'S MAJOR CATEGORIES
OF EDUCATIONAL DESIGN SITUATIONS[9]

Individual

C-1   An individual designs an activity for himself

C-2   An individual or a group designs an activity for another individual

Group

C-3   A group (with or without a continuing leader) designs an activity for itself

C-4   A teacher or group of teachers designs an activity for, and often with, a group of students

C-5   A committee designs an activity for a larger group

C-6   Two or more groups design an activity which will enhance their combined programs of service

Institution

C-7   A new institution is designed

C-8   An institution designs an activity in a new format

C-9   An institution designs a new activity in an established format

C-10   Two or more institutions design an activity which will enhance their combined programs of service

Mass

C-11   An individual, group, or institution designs an activity for a mass audience

---

Apprenticeship and Internship

One of the earliest forms of education, apprenticeship in its most literal meaning is a contractual relationship between an employer and an employee through which the employee is trained for prescribed work processes by practical experience under the supervision of master craftspeople and by formal instruction. Most apprenticeship agreements specify the number of hours per day for work and for study, graduated wage scales, and length of time for completion of the program (typically, four years). It is the format most commonly used for learning a skilled trade. More loosely, apprenticeship is also used to describe any kind of learning-on-the-job experience. For example, organizations frequently "apprentice" a newly selected officer or committee chairperson or staff worker to work for a period of time as an "understudy" of the person to be replaced.

Internship refers to a similar process of learning through supervised practical experience, but it tends to be used more narrowly in the context of managerial and professional roles.

Correspondence Study

A large number of commercial correspondence schools, several universities, and the United States Armed Forces Institute offer courses of every description in which the student engages in reading with the guidance of a syllabus, submits written assignments, and has these assignments reacted to by an instructor—all through the medium of the United States Postal Service. It is possible for any institution to enrich its pro-

Exhibit 19

DECISION POINTS AND COMPONENTS OF
AN ADULT-EDUCATIONAL FRAMEWORK[10]

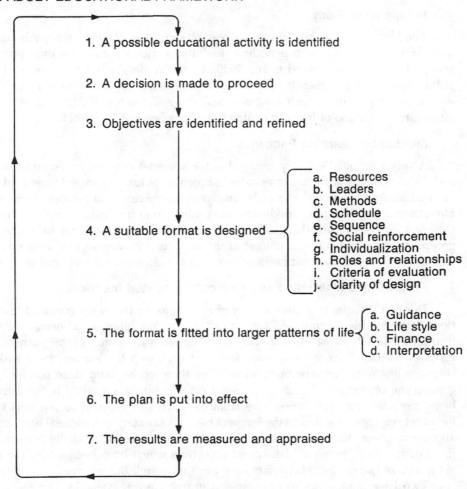

1. A possible educational activity is identified

2. A decision is made to proceed

3. Objectives are identified and refined

4. A suitable format is designed
   a. Resources
   b. Leaders
   c. Methods
   d. Schedule
   e. Sequence
   f. Social reinforcement
   g. Individualization
   h. Roles and relationships
   i. Criteria of evaluation
   j. Clarity of design

5. The format is fitted into larger patterns of life
   a. Guidance
   b. Life style
   c. Finance
   d. Interpretation

6. The plan is put into effect

7. The results are measured and appraised

gram of offerings to its clientele by providing a referral service to these established correspondence-study resources.

Counseling

Educational counseling—guidance in the selection of educational opportunities, and vocational counseling—guidance in occupational choices, are not so much formats for learning as administrative services. But clinical counseling, which typically involves a series of interviews over an extended period of time, and is concerned with helping an individual gain self-insights, can properly be classified as a format for learning. A number of institutions, such as family-service societies and casework agencies, use this format as their principal means for helping adults learn and grow. But an increasing number of schools, universities, industries, and other less-specialized institutions are

---

[10]Ibid., p. 47.

finding that clinical psychological counseling is a format through which their clients can meet certain of their learning needs more effectively than is possible through other formats.

Independent Study

The idea of developing tailor-made reading sequences to help individuals engage in self-directed inquiry, with periodic consultations with a mentor on their progress and problems, was pioneered in the 1920s by the readers' advisory services of our public libraries. Since then it has come into increasing popularity in our academic institutions, especially in their nontraditional study and external degree programs—often through the use of learning contracts as described in Chapter 11.

Multimedia Learning Packages

A very substantial industry emerged in the seventies devoted to the construction and distribution (through sale or rental) of sequences of learning experiences made up of combinations of printed materials, diagnostic instruments, audiotapes, films, slide films, microfiche, exercises, workbooks, and evaluation instruments. Many of them are designed for use by individuals, others by groups, and many by either individuals or groups. Packages are available in most of the subjects that have ever been taught, but the largest volume is in vocational and personal development subjects and languages.

Programmed Instruction and Computer-Assisted Instruction

During the sixties there was a surge of activity in the use of programmed instruction, through both programmed texts and teaching machines, as a format for self-instruction. In this format the material to be learned is presented to the learners in a series of carefully planned sequential steps. At each step the learners must make a response that tests their comprehension. They then receive immediate feedback regarding the correctness of their responses. Correct responses resulted in the learners being rewarded (or "reinforced") by being permitted to proceed to the next step; incorrect responses resulted in the learners having to restudy the material and choose another response. Each program is planned to bring the learners to the accomplishment of specified "terminal" behavioral objectives which have been set by the programmer, and when these behaviors have been mastered, the program is completed.

Two basic approaches to programmed instruction are available. The *linear* approach, espoused by B. F. Skinner and his followers, emphasizes reinforcement and "operant conditioning." This approach takes learners on a direct line to the terminal behavior, with cues or prompts that help them make the correct response in each small step. The *branching* approach, espoused by Norman Crowder and his followers, gives the learners choices which determine the material they will see next. The multiple-choice questions not only permit recognition of correct responses but also develop new paths of learning in the event that the correct response was not recognized.

Both approaches are used in a further development in which programs are tied in with computers—a method referred to as CAI (Computer-Assisted Instruction).

The popularity of programmed instruction began to wane in the seventies, and a number of corporations that invested heavily in producing the "hardware" and "software" of teaching machines went bankrupt. But many aspects of programmed instruction have been incorporated into other formats, and CAI remains in widespread use, especially in industry and technical education. Many of my students have found programmed instruction, especially when based on branching, to be an effective resource for self-directed learning when they take the initiative in using it and when they have one or more other persons to interact with while using it.

In the light of andragogical theory, I have reservations about the use of programmed instruction as it has evolved to date, especially the linear approach. The very notion of terminal behavioral objectives is discordant with the concept of continuing self-development toward one's full potential. And the notion of some programmer predetermining what is desirable behavior for an individual and then controlling the stimuli and responses so as to produce that behavior conflicts with the concept of an adult as a self-directing organism. But programmed instruction is still in a primitive stage of development. Perhaps as the technology comes under the influence of the humanistic psychologists, it will free itself from the constraints of the behaviorists and will develop ways to facilitate the learners engaging in a process of self-directed inquiry. Programming techniques, it is hoped, will provide more and more varied types of programs—some effective primarily for helping individuals discover basic facts and principles, but others effective for learning difficult aesthetic or critical discriminations, analytic skills, problem-solving abilities, and even creative approaches to problem solving.

Supervision

An interesting change has been taking place in recent years in the concept of supervision. Under the influence of such management theorists as Likert and McGregor, the conception of the role of the supervisor has been shifting away from a primary concern with controlling the behavior of subordinates toward a primary concern with developing the self-directing capacities of subordinates. Under the newer doctrine, the supervisor is seen as being essentially a teacher, and supervisory training focuses on helping supervisors gain the ability to serve as facilitators and resources for their subordinates' continuing self-development. Defined this way, supervision qualifies as a format for individual learning.

Formats for Group Learning

Most organized learning takes place in groups—largely because of the greater efficiency of operation afforded by dealing with people in collectivities and because of the richer resources and motivations for learning provided by a group. Two types of groups are used for purposes of adult education: those formed expressly to engage in learning, and those formed for purposes other than learning but which engage in learning as a supplemental function.

Action Projects

Many organizations contain groups formed primarily for the purpose of engaging in social action of some sort. For example, most churches have groups whose main purpose is to further some missionary work, to promote some moral cause, or to remedy some social injustice; and many civic organizations involve their members in various projects of civic improvement. Action groups of these sorts, which devote their total energy to achieving action targets, can hardly be classified as a format for learning. But many action groups engage in activities designed to increase their knowledge about the problems on which they are taking action, and often even to improve their skills as agents of change. When educational components of this sort are included in an action group's program, it seems to me that they can qualify as a format for learning.

Clinics, Institutes, and Workshops

Although these three terms are used quite loosely in the literature of the field, they convey some difference in emphasis in a basic format for learning. All these refer to a short, intensive, multiactivity, large-group learning experience. The clinic emphasizes the diagnosis, analysis, and solving of problems arising out of the participants' field experience. The institute emphasizes the development of knowledge and skill in a specialized area of concern or practice. The workshop (which may also be designated a "laboratory") emphasizes the development of individual competencies in a defined area of concern largely through a variety of small groups.

All three variations typically employ a pattern of activities that may include large meetings (general sessions), small groups (discussion groups, laboratory groups, special-interest groups, problem-solving groups, planning groups, skill-practice groups, instructional groups, etc.), reading periods, individual consultations, worship or meditational periods, and recreational activities. They vary in length from part of one day to several weeks, and are often residential—meaning that they take place in hotels, resorts, or conference centers in which the participants live while attending the event.

Clubs and Organized Groups

America has been dubbed a nation of joiners. Literally thousands of organized groups and clubs of every description dot every section of our map, and there is hardly a citizen who does not belong to at least one of them. The striking thing about American clubs is that almost all of them have the education of their members as a central objective.

These groups differ according to pattern of organization, ranging from the extremely informal arrangements of neighborhood friendship circles to the highly rigid structures of fraternal and service clubs. Some are completely autonomous and can decide on their form of organization and program policies for themselves. Others are affiliated with local, state, or national organizations that require varying degrees of conformity with established patterns of organization and that may even dictate program policies.

As a part of a comprehensive program of adult education, the club format for learning has several unique advantages. Because it is less formal in structure and has a larger social or fellowship component than most other formats, it is a way of reaching adults who might otherwise shy away from educational experiences. Because it goes on year after year, it provides opportunities for more continuous learning and for practicing what has been learned. For example, a person who has learned the basic facts and skills of photography or the French language in a course can develop them further and practice them in a photography or French club. Conversely, because clubs can be more flexible in their program content, they can serve as an effective instrument for helping members explore new interests that then may be pursued further in courses or other formats. Finally, because clubs tend to be more self-reliant and self-governing than other formats, they can be maintained in a comprehensive program with less administrative service. For example, the University of Minnesota General Extension Division has for many years provided program advisory services and materials to local and statewide clubs numbering many thousands of members for a fraction of the cost and energy required to service a few thousand students in its on-campus program.

Certain kinds of educational outcomes are especially appropriate for the club format for learning:

The acquisition of knowledge can be promoted by reading-discussion programs (e.g., the Great Books), lecture-discussions, motion pictures, exhibits, and tours. This is probably the educational objective that most clubs give an overwhelming priority to, and yet it is questionable if it is the one that most effectively exploits the unique properties of clubs as a format for learning.

A broadening of interests, through exposure to new ideas, experience with new activities, and other devices, is a function that many groups are performing well unless they have succumbed to the tendency to limit the scope of the program to the interests of a dominant few or to the tried-and-true activities of the past.

A deepening of cultural appreciation is accomplished partly through exposure to cultural interpretations, such as book reviews and lectures on the arts, but more effectively through cultural experience, such as participation in artistic activities or literary discussion.

An understanding of social issues can be pursued through having the issues defined and clarified by authoritative presentations and group discussion, but even more effectively by participation in action projects.

The refinement of certain skills, such as communications skills, group-participation skills, leisure-activity skills, leadership abilities, and human-relations skills in general can be furthered by providing opportunities for members to practice these skills and receive supportive feedback on their performance.

In this context, I'd like to suggest that the many boards and committees that exist primarily to do organizational work are a special case of the club format for learning, and that much better use than is typically the situation could be made of them as instruments for the growth and development of their members. A number of organizations have adopted the practice of setting aside blocks of time in their busy agendas for self-educational purposes, with beneficial results.

Conferences and Conventions

The conference or convention is one of the backbones of informal adult education in our country. Throughout the year thousands of organizations bring hundreds of thousands of their members together from across the cities, the states, or the nation to renew old friendships and make new ones, to review the work of the organizations during the past year and set their course for the next year, and to develop the competencies and build up the personal resources of their members. But unquestionably the full potential of conferences and conventions as formats for learning is far from being realized, largely because the conference planners don't perceive them as formats for learning. It may be helpful to examine, therefore, some principles for improving the value of the conference as an educational experience.

First, it is necessary to understand the various educational purposes a conference can serve, in order that those purposes can be selected that will best meet the needs of a particular group of participants. Among the possible functions a conference can perform are the following:

Presentation of information. This is probably the function that most people associate with conferences, since the most common pattern of conference organization consists of a series of meetings in which experts read papers or make addresses. There is reason to believe, however, that more faith has been placed in this form of education than is justified. On many occasions the presentation of facts is desirable and necessary, but other needs are probably more pressing than is usually recognized, and other forms of information giving may be more effective than formal speeches.

Inspiration. The mere meeting together of a large number of people with common concerns is often an inspiring experience. Inspirational goal-setting addresses or discussions may also help the delegates to raise their sights and gain new conviction.

Exchange of experience. The cross-fertilization of ideas that comes from exchanging experiences is a stimulant to improved practices. Delegates can learn a great deal from the successes and failures of others.

Training. Conferences are excellent instruments for helping delegates to learn new skills or improve old ones. They provide opportunities for gaining both knowledge and practice under controlled conditions and in concentrated doses.

Problem solving. Frequently delegates come to conferences with real problems, either of their profession, or of back-home operations, that can be solved better at a conference than in any other way. This is a function that has probably been undervalued more than any other in typical conference planning. The best kind of learning experience is provided in the solving of real problems.

Commitment to action. The conference provides one of the few opportunities most similar-minded groups of people have of coming together from a wide area to consider common problems, arrive at a common solution, and commit themselves and those they represent to common lines of action. This is, of course, the final step in education, and one that many conference planners also tend to undervalue.

There are probably very few occasions in which a conference could serve the needs of its participants by limiting itself to any one of the above functions. Indeed, it is difficult to imagine a conference in which all the functions are not needed.

As awareness of the great potential value of the conference as a format for learning has risen in recent years, increasing attention has been given by creative adult educators to providing guidelines to conference planners. The books cited in the bibliography at the end of this chapter are highly recommended.

Courses

The format that traditionally dominated our educational establishment is the course or class—a group with a definite enrollment (usually twenty students or more), meeting at specified times for a predetermined length of time (ten weeks, a quarter, a semester, a year) for study of a limited area of subject matter, under the direction of a continuing teacher. At one time a distinction was made between formal courses (for credit) and informal courses (learning for its own sake); but this difference has so largely disappeared in practice that it no longer serves a purpose to make the distinction.

In most comprehensive adult-education programs the course format is the predominant pattern in the design, but no longer to the extent that it once was. The course is still the most efficient and most acceptable unit for organizing most kinds of learning, and since it has been freed from the shackles of the traditional lecture-recitation-examination ritual, it has become a much more flexible and dynamic instrument for helping people learn.

Organizing a Course Program

There is a wide variety of practice in the organization of course programs, ranging from the staff-dominated organization of many schools to the completely participant-managed programs of such voluntary organizations as the League of Women Voters. Courses may be under institutional auspices, in which case their precise form of organization will be largely determined by the traditions and policies of the sponsoring institution. Or, they may be organized as completely separate and independent entities, without any predetermined pattern of organization, as in the Free Universities.

Frequently a course is organized and offered as an independent unit within some larger program. Thousands of organizations that depend on volunteer leadership, ranging from the Boy Scouts to political parties, bring their volunteers together periodically into leadership-training courses. Many churches sponsor courses for adults in subjects ranging from Bible study to religion and psychiatry. Numerous other organizations similarly have individual courses intermittently in their programs.

Although the discussion in this chapter is primarily in terms of programs involving groups of courses, many of the principles apply equally to independent courses.

There are many advantages in consolidating several courses into an integrated program, rather than presenting them as a series of individual offerings. Not only can the individual course be promoted more efficiently when it is one of a series, but the program has a greater impact on the individual and on the community. It seems more significant. There is an additional advantage if the program as a whole can be given an attractive unifying label such as "Lifelong Learning," "Hobby Nights at the 'Y'," "Learning for Living," "University of Life," "Summer School for Office Workers," or "Modern Industrial Institute."

A course program must be kept highly flexible if it is to adapt itself continuously to the changing needs of adults. The best course programs seem to operate on an almost perpetual "emergency" basis, responding within a few days to a change in the headlines, altering their plans on short notice to take advantage of the unexpected availability of a first-class instructor, or quickly organizing a new course to meet an unanticipated need that a small group of individuals has presented. This kind of flexibility is difficult to achieve if the course program is merely an appendage of some older, more routine type of program.

Determining What Courses to Offer

Sometimes there is little question about what subjects should be offered in a course program, owing to limitations inherent in the situation. For instance, an inservice training program in an industrial plant would automatically be concerned with the job skills involved. Usually, however, there is a wide choice of possible subjects. The program director and committee are then faced with the problem of deciding which subjects would be best. Several principles of curriculum building are suggested:

1. *A tentative goal should be set as to the total number of courses to be included in the program.* This goal will depend upon several factors, including capacities of the staff, number of meeting rooms, a realistic appraisal of the potential clientele, financial resources, and past experience. In general, it would seem to be sound advice to start a new program on a relatively small scale and to build slowly and soundly. The Learning for Living program in Chicago's Central YMCA started in 1946 with ten courses and added ten courses each quarter until the maximum of ninety had been reached. This seems to be a fairly typical pattern for community-center-type programs in large cities.

2. *Every program should be founded on a solid core of subjects in which there is a known need and interest, but should also include a small number of purely experimental subjects for the purpose of exploring new needs and interests.* The value of this principle is illustrated by a recent experience of a program director who found an expert instructor for a "sure-fire" course in interior decorating, but was persuaded by him to offer in addition a course in the expert's particular hobby, antiques. No participant had ever asked for a course on antiques, and the program director had no reason to believe there was much interest in it. When enrollments had been completed, however, the antiques course was filled to overflowing, while the course on interior decoration had only a moderate registration.

3. *A general program of courses should seek to present a more or less balanced variety of subjects.* It happens that people often have what might be called a secondary interest that would not in itself impel them to enroll in a course. But if they enroll in a course appealing to a primary interest and find that a course in their secondary interest is being given on the same night, they are attracted to it. For instance, a recent study of a group of adult students in a course on world affairs revealed that few of them would have enrolled in that course if they had not been coming to the center anyway for a course in public speaking, social dancing, or some other primary interest. Since one of the objectives of adult education is to broaden the interests of participants, it seems important to include as wide a variety of subjects as possible.

4. *Subjects should be selected that are in keeping with the policies of the sponsoring institution and the objectives of the program.* It is important for the program director and the committee to have a definite frame of reference in deciding whether or not a given subject would be a desirable one for that program. Once a program becomes established in the community, the director is likely to be deluged with requests for all kinds of courses by proponents of certain points of view or by people who would like jobs teaching. The director's life can be made miserable unless there is a definite set of policies to back him or her up in screening such requests. Furthermore, unless a consistent policy is followed, the program will lack integration.

5. *Subjects should not ordinarily be offered that will duplicate or conflict with the programs of other organizations in the community.* For a suggested set of criteria to apply in determining when duplication does or does not exist, see page 124, Chapter 7.

6. *Subjects should be limited to objectives that can be accomplished within the time limits set by the nature of the program.* Ordinarily, courses provide for between six and forty-five hours of instruction. It would obviously be a mistake to try to cover "Personnel Management" in six hours, whereas a more limited aspect of the subject, such as "Preparing Job Descriptions," might be treated quite adequately in that time.

Some subjects can be arranged into courses of progressive development, such as beginning, intermediate, and advanced. This system is most often employed in the case of languages. Wherever possible, however, the units should be arranged so that new students can be admitted at each level if they meet certain requirements, since there is an inevitable shrinkage in the original group as it passes from one level to another.

7. *Subjects can be delineated according to topical areas of knowledge or according to functional problems to be dealt with.* The traditional academic courses are almost entirely concerned with areas of knowledge, such as "Early American History" or "Elementary Physics." This system has carried over into adult-education-course programs to a large extent, but there is a growing tendency to supplant it with a problem approach. For example, "Getting Along with Others" is becoming more popular than "Principles of Applied Psychology." "Writing Short Stories" is preferred to "English Composition," and "Using Good English" is replacing "Basic Grammar." This represents a great deal more than mere playing with words. It shows that adult education is functional and is concerned with the real-life problems of people, not merely with abstract knowledge.

8. *There should be a balance between courses that produce an income and courses that require subsidy.* There are certain courses that attract large groups of people and are relatively inexpensive to operate, and so produce an income. Among courses of this nature are usually found those dealing with vocational improvement, public speaking, social dancing, music appreciation, and psychology. On the other hand, there are courses that almost always have to be subsidized because the enrollment in them is limited to small groups and they are expensive to operate. Many of the arts and crafts fall into this category, as well as public affairs, religion, and experimental courses. Sound financing requires that a sufficient number of the income-producing courses be included. But if a program is to offer a balanced variety of subjects and to be dynamic, it is also necessary to include a number of courses that require subsidy. By skillfully weighing the one against the other, both a balanced program and a balanced budget can be achieved.

9. *Subjects should be selected with a sensitivity to seasonal interests and to current developments in human affairs.* The seasonal variations are fairly constant and obvious. Courses on gardening are best in late winter and early spring; announcements of them should arrive shortly after the seed catalogs are delivered. Courses on interior decorating are usually most popular in the spring, when interest in spring cleaning is at its peak. Automobile driving is best in the fall or spring, at least in the North, because the roads are not in suitable condition for instruction during the winter.

People who plan courses ought to keep an eye on the headlines. A crisis in international affairs may be the signal for a new course on "How Diplomacy Works," or an outburst of racial tension may indicate a need and interest in that area, or a controversial election campaign may be a natural springboard for a course in practical politics. Such other events as the publication of a best-selling book or a new discovery may result in a wave of interest that will provide a natural stimulus for an informal course. During a depression the needs and interests of adult students are quite different from what they are during a boom.

10. *It is frequently good practice to arrange for one instructor to give two courses in an evening.* Usually it is more attractive to an instructor to spend a full evening teaching in the program, and to be compensated for two or three courses. Better instructors can often be recruited by offering them this added inducement. Sometimes, in the case of more popular subjects, the two courses might be in the same subject—an early and a late section. Frequently, however, good instructors have a secondary interest that would make a good experimental course. The case of the interior-decoration teacher who was also an expert on antiques has already been cited. Another instance is an instructor of vocabulary building who was also a champion chess player and who gave a very successful second course in "Learning to Play Chess."

11. *The selection of courses should be according to policies established by the directing committee, but should be made by the program director.* When a program consists of more than a few courses, the staff worker responsible should probably be granted a wide degree of latitude in the final determination of the subjects to be offered. For instance, the directing committee might express the desire that a certain subject be offered in the next series. The program director may not be able to find a first-rate instructor by the deadline for going to press, and should not feel under pressure to compromise with a second-rate instructor. On the other hand, the director should be free to include a new course for which a highly competent instructor suddenly becomes available, even though it has not been specifically approved by the committee.

Scheduling Courses

1. *When should course meetings be held?* The answer is, simply, when it is most convenient for the people being served. Evening hours prove to be most convenient to the vast majority of adults, although some courses are offered during the day for swing-shift workers, homemakers, and the elderly. At a downtown location, a luncheon meeting may be most convenient for some people. Almost all downtown programs schedule their courses to start at 6:00 or 6:30 P.M. Presumably, city workers find it more convenient to stay downtown after work, have a quick supper, and go right to class. Programs that take place in residential neighborhoods, on the other hand, schedule most of their classes to start at 7:30 or 8:00 P.M., allowing their participants time to have dinner at home before attending class.

2. *How long should the meetings last?* The general practice ranges from one to three hours, but the most common duration of class meetings seems to be an hour and a half. Several factors will determine which length of time is best in a given situation.

The element of fatigue must be considered in all cases. It is doubtful whether people who have just finished a hard day's work can concentrate very well for much longer than an hour and a half of unbroken study. With a ten-minute intermission, however, they frequently are ready for another hour and a half.

Another variable is the type of activity. Certain types of laboratory and arts and crafts courses require a considerable amount of preparation each evening, such as setting up apparatus, and therefore demand a longer period if the participants are to get in the allotted time for learning.

A third factor is concerned with length of time. When the duration of class periods is one hour, it is possible to schedule three sets of classes each evening. Hour-and-a-half and two-hour periods permit two sets. Longer periods will probably permit only one set of classes. In general, it seems desirable to have at least two class periods.

A fourth factor has to do with how late people can be expected to stay. The most general practice is to end all classes at ten o'clock, but this may vary an hour each way.

A general principle that seems to have merit might be stated as follows: class meetings should not be so short that too little will be accomplished nor so long that participants become fatigued.

3. *What days of the week are best?* The general experience seems to be that the earlier days in the week are the most popular, although there are many exceptions to this pattern. In fact, many programs have had great success with weekends. The habits of the particular group being served should be the determining factor.

4. *How frequently should classes meet?* The most common practice is to schedule class meetings once a week. Adults hesitate to set aside two evenings a week for education, unless there is a particularly strong motivation or a sense of urgency. Some programs, notably the Great Books courses, have experimented with holding meetings on alternate weeks. This practice may be desirable if a great deal of between-meeting preparation is required; but there is likely to be a higher rate of decrease in attendance, since it is more difficult for people to keep track of their schedules.

5. *How should subjects be grouped in the time schedule?* No general rule can be framed for guidance in answering this question, but it is a problem that deserves serious consideration. In a program that has two sets of courses each evening, each set should probably include a variety of subjects, but special attention should be given to subjects that seem to pair up nicely. For instance, many of the people who join the program for public speaking would probably also be interested in a course in discussion leadership. It would be wise, then, to schedule public speaking in the earlier period and discussion in the later period in the same evening, and to call attention to the combination both in the promotional literature and at the first meeting of the public-speaking course.

6. *How long should the terms or series be?* Terms range in practice from six to sixteen weeks. The same principle probably applies here that applies to length of meetings: terms should not be so short that too little will be accomplished nor so long that interest wanes. An examination of the program announcements of a number of course programs shows that ten weeks is the most frequent length of term, with eight and twelve weeks tying for second place.

Demonstrations

The demonstration format for learning evolved out of the work of Seaman A. Knapp and other pioneers in agricultural extension work around the turn of the century, who discovered that the most effective way to get poor farmers in the South to adopt better agricultural practices was to show them how to do them, let them practice them, and then visibly measure the better results. Demonstration has been the basic method of the Federal Extension Service ever since, and has been widely used in industry, the armed services, other government agencies, health agencies, and other institutions. Demonstration as a format is to be distinguished from the demonstration technique used in other formats, in that it is the basis of organization of the participants for learning; people are organized to participate in demonstrations either as experimenters or as observers.

The Federal Extension Service further distinguishes between method demonstrations and result demonstrations. As explained in *The Cooperative Extension Service,* the method demonstration

> . . . involves showing and telling simultaneously—visual and verbal explanation of a process or fact or idea. The demonstration shows how things are done. . . . A demonstration might show: how to organize a club, or how to lead a discussion, as well as how to take a soil sample, oil a tractor, figure hidden interest rates in time payments, or test the hardness of household water. . . . Where the group is small and the process long, it is frequently desirable for all members to perform a few steps as the demonstration progresses.[11]

And the result demonstration

> . . . is a demonstration conducted by a farmer, homemaker, or other person under the direct supervision of an extension worker to prove the advantages of a recommended practice or combination of practices. It involves careful planning, a substantial period of time, adequate records, and comparison of results. It is designed to teach others in addition to the person who conducts the demonstration.[12]

Both forms of demonstration have as their purpose the diffusion of improved ideas and practices throughout a given population. And the Extension Service has worked out a rather elaborate conceptualization and set of strategies for this diffusion process. The process itself is perceived as consisting of five stages: awareness, interest, trial, evaluation, and adoption. Any population is assumed to contain five categories of people in terms of their readiness to adopt new practices: innovators, early adopters, early majority, late majority, and laggards. A simplified version of the recommended strategy involves these steps: 1) alerting the population to the existence of the new practice through the mass media, meetings, visits, etc. (awareness stage); 2) arousing interest in the new practice through method demonstrations and other means (interest stage); 3) identifying a small number of innovators who are willing to try out the new practice in a result demonstration (trial stage); 4) organizing the early adopters to observe and evaluate the result demonstration (evaluation stage); 5) repeating the cycle with early majority, late majority, and laggard groups (adoption).

Naturally, many formats and techniques are used in carrying out this strategy, but the demonstration format is the core of the process.

Exhibits, Fairs, and Festivals

The essential feature of this format for learning is the displaying of ideas, products, or processes. The exhibit is basically a stationary sequential display, the fair a nonsequential mixture of exhibits and activities, and the festival a moving display. It is

---

[11]Loretta V. Cowden, "Method Demonstrations and Method-Demonstration Meetings," in H. C. Sanders et al., *The Cooperative Extension Service* (Englewood Cliffs, N.J.: Prentice-Hall, 1966), pp. 137–41.
[12]Ben D. Cook, "Result Demonstrations and Result-Demonstration Meetings," ibid., p. 129.

an effective format for reaching people who don't read publications, listen to broadcasts, or attend meetings, for the purpose of giving information, creating interest in new solutions to problems, promoting standards of excellence, showing the results of activities, enlisting community support, demonstrating processes, and getting new members for organizations. It is too transitory a learning situation to achieve educational objectives in much depth, but is probably one of the most effective formats for arousing interest.

For some institutions, such as museums and libraries, this is the primary format for achieving their educational objectives. But it is capable of being used as a supplemental format in any comprehensive program. For example, I am one of many thousands who have attended an autumn event sponsored by the Los Angeles public schools in the Hollywood Bowl with these features: a half-mile of booths lining the approach to the Bowl displaying the processor or products of dozens of adult courses; a parade of floats portraying the wide variety of activities available; and a festival featuring performances by students and faculty in music, drama, the dance, public speaking, motion-picture making, and physical education. In Hamilton, Ohio, all adult-education agencies join in sponsoring Adult Education Week activities including a parade, exhibits in downtown stores and public buildings, mass-media programs, official opening of the fall term by the mayor, and open-house parties at all the institutions.

Large Meetings

The large meeting is without doubt the one most widely used format for potential learning—defining "large meeting" as any assembly, regardless of number of people involved, in which the basic relationship is between platform and audience. Think of all the large meetings taking place this minute across the country—in the form of lecture sessions in schools and universities, congregational meetings in churches, weekly or monthly luncheon or dinner meetings of fraternal, civic, and professional associations, membership meetings of labor unions and voluntary associations, staff meetings in industrial concerns, government agencies, and hospitals, and meetings of dozens of other kinds. If it were possible to tally the total attendance at all such meetings in the course of a year, the figure would no doubt turn out to be several times the total population of the country, since each of us attends many large meetings each year. But I purposely qualify this method as a potential format for learning because I am convinced that relatively few of these meetings as they are now conducted produce much learning. Most of them consist simply of stereotypic speeches, occasionally with a formal question-and-answer period that usually falls flat.

I think that this is a situation that exists principally because the planners of large meetings don't have a good theory of large meetings, and that therefore it is a situation which could easily be remedied by the promulgation of an educational theory of large meetings. Accordingly, I should like to present a theory of large meetings as a format for adult learning.

Theory of Large Meetings

The basic premise of this theory is that the educative quality of a large meeting is directly a function of the quantity and quality of interaction in the meeting. This is to say, bluntly, that the more and better the interaction among the various elements of a large meeting, the greater the learning is likely to be. The second premise of the theory is that there are three loci or fields in which interaction can be manipulated: 1) the platform itself, 2) the audience itself, and 3) the relationship between platform and audience. Let us examine the possibilities of each in turn.

Interaction on the platform and between the platform and the audience is at its lowest ebb with a single speaker or film:

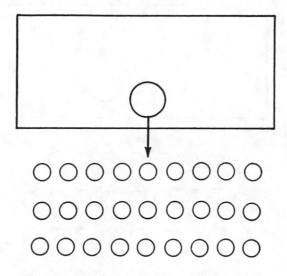

Lecture · Film · Audiovisual Presentation

The quantity of interaction on the platform (and, it is hoped, the quality, too, with good planning and coaching) can be moved up a notch by introducing a blackboard, flip chart, filmstrip, or some other visual aid for the speaker to interact with. Note, however, that the interaction between the platform and audience is not itself affected:

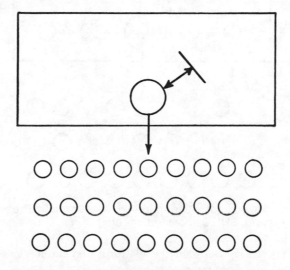

Visual Aid

The interaction strictly on the platform can be moved up a further notch by introducing one other person, so that two people are interacting before the audience in debate, dialogue, or interview:

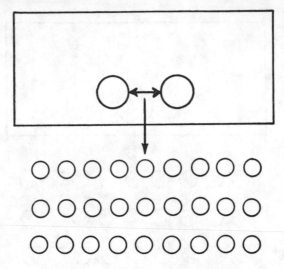

Debate · Dialogue · Interview

A next-higher level of interaction can be achieved by introducing two or more additional people to the platform in a symposium (series of statements), panel discussion, group interview, dramatic presentation, or demonstration:

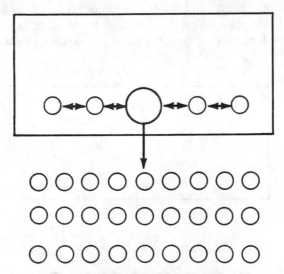

Symposium · Panel · Group Interview · Dramatic Presentation
(Role Playing, Skit, Demonstration, etc.)

So far, the interaction between the platform and the audience and among the members of the audience has remained constant.

Interaction between the platform and the audience is at its first level up from passive with the invitation to the audience to ask questions of the speaker or other platform resources, as illustrated in the case of multiple platform personalities:

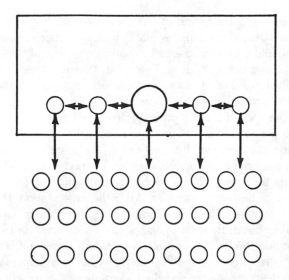

Symposium • Panel • Group Interview • Dramatic Presentation
(Role Players, Skit, Demonstration) with questions from audience
directed through chairman or directly to panel members, etc.

A still-higher level of interaction between the platform and the audience may be achieved by bringing representatives of the audience onto the platform to serve as reaction or watchdog teams. An audience-reaction team is asked simply to listen to the presentation and then to give their reactions either in a series of statements or through panel discussion. A watchdog team is asked to listen for language or concepts they think members of the audience might not fully understand, and to interrupt the presentation at any time and ask for clarification. To the extent that the people selected to serve on the panels are truly representative of the main characteristics of the audience (age, occupation, special interests, sex, geography), to that extent will the audience psychologically identify with the interaction on the platform:

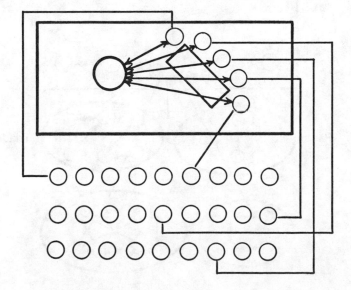

Audience Reaction or Watchdog Teams

Interaction among the members of the audience (which, incidentally, also further increases the interaction between the platform and audience) can be promoted in several ways. The audience can be asked to pair into groups of two, or get into a triad of three, or form buzz groups of from four to six persons without moving from their seats and perform any of several functions: 1) before presentation, they can be asked to identify problems or raise questions they would like the speaker to talk about, thus in effect outlining the speech for the presenter (which I refer to as an "inductive lecture"); 2) before a presentation the audience can be divided into four geographical sections and be asked to serve as "listening teams"—one section to listen to the presentation for points requiring clarification, another for points with which they disagree, another for points they wish to have elaborated on, and the fourth for problems of practical application they wish discussed. After the presentation, the teams are asked to "buzz" for a few minutes to pool their thinking about the points they want raised and select a spokesperson; then the spokespersons are called on to present the questions or issues to the speaker; 3) following a presentation, the audience can be asked to form buzz groups to discuss for a few minutes how they are going to apply the information contained in the presentation, and then a sample of the audience can be called on to report the ideas generated in the discussions.

Probably the highest level of interaction between all elements of a large meeting can be achieved by not having predetermined platform personalities at all, but by having the audience meet in separate rooms as work groups or committees to work on some common assignment and then come together in a meeting hall, with spokespeople for the groups (or a sample of them) going to the platform to report and pool their findings. The most effective device for accomplishing this composite reporting is not a series of separate reports, but an "inquiring reporter" interviewing the spokespersons as a group and polling the audience by a show of hands on issues and conflicts arising from the interview.

This optimal interaction pattern is portrayed graphically as follows:

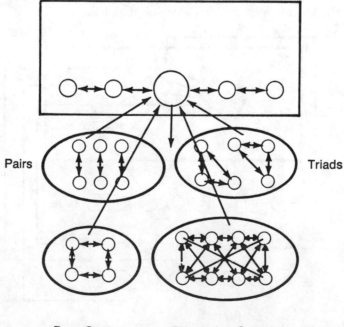

Pairs   Triads

Buzz Groups   Discussion Groups

Trips and Tours

Although trips and tours are a technique that can be used in several learning formats, they can be organized as a distinct format by serving as the basis of organization of participants for learning. For example, at West Georgia College ("The College in the Country") the "studycade" appears in the adult-education catalog along with courses, institutes, and other formats. If participants sign up for a studycade on community development, they are given a reading list, then meet several times to discuss their reading and identify questions for further inquiry, then they go in chartered buses for visits to community-development projects in surrounding states, and finally they have a series of discussions to consolidate their learnings. Or they may enroll in a studycade to Mexico or some other foreign country, in which case they become involved in months of preparation in the language, culture, and geography of the country they are going to visit. The Experiment in International Living at Putney, Vermont, has probably developed this format to its highest point, scheduling dozens of tours for young adults throughout the world each summer and including in their program the experience of actually living for a period of time with a family in the host country.

Community Development as a Format for Learning

Community development is closely related to the action project as a format for learning, but it is a much broader and richer concept. An increasing number of adult educators are coming to see total communities as their classrooms—as laboratories for learning, to see their educational objectives as being not only to help individuals learn to deal more effectively with their life problems, but to help communities as organisms learn to deal more effectively with their problems, and to see the process of community problem solving as a vehicle for accomplishing both educational objectives. Not all community-development activity is educational, just as not all social action is educational. To noneducator community-development workers the end is improving communities—solving community problems—and educational activities may be one of the means for achieving this end; to adult educators using community development as a format for learning, improving communities—solving community problems—is a means to the end of helping individuals and communities learn how better to solve their problems.

In the words of one of the pioneers in the shaping of community development as a format for learning, Dr. Howard Y. McClusky of the University of Michigan:

> . . . the adult educator is primarily interested in community development as a means of educating the community and the people who live there. For example, if a community sets up a project in improving health and recreational facilities, in the course of doing so there will be an opportunity (often unexploited) to learn a lot of facts about problems of health and recreation. If it conducts a survey of conditions essential for the attraction of new industry, the community should be in a position to acquire a lot of information about town and city planning, and so on for any area of living which it elects to improve. These are the factual learnings which community development may stimulate. At the same time, however, it is also possible to learn about how the community is put together and the methods by which it may achieve its goals. These are the process and contextual learnings of community development. Both kinds can be fruitful, but it is the second kind (process and contextual) which is currently most neglected by other forms of adult education, and to which community development can make a unique contribution.[13]

---

[13]Howard Y. McClusky, "Community Development," in Malcolm S. Knowles (ed.), *Handbook of Adult Education in the United States*, (Washington, D.C.: Adult Education Association, 1960), p. 419.

In the community-development format the professional adult educator serves as a consultant and resource person to citizen groups who may be self-organized or brought together under the auspices of some organization, such as a community council. The problems on which they work may be limited, such as improving sewers or housing, or they may encompass total rejuvenation of an entire area, such as Operation Bootstrap in Puerto Rico. The role of the adult educator is to help the citizen-participants diagnose the skills and knowledge they need in order to carry out a systematic program of community improvement and to help them marshal the resources required to accomplish these learnings. The key spirit of the whole enterprise, however, is self-help. Of all the formats for learning, this is the one that from the very beginning has been most congruent with the principles of andragogy.

Although community development had its beginnings in rural communities, and still is one of the principal methods used by the agricultural extension service in this country and by the Agency for International Development in rural areas of underdeveloped countries, this format for learning is being used increasingly in urban settings in this country and abroad. In fact, in the literature of urbanology the assertion is frequently made that the success of urban-development programs is highly dependent upon the use of adult-education processes. In recent years a number of universities—notably Washington, Southern Illinois, Michigan, Wisconsin, Earlham, West Virginia, California, Saskatchewan, British Columbia, and St. Francis Xavier in Nova Scotia—have established community-development centers staffed by adult educators who are specialists in this format for learning.

No doubt one of the major developments in the field of adult education in the years ahead will be the increased use of communities as laboratories for learning and the refinement and extension of community development as a vehicle for individual and community self-improvement.

A development that evolved in the seventies—the community education movement—is somewhat related to community development. It is not technically a format for learning so much as a way of organizing the learning resources of a community for the benefit of learners of all ages. In its ideal form, community education consists of a consortium of all the institutions, both public and private, with educational resources, which provides educational services to all citizens of all ages in locations and at times convenient to them. Often activities take place in school buildings, recreational centers, and other municipal facilities, but perhaps as often they can be found in churches, store fronts, shopping centers, and even homes. Participation by families as units is frequently encouraged.

Some Sample Designs of Comprehensive Programs

It might be helpful to examine how some of these principles of program design have been carried out in a few representative programs.

Let us start with the University of California Extension in Los Angeles, which is one of the best examples of excellence in program design—and of the conception of adult education as an art form—in the country. I have one of its spring catalogs before me now. Its cover is two-tone green, proclaiming "Lifelong Learning: A Program of Continuing Education for Adults" and describing the rich variety of formats—seminars, classes, counseling, short courses, lecture series, correspondence courses, conferences—being offered. The Table of Contents lists a wide range of subjects but under rather academic categories (often a price university extension divisions pay to gain academic acceptance)—agricultural sciences, anthropology, architecture, art, bacteriology, business administration, and so on. But then there is a center section of the catalog headed "Special Programs and Announcements," of which Exhibit H-1 in Appendix H is one page, with a completely different spirit and rhythm. Other features in this section include several lecture series on such broad-ranging interests as "Value of the Arts," "Land and Life in California Deserts and High Mountains," "Ancient Cities Rediscovered," "The Generation Gap," and a dozen other current concerns; a program consisting of a lecture series, a weekend seminar, and a trip to East Africa, on "East Africa: Its Land and People"; several workshops ranging from one day to several weeks for nurses, public-relations specialists, librarians, teachers, physicians, and parents; one-week and two-week leadership and human relations training laboratories; European tours; and special programs in the liberal arts. Obviously, when the program ventures away from the traditional territory of academia into the land of continuing education for adults, it suddenly becomes beautifully andragogical. That part of the program described in the thirty-two-page center section (which, incidentally, is set off from the rest of the catalog by being printed on colored paper) adds greatly to the line, space, tone, color, and texture of the whole program and endows it with a feeling of artistic quality.

Exhibit H-2 shows the imaginative attention to time scheduling by the Concord-Carlisle, Massachusetts, Regional School District Adult and Continuing Education Program. An even richer menu is displayed in the schedule of the Cambridge, Massachusetts Center for Adult Education in Exhibit H-3. Notice the variety of choices for moving in a sequence of interests from morning to afternoon to evening (starting from 5:30 to 7:30 and from 7:30 on) throughout the week.

An especially rich sensation of color and texture is given to the program design of the Miami-Dade Community College by the headings under which courses are grouped. For example:

Sounds Beautiful

Beginning Guitar
Intermediate Guitar
Jazz Band
Community Orchestra

For the Palate: Creative Cooking

Gourmet Cooking
Chinese Cooking
Vegetarian Cooking
Cooking Cuban and Spanish Food

For Your Body

Beginning Yoga
Tennis
Golf I
Slimistics/Nutrition/Diet Control

The Magic Eye

Beginning Photography
Advanced Creative Photography
Introduction to Professional
  Photography

Human Growth and Development

Hypnosis
Parent Effectiveness Training
Psychology in Business and
  Organization
Multi-Dimensional Awareness
Transactional Analysis
Parapsychology

I always enjoy seeing the catalogs of the Great Neck, New York, Public School Adult Education Program because of their artistic display of line, space, tone, color, texture, and unity in program design. Notice the variety of time sequences, the interesting tone, and the colorful titles in its program in Exhibit H-4.

The University of Wisconsin gets across a feeling of unity-in-diversity with this overview of its comprehensive extension program:

> University Extension is literally the direct extension of University teaching
> —through correspondence study
> —off-campus classes
> —centers
> —post-graduate seminars
> to equalize educational opportunity throughout Wisconsin.
> University Extension is applied research
> —through testing facilities
> —formal consulting
> —field surveys and studies
> to define community problems and uncover their solutions.
> University Extension is adult education
> —through study-by-mail
> —courses
> —evening classes
> —conferences, institutes
> —lectures
> —leadership training
> —counseling
> —publications, films
> to translate University resources into lifelong learning opportunities.
> University Extension is public service
> —through traveling libraries
> —radio and television
> —demonstrations
> —experts on leave to governmental bureaus
> —area agents
> —a wide range of informal instructional liaison with individuals, communities, institutions, agencies, and groups
> to fill in the interstices of the state's educational program.[14]

Similar examples of comprehensive designs could be added from libraries, business and industry, governmental agencies, and other institutional settings if space permitted. But the reader can easily obtain additional examples by writing to relevant institutions and asking for copies of their program announcements.

---

[14]University of Wisconsin Extension, *Education for Continuing Change*, p. 17.

For Your Continuing Inquiry . . .

Regarding Art Principles

Langer, Susanne K. *Problems of Art*. New York: Scribner's, 1957.
Rasmusen, Henry M. *Art Structure: A Textbook of Creative Design*. New York: McGraw-Hill, 1950.
Scott, Robert G. *Design Fundamentals*. New York: McGraw-Hill, 1951.
Teague, Walter D. *Design This Day*. New York: Harcourt, Brace, 1949.

Regarding Formats for Learning

Aker, George F. *Adult Education Procedures, Methods, and Techniques: An Annotated Bibliography*. Syracuse, N.Y.: Library of Continuing Education, Syracuse University, 1965.
Armsey, James W., and Dahl, Norman C. *An Inquiry into the Uses of Instructional Technology*. New York: The Ford Foundation, 1973.
Beal, George M., et al. *Social Action and Interaction in Program Planning*. Ames, Iowa: Iowa State University, 1966.
Benne, Kenneth; Bradford, Leland; and Lippitt, Ronald. *The Laboratory Method of Changing and Learning*. Palo Alto, Cal.: Science and Behavior Books, 1975.
Berridge, Robert I. *Community Education Handbook*. Midland, Mich.: Pendell, 1973.
Blocher, Donald H. *Developmental Counseling*. New York: Ronald Press, 1966.
Burke, W. Warner, and Beckhard, Richard (eds.). *Conference Planning*. 2nd ed. New York: NTL Institute of Applied Behavioral Science, 1970.
Cary, Lee J. (ed.). *Community Development as a Process*. Columbia, Missouri: University of Missouri Press, 1970.
Craig, R. L. (ed.). *Training and Development Handbook*. New York: McGraw-Hill, 1976.
Cross, K. Patricia, and Valley, John R. (eds.). *Planning Non-Traditional Programs*. San Francisco: Jossey-Bass, 1974.
Davis, Larry N., and McCallon, Earl. *Planning, Conducting, Evaluating Workshops*. Austin, Texas: Learning Concepts, 1974.
Duley, John (ed.). *Implementing Field Experience Education*. New Directions for Higher Education, No. 6. San Francisco: Jossey-Bass, 1974.
Eisner, E. W., and Vallance, E. (eds.). *Conflicting Conceptions of Curriculum*. Berkeley: McCutchan Publishing Corp., 1974.
Franklin, Richard. *Patterns of Community Development*. New York: Public Affairs Press, 1966.
Godbey, Gordon C. *Applied Andragogy: A Practical Manual for the Continuing Education of Adults*. College Station, Penn.: Continuing Education Division, The Pennsylvania State University, 1978.
Houle, Cyril O. *The Design of Education*. San Francisco: Jossey-Bass, 1973.
Jones, G. Brian, et al. *New Designs and Methods for Delivering Human Development Services*. New York: Human Sciences Press, 1977.
Jack, Homer A. *Primer for Social Action*. Boston: Beacon Press, 1950.
Klevins, Chester (ed.). *Materials and Methods in Continuing Education*. Canoga Park, Cal.: Klevins Publishing Co., 1978.
Loughary, John W., and Ripley, Theresa M. *Helping Others Help Themselves: A Guide to Counseling Skills*. New York: McGraw-Hill, 1979.

MacKenzie, Ossian, and Christensen, Edward L. (eds.). *The Changing World of Correspondence Study: International Readings*. University Park, Penn.: State University Press, 1971.

Malone, Violet M., and Diller, Mary Ann. *The Guidance Function and Counseling Roles in an Adult Education Program*. Washington, D.C.: National Association for Public Continuing and Adult Education, 1978.

McLagan, Patricia A. *Helping Others Learn: Designing Programs for Adults*. Reading, Mass.: Addison-Wesley, 1978.

Nadler, Leonard, and Nadler, Zeace. *The Conference Book*. Houston: Gulf Publishing Co., 1977.

Rossi, Peter, and Biddle, Bruce (eds.). *The New Media and Education*. Chicago: Aldine Publishing Co., 1966.

Rountree, Derek. *Basically Branching: A Handbook for Programmers*. London: Macdonald, 1966.

Ruskin, Robert S. *The Personalized System of Instruction: An Educational Alternative*. Washington, D.C.: American Association for Higher Education, 1974.

Russell, James D. *Modular Instruction*. Minneapolis: Burgess Press, 1974.

Sanders, H. C., et al. *The Cooperative Extension Service*. Englewood Cliffs, N.J.: Prentice-Hall, 1966.

Seay, Maurice F., et al. *Community Education: A Developing Concept*. Midland, Mich.: Pendell, 1974.

Smith, Robert, et al. *Handbook of Adult Education in the U.S.* New York: Macmillan, 1970.

Verner, Coolie. *A Conceptual Scheme for the Identification and Classification of Processes*. Washington, D.C.: Adult Education Association of the U.S.A., 1962.

9
Operating
a Comprehensive
Program

The Art of Administration

The process of translating a program design into a flow of people and materials through a system of activities is the function of administration, and it is in this process that the principles of andragogy are most frequently ignored or violated. This is because the early evolution of administrative theory and practice in this country was dominated by adherents to the cult of efficiency, for whom the highest value was to achieve the highest production at the least cost regardless of the consequences to such human values as self-esteem, love, and self-actualization. Fortunately, the influence of the modern humanistic management theorists, such as Barnard, Drucker, Likert, McGregor, and Odiorne, has begun to shift the pendulum in the opposite direction. But it is my impression that educational administration has lagged behind industrial management in establishing a balance between the values of human growth and satisfaction on the one hand and operational efficiency on the other.

This is not to suggest that these are mutually exclusive values, and that the educational administrator should not be concerned with efficiency of operation. It is to suggest, however, that the American tradition has been to overemphasize efficiency, and that this overemphasis has often had the consequence of interfering with the educative quality of the environment created expressly to help people learn. Let me illustrate this proposition very simply. The most efficient procedure for registering students (efficiency as measured by the number of student units processed in one unit of time) is to have the students line up to receive the registration forms, take them to a table and fill them out according to their best judgment about activities they should enroll in, then line up again to have the forms checked by a registrar. But this procedure is not conducive to effective learning for at least two reasons: 1) it deprives the student of informed assistance in selecting activities, with the result that the misfit rate is higher; and 2) it causes so much resentment on the part of the students at being treated like cattle (or children) that they enter their courses with so much resistance to influence that it may take even the most effective teachers weeks to remedy the damage.

It was suggested in Chapter 5 that the basic characteristics of an educative environment are: 1) respect for personality, 2) participation in decision making, 3) freedom of expression and availability of information, and 4) mutuality of responsibility in defining goals, planning and conducting activities, and evaluating. This chapter will be concerned with applying these conditions to five aspects of program operation: 1) recruiting and training leaders and teachers, 2) managing facilities and procedures, 3) counseling, 4) promotion and public relations, and 5) budgeting and financing.

Recruiting and Training Leaders and Teachers

Probably the one most obvious—and, I believe, central—consequence of the andragogical theory propounded in this book is that it requires a drastic redefinition of the role of the teacher in the learning-teaching relationship. Under this theory, teachers can no longer see their role as being primarily that of transmitters of knowledge, attitudes, and skills. Their role is now defined as facilitators and resources in the process of self-directed inquiry by the learners. But this new role is one that few of the people available to adult-education institutions as potential teachers have been exposed to. Most people recruited to teach adults, whether from educational institutions or their fields of practice, would (if left on their own) teach as they were taught—according to principles and practices of pedagogy. This fact places a heavy burden on a conscientious adult-education administrator to be more creative and industrious than is typically required of other educational administrators in the selection, training, and supervision of teachers and leaders.

Selecting Leaders and Teachers

To simplify the discussion in this chapter, let us refer to all the leadership personnel in an adult-education program, whether teachers of organized courses or leaders of clubs and groups as "instructors"—since the role of both categories is to facilitate and serve as resources in the process of self-directed inquiry by groups of learners. A number of questions arise and must be dealt with concerning the selection of instructors:

1. *What are the best sources of instructors?* For programs tending toward academic subject matter, the best source of instructors will probably be the formal educational institutions—high schools, colleges, and universities. For programs that are based on problems of living, the best sources of instructors will probably be those places in which people are doing the kinds of things they are to teach. For example, for a course in "Using Psychology in Everyday Living," the best instructors are likely to be found in psychological clinics or psychiatrists' offices, where real problems are being handled. A good wood-carving instructor is likely to be found in a furniture factory, a public-speaking instructor in a radio station, a creative-writing instructor in an advertising agency, a business-mathematics instructor in an accountant's office, and an interior-decoration instructor in a department store.

Probably the best teachers of adults are people who are enthusiastic amateurs in their subject—at least, amateurs at teaching it. This is not to say that good teachers of informal courses cannot be found in formal educational institutions. Some of the very best teachers in informal course programs have been full-time teachers in high schools and universities. But it should be emphasized that there is considerable danger that a university professor might merely repeat to a group of adults the lectures he has prepared for undergraduate students. And the chances are very high that, if this happened, the adults would soon stop attending.

2. *How does one determine who will be a good instructor?* Certainly it is necessary to gather all the usual information about an instructor's education, experience, and character, just as with any other type of employee, through interviews, academic transcripts, and letters of recommendation. These data will have to be evaluated, however, in terms of the unique qualities that make for success as a teacher of adults. A good

academic record might not carry the same weight in this situation as it would in the case of a high school teaching job. It is necessary, therefore, that the program director have a clearly stated set of criteria by which to judge the qualifications of candidates for teaching positions. The following is a sample set of criteria developed by one adult-education program.

a) Instructors must not only have knowledge but must be successful practitioners of their subject or skill.

b) They must be enthusiastic about their subject, and about teaching it to others.

c) They must have—or be capable of learning—an attitude of understanding and permissiveness toward people. They must have such other traits of personality as friendliness, humor, humility, and interest in people, that make for effectiveness in leading adults.

d) They must be creative in their thinking about teaching methods. They must be willing to experiment with new ways to meet the changing needs and interests of adults. They must be concerned more with the growth of the individual than with the presentation of facts.

e) Such standard requirements as status in the community or occupational group, previous teaching experience, etc., are desirable only when they are compatible with the characteristics described above.

f) They should be intrigued with the notion that adults are different from children as learners, and express positive pleasure at the prospect of participating in an inservice training program on the teaching of adults.

A simple tool that might be helpful, if used properly, in the selection process, is an "Educational Orientation Questionnaire" that was developed and validated by one of my former students, Dr. Herschel Hadley. The EOQ enables individuals to place themselves on a scale from "pedagogical orientation" to "andragogical orientation" as regards their beliefs about the teaching-learning process. I believe it should be used as a diagnostic instrument—providing clues as to what inservice education activities or reading might be recommended to teachers leaning toward the pedagogical orientation—rather than used as a screening device.

The EOQ has been used effectively in workshops and courses in helping participants identify issues—different views of the teaching-learning process—that are important for their practice. When this is supplemented by open examination of these issues, and issues that grow out of them, it is astonishing what a productive learning situation is created. The results provide a basis for constructing projects to investigate these issues more in depth, either by individuals or in collaborative groups.

A copy of the Educational Orientation Questionnaire, with a scoring sheet, can be obtained from Dr. Herschel Hadley, 45 Martin Street, Acton, Massachusetts 01720.

3. *Should instructors be volunteer or paid?* The majority of instructors in institutional programs are paid. As a rule, having an instructor on the payroll seems to result in better administrative relationships in organized classes. The director feels freer to make demands on paid instructors for the good of the program. There are some instances, however, in which volunteer instructors have made outstanding contributions in institutional programs. It sometimes happens that very prominent people, who could not possibly be motivated by economic considerations, can be persuaded to instruct a course as a community service. It would be a mistake, of course, to have a hard-and-fast rule that would eliminate such people. Volunteer instructors are found frequently in church, civic organizations, and club programs, are usually closely iden-

tified with the sponsoring organization, and are highly motivated by a sense of loyalty to their group.

4. *Who should hire and fire instructors?* It is generally accepted as good practice in all types of organizations that the responsibility for the employment and supervision of workers should be centralized in a single executive. The program director should have the final authority to employ and dismiss teachers. It has been my personal experience as a program director, however, that my selections have almost always been better when I had a sample of students and committee members interview prospective instructors and give me their advisory opinions about them.

5. *Should there be a written contract?* It is generally found to be desirable to have some kind of written agreement between the instructor and the organization, so as to avoid any possible misunderstanding. The sample letter of appointment in Appendix I, Exhibit I–1, will illustrate the kinds of information such an agreement might contain.

Compensation of Instructors

There are several methods of compensating instructors, including the per-hour or per-course basis, the per-student basis, the percentage-of-income basis, and the flat salary basis. Full-time faculty members of an educational institution may be compensated for their part-time adult-education service either as a part of their regular course load or on an overtime basis proportionate to their regular salary. Usually part-time instructors are paid a fee per hour of instruction or per course (which is basically the same thing). The difficulty of this method is that there may not be a large enough enrollment in a given course to cover the instructor's fee. It is generally accepted as poor practice, however, to request that the instructor accept less than the fee originally agreed upon, and so the program director is faced with the alternatives of subsidizing or discontinuing the course. By good planning it is usually possible to balance income-producing against subsidy-requiring courses. Often an understanding with an instructor is reached in advance that, if the course fails to attract a sufficient number of students, it may be canceled without obligation beyond compensation for the actual number of hours of instruction given.

The practice of compensating instructors on the basis of the number of students enrolled in their courses or on the basis of a certain percentage of income produced by each course is generally frowned on as introducing an undesirable element of commercialism into the relationship of the instructor with the program; it tends to induce a force on the instructors to perceive their students as economic units rather than self-actualizing learners. Most adult educators prefer to regard their instructors as professional people who are entitled to a certain fee for services rendered.

The exact amount of compensation that will be best in a given situation will depend upon such factors as these:

1. *The standard practice among other organizations in the community.* Although compensation practices varied widely both among communities and among organizations within the same community not long ago, there has been a growing tendency toward a narrowing of the range. A recent study of practices in public schools across the country, for example, revealed these facts: in most of the large-city systems compensation is based on the standard scale for all teachers and is graduated according to length of service; frequently, noneducational institutions have to offer a higher rate of compensation to attract the best quality of instructors to make up for the factor of academic prestige.

2. *The amount necessary to attract an individual instructor with special qualifications.* To obtain the services of psychiatrists, it may be necessary to offer a higher compensation than is offered most other types of instructors. In this case, one would be competing for their services not merely with other educational institutions, but with private patients.

3. *The tuition rates the participants can afford to pay.* This consideration will greatly influence the rates one can pay instructors, unless there will be outside sources of income with which to subsidize the program. If the participants of a course are to be high-income businessmen who have strong motivation to take the course, then one can probably afford to pay an unusually good instructor at an unusually high rate. On the other hand, if the clientele is that of a neighborhood settlement house, tuition rates will have to be very low and the rate of compensation for instructors will have to be in proportion—except that in this case one may be able to interest the "best" instructors in giving courses as a public service.

The question is often raised: Should all instructors be paid at the same rate, or should there be a flexible scale with certain types of instructors receiving higher rates than others? There are some adult educators who feel that the only fair thing to do is to pay all instructors at the same rate, and they criticize scales as promoting a caste system. There are others who feel that one must face the fact that people who have achieved a higher pay scale in their regular work expect a higher rate of compensation than those whose normal income is lower. They point out that it is necessary to pay more to interest a highly trained professional person than to interest a highly competent arts and crafts teacher. Similarly, a psychiatrist will generally demand a higher rate than a psychologist. If a program is to be enriched with this kind of leadership, the pattern of different rates of compensation that has been established in our society may have to be accepted.

If the flexible scale of compensation is adopted, it would probably be advisable to establish quotas for each level of compensation. In a given program the quotas might be twenty instructors at $10 per hour, ten at $15, five at $20, and two at $25. In this way the tendency to move all the instructors toward the top rate would be avoided.

Training and Supervision of Instructors

The selection of good instructors is only the first step in producing a good teaching staff. Even the best instructors cannot do their best unless they have been properly oriented into the program. They should understand its objectives, its philosophy of education, its methods, and exactly where they fit into the organization. During their entire tenure they should have a progressive sense of belonging and of personally growing. How can such an orientation be achieved? Several methods can be suggested.

Individual Conferences

The basic tool of supervision and training is the periodic interview with individual instructors. Certainly the program director should have one or more extended interviews with an instructor between the time of employment and the first meeting of the course. During these interviews the instructors should be given an understanding of the background of the organization—its history, purpose, and total program. They should be given some insight into the nature of the adult students they will be teaching, and what they are likely to expect of the faculty. They should be acquainted with the physical and staff resources that will be available. Above all, they should be injected with the spirit of the program. They should be challenged to do a creative job of meeting the real needs of the participants. They should be told that the courses are their personal responsibility, that they do not have to follow a stereotyped outline developed by someone else, but can try out their own ideas and the ideas of course members. They should be assured that the program director will stand ready to discuss their plans with them and make suggestions, but not to impose an authoritarian pattern.

Following the initial orientation interviews, there should be subsequent interviews—in decreasing frequency as the instructors gain experience—to help them evaluate their progress and to make suggestions growing out of the program director's experience with other situations. These interviews need not be formally scheduled but might take place in the hallway between classes or at the end of the evening.

Printed Materials

At the time of employment, each instructor should be given copies of printed materials describing the organization and its program, including folders, reports, activities schedules, and other descriptive materials. All instructors should be put on the mailing list to receive subsequent printed materials as they are issued. Many adult educators also make it a point to obtain reprints of articles and reports bearing on subjects concerning adult education as a movement, teaching methods, or specific courses, and to circulate these among their instructors.

Some of the larger institutions have produced faculty manuals that are given to new instructors upon employment; and some state departments of education have produced a handbook for distribution to all public-school adult-education personnel.

Internal Memoranda

If judiciously used, internal memoranda can be a valuable tool of good administration. They can be used to acquaint instructors with new policies, procedures, and activities. They may contain announcements to be made to the classes. Certainly each instructor should have an explanation in writing before the opening of his part in the registration and opening-night processes. Appendix I, Exhibit I-2, contains an example of such an orientational memorandum that is used by one institution.

Faculty Meetings

Faculty meetings are usually more difficult to schedule in adult-education programs than in formal schools, where the teachers are employed full-time. The teachers of evening courses are usually busy people, and it is difficult to bring them together as a group at any one time. Faculty meetings have many advantages, however, over other methods of training, and should be held at least two or three times a year. During the two or three weeks between terms is usually a propitious time, since courses are not in session.

Probably the best type of faculty meeting is that in which there is a free discussion by the teachers of problems that concern them. One very successful faculty meeting, for instance, was devoted entirely to a discussion of "What is a good learning situation?" After a two-hour discussion this faculty had listed over a dozen characteristics of the "ideal" learning situation and, in the process, had developed a much better feeling of esprit de corps and unity of purpose. Faculty meetings can also be used for training teachers in the use of audiovisual aids, for discussing case problems, for participation by the teachers in policy determination, for giving special recognition, and for joint planning.

Course Plans and Process Designs

A device that is useful in helping an instructor to a good start is a written course plan outlining the units of content to be included in the course. Most people have had some experience with content outlines of this sort, either as students or as teachers, or both, and so they usually don't find them difficult to construct. But a content plan by itself is not enough; in fact, it may lead instructors to feel that their job is to "transmit the content." Early in my experience as a program director I learned to insist that my instructors also construct a "process design," in which they would describe the procedures they would use to create a climate that would be conducive to adult learning and to involve the learners actively in planning, learning, and evaluating. Exhibit I–3 is a reproduction of this "Teacher's Process Plan."

The way I used it was to ask the teachers well in advance of their opening sessions to write out the answers to the questions and then get together with me to go over their answers. I found that in these follow-up interviews (sometimes even on the telephone) I could frequently make suggestions about other procedures they might try; but most important, I found that just by having to think about what procedures they would use, overnight they became process-oriented, whereas otherwise they would be completely content-oriented.

Class Visitation

Adult-education administrators do not agree as to the desirability of direct observation by members of the staff of classes in session. Some administrators feel that it is only by visiting classes that they can really know what is going on in their program. They also feel that the instructors appreciate having the administrative staff show enough interest in their work to drop around and see them in action. Other administrators feel that instructors resent their visiting classes and think of it as snooping. They also hesitate to cause the interruption that is involved when a strange person enters a class in session. Probably the only solution to the problem is to let the faculty decide for themselves, individually and as a group, whether they would find class visitations a help or a hindrance.

Observation

An alternative to class visitations by members of the staff is periodic controlled observation by graduate students from a nearby university, by members of the directing committee, or by other impartial outsiders. It would seem advisable, however, to arrange such visitations only with the cooperation of the faculty, and to make their reports available to the faculty.

Narrative Records

A simple narrative account of each course meeting serves several purposes: 1) it enables the instructors to communicate their concerns and observations to the supervisor; 2) it enables the supervisor to keep in touch with what is happening in every course; 3) it provides a convenient method for bringing to the attention of the supervisor any needs of course members, such as the need for counseling, that should be taken care of outside the course; 4) it helps the instructors to evaluate themselves and to measure the progress of the group.

Narrative reports may follow a standard form, with each instructor answering the same set of questions, or they may be free-running expressions. A degree of uniformity is required, however, if the supervisor wishes to make comparisons among courses. The minimum information a supervisor should be able to get from narrative reports is the following:

1) subject matter development
2) methods, techniques, and materials used
3) group behavior and growth
4) individual behavior and growth
5) interpretations of the instructor
6) individual and group problems requiring further attention

Systematic Inservice Training Programs

The task of converting pedagogues into andragogues is probably too heavy a burden to be carried entirely by the procedures described so far. Increasingly, progressive adult-education agencies are finding that they have to supplement these procedures with a systematic program of inservice training to get the job done.

Northeastern University's University College, for example, has followed the practice for several years, with visibly rewarding results, of holding a faculty institute prior to the opening of classes each semester. The institute is held on Friday and Saturday evenings, with the option open to each instructor—new and veteran alike—to attend whichever evening is more convenient. To add to the inducement a program is offered for spouses (such as a play, a musicale, a film) parallel to the institute, with both groups coming together at the end of the evening for refreshments. Because of this split-session option, the university reaches most of its faculty once each semester. The design of one of these institutes, in which I participated as a resource person, is reproduced in Appendix I, Exhibit I-4.

A considerably more intensive design I have used extensively in faculty-development programs in educational institutions, industry, government agencies, and voluntary organizations, is launched with a one-day workshop in which the participants get an exposure to the concepts of andragogy, self-diagnose their competency-development needs (using the model in Appendix B), and develop a learning contract. The design of this workshop is contained in Appendix I, Exhibit I-5. Every faculty member leaves the workshop, therefore, with a plan of continuing self-development. Some institutions also have the faculty members form "learning networks" of from two to six people to meet periodically to monitor and help further one another's progress. A number of the institutions have also convened follow-up clinics a couple of months after the original workshop for the purpose of having the participants share their experiences, identify and get help on problems, and suggest additional needed resources. One institution, Gordon College, in Wenham, Massachusetts, has built its faculty-development program entirely around the use of what they call "growth contracts."

Building Faculty Morale

Certainly one objective of the whole process of training and supervision is to build good faculty morale—to bring about an enthusiastic pooling of effort toward a common goal. Good morale is largely achieved when the instructors have a clear understanding of the objectives of the organization for which they are working and subscribe wholeheartedly to them. This puts a burden on the program director constantly to interpret these objectives and to give them a sense of significance. Good morale also involves a feeling of belongingness on the part of the faculty members. This feeling can be produced by giving them an opportunity to take part in the making of decisions affecting them, by inviting their participation in ceremonial occasions, and by extending to them the privilege of participating in other regular activities of the institution. Their morale is likely to be improved, also, if they are given a sense of being a part of the important larger movement of adult education through being invited to attend meetings and conferences sponsored by adult-education councils and associations.

Managing Facilities and Procedures

Providing Good Physical Facilities

As was emphasized in Chapter 4, to be congruent with the principles of andragogy, the physical setting in which adult education takes place should "smell" adult. Let me illustrate how literally this figure of speech might well be taken. The director of a new adult basic-education program in a small town in West Virginia reports that the first contingent of students from the "hollows" refused to attend classes in a former red-brick elementary school, which he had redecorated and re-equipped for adult students. When he asked them why, they replied that it "smelled like a school," referring clearly to the sawdust-and-oil that was used to sweep the floors. The director reports that when he quickly arranged to have the program moved to an abandoned warehouse, into which he moved his comfortable new equipment, and sent word back into the hollows that the program was not meeting in a place that smelled like a school, a full complement enrolled.

The physical setting in which a program takes place and the quality of equipment available for program use unquestionably affect the quality and effectiveness of the experiences the participants will have. While there is wide variation in the space requirements of different types of programs, certain criteria apply to all of them—especially those of comfort, convenience, personalization, and maximization of interaction.

Meeting Rooms

A curious tradition has come to pervade our culture that the ideal classroom or meeting setup is straight rows of chairs facing a podium or platform. In fact, if you make reservations for educational meetings in hotels, most schools and universities, and public buildings, you automatically get rooms that are set up this way. Consequently, I spend a good deal of my time as a practitioner drawing pictures for custodians depicting how I want the rooms arranged. Exhibit 20 reproduces a sample of pictures I draw for small meeting rooms and Exhibit 21 shows several arrangements for large meetings.

The ideal situation, andragogically, is for all participants and resource people to be on one level, with nobody looking at the back of another (as in a circle), and with maximum flexibility of movement of chairs back and forth from a large circle to small circles. This ideal must be compromised somewhat when the numbers are too large or when visual aids must be used that everybody can see simultaneously. But the compromise need not be total, as has been imaginatively demonstrated at the Kellog Center for Continuing Education at the University of Oklahoma (which, incidentally, was planned by a team of architects and adult educators who expressly set themselves the challenge to translate principles of adult education into bricks and mortar), where all small meeting rooms are hexagonal in shape, with hexagonal seminar tables, and where the auditoriums are bowl-shaped, with swivel chairs.

Exhibit 20

SMALL MEETING ROOM ARRANGEMENTS

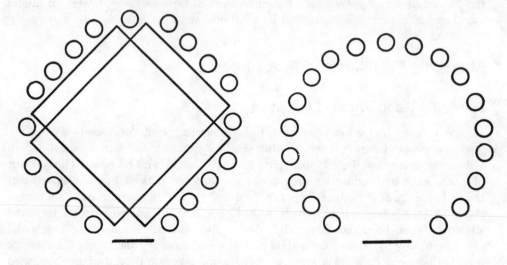

Tables in Diamond

Chairs in Circle

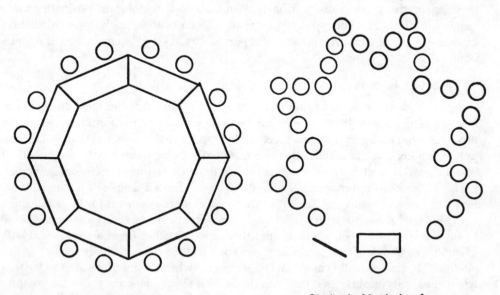

Tables in Octagon

Chairs in Maple Leaf
(For ease in subgrouping)

Exhibit 21

LARGE MEETING ROOM ARRANGEMENTS

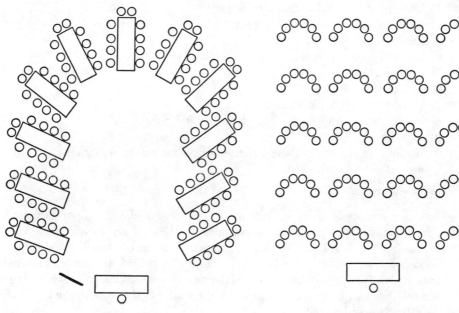

Tables Fan-shape

Chairs in Small Semicircles
(For easy subgrouping)

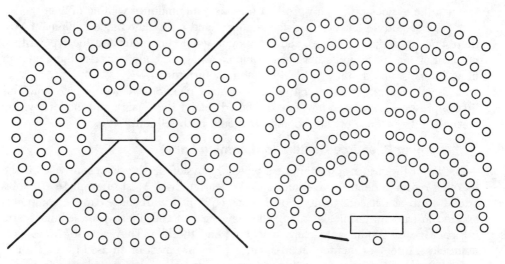

Theater-in-the-round
(or Bowl)

Semicircular Theater

Auxiliary features. In a survey made in preparation for a national conference on "Architecture for Adult Education" in 1958, a sample of two hundred adult educators identified the following features of their physical facilities as generally least satisfactory.

1) Uncomfortable and stationary seating;
2) Insufficient and inflexible equipment;
3) Inadequate lighting;
4) Inflexible space layout;
5) Inadequate parking space;
6) Unattractive decor;
7) Inadequate ventilation;
8) Poor acoustics and interference from outside noises;
9) Poor library facilities;
10) Inadequate storage facilities for equipment, materials, and adult-sized clothing.[1]

Office Facilities

The office arrangements in institutional programs also play an important part in setting the spirit of a program. The two extremes are the cold and formal but efficient office on the one hand, and the informal but "messy" office on the other. Ideally, an office should be both efficient and friendly. How can this ideal be accomplished?

First, the type of decorations influences the general tone. Is the color scheme light and cheerful? Are there attractive pictures on the walls? Is the light adequate? Is the furniture attractive and comfortable?

The general layout is important to both efficiency and appearance. Are the desks placed in such a way as to reflect a desire to serve people conveniently and pleasantly? Are the desks neat? Are the filing cabinets and other office equipment inconspicuous but convenient? Is the whole office arranged so that there is a smooth flow of traffic through the various procedures, so that there is a minimum of waiting in line?

Care should be taken to provide adequate and up-to-date office equipment. Are there enough desks and tables, and are they in good condition? Are the typewriters, duplicating machines, and other office equipment in good condition? Are there enough filing cabinets, and do they fit in with the other furniture?

Usually the office is the first point of contact poeple have with a program. This first impression is an important one. It should reflect the quality and modernity, the warmth and efficiency of the program. It should both sell and serve.

Learning Resource Centers (or Learning Labs)

One of the fastest-spreading new types of physical facility in recent years is the learning resource center, sometimes called a learning lab. Most often these are areas added on to or adjacent to libraries that are equipped with study carrels, computer-assisted instruction terminals, microfiche viewers, film and filmstrip projectors, learning packages or modules, teaching machines, and the like. They almost always have counselors, tutors, or mentors in attendance. They are most often used for individualized instruction for remedial or "developmental" purposes, but in at least one School of Medicine (McMaster University, Hamilton, Ontario) the center has replaced the classroom as the site of advanced study.

---

[1] *Creating a Climate for Learning: A Report of the National Conference on Architecture for Adult Education* (Washington, D.C.: Adult Education Association, 1959).

Resource File

Good organization is greatly facilitated by an efficient filing system. While the exact types of files will vary with the types of programs, one file that every organization, large or small, should have is a resource file.

This is an organized compilation of information about sources of speakers, materials, and other resources for program building. Such a file might be in the form of folders containing letters, announcements, and pamphlets. Even better is a card file, with cards containing essential data about each resource and divided according to subject matter. Here is how such a file works:

1. A supply of three-by-five cards is mimeographed in the form illustrated below:

Exhibit 22

```
┌─────────────────────────────────────────────────────────────────┐
│                       RESOURCE RECORD                             │
│                                              ─────────────────    │
│                                              Classification        │
│   Organization or name: _____    │
│   Bus. address: _____  Zone _____       │
│   Bus. tel. _____  Home tel. _____      │
│   Home address: _____     │
│   Nature of resource: _____     │
│   ─────────────────────────────────────────────────────────────   │
│   Conditions of use (fee, equipment required, etc.) _____      │
│   ─────────────────────────────────────────────────────────────   │
└─────────────────────────────────────────────────────────────────┘
```

2. On about fifty blank three-by-five cards are written the subject-matter classifications of the types of resources used in the program. These may be:

Adult-Education Agencies	Labor	Printers
Advertising	Languages	Psychology
Arts & Crafts	Law	Public Affairs
Business	Leaders	Public Relations
Camera Clubs	Literature	Radio
Clubs, Fraternal	Magic	Reading
Economics	Mailing Lists	Real Estate
Education	Mailing Services	Religion
Entertainment	Marriage	Science
Films	Materials and Supplies	Sign Painters
Forums	Music	Speakers Bureaus
Group Work	Newspapers, Community	Typewriter Repair
Health	Newspapers, Daily	Vocational Guidance
Hobbies	Newspapers, Industrial	Woodcarving
Insurance	Photography	Writing
International		

3. Records are made out for all resources now in the files, showing the classification in the upper right-hand corner. A given resource might appear under several classifications. For instance, Dr. John Doe of the Family Relations Clinic might have cards under both "Marriage" and "Psychology." The card is then placed behind the right classification tab card.

4. Be alert for new resources—e.g., watch the newspapers for reports on speakers, scan the program announcements from other organizations—and when a resource that might fit into the program is spotted, enter it on a card.

5. Go through the resource file periodically, culling the deadwood and noting on the reverse side of each card a brief evaluation of each resource that has been used.

Such a resource file is an invaluable aid in program planning. It makes the information readily available to lay leaders and to other professional workers. It is flexible and easy to keep up-to-date.

Registration Procedures

Forms and Records

Careful thought should be given to drafting the forms required for registration of students. They should be as simple as possible and should ask for only the minimum amount of information needed for efficient administration. Most institutions would be happy to send you copies of the forms they are now using, which you can use as models in drafting your own.

Sequence of Service

The process of registration should be carefully worked out in advance, if a large number of participants are expected, in order that there will be a smooth and efficient movement of registrants. Since the first personal contact most students will have with your institution is at registration, it is crucially important that the experience be a pleasant one; and yet it is at this point that more damage is done to the "climate for learning" referred to in Chapter 4 than at any other point. Negative attitudes can be engendered by disrespectful treatment during registration that will require weeks of classroom experience to remedy. A sufficient number of registration helpers should be recruited (faculty members and veteran students providing a handy supply) to greet new registrants personally and help them through the process. Long lines (like cattle waiting for slaughter) should be avoided at all costs.

Control of Class Size

Usually in informal classes a limit is placed on class size—below a certain minimum the course will be canceled and above a set maximum either enrollments will not be accepted or additional sections will be opened. In order that the program director may know at any time how many students are enrolled in each class, a simple enrollment chart can be maintained by the registrars. As they make out a class card for each enrollment, they merely place a tally mark after that course in the chart, as shown in Exhibit 23.

Exhibit 23

ENROLLMENT CHART

Course	Enrollments	Limit
Painting as a Hobby	_____ _____ _____ _____	18
Section No. 2	_____ _____ _____ _____	18
Current Events	_____ _____ _____ _____ _____	25
Speaking in Public	_____ _____ _____ _____ _____	25

It may be desirable also, in the case of courses that have reached their maximum quota of enrollments and in which additional sections cannot be opened, to maintain a waiting list of people who would like to enroll in the course if one of the present enrollees drops out.

Reservations

Most informal course programs stipulate that reservations cannot be made in courses without either full or partial payment of tuition fees. They have found from experience that much grief usually comes from accepting reservations without payment.

Time of Registration

Should registration be permitted only during a specified period, say for three evenings in the week preceding the opening of the term, or should registration services be available during normal working hours continuously for a period of a week or two before and after classes start? Both systems have wide acceptance and each has certain advantages.

When registration is concentrated into a short period in advance of the starting of classes, there is likely to be a high percentage of advance registrations, which means less confusion on opening nights. Also, concentration makes possible the more efficient use of the personnel, clerical and advisory. It has certain disadvantages, however, including the greater inconvenience to enrollees, more waiting lines, and more tendency to hurry the process of registration. In addition, there will always be a large percentage of people who will not come in to register before the opening night anyway.

When registration is permitted any time during working hours, including certain evening hours, for a week or two prior to the start of the term, the adult students will be able to come in at a time more convenient to them. The process is likely to be less hurried and more informal, and there will probably be less waiting. This system, however, involves the scheduling of more staff time for registration. The experience in institutions following this policy has been that about one half of the total enrollments take place in advance of the opening night (with plenty of urging in the literature to "enroll in advance, save time, and be sure of a place"). Most of the remaining enrollments occur during the first week, but there are some stragglers as long as three weeks after the opening date.

Registration by Mail

A number of programs permit students to register simply by sending in a written request accompanied by a check or money order. It is difficult to understand how the evils arising when students are not properly counseled can be avoided if this practice is followed. Several program directors report that the percentage of dropouts and complaints is considerably higher among students who register by mail than it is among those who register personally.

Opening-Night Procedures

Every program director should be prepared for a series of crises during the opening week of a program. It seems that some are inevitable, although good planning can reduce them to a minimum. Here are some suggestions that may be helpful:

1. Have directional signs in strategic spots pointing out the flow of traffic.

2. Have the doors of activity rooms clearly marked, preferably with signs indicating the courses meeting in them.

3. Have members of the committee or former students who know the physical facilities posted in lobby areas to help new students find the proper locations.

4. Be prepared to discontinue courses that have insufficient enrollment quickly and without embarrassment. It is wise to have established in advance a chart of minimum enrollments for each course. In some cases it may be desirable to continue a course with a borderline number of enrollments, because of its intrinsic worth in a balanced program, or an unusual degree of enthusiasm among the students, or some other extenuating circumstances. It may sometimes be desirable to carry a course conditionally for another week, especially if there is good indication that additional students can be recruited. Program directors should feel no embarrassment in closing courses if they accept the fact ahead of time that there will always be a certain percentage of failures in a program that is courageous in exploring new needs and interests. Students enrolled in courses that are discontinued should be offered their choice between a cash refund or transferring to another course (the latter alternative is a much more likely possibility if the course is discontinued early in the opening meeting).

5. Prepare the instructors carefully to handle their responsibilities during the opening meetings. These duties will usually consist of collecting admission cards, introducing themselves and the subject, establishing a friendly group feeling, and determining the needs and interests of the students. This latter objective might be greatly advanced by the use of a simple information card for students to fill out as they are waiting for class to begin (thus sparing them the discomfort of sitting idly while the class assembles). Exhibit 24 illustrates such a card.

Exhibit 24

INSTRUCTOR'S INFORMATION CARD
Adult Education Program

Name of Student _____

Address _____

Employer _____

Type of Work (position) _____

Age _____ Marital Status _____

Education _____

_____

What do you want to get out of this course? _____

_____

_____

Attendance Records, Grades, and Certificates

Some adult educators object to keeping attendance records in informal course programs for the reason that it introduces an element of formality and, by implication, of compulsion that is foreign to the spirit of voluntary adult learning. Many program directors, however, feel that attendance records are necessary to efficient administration. Attendance records give an indication, for instance, as to how well the individual instructors are maintaining the interest of their students.

Simplified standard attendance records can be obtained from any school supply house. The names of the students enrolled in each course should be entered at the end of the second or third week (after the enrollment has stabilized) by the office clerk, from the class cards on file. It is advisable to have the instructors leave the attendance records in the office between class meetings in order that the program director can check them periodically.

Attendance records can also be valuable in following up on absentees. In some institutions it is the practice to send a friendly postcard to each student who has been absent for two consecutive meetings. Experience has shown that frequently students have simply grown out of the habit of coming to class and that such a reminder revives their interest.

Attendance records are obviously necessary where it is a policy to refund tuition to students who maintain a certain percentage of attendance (a practice fairly common in public high school evening course programs) or when certificates of attendance are awarded. This latter practice, while not yet very common, has much to recommend it. For, although informal courses do not carry any credit, there is a strong feeling on the part of many adults that they would like to have something to show for their efforts. A simple attendance certificate, stating specifically the nature of the achievement, as illustrated in Appendix I, Exhibit I-6, will often fill a real need.

Should grades be given in informal courses? The general practice is against it. Adults engage in education because they want to learn something. The test of their achievement, then, is not whether they can learn better than someone else, but whether they have learned what is useful to them. It is important for adults to have some way to measure their own progress, and for teachers to be able to appraise development, but there are more natural and meaningful ways of doing this (see Chapter 1) than grades. The use of grades introduces an element of formality and competition that runs counter to the very spirit of andragogy.

It may be impossible for a program director to avoid the use of grades if the courses are closely associated with credit programs or if grades are required by law. In such a case, provision must be made in the record system for the recording of grades.

Educational Counseling

Educational counseling, as it is used here, should be distinguished from the counseling format for learning as described in Chapter 8. In its narrowest sense, educational counseling simply means helping people select activities in a given program. It is an administrative service that is part of the registration process.

But adult education will never achieve its full potential as the fourth level of our national educational enterprise if its institutions limit their educational counseling to activity guidance. For, in the last analysis, it is only through a sophisticated process of educational counseling that individuals will be able to engage in an integrated, sequential program of lifelong learning. In education of children and youth, the sequence from one learning to another and the integration of one category of learning with another are presumably inherent in the articulation of subjects from one grade level to another and in the patterns of curricular organization (e.g., core curriculum, liberal-arts and sciences curriculum, engineering curriculum, etc.). In adult education there are no grade levels, and the curriculum is a random mosaic of unrelated resources scattered among scores of institutions. There is no inherent pattern that provides sequence and integration; individuals have to mould their own patterns, and the only source of help in this complicated undertaking is educational counseling.

Education counseling, therefore, is really the program-planning process applied to an individual. It involves the same steps: 1) establishing a climate conducive to self-analysis and self-direction; 2) assessing the needs and interests of individuals for further learning in the light of their models of what they want to become; 3) helping them formulate step-by-step learning objectives; 4) helping them identify the resources available to them and map out a sequence of learning experiences; and 5) helping them continuously to evaluate their progress toward their objectives and to repeat this cycle.

The Role of the Counselor

The notion of an educational counseling function (as contrasted to a registration function) being an essential feature of an institutional adult-education program is so new that the role of educational counselor has not yet been well defined. The following pioneering attempt to define the duties of the adult-education counselor in the Baltimore public schools suggests the breadth of contribution such a role can make:

A. Interviews
   1. Students
      a. Registration procedures
      b. Long-term educational planning
      c. Credit evaluation for graduation requirements
      d. College entrance requirements
      e. Educational requirements to meet vocational plans
      f. Curriculum adjustment
      g. Interpretation of test results
   2. Others
      a. With administrators to discuss the implications of facts discovered through the interview or through follow-up studies as a basis for curriculum modification, expansion, or adjustment
      b. With faculty members to discuss the adjustment problems of individual students
      c. With leaders in the community to interpret programs, courses, or cooperative action
B. Group Meetings
   1. With students to present
      a. Registration procedures
      b. Educational opportunities in the school
      c. Graduation requirements
      d. Educational opportunities in other schools and colleges
      e. College entrance requirements
      f. The High School Equivalence Examination (application procedures, the scope of the tests, the values)
      g. The guidance services
      h. Solution of problems, analyzation of problems, and checks on conclusions
   2. With faculty members on
      a. Registration procedures and information
      b. Policies and procedures of guidance services
   3. With civic, social, and professional groups to present and discuss pertinent facts about adult education programs
C. Placement and Referrals
   1. The value of cooperative placement work with state and federal employment agencies should be explored and developed at the earliest possible time.

2. Every adult-education counselor needs a comprehensive acquaintance with all other civic, social, professional, and welfare agencies, or organizations which have services to help adults meet particular problems. This knowledge is the base from which a creative referral can become part of the counselor's work.
3. The counselor may wish to sponsor occupational conferences, assembly programs and similar activities designed to bring information to the students of an educational or vocational nature, or to acquaint them with community services.[2]

And a hint as to the range of services that might be provided by a comprehensive counseling program is given in the following statement by Mr. Preston Amerman of the Detroit Edison Company:

> The philosophy of counseling in industry is to help the individual resolve his own problems and make his own decisions. The counselor does not give the individual direct aid but helps him stand on his own two feet by strengthening his decision-making abilities. The counseling process usually begins at the supervisory level where there is day-to-day contact with the individual's problems. Counseling services at Edison encompass the following areas:
>
> Educational Counseling: This type of counseling is especially important for the person in his thirties who begins to wonder what he has missed and where he is going. He may be seeking additional education or training in order to move up the ladder within the company.
>
> Emotional Counseling: The company employs a full-time psychologist who deals with many personal problems. One of the most frequent is alcoholism. Many of the individual problem situations dealt with concern interpersonal relationships within the company, such as relations with the boss or other employees. Personnel know that they can come to the counseling office and their confidence will be kept.
>
> Pre-retirement Counseling: This type of counseling is gaining greater importance. It is frequently a traumatic experience for employees to leave the company after many years of service.
>
> Legal Counseling: The company will give legal assistance to the individual experiencing legal difficulty. Income tax assistance is also given.[3]

Another dimension of the counseling function that has been receiving increasing attention in recent years is assistance in career planning. One of the most elaborate programs of this sort that I know of is General Electric Company's Career Dimensions program, the essential features of which are described in Appendix I, Exhibit I-7.

It is my deep conviction that the scope of the counseling function and the role of the educational counselor in adult education will expand and become increasingly refined as a major thrust of the adult-education movement in its next phase of evolution. Indeed, I foresee the time when counseling will be the central, integrative function for the entire field.

The Use of Tests

Although most of the tests available as a resource in educational counseling—tests of mental ability, academic aptitude and achievement, vocational aptitude and interest,

---

[2]From a section prepared by Mrs. Hildreth Lambert, supervisor of adult guidance, for the Adult Education Handbook for Principals, Viceprincipals, Teachers-in-charge, and Counselors of the Division of Adult Education of the Baltimore City Department of Education, as quoted in *The Swap Shop* (Washington, D.C.: National Association for Public School Adult Education, May, 1957).

[3]Thomas Van Sant, "Counseling Adult Students," in National Association for Public School Adult Education, *Public School Adult Education: A Guide for Administrators* (rev. ed.) (Washington, D.C.: National Association for Public School Adult Education, 1963), p. 121.

and other types—are geared to the developmental stages of childhood and youth, an increasing number are being developed specifically for use with adults. Information about these tests can be obtained from the current editions of Oscar K. Buros, editor, *Tests in Print* and *Mental Measurement Yearbook*, both published by the Gryphon Press, Highland Park, New Jersey. But the use of psychological tests is a highly technical undertaking that should be restricted to trained psychometrists who subscribe to the basic philosophy that their purpose is to produce information that will help the individual diagnose his own needs and realities as regards learning.

Organizing a Counseling Service

Since so few institutions presently have a full-fledged counseling service, I thought it might be helpful to reproduce in full the following step-by-step outline developed by Carl R. Johnson of the Warwick, Rhode Island, public schools as a proposed plan of action for the establishment of an adult counseling service.

I. Establish a tentative counseling service organizational philosophy.
  A. This philosophy to be developed by the program administrator initially.
  B. This philosophy to be cognizant of, and within the scope of, the organizational philosophy of the total adult education program in this community.
  C. This philosophy to serve as a starting point for the Counseling Service Planning Committee. They will modify or replace it as they deem necessary.
II. Assessment of the needs and interests to be served by the counseling service.
  A. Assess through current adult-education clientele.
    1. By questionnaire to extract stated needs and interests. To ascertain level of intellectual awareness of the needs.
    2. By interview to ascertain conflicts, voids, anxieties, which could be served by educational, vocational, personal counseling.
    3. By having students participate as members of the Counseling Service Planning Committee.
    4. By observation in class situation of students in the program of adult education (by trained observer).
  B. Assess through employers and employers' representatives (personnel managers).
    1. By questionnaire to determine their views and observations of the interest in and need for help in vocational, educational, and personal lives of their labor force.
    2. By interview to obtain more depth of reaction and observation from the employer.
    3. By having selected employers or personnel managers serve as members of the Counseling Service Planning Committee.
  C. Assess through the adult-education teachers.
    1. By questionnaire to gain insight into the extent to which they recognize situations in past classes which would have benefited from a counseling relationship.
    2. By interview to examine the types of counseling which they feel might be needed.
    3. By having selected teachers serve as members of the Counseling Service Planning Committee.
  D. Assess through the adult-education administrator.
    1. By examination and study of drop-out records.

2. By examination and study of attendance patterns.
3. By examination of literature in the field pertinent to organization of and practice of adult counseling.
4. By consultation with other adult-education administrators in comparable communities.
5. By study of reports and studies about the community and its social, economic, and political patterns.

E. Assess through other educational and/or counseling entities in the community to determine the extent of their facilities and their emphasis within the counseling function, i.e., vocational, educational, personal, social, emotional, familial.
  1. USES local office.
  2. Churches within the community.
  3. College and extension services.
  4. Veteran's Administration.
  5. Community Guidance Clinic.
  6. Warwick YMCA.
  7. Armed forces recruiting offices.
  8. Local and state labor unions.
  9. City welfare department.
  10. State mental hospital.
  11. Probation office of the District Court.
  12. State Office of Vocational Rehabilitation.
  13. Bradley Hospital.
  14. Family Service Inc.

F. Assess through a Counseling Service Planning Committee.
  1. Membership consisting of those mentioned in A through D above.
  2. To assemble and evaluate those data obtained in A through E above.

III. Formulation of counseling service objectives.
  A. By the Counseling Service Planning Committee.
  B. Based upon evaluation and interpretation of those data obtained.
  C. Upon what types of counseling will the emphasis be placed?
    1. Vocational.
    2. Educational.
    3. Personal (emotional, social).
  D. Delimit tasks and scope of tasks ascribed to the counseling service.
  E. Describe the relationship of the counseling service and the adult-education administration.
  F. Specify desired outcomes for the counseling service.
    1. Improved attendance patterns.
    2. Improved drop-out rate.
    3. Increased job efficiency.
    4. Increased community interest and activity.
    5. Increased independence by counselees from the counseling service.
  G. Provisions for growth of the counseling section.
    1. Integrate test and measurement section.
    2. Placement service.
  H. Attitude of the counseling service toward community service and community acceptance.
    1. Actively stimulate awareness and understanding of personality problems and mental hygiene principles.

IV. Design organizational structure of the counseling service.
  A. Structure will be dependent upon the needs and interests in II.
  B. Structure will be dependent upon the objectives formulated in III.
  C. Structure will spell out relationship to and responsibilities to the administrative hierarchy of the adult-education program.
  D. Structure will be limited initially by requirements imposed by financial support and physical facilities.
 V. Evaluation (if the counseling service were to become a reality, the evaluation would follow the selection of counseling and clerical personnel, and the recruitment of clientele, and one year of operation).
  A. A segment of the planning committee retained for a one-year follow-up.
    1. Evaluation of data accumulated by the counseling service.
    2. Evaluation of their personal contact with adult students and their views of and experiences with the counseling service.
    3. Conduct survey of clientele and teachers via questionnaire and interview re: view of and use of counseling service.
    4. Implications for educational program change.
  B. Administrative evaluation.
    1. Comparative drop-out study.
    2. Comparative study, control group vs. experimental group.
    3. Study of patterns of attendance—persistence, satisfaction.
    4. Informal evaluation.
      a. Examination of anecdotal records.
      b. Growth of the demand for the service.
      c. Discussion with teachers and students.
    5. Implications for educational program change.

Promotion and Public Relations

Many good programs have failed because of poor promotion—people just never heard about them or did not realize how good they were.

Good promotion goes deeper than merely describing a program. Adult education has to be "sold." One of the major functions of adult education is to sell to people the idea of continuing to learn. It is important to society and to each individual that people be enthusiastic about the possibilities in adult education.

Looked at in this light, the promotion of adult education becomes something of a crusade. Adult educators are challenged to learn the skills developed by the advertising business in behalf of mass entertainment, and to apply them, when they are fitting, to their own worthy cause. There is no reason for program directors to be ashamed of selling their wares—provided, of course, the wares are worthy.

The well-tested methods at our command involve four basic steps: 1) defining the clientele, 2) planning the campaign, 3) preparing and distributing materials, and 4) evaluating results.

Defining the Clientele

Defining the clientele is an essential first step. This is simple if the program is designed for the members of a single organization, such as a church or an industrial plant. Even then, it is helpful to know the age, sex, marital status, educational background, economic status, and interests of the potential participants, in order that promotion materials may be designed to appeal to them.

If the program is communitywide, the problem is more complex—and requires greater care. The most effective promotion is "rifle-shot" promotion, aimed directly at specific persons or groups. If an appeal is to be made particularly to young people, a list of youth-serving organizations will be needed and special promotion materials will be directed to them. Other lists would be required for appeals to members of labor unions, various occupational groupings, professional people, college graduates, members of minority groups, and other special groupings. The University College of the University of Chicago determined that it wanted to attract and serve the leaders of the community. This necessitated the development of a list of the officers of hundreds of different organizations.

The more precisely the clientele is defined, the more effective the promotion campaign will be.

Planning the Promotion Campaign

Whether the goal is to attract fifty people to a club lecture series or five thousand to a university extension program, careful advance planning results in more effective effort and makes the promotion job easier. It reduces the strain and tension on the director, it facilitates dividing the work among a number of people, and it makes it possible to prepare much of the material considerably in advance. Probably the soundest policy is to develop a general plan for the year and then to map out more specific plans for each month, series, quarter, or semester.

The plan is likely to be more effective if it is the result of group thinking than if it is developed entirely by an individual. The directing committee, or a special subcommittee on promotion, and the staff are logical groups to bring into the planning process.

The planning of promotion involves two steps, the first of which is building the promotion budget. How much money should be spent on promotion? In some situations this figure may be set by some higher authority, such as legislation or headquarters policy. In others, it is an open question, and frequently a very troublesome one. The tendency is to be too conservative. As a result, many programs fail to reach the number of people they should and could reach, and the materials are so cheap that they do justice neither to the organization they represent nor to adult education as a movement.

Various formulas have been devised for calculating the amount of money to spend on promotion. For instance, one organization sets its promotion allowance automatically at 15 percent of the total budget. Another figures that it must spend $1.50 on promotion for each enrollment it hopes to receive. Still others map out the kind of promotion campaign they feel will attract the number of people they want, and then allocate whatever amount of money is required. Situations vary so widely according to community, type of organization, and type of program that it is futile to try to state a rule that would apply to all.

One way to go about solving the problem in any situation is to use this process:

1. Estimate the number of people needed to make the program a success.

2. Estimate the amount of promotion (number of printed announcements, advertisements, etc.) that will be required to attract this many people. The experience of similar organizations in the community may be helpful in making this estimate. In general, a 10 percent response on direct-mail promotion is considered excellent.

3. Determine the cost (printing, mailing, advertising, etc.) of this amount of promotion.

4. If the resulting figure is so high as to be completely out of line it will, of course, have to be reduced, with an equivalent curtailment of the promotion campaign. Keep in mind, though, that it is more common to spend too little on promotion than too much.

It is generally true that the per-capita cost of promotion is higher in the early stages of a new program, and that it tapers off as the number of participants increases. As soon as a body of satisfied customers is developed, they will promote the program by word of mouth.

After settling on the amount of money to spend on promotion, the next problem is to decide how to spend it. How much should be earmarked for newspaper advertising, how much for direct mail, how much for the other media? There is no general rule that applies to all situations. The best guide is experience—the experience of other organizations with similar problems and the experience that comes from trial and evaluation.

The promotion budget should grow out of a general plan of promotion. If the available funds are to be divided intelligently among the various media, it is essential that the total promotion picture be seen. One method of developing an overall plan of promotion is to devote an entire meeting of the planning group to listing the promotion possibilities for the program as a whole and for each specific activity. For a lecture series, for example, the group first lists the individuals and groups it feels would be interested in the series as a whole. Then it considers each meeting topic and thinks of additional groups having a specific interest in particular topics. The same process is used in course programs, club programs, forums, and conferences. Exhibit 25 illustrates this kind of overall plan.

It is possible, by doing some rough estimating, to determine what proportion of the promotion funds should be allocated to each medium—subject to the testing and adjustment of the proportions in the light of experience. Exhibit 26 shows a promotion budget formulated on this basis.

The second step in planning the promotion campaign is to draw up specific schedules showing exactly when and how the general plan is to be accomplished through each medium. A well-rounded campaign usually has at least three types of schedules: newspaper advertising; newspaper, television, and radio publicity; and direct-mail promotion.

In drafting the promotion schedules, thought should be given to the most effective timing of the various elements. Experience indicates that if printed materials are received too far in advance, people put them aside and forget about them. No immediate action of any kind is required. On the other hand, if the notice is too short, the prospective participants may either have other plans already made or feel that they need more time to think it over. The right time for a given program has to be determined by trial and error, but about three weeks' advance notice for the printed materials seems to be effective in most cases.

Since the printed announcement is the final salesperson of a program, all other promotion efforts must be keyed to it. The chief purpose of advertising, publicity, posters, and other promotion devices is to bring in requests for the program announcements. Assuming that printed materials are more effective if put into the hands of prospects about two or three weeks before the opening of the program, it seems to be sound practice to start the campaign with advance promotion about six weeks before the opening. The intensity of the campaign should rise gradually to a climax about two weeks before opening.

Exhibit 25

GENERAL PLAN OF PROMOTION
XYZ Community Center

Groups to be reached	Methods of reaching them
1. *General promotion*	
Community Center membership	Direct mail
General public	Newspaper advertising and publicity, TV and radio spots
Employees of larger businesses	Posters, publicity in house organs, letters to personnel managers
Library users	Posters, letters to librarians
2. *Forum promotion*	
Labor union members	Special flyer on labor meeting; direct mail
Real-estate owners and operators (concerning housing debate)	Letter to members of Real Estate Board; classified ads in daily papers; display ad in real estate journal
League of Women Voters	Letter to president; news story in monthly paper
3. *Promotion of parent-education course*	
Parent-Teachers' Associations	Special folder; direct mail
Schoolteachers	Letters to principals

Exhibits I-8 to 11 in Appendix I show how these principles worked out in various promotion schedules in the adult-education program of Central YMCA, Chicago. While these schedules are more extensive than some adult-education programs require, they illustrate the process that should be followed, regardless of the size of the program. Notice that the publicity stories, advertisements, posters, and institutional mailings started from four to six weeks in advance of the opening date. About three weeks in advance of the opening, direct mailings to individuals were sent out, and the publicity and advertising insertions became more frequent. Then there was a postcard reminder in the last week. Publicity stories kept the campaign rolling during the term.

Integrating the Program with a Theme

A program is more effective if its parts are tied together with a theme, slogan, title, or symbol. This theme may be expressed in words with distinctive lettering or by a design. It should appear on all promotion pieces—advertisements, printed materials, and letterheads—in order that the relationship among the various pieces is immediately evident.

The University Extension of the University of California heads all its materials with the caption "Lifelong Learning." The YMCA Community College of Chicago uses "Learning for Living" as the trademark of its adult-education program, with a design featuring the triangle, and this symbol appears on all of its promotion materials.

Getting Expert Advice

It has been stated that the planning of a promotion campaign should be done by a group. A corollary to this principle is that the thinking should be as expert as possible. Skillful and experienced advertising representatives, newspaper people, and direct-mail specialists often are willing to serve on committees for causes in which they are interested.

Another method of obtaining expert advice on promotion is to employ the professional services of public-relations experts. Usually these experts do not charge for handling newspaper advertising, since in most cases they receive a commission from the publishers. They can be very helpful, in addition, in increasing the effectiveness of the direct-mail and publicity campaigns, at relatively small cost. Not only can public-relations experts bring creative ideas and skilled services to the promotion campaign, but their experience with other situations can help to make estimates more accurate and errors less costly.

Preparing and Distributing Promotion Materials

The development of a general plan, the mapping out of a promotion campaign, and the drawing up of schedules are the preliminary steps in promoting a program. The major task is then to prepare and distribute promotion materials.

A wide variety of choices is open in the use of the various promotion media. A knowledge of a few principles that apply to each medium will help the director to use it with judgment and imagination.

Newspaper Advertising

Newspaper advertising is a "shotgun" medium—it reaches out to the public at large. It is useful in attracting the attention of people with whom an organization does not now have contact. It is an effective way to build prospect lists for direct-mail campaigns. Various types of newspapers, ranging from house organs and neighborhood weeklies to metropolitan dailies, accept advertising. All should be considered in the light of the needs of a given promotion campaign.

Program directors seem to get the best results from newspaper advertising when they observe the following principles:

1. A definite schedule of advertising should be carefully drafted. (See the previous section dealing with scheduling.)

2. A large number of relatively small display ads (one to three inches) seem to be more effective than a small number of larger ads.

3. The display ad should have an eye-catching headline or reverse-plate banner, but should be dignified.

4. The copy should be easy to read and have sales appeal, but most of the space should be devoted to a listing of specific activities—not generalizations about the program. A person will be more attracted to a course on public speaking, if that's what he or she wants, than to a program of adult education in the abstract.

5. Classified ads are effective when they can be directed to special groups of readers concerning particular activities designed for them.

6. Display ads may be general, concerning the program as a whole, or specific, featuring only one type of activity, such as business courses. The general ads can appear on

Exhibit 26

PROMOTION BUDGET, FALL
XYZ Community Center

Newspaper advertising

Display ads, daily papers	$150	
Classified ads, daily papers	150	
Display ads, neighborhood and trade papers	150	
Total	——	$450

Newspaper publicity

Mimeographing	$200	
Postage	150	
Total	——	350

Direct mail promotion

Printing	$350	
Mimeographing	150	
Addressing	150	
Postage	220	
Total	——	870

Posters, displays, and exhibits

Printing	$300	
Sign painting	150	
Distribution	100	
Total	——	550
Grand total		$2220

any page in the paper, but the specific ad is more effective if it appears on the page concerned with the subject of the ad. For instance, an ad on business courses should appear on the finance page, an ad on interior decoration on the home furnishings page.

7. Advertisements in community newspapers, trade journals, house organs, church papers, club news sheets, labor-union publications, concert programs, etc., are especially effective when they can appeal to a specialized interest of the readers of the particular paper.

8. Professional advice should be obtained on the layout, typography, size, frequency, and other aspects of advertising. Such service can be obtained from public-relations agencies or the newspaper advertising departments.

Newspaper Publicity

Publicity is closely related to advertising, but should never be thought of as replacing it. Rather, publicity supplements and fortifies advertising. Here are a few helpful principles:

1. A definite publicity schedule should be carefully drafted for the entire duration of the program. (See the previous section dealing with scheduling.)

2. An essential part of publicity is personal contact. Get to know the city editors, department editors, columnists, etc., of the papers in the community.

3. Develop a master list of the sources of publicity in the community, including the daily papers, trade journals, house organs, labor-union publications, church, club, and civic organization news sheets, professional-society papers, etc. Each type should be classified separately and in a form convenient for addressing (three-by-five-inch cards are handy).

4. Develop a file of good action photographs that can be used with news stories.

5. Be on the alert for good human-interest stories and invite an individual paper to assign a feature writer to cover it. If there are two or more newspapers serving the community, be sure to spread the stories among them.

6. Invite the press to newsworthy events—anniversary celebrations, special presentations, etc. It is legitimate to arrange such events with an eye to their publicity value.

7. Find out how particular papers prefer press releases to be written and write them that way. Make them short, to the point, and interesting. Write from the point of view of the readers and their interests. Give facts. If the paper is published weekly, be sure the release is delivered well in advance of the deadline set by the paper.

8. Use all sources of publicity, not just the big ones. Slant the story according to the special interests of the public served by each source.

9. Send in both general stories announcing the program as a whole and special stories featuring specific activities (these might be directed to departmental editors, such as homemaking, financial page, etc.).

10. Count on not more than 25 percent of the releases ever getting into print.

11. Prepare the releases on 8½-by-11-inch typing paper of good quality, preferably sending each editor an original typed copy. Releases should be double or triple spaced, with about two inches left blank at the top for the editor to write in a headline.

12. Never try to trade advertising for publicity. Publicity should stand on its own merits as news. Good editors resent people who try to buy publicity with advertising.

13. Names make the news. It is frequently considered good practice to build up a committee chairperson or program director as a newsworthy figure to symbolize the program to the public. It is also rewarding to build a news release around interesting events or achievements in the lives of individual leaders, instructors, or staff members.

Exhibit I-12 in Appendix I shows an acceptable form for the preparation of releases. Note that the source of the release is given and that release instructions are specified. (A definite date for release should be given only if damage would be done by publication before a set date; otherwise, leave the timing up to the editor.) Exhibit I-13 describes an imaginative procedure for generating publicity through your faculty.

Radio and Television

Many of the principles given for newspaper advertising and publicity apply to radio and television with appropriate adaptation. Brief spot announcements serve the same purpose as the small display advertisements in newspapers—to get people to write in for materials. Special skill is required for writing radio and television script, however, so the services of an expert should be obtained for this undertaking.

Publicity by radio and television offers unique opportunities of a type not possible through the printed word. For instance, one adult-education institution I know produces a regular weekly half-hour program on its local educational television station in which instructors and participants from the different courses discuss or demonstrate the subject treated in their courses. A forum program in the Midwest makes a tape recording of each of its programs for rebroadcasting later in the week, with an invitation to listeners to attend the next forum. The public schools of Philadelphia, as well as a number of community colleges and universities across the country, sponsor "telecourses" in which regular class sessions are broadcast and listeners may enroll as regular students.

Other publicity ideas that have proved successful include plugs by commentators (one classical-recording announcer lists the music-appreciation courses of institutions in his city), interviews with staff members, instructors, or participants, and presentations by staff members or instructors.

Direct Mail and Printed Materials

Direct mail is usually the most costly item in the educational promotional campaign in terms of time, energy, and money. Program directors report almost unanimously that most of their participants are obtained through direct mail. The chief purpose of all other promotion is to set the stage for printed materials. Direct mail is the "door-to-door salesperson" for a program.

What kinds of printed materials should a program have? One generalization applies to all types of programs: printed materials should reflect the quality of the program they represent. A high-quality program should not be burdened with poor-quality printing. The impression given by printed materials is the first impression people will usually have of a program.

The kind of printed materials depends upon the size and the nature of the program. If it consists of an extensive list of activities, a folder or booklet is probably needed. If it is a single activity, a simple one-page flyer or even a letter might do. Here are some suggestions for each type of printed material.

Folders and Booklets

What size should a folder be? This will depend upon how much material must go into it, how the paper will cut, and what kind of envelope is to be used. A popular size for larger programs is 6 by 9 inches, which requires an outsize envelope for mailing. Another popular size is $4\frac{1}{2}$ by 6 inches, which also requires a special envelope unless it is self-mailed. Probably the most extensively used size is 4 by 9 inches, which will fit into a business envelope. Another common size is $3\frac{1}{2}$ by $6\frac{1}{4}$ inches, which will fit into a correspondence envelope.

One advantage of the smaller booklet is that it is more convenient for the recipients to put into their pockets or handbags; but if it is too small it is more likely to be overlooked and the type may have to be crowded. The mailing weight of the booklet must be considered in determining the size. If it goes over two ounces, it cannot be sent by third-class permit mail. These are problems that a printer can give good advice on.

What should be the style of the folder be? Good layout, typography, and artwork do much to increase the attractiveness and appeal of a folder. Expert advice should be obtained from a good printer or layout artist. If it costs extra it will be well worth the expense. Here are some general principles, however, that may be helpful:

1. The cover should attract attention (by means of special effects in type, reverse-plate printing, illustrations, and color) but be dignified. It should tell enough of the idea of the program to cause a reader to want to turn the page, but the less printing on the cover the better.

2. Careful attention should be given to the selection of paper stock and ink. A good-

quality book stock is generally preferred if there is to be only printing or line drawings, but an enamel stock is required if photographs are to be reproduced. Using two colors of ink, one for captions and the other for body type, makes a more appealing folder but is expensive. Somewhat the same effect can be accomplished by printing an attractive colored ink on tinted paper.

3. The type used in printing the folder should be large and readable. The type used in captions should be bold enough to stand out from the body type.

4. The material in the folder should be organized so that it is easy to understand and follow. Good layout will enhance good organization through the use of spacing, different type fonts and sizes, and indentation.

5. Line drawings or photographs will greatly increase the appeal of a folder, provided they are skillfully executed and in good taste.

6. There should be plenty of white space in the folder. It should never give the impression of being crowded.

Exhibit I-14 illustrates many of these principles.

What should the folder say? The folder should give all the information a reader needs to understand the program and to enroll in it. Here is a checklist of questions that should be answered in a folder:

What is the purpose of the program?

What specific benefits can an individual expect to derive from it?

Who is sponsoring it?

What are the activities?

What kinds of people is it designed to serve?

Who are the speakers, instructors, or leaders?

How much does it cost?

When do the activities take place? Where?

How does one affiliate?

The way in which a folder says these things is all-important. The very titles given to the activities can attract or repel, inform or misinform. The best titles generally: 1) give an accurate idea of the substance of an activity, 2) have a suggestion of action in them, 3) are stated in terms of a problem or function, and 4) are personalized. For example, "Writing for Pleasure and Profit" is a better title for a course than "English Composition." "Starting Your Own Business" is better than "Elementary Business Management." "Will You Have to Fight Russia?" is a better forum title than "The Russian Foreign Policy."

The importance of selecting good titles is illustrated by numerous instances in which activities have failed under one title and have attracted large groups under another. Speakers have found that their audiences are usually small when their topics are dull. The most successful program directors give a great deal of thought to the selection of titles for their activities.

Equally important is the way an activity is described. The description should be informative and accurate; it should tell the readers exactly what to expect. But it should do more. It should tell them why they should take part in the activity, why they need it, what it will do for them. The readers' interest should be aroused to the point that they will want to do something about it. The words should be directed to an individual reader—"you" should appear several times in every description. This is what is known as sales copy, and its function is unashamedly to sell a worthy activity. Be sure, however, never to oversell; never promise results that cannot be achieved.

Here are two examples of actual descriptions of adult-education courses. The first is in line with the suggestions made above, and the second violates most of them. Which course would you enroll in?

Painting as a Hobby

One of the most satisfying, creative, and convenient of all hobbies, painting is ideally suited for those priceless hours of relaxation after a hard day at the office. It takes little energy, is easy to learn, and rewards with much pleasure.

It does not matter whether you have ever before painted a picture; you will start out wherever your interest lies and will be helped to develop your own style. You will learn the meaning of color, line, composition, light and dark, and how they combine to make your picture. You may try out different media: pastels, oils, watercolors, or charcoal.

Elementary Painting

Painting in oils and watercolors for recreation; color theory and mixing. Various methods of painting, handling colors compositionally, and individual criticism.

In writing activity descriptions, keep in mind that adults have a natural sales resistance to education. They have visions of rigidly formal classrooms, embarrassing questions by a domineering schoolmaster, difficult assignments, and dull lectures. The description must convey to them the friendliness and informality, the respect for personality, the practice of learning by doing, that characterize modern adult programs. Many adults are timid about their ability to keep up with the others, because they have been out of school so long. They must be reassured that they will be able to participate without embarrassment. (The "individual criticism" in the second illustration above must have scared away a lot of people.) Good copy writing involves putting oneself in the readers' shoes.

One of the strongest selling points in any program is—or should be—the faculty. People reading about a program that is new to them will feel much less as outsiders if the catalog introduces them to the instructors in such a way that the readers feel they almost know them. Ideally, the readers should know these things about the instructors before they ever meet:

Their names;

Who they are—what their backgrounds are, their occupations, their present employer;

Why they are qualified to teach or lead a particular activity;

What kinds of people they are; an anecdote or human-interest story about each one will help to "humanize" the faculty.

The instructors might be described as part of each activity description, or they might be grouped together in a special part of the catalog.

Flyers

There are occasions when it is desirable to promote a single activity or a group of related activities among large numbers of people with specialized interests. A simple single-sheet flyer can be produced in quantity at low cost and distributed more widely than expensive catalogs. The University of California Extension, Riverside, is especially noted for its use of this technique. Some examples of its flyers are displayed in Exhibit I-15.

Form Letters

Form letters can perform two important functions in the promotion campaign: 1) as covering letters mailed with folders, directing the reader's special attention to certain activities, form letters focus the appeal of the folders on the known interests of particular groups of people; 2) as separate mailing pieces, form letters can make an inexpensive but personalized appeal to special groups of people.

Good form letters are usually short and concise. They should be written in a conversational tone and should refer directly to the particular interests or backgrounds of the group to which they are directed. It is probably better to state frankly in the heading the nature of the group for whom the letter is intended. Form letters should be individually signed, if possible.

How form letters can be fitted into the general promotion campaign is illustrated in the direct-mail schedule reproduced in Exhibit I-8. Note that form letter No. 1 was sent to the institutional list, letter No. 2 to the personnel managers, etc., as covering letters for printed materials. Exhibit I-9 shows that separate form letters were sent to former painting students, former music students, and so forth.

Mailing Lists

The names and addresses of people who are potentially interested in a program can be accumulated from a variety of sources. Requests for printed materials that come in as a result of advertising, publicity, and direct mail constitute the very best kind of individual-prospect mailing list. Present participants will often give the names and addresses of friends. Another fruitful source is the membership lists of various clubs, church organizations, business and professional societies, alumni associations, labor unions, and other groups. Frequently these organizations will not give out their membership lists but will address envelopes at cost. It is possible, also, to purchase mailing lists from commercial letter services.

Mailing lists should be separated in such a way that it will be easy to address envelopes according to different categories. The following categories have been developed by one institution:

public-service institutions
selected personnel managers
high school principals
university registrars
former participants (of this program)
current prospects
public libraries
social agencies
daily newspapers
community newspapers
industrial house organs
labor-union papers
clergy, by faith
members of Adult Education Council
members of University Club
bookstores
nurses' homes
members of Chambers of Commerce
women's clubs
PTA's

To be most effective, mailing lists must be continually cross-checked to avoid duplication, and changes in status or address should be entered as they occur. The whole process of keeping and using mailing lists will be greatly simplified if the lists are entered into one of the electronic devices designed for this purpose.

Methods of Mailing

There are several methods of mailing printed materials. Booklets and folders can be printed in such a way that the address can be fixed directly to the piece and it can be self-mailed without an envelope. Or printed material may be inserted into a special permit envelope, a flap of which is removable for inspection purposes, and mailed, provided it weighs less than two ounces. Both of these methods require special handling and bundling and may be delayed in delivery.

Another method is to use a regular business envelope with the flap tucked in instead of sealed. This will go third class if it weighs two ounces or less. Larger supplies of materials may be mailed third or fourth class in large manila envelopes or wrapped packages. First-class mailing is more expensive but also more efficient and convenient.

The opinion is sometimes expressed that third-class mailings are not read by the recipients. It seems to be the consensus of direct-mail experts, however, that if the cover of the piece or the envelope in which it is inserted is appealing, the material will be read. They indicate, in addition, that a piece which is enclosed in an envelope is more effective than self-mailing pieces, and that a covering letter will further increase the pulling power of a folder.

Without question the great majority of all adult-program materials are mailed third class. Highly personalized form letters and materials sent to "prestige" lists should, however, be mailed first class.

The local postmaster is the best source of advice on the proper method of mailing in a given situation.

Posters, Displays, and Exhibits

Posters can be used to attract attention and to obtain prospects. One of the most prolific sources of names and addresses for the Central YMCA of Chicago was a printed poster about eleven by twelve inches which splashed the name of the program across the top in reverse plate and then listed the types of activities. A small supply of business-reply postcards requesting the institution to send a folder was placed in a slit at the bottom. This poster was placed on bulletin boards in offices and factories, libraries, public buildings, clubs, and social agencies.

Individually painted posters can be used to arouse interest in special activities among present participants. A good quality of workmanship in layout, copywriting, and art work is as important in a poster as in a piece of printing.

Displays can sometimes be placed in a window, lobby, or other area frequented by the public, with good effect. To arouse interest in a lecture series on "How to Buy a House," for instance, models of various types of houses were obtained from a real-estate company and set on tables in the lobby of the sponsoring institution. Descriptive folders were placed on the table with the display.

Exhibits of work done by present participants in such activities as arts and crafts, painting, sewing, and photography not only arouse the interest of the spectators, but help to give them the feeling that maybe they can do it, too.

Personal Contacts in the Community

Usually we do not think of our relationships with other groups in the community as a part of the promotion campaign. Personal contacts are, however, a very effective instrument of promotion. Every time staff members, committee members, leaders, or students appear at a meeting or make a speech as a representative of an organization, they are in effect advertising the program. Larger institutions frequently seek out and schedule speaking engagements and arrange organizational or committee memberships for their staff as conscious promotion strategy. A personal-contact campaign can be planned almost as definitely as a publicity campaign, and as much care should be taken to see that the proper impression is made.

Enlisting the Support of Participants

A body of satisfied customers is a most effective instrument of promotion. Word-of-mouth advertising of people who have participated in a program and are enthusiastic about it is the most important factor. Numerous studies of how people first learned of a program list "friends" at the top. How can the support of present (and past) participants be cultivated?

The first requirement is, of course, that they be enthusiastic about the program. Obviously, this means that the program has to be good. But more than that, it means that people must be guided into the right activities. Regardless of how good a program is, if it is not what individuals want and need, they will not be satisfied with it. It is a mistake to rely on the printed materials to guide people into the right activities—even the most experienced program directors are continually amazed at how differently an activity description can be interpreted by different people. The most satisfactory solution to this problem is to provide competent counselors—committee members, staff members, and former participants can be trained—during the registration period.

In addition, the participants should be injected with some of the spirit and philosophy of the program if they are to interpret it well to others. Through printed materials, interpretation during registration, and experiences in committee work, participants can be given a better understanding of the purposes and program of the organization. Every opportunity should be given to participants to get a sense of belonging. This effect may be accomplished by inviting them into membership in the organization, by giving them leadership responsibilities, by offering them opportunities to serve on committees and councils, and by inviting them to special events and ceremonial occasions. Asking participants periodically to fill out interest questionnaires is another method of increasing their sense of participating.

Present participants can be asked directly to help spread the word. Toward the end of a series they can be asked to write on small cards the names and addresses of friends they think would be interested in receiving the announcement of the next series. Or, when present participants are mailed their copies of the new announcements, an extra copy can be enclosed and the covering letter can ask them to pass it along to someone else in their neighborhood or at work. Both devices have produced excellent results in actual practice.

The Telephone Committee

A potent instrument of promotion that should never be overlooked is an organized telephone campaign. In a small organization this may be just about the only promotion that is needed to draw a group of the desired size together. But even in large organizations a few dozen telephone calls may mean the difference between failure and success.

A telephone campaign can be organized by enlisting the services of a large enough number of people so that no one person has too heavy a burden. Each person is given a list of the names and numbers of people to call. These names may be either members of the organization or prospects, and the call may be made either as a reminder or as an invitation.

This technique injects a degree of personal interest and interaction into the promotion campaign that cannot be duplicated through printed materials.

Evaluating a Promotion Campaign

It would be very helpful to know exactly what results are being produced by the various elements of the promotion campaign, in order that time and money could be spent where it would do the most good. There is, unfortunately, no completely satisfactory way to evaluate a promotion campaign. But there are several methods of getting good clues. For instance, newspaper advertisements can be keyed. In newspaper A, the advertisements can say, "Write for catalog A," and in newspaper B, "Write for catalog B." Some newspapers object to this device because the results are never very reliable. Many people know it is a key and refuse to specify "A" or "B." Much the same procedure can be followed on some direct-mail pieces. Flyers or business-reply postcards can be marked to indicate where they were displayed when they were picked up. The results of this method are likely to be more accurate in direct mail than in newspaper advertising, since the key is fixed to the printed material, but it involves a lot of extra labor.

Another method of tabulating the sources of information about the program is to ask people at the time of registration where they first heard about it. Information obtained in this way is probably the least reliable of all, but it may give some interesting clues that can be checked against other data. Usually considerable time has elapsed between the individuals' first learning about the program and time of registration, and they will make a guess at how they first heard about it. Several times people have actually brought in clipped ads or news stories that appeared only in one paper, and have maintained that they clipped them from another.

It is fairly easy to check the effectiveness of the promotion in a given company or place of residence merely by tabulating the places of employment or residence on the students' registration cards. This information is, of course, highly accurate.

There is no foolproof method of determining the exact number of sales made by any single instrument of promotion. In a given situation there may be clues indicating that one or another of the media is yielding better results than the others. But it would be a mistake to assume that any phase of the promotion campaign could therefore be eliminated. It is the total impact of all phases that produces results, and every phase supports every other phase in making this impact. For example, a printed announcement may be more meaningful to some recipients because they have recently seen a newspaper advertisement that established the prestige of the organization in their minds or because a friend spoke to them about it, or because they saw a poster.

Adult-education workers should evaluate the results of their promotion efforts periodically, and should constantly seek to improve their promotional skills. The promotion of adult-educational activities is not only essential to the success of the activities themselves, but is important to the extension of adult education as a force in our society.

Interpreting and Reporting

Every organization has a public that it has spent time, energy, and money to cultivate. This public consists of participants in the program, members of the larger organization, committees, state and national headquarters, and various individuals and groups in the community at large. If the interest of this public is to be maintained, it should be informed periodically of the work of the organization.

Reports may be oral, to a directing committee or to a gathering of the participants; or they may be written and distributed more or less extensively. Some of the most effective interpretive reports are in the form of pageants or tableaux at annual meetings, graduation exercises, or open-house programs.

General principles suggested for guidance in preparing reports are:

1. Reports should be made frequently to individuals and groups intimately involved in the program, at least annually to the larger public.

2. The aim of each report should be clearly formulated before it is prepared. What is its audience? What results should it accomplish? What will be its scope?

3. The report should be based on accurate facts.

4. The process of preparation should involve as many people as possible. It should be based on the cooperative efforts of staff, committees, leaders, and participants.

5. The style of the report should be clear, concise, and readable. It should be dignified but dramatic. Charts, graphs, case histories, and photographs will greatly enhance its effectiveness.

6. The content of the report might be concerned with any or all of these items:
    —objectives of the program
    —nature of the program
    —resources used—human and physical
    —financial experience
    —methods employed
    —results accomplished
    —plans for the future
Especially outstanding examples of annual reports are those of the Adult Education Council of Metropolitan Denver, the Mott Program of the Flint, Michigan, Public Schools, the Extension Division of the University of Wisconsin, and the University of Georgia Center for Continuing Education.

Budgeting and Financing

Financial requirements and practices vary widely according to the type of program and sponsoring institution. Some programs are completely subsidized. Others must show a profit.

Some organizations, particularly churches and settlement houses, are able to produce educational programs with almost no financial budget, because of their ability to attract volunteer leaders. Others, including public schools and industry, provide educational programs that are completely subsidized. In between are thousands of organizations that are constantly battling with the problem of how to raise enough money to pay for the speakers, staff, instructors, rent, promotion, equipment, and other expenses.

There is no pat formula for solving the problem of financing an educational program. Some general principles, however, apply to all types of programs:

1. A financial goal should be set, based on consideration of estimated necessary ex-

penses and of possible income. A women's club that sponsors six educational meetings a year will have a much smaller financial goal than the community center that offers over a hundred courses; but unless a goal is set in both cases, financial planning is almost impossible.

The typical practice in informal adult education is to set a goal that is too low. There seems to be an expectation that educational programs cost very little money, with the result that many of them are poorly financed, poorly promoted, and provided with second-rate leadership. This accounts for many disappointments.

On the other hand, there is ample evidence that when a financial goal is set high enough to provide a program with high quality, the funds necessary to achieve the goal are forthcoming. People are willing to pay for programs that are interesting and that meet their needs.

2. A detailed plan should be formulated for producing whatever income is required. Some of the sources of financing open to various kinds of organizations are as follows:

a) Charges to participants. In organized classes, this is usually a tuition fee. In lecture series and forums, it may be either free-will offerings or admission fees. In clubs and ongoing groups, it may be membership dues or special assessments.

b) Appropriations from the general funds of an organization. When the educational program is a part of a larger organization, such as a social agency, church, women's club, and the like, a share of its total income may be set aside for the educational program.

c) Contributions from outside sources. Many organizations that do not limit their services to their own members may go directly to the community for support. This support may be from the United Way if the organization is eligible, or from foundations, or from individual contributions. A most common practice is to conduct a campaign for private contributions.

3. A budget should be prepared to serve as a basis for financial planning and control. A reasonable estimate of both expenditures and income, broken down into specific items, should be prepared. Sample budgets are given in Exhibits I-16 and 17, and a simple budget planning form is reproduced in Exhibit I-18.

4. Expenses should be incurred only under proper authorization. The approval of a budget by a policy-making committee is general authorization for the incurring of expenses. Beyond this, however, there should be a clear understanding as to what persons are authorized to expend funds and under what conditions. For example, it is common practice for authorized individuals to be permitted to spend up to a fixed maximum without specific approval, but expenditures over this amount must be approved individually by the policy-making authority.

5. Adequate records of all financial transactions should be kept. These records should be accurate, clear, as full as necessary, and as simple as practical. Transactions should be recorded as they occur and should be supported by vouchers and receipts. The accounting system should guard against fraud and mistakes.

6. The accounts should be audited by a CPA or an auditing committee at least once a year.

7. A financial report should be published at least annually. This report should consist of an itemized list of actual income and expenses, accompanied by interpretive or explanatory comments.

Establishing an Overall Financial Policy

The same principles of good business management should be applied to adult-education programs that pertain to any other activity involving financing. One of the primary requirements of good business management is a clear general financial policy. This policy ought to include at least the following elements:

1. Source of authority for budget approval and financial policy determination;

2. Limitations, if any, on specific budgetary items (in some governmental programs, for instance, the amount that can be allocated to administrative expense is limited to a percentage of the total budget);

3. Prorating of overhead costs where other programs or services are being operated under the same sponsorship;

4. Degree of self-support that will be aimed for, limitations on the subsidy that will be forthcoming;

5. Methods and standards of accounting;

6. Bases for computing fees charged to participants;

7. Sources of income other than fees, and conditions under which they are to be exploited;

8. The nature and frequency of financial reports that will be required.

Establishing Fees

There is a general lack of agreement among adult educators as to the proper basis for determining the proportion of costs that should be carried by the participants.

Attempts have been made to develop formulas that will yield the proper tuition charges in a given situation, but none has yet been produced that has met the test of varied experiences. Factors that enter into the determination of fees include:

1. *Amount of subsidy available.* In many governmental and public-school programs, more or less liberal allotments are made for adult education, frequently with limitations placed on the charges that can be made. In some voluntary organizations contributions are received from the community chest or private subscribers, on the understanding that charges to participants will be held to a minimum. In industry the total cost is usually borne by the company.

2. *The nature of the clientele being served.* Tuition rates should not be set so high that they will act as an economic barrier to the participants one wishes to attract to the program. On the other hand, the charge should not be so low as to depreciate the value of the course. It seems to be a characteristic of our culture that people tend to value articles or services according to their cost.

3. *The intensity of motivation in the adult students.* In some subjects, such as public speaking and courses leading to vocational advancement, the motivation seems to be almost universally high. It is considered good practice by many adult educators to charge at a high rate in these types of courses, in order to be able to carry other subjects which should appear in a well-balanced program but which seldom pay their own way, such as many of the cultural courses, arts and crafts, and public affairs.

4. *The cost of instruction.* As has been pointed out in the section dealing with compensation to instructors, it is necessary to pay more to certain types of instructors than to others to interest them in teaching. These higher costs can be reflected in the tuition charges for those courses, provided the motivation is proportionately higher on the part of the students. (And students would frequently prefer to pay more to study under X than to pay less for a course with Y.)

5. *The standards set by similar organizations in the community.* While the tuition charges in other informal course programs in the community should not necessarily be an inflexible criterion in determining the fees of a program, it would be advisable to study them and to depart from them only for good reason. It may be that a new program will be of a different quality or is designed for a different clientele. On the other hand, the factor of competitive pricing might enter in.

Determining Costs

Loose practices of cost accounting are common. Many course programs are operated as extensions of the larger programs of sponsoring organizations and use space and administrative services that are not charged directly to them. It is therefore practically impossible to make any kind of meaningful study of the comparative costs of operation of different adult-education programs. This practice also makes it difficult for the sponsoring organization to arrive at any accurate estimate of the cost of operating a program.

Good business practice requires that the budget of an adult-education program include its prorated share of such institutionwide costs as building operation, administrative services, and other overhead items.

Sources of Income Other Than Tuition

In actual practice, adult-education programs are rather heavily subsidized. Some of the chief sources of support in addition to tuition income are as follows:

1. *Federal funds* for programs sponsored by federal agencies and for the subsidizing of such local programs as agricultural extension.

2. *State funds* directly supporting such state-supported programs as university extension and indirectly supporting local public-school programs through legislative grants.

3. *Public-school funds,* limited usually to the support of public-school programs.

4. *Industrial funds.* These are used in three ways: a) to support programs sponsored by industries for their own personnel; b) to subsidize nonindustrial programs through contributions; and c) to pay the tuition charges in whole or in part for the enrollment of their own personnel in programs in educational institutions. Many community agencies receive generous support from industries whose workers they serve.

5. *Community funds and private contributors.* A willingness has been shown on the part of many community chests and private contributors to support adult-education programs when they can demonstrate that they are providing valuable service to the community.

6. *Grants from foundations* for research projects, publications, and experimental programs.

7. *Profits from the sale of books and materials.* In larger programs this may be a worthwhile source of income. Many adult educators feel, however, that they should supply books and materials at cost.

While it may be desirable as a general goal for adult-education programs to become self-supporting, it is unwise in most cases for a new program to be started without some source of support other than tuition. The process of building up a new clientele requires investment. Few programs have achieved a balanced budget during the first year or two of their existence. Probably the most common method of obtaining this additional support among private organizations is to estimate the amount of subsidy that will be required during the first year and then to conduct a well-planned finance campaign to raise the required amount from private contributors.

Payment Practices

Good will can be made or lost in the financial relationships an organization establishes with its participants. If policies regarding payments are too lenient, they are likely to leave an impression of carelessness and poor administration. If they are too hard and inflexible, they are likely to give an organization the stigma of commercialism. As in most things, the golden mean is probably best, though not always easy to achieve.

Whatever financial rules are finally decided on should be stated clearly and circulated conspicuously, in order that the chances of misunderstandings are reduced to a minimum. Even then, the program director should be prepared for a small proportion of people who will demand special favors and refuse to abide by the rules.

Deferred Payments

The practice of permitting students to pay their tuition charges over an extended period of time may add to the convenience of many students and reduce the economic barrier to their enrollment, but it involves a number of dangers and disadvantages. It complicates the accounting system required and involves unpleasantness in the collecting of overdue bills. It may encourage marginal participants to encumber themselves with debt when they should really be helped with scholarships. Some adult educators claim that the percentage of drop-outs among students making deferred payments is much greater than that among students who have paid in advance.

The practice regarding deferred payments is largely determined by the size of tuition charges. Most programs in which the tuition is fifty dollars or less make no provision for deferred payments, while a majority of those with tuition charges greater than fifty dollars have some kind of extended-payment plan. These plans usually require payments in two or three installments before the end of the term and make an accounting charge of one to three dollars for the privilege.

Single-Admission and Guest Passes

It is common practice to permit new students to attend single meetings of classes upon purchase of a single-admission ticket (which is taxable, by the way, whereas tuition is not). This practice is seriously questioned by some program directors because it encourages "shoppers" and adds greatly to the confusion of opening meetings. They maintain that if a good job is done in counseling new registrants, single admissions are not necessary. There may arise exceptional situations, however, in which observation of a class would be helpful in determining whether or not a certain student belongs in it. In this case, it may be desirable simply to issue a guest pass with no charge.

When single-admission tickets are sold, the amount paid can usually be credited toward the course tuition if the course has not reached its quota.

Refunds

Refunds are so annoying that it is becoming general practice to have a flat norefund policy. Even the hardest-headed program directors find it almost impossible, however, not to grant special exceptions in the case of authenticated disability or removal from the city. One way to ameliorate the effect of a rigid no-refund policy somewhat is to grant certificates of credit, enabling the student who wishes to drop a certain course to apply the money paid on it to any other course within a specified period, usually one year. This alternative has gone a long way in preserving good will. It is always understood, of course, that refunds will be granted in full when courses are discontinued by the organization.

Transfers

Most organizations are very liberal about allowing students to transfer from one course to another, provided the quota for the second course has not been filled and provided the transfer is requested within a reasonable time after the beginning of the term. Special procedures must be established for transfers, since registration and financial records will have to be changed.

Scholarships

Most adult-education programs, especially if their tuition charges are relatively high, make some kind of provision for the granting of full or part scholarships to individuals who would otherwise be barred from the programs. It is general practice either to set aside a certain amount in the budget or to obtain special contributions for this purpose. The conditions under which scholarships are to be granted should be clearly stated by the policy-making committee.

The financial policies of the Cambridge Center for Adult Education, as described in the "General Information" page of its catalog reproduced in Appendix I, Exhibit I-19, represent a moderate position on this complex issue.

For Your Continuing Inquiry . . .

Regarding Administration

Craig, Robert L. *Training and Development Handbook.* 2nd ed. New York: McGraw-Hill, 1976.

Eble, Kenneth E. *The Art of Administration: A Guide for Academic Administrators.* San Francisco: Jossey-Bass, 1978.

Gross, Bertram M. *Organizations and Their Managing.* New York: The Free Press, 1968.

Hicks, Herbert G. *The Management of Organizations.* New York: McGraw-Hill, 1972.

Hoppe, W. A. (ed.). *Policies and Practices in Evening Colleges, 1969.* New York: Scarecrow Press, 1969.

Knowles, Asa S. (ed.). *Handbook of College and University Administration.* Vols. I and II. New York: McGraw-Hill, 1970.

Shaw, Nathan. *Administration of Continuing Education.* Washington, D.C.: National Association for Public Continuing and Adult Education, 1969.

Regarding Recruiting and Training Instructors and Leaders

Conroy, Barbara. *Library Staff Development and Continuing Education: Principles and Practices.* Littleton, Col.: Libraries Unlimited, 1978.

Freedman, Mervin (ed.). *Facilitating Faculty Development.* New Directions for Higher Education, No. 1. San Francisco: Jossey-Bass, 1973.

Gaff, Jerry G. *Toward Faculty Renewal: Advances in Faculty, Instructional, and Organizational Development.* San Francisco: Jossey-Bass, 1975.

Harris, Ben M., and Bessent, Wailand. *Inservice Education: A Guide to Better Practice.* Englewood Cliffs, N.J.: Prentice-Hall, 1969.

Hei, Harold; Sweet, David; and Carlberg, R. Judson. *Professional Development through Growth Contracts: Handbook.* Wehnham, Mass.: Gordon College, 1979.

Kaslow, Florence, et al. *Supervision, Consultation, and Staff Training in the Helping Professions.* San Francisco: Jossey-Bass, 1977.

Kirkpatrick, Donald L. *A Practical Guide for Supervisory Training and Development.* Reading, Mass.: Addison-Wesley, 1971.

Leslie, David W. (ed.). *Employing Part-Time Faculty.* New Directions for Institutional Research, No. 18. San Francisco: Jossey-Bass, 1978.

Miller, Harry G., and Verduin, John R. *The Adult Educator: A Handbook for Staff Development.* Houston: Gulf Publishing Co., 1979.

O'Bannion, Terry (ed.). *Developing Staff Potential.* New Directions for Community Colleges, No. 19. San Francisco: Jossey-Bass, 1977.

Yarrington, Roger (ed.). *Educational Opportunity for All: New Staff for New Students.* Washington, D.C.: American Association of Junior and Community Colleges, 1973.

Regarding Managing Facilities and Procedures

Alford, Harold J. *Continuing Education in Action.* New York: John Wiley & Sons, 1968.

Birrin, Faber. *Light, Color, and Environment.* New York: Van Nostrand-Reinhold Co., 1969.

Castaldi, Basil. *Creative Planning of Educational Facilities.* Chicago: Rand McNally, 1969.

Creating a Climate for Adult Learning. Washington, D.C.: Adult Education Association of the U.S.A., 1959.

Dale, Edgar. *Building a Learning Environment.* Bloomington, Ind.: Phi Delta Kappa, 1972.

David, Thomas G., and Wright, Benjamin D. (eds.). *Learning Environments.* Chicago: University of Chicago Press, 1975.

Meyer, Marshal, et al. *Environments and Organizations.* San Francisco: Jossey-Bass, 1978.

Moos, Rudolph H. *Evaluating Educational Environments: Procedures, Measures, Findings, and Policy Implications.* San Francisco: Jossey-Bass, 1979.

White, Sally. *Physical Criteria for Adult Learning Environments.* Washington, D.C.: Adult Education Association of the U.S.A., 1972.

Regarding Counseling

Arbeiter, Solomon, et al. *Telephone Counseling for Home-Based Adults.* Princeton, N.J.: College Board Publications, 1978.

Career Education Counseling and Guidance for Adults. Portland, Ore.: Northwest Regional Educational Laboratory, 1974.

Jeffer, Frances C. *Guidelines for an Information and Counseling Service for Older Persons.* Durham, N.C.: Center for the Study of Aging and Human Development, Duke University Medical Center, 1970.

Loughary, John W., and Ripley, Theresa M. *Helping Others Help Themselves: A Guide to Counseling Skills.* New York: McGraw-Hill, 1979.

Malone, Violet M., and Diller, Mary Ann. *The Guidance Function and Counseling Roles in an Adult Education Program.* Washington, D.C.: National Association for Public Continuing and Adult Education, 1978.

Matthews, Esther E. *Counseling Girls and Women Over the Life Span.* Washington, D.C.: National Vocational Guidance Association, 1972.

Schlossberg, Nancy K., et al. *Perspectives on Counseling Adults: Issues and Skills.* Monterey, Cal.: Brooks/Cole, 1978.

Thoroman, E. C. *The Vocational Counseling of Adults and Young Adults.* Boston: Houghton Mifflin, 1968.

Ways and Means of Strengthening Information and Counseling Services for Adult Learners. Los Angeles: University of Southern California College of Continuing Education, 1977.

Regarding Promotion and Public Relations

Barton, David W., Jr. (ed.). *Marketing Higher Education.* New Directions for Higher Education, No. 21. San Francisco: Jossey-Bass, 1978.

Dapper, Gloria. *Public Relations for Educators.* New York: Macmillan, 1964.

Regarding Budgeting and Financing

Carlson, Daryl E., et al. *A Framework for Analyzing Post-Secondary Education Financing Policies.* Washington, D.C.: Government Printing Office, 1974.

Chambers, M. M. *Higher Education: Who Pays? Who Gains? Financing Education Beyond the High School.* Danville, Ill.: Interstate Printers, 1968.

Kidd, J. R. *Financing Continuing Education.* New York: Scarecrow Press, 1962.

Lombardi, John. *Managing Finances in Community Colleges.* San Francisco: Jossey-Bass, 1973.

Robins, Gerald B. *Understanding the College Budget.* Athens, Ga.: Institute of Higher Education, University of Georgia, 1973.

10
Evaluating Comprehensive Programs

Confronting a Sacred Cow

Nothing in all the practice of educators in general and of adult educators in particular has produced more feelings of guilt, inadequacy, and frustration than evaluation. But, to put it as bluntly as I know how, *I think that evaluation has become a much overemphasized sacred cow.* Furthermore, I think that this very overemphasis has caused an underproduction of practical, feasible, and artistic evaluation in terms of program review and improvement.

First, regarding overemphasis. Pick up almost any book on training or adult education and you will find statements like these.

From the down-to-earth field of agricultural extension:

> When attempts are made to educate a person, responsibility is taken for making changes in a human being. This is the highest level of responsibility in our society because people are considered important. Because of this, teachers should want to evaluate their work, not hesitate to do so. . . . They should want also to evaluate their efforts in a scientific manner. . . . Being scientific in an approach to problems and to evaluation of them keeps one from seeing only what one wants to see. This latter attitude, very strong in most people, is one of the greatest barriers to useful evaluation. Following strict rules prevents this attitude from governing the process that is used.[1]

An even sterner exhortation to observe the rigors of science from adult-education professors:

> Adequate and meaningful evaluation of adult education involves rigorous social scientific research procedures to develop and test a variety of instruments for measurement that are suited to the infinitely numerous and varied objectives which characterize adult education. Anything less than the most rigorous scientific research is of lesser value. . . . It is better not to evaluate at all than to do so unwisely and ineptly.[2]

---

[1] Laurel K. Sabrosky, "Evaluation," H. C. Sanders (ed.), *The Cooperative Extension Service* (Englewood Cliffs, N.J.: Prentice-Hall, 1966), p. 342.

[2] Coolie Verner and Alan Boothe, *Adult Education* (Washington, D.C.: Center for Applied Research in Education, 1964), p. 95.

A somewhat gentler critique from a public-school adult educator:

Evaluation is an essential and inescapable part of the process of administering an adult program. Every intelligent administrator constantly makes value judgments about the things and the results he seems to get. . . . Too often he relies on snap judgments based upon limited evidence; no systematic procedure is used, and no references to goals or objectives are made.[3]

From business and industry, the threat of an impending day of reckoning:

Managers, needless to say, expect their manufacturing and sales departments to yield a good return and will go to great lengths to find out whether they have done so. When it comes to training, however, they may expect the return—but rarely do they make a like effort to measure the actual results. Fortunately for those in charge of training programs, this philanthropic attitude has come to be taken for granted. There is certainly no guarantee, however, that it will continue, and training directors might be well advised to take the initiative and evaluate their programs before the day of reckoning arrives.[4]

Finally, from my own writing at an earlier stage of development (1950):

Informal adult education, as carried on by thousands of organizations of many kinds, has produced important and lasting results in helping our people and our society to improve themselves. How good a job has been done cannot be described specifically, because until now those in adult education have been too busy *doing* to give much time to evaluating. This is excusable in a movement that is in its infancy, but adult education is coming of age.[5]

Is not the cumulative effect of these statements the welling up in you of a deep sense of guilt and inadequacy?

What this all means, as I now see it, is that we all know that theoretically it is desirable—in fact, it would be wonderful—to be able to demonstrate with hard data (collected, quantified, and tested for significance by the most rigorous statistical procedures) what our programs are accomplishing. But we also know that: 1) human behavior is too complicated, and the number of variables affecting it are too numerous, for us ever to be able to "prove" that it is our program alone that produces desired changes; 2) the social sciences have not yet produced the "rigorous research procedures" and measurement instruments for getting the kind of hard data required for evaluating many of the subtle and more important outcomes of a comprehensive program of adult education; 3) the kind of intensive and scientific evaluation these statements are advocating requires investments of time and money that many institutional policymakers are unwilling to make simply to document the worth of training which they can *see* is valuable; and 4) adult education is, unlike youth education, an open system in which participation is voluntary, so that the worth of a program is more readily tested by the degree of persistence and satisfaction of its clientele.

These practical obstacles do not lead me to the other extreme end of the spec-

[3]John H. Thatcher, "Evaluation," National Association for Public School Adult Education, *Public School Adult Education* (Washington, D.C.: National Association, 1963), p. 175.

[4]Daniel M. Goodacre III, "The Experimental Evaluation of Management Training: Principles and Practice," *Personnel*, B. F. Goodrich Co., May, 1957.

[5]Malcolm S. Knowles, *Informal Adult Education* (New York: Association Press, 1950), p. 252.

trum—a position taken by a national leader of our field in 1951 (a position he would probably not take today):

> To a major extent adult education stands on its own merits. It responds to changing needs of society to whatever extent people can articulate those needs clearly in educational terms. In the final analysis there is no need for elaborate schemes of evaluation of adult education in the United States, or in any nation in which adult education responds to the eternal search by individual human beings for redeeming life from insignificance. It must add significance to the life of the adult momentarily or permanently, or it does not continue.[6]

My own position is that it is good to hold out the goal and vision of deep, continuous, and scientific evaluation; but that great damage is done by raising the expectation that it is feasible and even perhaps desirable now in every situation. The difference between a goal and a promise is a subtle one, but I think we must work at making that difference clear. When we promise what we cannot yet deliver, we create resentment in others and self-punishment in ourselves, as is partly illustrated by a survey of federal training personnel:

> Without exception training officers and management officials expressed a strong belief in the efficacy of and necessity for evaluation. Also without exception they expressed a belief that not enough was done and what was done was inadequate to the purpose. The strong convictions, coupled with a feeling of ineffectiveness, created conditions ranging from vague uneasiness to deep-seated concern about what could be done.[7]

Similar sentiments were revealed in a survey of techniques being used by business, industry, and government in the evaluation of their training programs, in which it was found that:

> Approximately 77 percent of the responding organizations measured reaction to determine how the trainees feel about the program . . . 50 percent attempted to measure learning that takes place in the classroom . . . 54 percent attempted to evaluate their programs in terms of changes in on-the-job behavior (but only twelve firms indicated that they measured behavior before the program as well as after; only one used a control as well as an experimental group, and only two did any statistical analysis) . . . 45 percent attempted to measure the results achieved from the programs.[8]

The recurrent theme in the many discussions on evaluation in which I have participated at adult-education meetings across the country has been the frustration we experience over being told (and telling ourselves) we ought to be doing more scientific evaluation than we know we can do.

If any of my readers are at this point feeling that I may be exaggerating or caricaturing the situation regarding evaluation of programs, I urge you now to turn to Appendix J, Exhibit J-1, in which one of the most cogent analyses of the issues to appear in our literature, by an evaluation expert who has devoted years to evaluating University of Wisconsin Extension programs, is presented.

---

[6]Paul L. Essert, *Creative Leadership of Adult Education* (Englewood Cliffs, N.J.: Prentice-Hall, 1951), p. 161.
[7]Henry J. Duel, "A Staff Report on Evaluation of Training and Education in Federal Agencies," *Self and Service Enrichment Through Federal Training* (Washington, D.C.: U.S. Civil Service Commission, 1967), p. 424.
[8]R. F. Catalanello and D. L. Kirkpatrick, "Evaluating Training Programs—The State of the Art." Reprinted by special permission from the May, 1968, issue of the *Training and Development Journal*. Copyright © 1968 by the American Society for Training and Development.

Conflicting Values in Evaluation

Clearly, what we are confronting in this controversy over evaluation is a conflict of values. At one end of the spectrum is an emphasis on the values of control, precision, "proof," hard data, "science"—values of high priority to the Taylorian[9] efficiency proponents, behaviorist psychologists, experimental researchers, and cost accountants. At the other end of the spectrum is an emphasis on the values of self-actualization, artistic intuition, free play of natural forces, and creative ambiguity—values of high priority to the humanistic management theorists and psychologists, politically oriented administrators, lazy practitioners, overworked practitioners, and artistic practitioners.

Obviously, both sets of values are present and appreciated in our culture, with one end of the spectrum or the other being given greater weight by different individuals, different organizations, and different subcultures at different times. So a position somewhere near the middle of the spectrum, such as is suggested by this statement in the same report on federal training, is probably most functional for most adult educators:

> Certainly within the realm of present knowledge there are many outcomes of training and education which cannot be effectively assessed. Time is only one of the many factors which complicate the problem. Is the resultant of training and education applied immediately, in one year, in five years, in ten years? However, because the full impact of training and education cannot be assessed, this does not mean we should ignore that which is already measurable through known techniques.[10]

Fundamentally, however, the issue as to how much and what kind of evaluation given adult educators will engage in will be resolved by reference to their philosophy of education—indeed, their very definition of education. If they define it as a process of educating a person, of taking responsibility "for making changes in a human being," as it was defined in one of the preceding quotations, then they do certainly incur an obligation to measure as precisely as possible what they are doing to that person and subject their findings to ethical review. Their evaluation will also be greatly concerned with efficiency—with obtaining data to determine whether or not they are producing maximum change in the shortest possible time at the least cost. Their dominant theme will be quantification.

But if they define education as a process of facilitating and providing resources for self-directed inquiry and self-development, they incur an obligation to involve the participants in collecting data that will enable them to assess the effectiveness of the program in helping them accomplish their objectives. Their dominant theme will be involvement.

The philosophical issue here is essentially the conflict between the assumptions of traditional pedagogy and the assumptions of modern andragogy. Since the position taken in this book is clearly the latter, let us examine the purposes, procedures, and tools of evaluation as applied to programs of adult self-development.

[9]Frederick W. Taylor, founder of "scientific management."
[10]Henry J. Duel, op. cit., p. 429.

Purposes of Evaluation

One of the problems in discussing evaluation is the need to treat it as a single entity—as we have done so far in this chapter—when in actual practice, "evaluation" is a term used to describe several different processes for several different purposes.

Stufflebeam proposes that evaluation has two purposes. The first is *accountability*—justification of the value of the program to employers, sponsors, the clientele, or society. This he calls summative evaluation. The second purpose is to improve *decision making* by providing information to the program managers that will enable them to improve the quality of the program. This he calls formative evaluation. Both types of evaluation must take into account four elements of the program: goals, design, process, and product. His basic framework is illustrated in Exhibit 27.

Exhibit 27

STUFFLEBEAM'S EVALUATION SCHEMA[11]

	Goals	Design	Process	Product
Accountability (Summative)				
Decision making (Formative)				

Kirkpatrick sees evaluation as consisting of four types, each of which is one step in a total evaluation process: 1) *reaction evaluation,* which ideally takes place periodically during a program and provides data to the program managers about how the participants are feeling about the program—data that can be used to make changes in design, methods, personnel, facilities, and the like, as the program moves along; 2) *learning evaluation,* which provides data, ideally through pre- and posttests, about what knowledge, skills, attitudes, and values have been acquired by the participants; 3) *behavior evaluation,* which provides data—also ideally through pre- and postmeasures—to show what changes in actual performance have been produced; and 4) *results evaluation,* which provides data about the tangible results of the program in terms of reduced cost, improved quality, increased productivity, lowered accident rates, and the like.[12]

As I see it, however, with the focus in this book on the delivery of the highest possible quality of educational services to adult learners, program evaluation has two principal purposes: 1) improvement of organizational operation, including such aspects as its planning process, structure, decision-making procedures, personnel, physical facilities, finances, recruitment, training, public relations, and administrative management; and 2) improvement of the program, including such aspects as objectives, clientele, methods and techniques, materials, and quality of learning outcomes. But evaluation can also be used for such secondary purposes as defense against attack, justification for expansion, support for the status quo, boosting of morale, personnel

---

[11]Daniel Stufflebeam, "Evaluation As a Community Education Process," *Community Education Journal,* V, 2 (March, 1975), pp. 7–12.
[12]Donald L. Kirkpatrick, "Evaluation of Training," in Robert L. Craig (ed.), *Training and Development Handbook* (New York: McGraw-Hill, 1976), pp. 18–27.

appraisal and promotion, and institutional reorganization. Concerning these secondary purposes, Kempfer issues this warning:

> The basic purpose of evaluation is to stimulate growth and improvement. Whatever other worthy purposes exist are only facets of the all-inclusive effort to assess present conditions as a basis for achieving better ones. Evaluation that does not lead to improved practice is sterile.
>
> An attempt to appraise a program by comparing it with another, or with several others, perverts the basic purpose of evaluation and usually leads to unsound conclusions. . . . Evaluation intended to show the effectiveness of an operation in order to win budget support, to justify program expansion, or to defend the current program can easily fall into the traps of program comparison.[13]

If we reject the validity of evaluating a program according to external criteria, such as comparison with other programs or "objective" standards established for other educational enterprises (such as by college accrediting agencies), as Kempfer quite properly counsels us to do, we are left with a program's own objectives as the only legitimate basis for evaluation. The point at which program evaluation starts, therefore, and the point to which it continuously returns, is each program's objectives. As described in Chapter 7, these are of two types: 1) operational objectives, and 2) educational objectives. Let us then explore the processes and tools for assessing the extent to which these two types of objectives are being achieved.

The Evaluation Process

The evaluation process consists of several apparently simple steps: 1) formulating the questions you want answered (or establishing the criteria, yardsticks, or benchmarks); 2) collecting the data that will enable you to answer those questions; 3) analyzing the data and interpreting what they mean as answers to the questions raised; and 4) modifying your plans, operation, and program in the light of your findings. But this is not merely a mechanical and automatic step-taking process; decisions have to be made repeatedly as to when to evaluate what and who should be in on the evaluation.

When to Evaluate

Informal evaluation is actually going on all the time. Some kinds of judgments are being made continuously about the worth of a program. Participants are constantly making complaints or paying compliments. Teachers and leaders are never without feelings about how well or how poorly things are going. The directors of programs are sensitive both to these judgments and to their own feelings. This continuous but almost unconscious evaluation results in many on-the-spot improvements, provided the staff has developed skill in nondefensive listening. But it does not serve the same purpose as periodic, systematically planned evaluation.

Probably most well-run programs have some form of feedback from participants and instructors at the end of a program unit—each series, each term, each semester, or each year. This feedback typically taps information about a sample of both operational

---

[13]Homer Kempfer, *Adult Education* (New York: McGraw-Hill, 1955), p. 399.

and educational objectives and tends to produce what in the federal agencies is referred to as "happiness data." On the whole, this kind of feedback is most useful in providing a general sense of trends in morale and satisfaction, but it frequently turns up specific and practical suggestions for improvement in the general program or in specific activities; and it may reveal problem points that call for deeper evaluation.

In actual practice, really serious evaluation probably most often takes place when crises are imminent or occur. When the drop-out rate goes up or enrollments fall sharply, the resources are likely to be quickly found for reassessing the extent to which the program is meeting the needs of the participants. When the budget starts running a deficit, energy is likely to be made available for a comprehensive evaluation of operational efficiency. The ideal, of course, is to have a continuous evaluation process in operation that would detect trouble spots before they reach crisis proportions. But real life is not that ideal, and so evaluation-by-crisis is an actuality.

Usually, in the process of planning the next year's program it is possible to identify the half-dozen or so aspects of the program that it would be most useful to subject to systematic evaluation, and to focus the organization's evaluation energies on these focal points. This approach of reasonableness is the one followed by the Cooperative Extension Service, as explained in the following:

> . . . no attempt is made in Extension Service work to evaluate all educational efforts every year. The most efficient use of time spent on evaluation is in evaluating during a given year a limited number of educational and organizational objectives, teaching methods, and situations. Usually, one or two of each fills the time which should be devoted to organized evaluation. These evaluations are carried out carefully, through the reporting stage. Throughout the year, the remainder of Extension work is continually being evaluated informally. The most important observations and findings are recorded. [14]

Who Should Evaluate?

Every person who is in a position to make any kind of judgment about a program should be brought into the evaluation process in some way. One or more of these groups are usually involved, depending upon the type of program:

The participants. The judgments of students, group members, or audience participants can be obtained from them individually through interviews or questionnaires. Or they may be funneled through a representative council.

The leaders or instructors. Those who are directly responsible for the growth of the participants are, next to the participants themselves, in the best position to judge the results achieved. These judgments also can be obtained individually through interviews or written forms, or through group meetings of the faculty or leaders' corps.

The program director and staff. Those who are responsible for the administration of a program are in a key position to observe the results of the program as a whole. They will naturally make judgments of their own and report them in staff meetings, committee meetings, and written reports. In addition to making their own judgments, however, the staff members will initiate and facilitate the collection of judgments from all other sources and will compile them into a composite evaluation.

The directing committee. Because it is responsible for establishing objectives and

---

[14]Laurel K. Sabrosky, op. cit., p. 350.

policies, the directing committee is particularly concerned with evaluation. If it is to be in a position to determine new objectives and policies intelligently, it should have the opportunity both to observe results directly and to examine the judgments from all other sources.

Outside experts. It is frequently desirable to call in specialists from the universities, coordinating councils, and other sources to assist in the evaluation process. Controlled observations of classroom procedure by graduate students from teacher-training institutions have often yielded valuable information. Many kinds of organizations are required to submit information to higher authorities, such as state and national headquarters, community councils, and contributors of funds, in order that these authorities may make evaluations of their own.

Supervisory and management personnel. In the case of inservice education programs, such as in industry, government agencies, hospitals, and voluntary agencies, the line supervisors of the trainees are primary sources of data and of judgment in an evaluation process.

Community representatives. In programs that are serving the general public, especially in the format of community development, spokesmen of major community interests are an essential resource.

What the best mix from these several population groupings would be for a given evaluation of administrative operations would probably best be served by representatives of the first four groups; whereas a comprehensive assessment of the adequacy of a program in serving a community would have to involve representatives of all groups.

Many program directors have learned the hard way that it is a mistake to perceive these populations merely as sources of data for the use of others in making an evaluative judgment. It is crucial to their ego-involvement and to the validity of the results that they be included also in the process of analyzing the data and interpreting and applying the findings.

Formulating Evaluative Questions

The starting point of all research is a good question that can be answered by data. And since evaluation is a form of research, I prefer the formulating of evaluative questions as the starting point of the process rather than, as some other writers prefer, the formulation of criteria, benchmarks, or yardsticks. A good evaluative question implies the criteria by which the data will be judged.

Listed below are some sample evaluative questions, but I want to emphasize that these lists are stimulative rather than exhaustive in intent. Indeed, a good deal of the value of engaging in an evaluative process comes from involving key people in figuring out for themselves the important questions to ask about a particular program at a given time.

In Terms of Operational Objectives

Operational objectives tend to be more implicit than explicit. For example, I do not believe I have ever seen "to achieve a balanced budget" in writing in a list of instructional objectives, but everyone understands that it exists. Perhaps one of the bonus benefits of formulating evaluative questions is that many of these implicit objectives are brought to the explicit level.

Using the system of categories on the basis of which this book is organized, the following kinds of questions might be asked in relation to operational objectives.

Concerning Organizational Climate and Structure

Objective: to maintain a dynamic policy base for adult education in our institution.

Evaluative Questions: Does the present policy statement convey a clear commitment to adult education? Does it define purposes relevantly to contemporary needs and conditions? Does it accord adequate status and influence to the adult-education function? Has it been reviewed by the policymakers within a reasonable period of time?

Objective: to assure participation of all relevant parties in policymaking and management of the adult-education operation.

Evaluative Questions: What would be the ideal committee structure for this enterprise? Where does the present structure fall short of this ideal? Are all committees' functions clearly stated and understood by their members? Do the committees function well as groups—do they accept responsibility as groups, think cooperatively, and make decisions efficiently? Are the individual committee members personally involved in the organization—do they subscribe to its objectives, do they give active service? Are staff services to committees adequate? Are notices of meetings sent in time? Are adequate records kept? Is there follow-up on decisions? Are the committees working on significant matters? Are they being challenged to be creative? Are the committees' memberships representative of all parties with a stake in the program?

Objective: to provide staff service to the program at a high level of excellence.

Evaluative Questions: Is the staff personnel adequate in number to the needs of the program? Are all necessary staff services performed? Is there adequate differentiation and yet flexibility in role definitions? Is there a spirit of teamwork? Are staff members involving participants and committee members in sharing responsibilities and rewards imaginatively? Are there good working conditions, adequate salaries, and sound personnel policies and practices? Are staff members paying adequate attention to their own continuing self-development? Are they good role models for continuing learners?

Objective: to maintain an institutional atmosphere that is conducive to adult learning.

Evaluative Questions: Are participants treated with warmth, dignity, and respect at all points of contact? Is the rich experience of participants being made use of to the full extent possible in policymaking, planning, management, learning, and evaluation? Do we know in what ways the participants feel they are being treated as more or less adult in their experience with us?

Concerning Assessment of Needs and Interests

Objective: to maintain an up-to-date inventory of the individual needs and interests, organizational needs, and community needs our program should be serving.

Evaluative Questions: Have surveys of these three types of needs (and interests) been made within a reasonable period? Is some individual or group taking responsibility for sensing changing needs and interests from contacts with community leaders, the mass media, and professional literature? Are the techniques we are using for the collection and analysis of data about needs and interests keeping up with advancing survey technology? Do the assessed needs include predicted future needs as well as identified present needs?

Concerning Definition of Purposes and Objectives

Objective: to maintain an up-to-date statement of purposes that will provide direction, coherence, and relevance to the program.

Evaluative Questions: Has the present statement of purpose been reviewed within a reasonable period of time? Does it delineate the role of adult education in the institution clearly? Does it specify the long-run goals and constituency clearly? Does it express a philosophy of education that is congruent with modern knowledge about adults as learners? Are the purposes significant and relevant in the light of contemporary conditions?

Objective: to develop and promulgate operational and educational objectives that provide clear guidance in current program development, operation, and evaluation.

Evaluative Questions: Have the objectives been reviewed within a reasonable period of time? Are they clearly related to assessed needs? Are they stated in terms of measurable outcomes? Are they known, understood, and accepted by policymakers, leaders and instructors, and participants?

Concerning Program Design

Objective: to maintain a sense of artistic quality in the program design.

Evaluative Questions: Is a sense of *line* provided by a dynamic theme, activity sequences, and time schedule? Does an interesting *space pattern* emerge from the rhythm of activities, varying depth of activities, control of size of activities, etc.? Is the *tone* of the program one of warmth, varying emphases, and personalization? Is the *color* of the program bright and warm, as conveyed by publicity materials, the arrangement and decoration of physical facilities, and the personnel? Is the *texture* of the program interesting, rich, and functional? Does the design make appropriate use of a variety of formats for learning? Does the program design have a sense of unity, balance, and integration?

Objective: to maintain a program that serves the purposes and meets the needs for which it was intended.

Evaluative Questions: Are the activities in the program design consistent with the institution's purposes? Do they achieve these purposes? Are the activities based on the stated objectives? Do they carry out these objectives? Is the program design adequate in scope and emphasis? Is the design flexible enough to adapt quickly to changing needs and conditions? Is provision made for participants to influence the program design?

Concerning Program Operation

Objective: to provide the highest quality faculty of leaders and instructors possible.

Evaluative Questions: Are the criteria of selection clear, adequate, and in keeping with principles of andragogy? Are they applied? Is compensation on a professional basis? Is it competitive with other institutions? Are new instructors and leaders given adequate orientation and individual coaching? Is adequate inservice training and supervision given the entire faculty? Do they perceive it as a program of continuing self-directed self-development? Is the performance of faculty members periodically assessed?

Objective: to provide physical facilities that make an environment conducive to adult learning.

Evaluative Questions: Are the meeting rooms adequate in number, size, flexibility, comfort, and attractiveness? Are leaders and instructors helped to arrange rooms for maximum informality and interaction? Are the lighting, ventilation, and storage facilities adequate? Are the physical facilities maintained in good condition? Is there adequate instructional equipment? Is it properly safeguarded and maintained in good condition? Is the faculty given sufficient help in using it well? Is provision made for the replacement or renewal of physical facilities before they deteriorate? Are the space and equipment used as close to capacity as is practicable? Are the office facilities adequate, attractive, and efficient?

Objective: to provide administrative services that facilitate the educational objectives of the program.

Evaluative Questions: Are the office services adequate in quantity and quality? Does correspondence get answered promptly? Is filing efficient? Are inquiries and registrations handled promptly, courteously, and with dignity? Are records accurate, as comprehensive as necessary, as simple as practicable, and accessible? Is adequate educational counseling service available to participants? Are participants given personalized attention during registration and opening sessions? Are veteran participants used as hosts and hostesses?

Objective: to provide promotion and public-relations services that will advance the objectives of the program.

Evaluative Questions: Is the desired clientele clearly defined? Is the present promotion program recruiting this clientele? Is the promotion campaign adequately planned and efficiently carried out? Do the promotion materials accurately reflect the quality and spirit of the program? Do they help to set the proper expectations and climate for learning? Are the various media being used appropriately and effectively? Are the results of the various elements of promotion evaluated adequately? Is the program being adequately interpreted to the public?

Objective: to provide adequate financial resources and procedures to maintain a high-quality program.

Evaluative Questions: Are the financial goals adequate and realistic in terms of the program's objectives? Are the program goals reflected accurately in the financial budget? Does the budget provide sufficient guidance, flexibility, and control? Are adequate financial procedures and records maintained? Are the financial policies clear, realistic, and in keeping with the nature of the clientele and the spirit of the institution? Are all possible sources of income being drawn upon? Is the financial experience of the program being adequately reported and interpreted?

Concerning Program Evaluation

Objective: to obtain information that will promote continuous program improvement.

Evaluative Questions: Are the purposes of any proposed evaluation clear and understood by all parties who will be involved? Have plans for evaluation been made as part of the program-planning process? Have realistic priorities been set that will result in the most important improvements? Have all parties who will be affected by evaluation been represented in planning it? Have the most efficient and reliable means for getting the desired data been used? Are the data being adequately analyzed and the findings being fed back into the planning process? Are those from whom data were obtained being kept informed about the findings and the use that is being made of them?

In Terms of Educational Objectives

Educational objectives always define behavioral changes an educational experience is designed to help participants achieve. In youth education the focus tends to be on broad, general objectives:

Attaining maximum intellectual growth and development.
Becoming culturally oriented and integrated.
Maintaining and improving physical and mental health.
Becoming economically competent.[15]

or:

The development of effective ways of thinking.
The acquisition of important information, ideas, and principles.
The development of effective work habits and skills.
The development of increased sensitivity to social problems and aesthetic experiences.
The inculcation of social rather than selfish attitudes.
The development of appreciation of literature, art, and music.
The development of increasing range of worthwhile and mature interests.
Increased personal-social adjustment.
Improved physical health.
The formulation and clarification of a philosophy of life.[16]

The objectives of each unit of learning, such as a fifth-grade unit in arithmetic or a tenth-grade course in social studies, are derived from and expressly geared to contribute to the achievement of these general objectives. Evaluation of the extent to which educational objectives are being achieved, therefore, is mainly across units—indeed, across school systems. Nationally standardized tests of verbal ability, mechanical ability, subject knowledge, academic achievement, quantitative ability, social adjustment, occupational and leisure interests, social attitudes, critical thinking ability, and a variety of other attributes are administered to students at every grade level to assess the extent to which the school's objectives are being realized. Of course, tests are administered in most individual units as well, but more for the purpose of giving the students a grade and evaluating their readiness to be promoted to the next-higher level than for the purpose of evaluating the effectiveness of the course in accomplishing its objectives.

In adult education the situation is the reverse. There are few objectives that are programwide. In fact, there are just two kinds of general objectives that I think are (or should be) universal to all adult-education programs. One is to facilitate the continuous maturing of every participant along the dimensions illustrated in Chapter 3, such as from dependence toward autonomy, from passivity toward activity, from subjectivity toward objectivity, from ignorance toward enlightenment, and so on. The other is to help the learners continuously to augment their ability to engage in self-directed inquiry. Every unit in every adult-education program, regardless of its particular goals, should contribute to these two general objectives. I do not know of any systematic attempt ever being made to evaluate a program in terms of its accomplishment of these objectives, but I believe that such an evaluation would be the deepest measure of a program's worth, and I hope that someone soon will be challenged to develop and test procedures and instruments for doing it.[17]

---

[15] Will French et al., *Behavioral Goals of General Education in High School* (New York: Russell Sage Foundation, 1957), p. 88.

[16] E. R. Smith and R. W. Tyler, *Appraising and Recording Student Progress* (New York: Harper, 1942), p. 18.

[17] An instrument that was developed for the purpose of assessing readiness for self-directed learning might also be used to measure changes in that readiness. It is the "Self-Directed Learning Readiness Scale" by Dr. Lucy M. Guglielmino, 734 Marble Way, Boca Raton, Florida 33432.

As it stands now, the most feasible way available to most of us for the evaluation of the educational outcomes of a program to be accomplished is by summing up the separate evaluations of the individual learning units. A heavy burden, therefore, is on individual instructors and activity leaders to be skillful and conscientious in negotiating clear behavioral objectives with their students, getting reliable baseline data (as through diagnostic exercises) on the level of performance of the students at the beginning of the experience, and then getting good data (as through rediagnosis procedures) on level of performance at the end of the experience (or, even better, after the learning has been applied in the field). Specific techniques to help instructors in this endeavor are discussed below and in Chapter 11.

Methods of Data Collection

A wide variety of methods can be used for obtaining the information necessary to evaluate. Most of these methods are geared to retrieve the personal judgments of people, and therefore are subject to error, bias, and difference in outlook. Many instruments of evaluation are designed to measure only certain kinds of results. A thoroughgoing evaluation, therefore, requires the use of a combination of methods.

Obtaining the Reactions of Participants

The opinions and feelings of the participants in a program, while they are completely subjective, are a primary source of information on which to base an evaluation. Experienced leaders recognize that in almost any group of people there is a certain proportion of chronic complainers to whom nothing is satisfactory, as well as a certain proportion of Pollyannas to whom everything is wonderful.

One of the most helpful concepts for those who have to weigh judgments is that of the *curve of normal distribution* (or of *normal probability*). This curve describes the probable distribution of phenomena and traits in an unselected population—or according to pure chance. It indicates that about 34 percent of the cases (in terms of such characteristics as height and weight, or intelligence, or emotional adjustment, or almost any other physical or psychological trait) will fall within one standard deviation above or below the mean. Two standard deviations will mark off another 14 percent on each side of the mean, and three standard deviations, another 2 percent. A typical curve of normal distribution is illustrated in Exhibit 28.

While there are few situations in adult education in which the selection of participants is according to pure chance, there is a general tendency for the characteristics of

Exhibit 28

CURVE OF NORMAL DISTRIBUTION

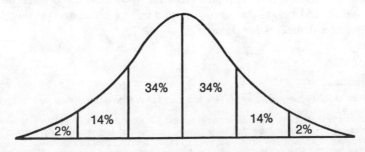

our participants to be grouped more or less as depicted by the curve of normal distribution. This being so, program directors do not become disturbed when they receive a normal number of negative reactions. Nor do they rejoice unduly when they receive a normal amount of praise. According to the curve of normal distribution, about 2 percent will be extremely negative and 2 percent will be extremely complimentary; about 14 percent will be fairly negative and 14 percent will be quite enthusiastic; and about 68 percent will be moderately positive. Thus, although conscientious program directors will respect the criticisms of the habitually negative people and will try to eliminate the causes of their discontent, they will not become alarmed until the proportion of criticism goes above 16 percent. This concept has made such a difference in my own state of mind as a practitioner that I call it my ulcer-saver.

Some practical methods for obtaining the judgments of the participants as to the value of the program are as follows:

1. *Interviews.* There are many opportunities for talking more or less informally with participants during office contacts, in the halls, and in the meeting rooms. Alert staff workers, leaders, and teachers can obtain valuable information by sounding out the participants on these occasions. In many instances there are opportunities for more formal and deeper interviews through personal counseling activities or through the use of highly structured interview schedules with a scientifically selected sample of participants. The advantage of this latter approach is the greater uniformity of the data that will be obtained and, therefore, the greater ease of analysis and interpretation.

2. *A representative council.* When it is possible to have group discussion by representatives of the various activities, a more comprehensive picture of how the participants feel about the program can be obtained. Usually such a council has planning and service functions in addition to responsibility for evaluating, so that its members are able to translate their ideas into action.

3. *Questionnaires.* Various kinds of questionnaires can be used for obtaining information from the participants, ranging from those seeking specific data about behavior to those seeking general opinions. As a rule, the more specific the questions are the more reliable the information will be, especially if they are directed at measuring actions rather than obtaining opinions. ("What things do you *do* as a result of your learning?" is likely to produce better answers than "What do you *think* you learned?")

Exhibit 29 illustrates a simple form that is used to detect the feeling tone of the participant at the end of each meeting. It gives the leader or instructor some clues as to how well the interest of the group is being maintained.

More complex types of questionnaires are illustrated in Exhibit J-2 in Appendix J. These forms are used in programs of organized courses and are distributed at the last meeting of each term.

Questionnaires have several limitations. They cannot be used too often without interfering with activity and arousing the resentment of the participants. They are probably most reliable when the name of the participant is not requested, but this anonymity prevents cross-checking. Their value depends largely on their phrasing, and great care must be exercised to make them clear, concise, and specific. There is always danger that the answers on questionnaires will be misinterpreted.

4. *Instructional procedures.* Many opportunities arise in the course of the teaching or leading of a group to obtain continuous evaluations by the group members. These opportunities range from more or less informal discussions (for which, incidentally, I find buzz groups most effective, since the individual source of an opinion remains anonymous) to more or less elaborate written course-evaluation forms.

Exhibit 29

END-OF-MEETING EVALUATION SLIP

ACTIVITY _____ Date _____

Would you give us just one minute of your time to let us know how you feel about tonight's meeting? It will help us in improving our program.
Please *circle* the phrase that best describes how you feel:

1. I think that in this session I learned
    a great deal   *quite a lot*   *some*   *a little*   *nothing*

2. On the whole, tonight's session was
    excellent   *pretty good*   *average*   *poor*   *no good*

3. I am leaving this meeting feeling
    enthusiastic   *encouraged*   *all right*   *disappointed*   *frustrated*

4. As of now, the activity interests me
    intensely   *quite a bit*   *somewhat*   *a little*   *not at all*

Comments:

Measuring Changes in Individuals

The final measure of the value of any educational program is, of course, the actual changes in behavior it helps the participants to accomplish. And this is where the complexity of human nature (as compared, for example, with rats or pigeons) causes so much frustration. For a person might "learn" a great deal (such as knowledge about the political-party system in the democratic process of government) and behave no differently in important respects (such as giving time, energy, and money to a political party). Program directors can easily be trapped into assuming that because they can demonstrate that students acquired substantial quantities of new knowledge (through before-and-after tests), there have been effective behavioral changes. Evaluators in adult education, therefore, cannot be satisfied with measuring changes in knowledge, understanding, attitude, skill, values, and interests; they have to be concerned with the transfer of these kinds of learnings to behavioral performance.

A further complication arises from the fact that the overt or primary objectives of a learning experience may not be the objectives that are really accomplished. Brunner et al. provide a classic example of this phenomenon:

> The French course may not teach a student enough French to buy a pack of cigarettes in Paris, much less allow him to read French classics, but it might meet other goals successfully. One of these might be improving "international understanding for peace," and who is to say this is a less important goal than learning French?[18]

Studies of the outcome of youth education indicate that the chief learning derived for some students from an English course was "to hate poetry," from a mathematics course "that I'm dumb about numbers," from a civics course "that politics is dirty," and from a music-appreciation course that "good music is boring."

---

[18]Edmund de S. Brunner, et al., *An Overview of Adult Education Research* (Washington, D.C.: Adult Education Association, 1959), p. 247.

These secondary outcomes or "deuterolearnings" may therefore be either positive or negative, and may well be the most important products of a learning experience—especially when related to the dimensions of maturation discussed in Chapter 3. An adequate evaluation of behavioral change will take them into account.

Methods available for obtaining data about behavioral changes include the following:

1. *Standardized tests.* An increasing number of national test publishers are developing tests at the adult level designed to get data about individuals that can be compared with national norms in many areas:

Subject knowledge (language, mathematics, fine arts, physical sciences, social sciences, biological sciences, and various occupational and professional fields)

Attitude characteristics

Academic achievement and general educational level

Aptitudes (verbal, quantitative, mechanical, vocational)

Interests (occupational, social, recreational)

Skills (verbal, computational, critical thinking, psychomotor, interpersonal, reading, etc.)

Through administration of appropriate tests before and after a learning experience, some data may be obtained that will provide clues as to changes that are taking place along these dimensions. But tests often smack of childhood schooling to adult learners, and so should be used with caution and preferably with the participants' full participation in the decision, administration, and analysis. Information concerning the sources of standardized tests is given in the references listed at the end of this chapter.

2. *Tailor-made tests.* Tests that are constructed specifically in terms of the objectives of a given learning experience will in many cases produce data more directly relevant to the behavioral changes for which that experience was designed. Traditionally, these tests have always been constructed by the teachers (or a curriculum committee of the faculty) and have been used most often to compare one student with another for the purpose of giving grades to the students. But they do not have to be used in such an antiandragogical way. The tests can be constructed for before-and-after administration so as to produce information for the students' own edification regarding relative gains they made in accomplishing the various objectives of the learning experience. And I have had generally successful experience in having the students construct their own tests, either for themselves or their fellow students, individually or in teams. Some guidelines for constructing tailor-made tests are suggested in references listed at the end of this chapter.

3. *Performance tests.* Probably the oldest form of testing—and the only one used in primitive societies—but one that is in the ascendancy in adult-education practice, is the construction of situations in which the participant actually performs a sample of the behaviors a given learning experience is concerned with. This may be a real situation, in which an actual work sample, such as operating a machine or carrying out a procedure, is performed and the performance is rated by observers, timed, or otherwise measured. Or it may be a simulated situation, in which conditions as much like those in "the real world" as possible are created for the demonstration of performance. Some fairly standardized simulation situations and materials are available, including critical-incident cases, business games, in-basket exercises, role-playing skits, and response-inviting audio or video tapes. These usually present situations that typically must be handled by supervisory and executive personnel in government, industry, educational institutions, and hospitals—such as interviewing, making decisions, delegating, giving instructions, and resolving conflicts. Sources of published simulation materials are given in the list of references at the end of this chapter. But simulation situations can readily be constructed by instructors and participants, together or separately, for a given learning experience. These are most effective when performed early in a learning experience for diagnostic purposes and then repeated later in the experience for evaluation of changes in behavior (which, as I have said in a previous chapter, I prefer to designate as "rediagnosis"). Some specific suggestions for this use of simulation exercises are made in Chapter 11.

4. *Case studies.* By obtaining rather complete records of students' life patterns at the time they enter a learning experience, and adding to it continuously until after they have completed the experience, it is possible to detect significant changes—especially in the areas of adjustment, outlook, and habits. Complete case studies require so much time and such skilled interviewers that they are practicable only for a sample group of the total participant body. Case studies have the advantage, however, of giving a much better picture of the effect of the learning experience on the whole person than do any of the more specific methods of evaluation.

5. *Student products.* For some kinds of learning experiences artifacts of the students' own work may provide the most revealing evidence of behavioral change. For example, in a course on oil painting an exhibit of the pictures produced in the early, middle, and later phases of the course would give such evidence; in a course on public speaking, tapes of speeches in a sequence of time; in a course on writing, a collection of compositions. A type of student product that is especially useful in other situations, such as human-relations training, is a running diary that can be analyzed by content-analysis procedures to reveal changes in feelings, perceptions, self-concept, and interpersonal relations. A more elaborate form of student product is the student-collected portfolio of evidence used in contract learning, which is described in the next chapter.

6. *Job performance records.* In some situations, particularly in government and industry, where the learning experiences are directly related to work, some of the best evidence of behavioral changes can be obtained from such routine records as production reports, safety reports, equipment-breakage reports, and grievance records. Comparisons can be made either between the performance of given individuals before and after training or between groups of individuals who have received certain training with those who have not. The observations of the supervisors, associates, and subordinates of participants in a training program—obtained through questionnaires, interviews, or regular personnel-appraisal procedures—may also provide excellent evidence of behavioral changes.

7. *Instructor evaluations.* The people who are in an especially good position to observe results achieved are the leaders or instructors. Their great shortcoming as observers, however, is that they are personally involved in the outcome of the evaluation, so that it may be difficult for them to be objective. They may tend to overlook instances in which desired changes are not being produced and to emphasize minor successes. While this limitation must be recognized, there is no doubt that the observations of the leaders and teachers are an essential source of data for evaluating a program. In addition, involving the faculty in the evaluation process is an excellent method for stimulating self-analysis and promoting their own personal growth.

Although a great deal of valuable information can be obtained from leaders and teachers through interviews and group meetings, many administrators have found that more comprehensive information can be obtained through written evaluation forms that are distributed at the end of each term. These forms are especially helpful if they are correlated with the course plan made up at the beginning of the term. An outline for a leader's or teacher's evaluation that has been used by several organizations is provided in Exhibit J-3, Appendix J.

Analysis of the Data

How the data will be handled after they have been collected will depend on the nature of the evaluative questions asked. Many of them—particularly those having to do with operational objectives—require simply a pooling of judgments of relevant parties, such as committee members, staff, faculty, participants, supervisors, and community leaders. Other evaluative questions—particularly those having to do with the measurement of specific behavioral changes in terms of educational objectives—will require more or less elaborate quantification and statistical procedures. Suggestions regarding these procedures are contained in the references listed at the end of this chapter.

Outcomes of Evaluation

The process, yardsticks, and methods of evaluation involve a great deal of planning and labor on the part of a number of people. Is evaluation worth all this trouble? What can be accomplished by evaluation?

There would be no point in evaluating if it did not result in action of some sort. Several kinds of action can be taken on the basis of information obtained through the evaluation process.

For one thing, the program can be changed. The objectives can be altered in the light of the new needs and interests of participants that have been revealed through evaluation process. They should be altered also in the light of developments in the institution and in the community. The operational efficiency of the organization can also be improved as a result of information acquired through the evaluation process.

A second kind of action that should be taken as a result of evaluation is the reporting of the findings to the participants and all others interested in the program. Those who have contributed to the evaluation have a right to know what the composite judgment turns out to be, and what actions have been taken as a result. Furthermore, their interest will be heightened if they are informed.

A third kind of action affects the leaders and teachers. While many of the recommendations growing out of evaluation will be concerned with improvement in the program as a whole, probably the largest number will be concerned with improvements in individual courses or activities. These improvements can be carried out only by the leaders and teachers themselves. Accordingly, complete and frank reports should be made to every leader concerning judgments made about activities for which they are responsible. If these reports are presented as objective findings posing problems to be solved, rather than indictments, they will be accepted by the leaders without defensiveness and will result in constructive action.

For Your Continuing Inquiry . . .

Regarding Evaluation Research and the Evaluation Process

Abt, Clark C. *The Evaluation of Social Programs.* Beverly Hills, Cal.: Sage Publications, 1977.

Adams, R. E. *DACUM: Approach to Curriculum, Learning, and Evaluation in Occupational Training.* Yarmouth, Nova Scotia: Canada Newstart Program, 1972.

Anderson, Scarvia, et al. *Encyclopedia of Educational Evaluation.* San Francisco: Jossey-Bass, 1974.

Anderson, Scarvia B., and Ball, Samuel. *The Profession and Practice of Program Evaluation.* San Francisco: Jossey-Bass, 1978.

Baird, Leonard L. (ed.). *Assessing Student Academic and Social Progress.* New Directions in Community Colleges, No. 18. San Francisco: Jossey-Bass, 1977.

Bloom, B.; Hastings, J.; and Madaus, G. *Handbook of Formative and Summative Evaluation of Student Learning.* New York: McGraw-Hill, 1973.

Borich, Gary D. (ed.). *Evaluating Educational Programs and Products.* Englewood Cliffs, N.J.: Prentice-Hall, 1974.

Caro, F. G. *Readings in Evaluation Research.* New York: Russell Sage Foundation, 1970.

Clark, Noreen, and McCaffery, James. *Demystifying Evaluation.* New York: World Education, 1978.

Craig, Robert L. (ed.). *Training and Development Handbook.* 2nd ed. New York: McGraw-Hill, 1976.

Davis, Larry N., and McCallon, Earl. *Planning, Conducting, Evaluating Workshops.* Austin, Texas: Learning Concepts, 1974.

Denova, Charles D. *Test Construction for Training Evaluation.* New York: Van Nostrand Reinhold, 1979.

Dressel, Paul L. *Handbook of Academic Evaluation: Assessing Institutional Effectiveness, Student Progress, and Professional Performance for Decision Making in Higher Education.* San Francisco: Jossey-Bass, 1976.

Guttentag, Marcia, and Struening, Elmer L. *Handbook of Evaluation Research.* Beverly Hills, Cal.: Sage Publications, 1975.

Heyman, Margaret M. *Criteria and Guidelines for the Evaluation of Inservice Training.* Social and Rehabilitation Service, U.S. Department of Health, Education and Welfare. Washington, D.C.: Government Printing Office, 1967.

Hoepfner, Ralph, et al. *CSE-RBS Test Evaluations: Tests of Higher-Order Cognitive, Affective, and Interpersonal Skills.* Los Angeles: Center for the Study of Evaluation, University of California Los Angeles, 1972.

Inbar, Michael, and Stoll, Charles. *Simulation and Gaming in Social Science.* New York: The Free Press, 1971.

Kirkpatrick, Donald L. *Evaluating Training Programs.* Madison, Wis.: American Society for Training and Development, 1975.

Knox, Alan B. (ed.). *Assessing the Impact of Continuing Education.* New Directions for Continuing Education, No. 3. San Francisco: Jossey-Bass, 1979.

Lake, Dale G.; Miles, Matthew B.; and Earle, Ralph B., Jr. (eds.). *Measuring Human Behavior.* New York: Teachers College Press, Columbia University, 1973.

Lein, Arnold J. *Measurement and Evaluation of Learning: A Handbook for Teachers.* Dubuque, Iowa: William C. Brown Co., 1967.

Mezirow, Jack, et al. *An Evaluation Guide for Adult Basic Education Programs.* Washington, D.C.: Government Printing Office, 1972.

Miller, Richard I. *Evaluating Faculty Performance.* San Francisco: Jossey-Bass, 1972.

_____. *Developing Programs for Faculty Evaluation.* San Francisco: Jossey-Bass, 1974.

Mullen, Edward J., et al. *Evaluation of Social Intervention.* San Francisco: Jossey-Bass, 1972.

National Institute for Mental Health. *Guidelines for Evaluation of Continuing Education Programs in Mental Health.* Washington, D.C.: NIMH, Continuing Education Branch, 1971.

Oppenheim, A. N. *Questionnaire Design and Attitude Measurement.* New York: Basic Books, 1965.

Pace, C. Robert. *Evaluating Learning and Teaching.* New Directions for Higher Education, No. 4. San Francisco: Jossey-Bass, 1973.

Patton, Michael Q. *Utilization-Focused Evaluation.* Beverly Hills, Cal.: Sage Publications, 1978.

Payne, David A. *The Specification and Measurement of Learning Outcomes.* Waltham, Mass.: Blaisdell Publishing Co., 1968.

Popham, W. James. *Evaluating Instruction.* Englewood Cliffs, N.J.: Prentice-Hall, 1973.

_____. *Educational Evaluation.* Englewood Cliffs, N.J.: Prentice-Hall, 1975.

Rippey, Robert M. *Studies in Transactional Evaluation.* Berkeley, Cal.: McCutchan, 1973.

Rutman, Leonard (ed.). *Evaluation Research Methods: A Basic Guide.* Beverly Hills, Cal.: Sage Publications, 1977.

Sanders, H. C., et al. *The Cooperative Extension Service.* Englewood Cliffs, N.J.: Prentice-Hall, 1966.

Schid, E. O., and Boocock, Sarane. *Simulation Games in Learning.* New York: Sage Publications, 1970.

Scriven, M. (ed.). *Evaluation in Education.* Berkeley, Cal.: McCutchan, 1974.

Shaw, Marvin E., and Wright, Jack M. *Scales for the Measurement of Attitudes.* New York: McGraw-Hill, 1967.

Steele, Sara M. *Contemporary Approaches to Program Evaluation.* Washington, D.C.: Capital Publications, 1973.

Steele, Sarah M., and Brack, Robert E. *Evaluating the Attainment of Objectives: Process, Properties, Problems, and Projects.* Syracuse, N.Y.: Publications in Continuing Education, Syracuse University, 1973.

Stufflebeam, Daniel, et al. *Educational Evaluation and Decision Making.* Itasca, Ill.: Peacock, 1971.

Suchman, Edward A. *Evaluative Research: Principles and Practice in Public Service and Social Action Programs.* New York: Russell Sage Foundation, 1967.

Thorndike, Robert (ed.). *Educational Measurement.* 2nd ed. Washington, D.C.: American Council on Education, 1971.

Thorndike, Robert, and Hagen, Elizabeth. *Measurement and Evaluation in Psychology and Education.* New York: John Wiley & Sons, 1977.

Tracey, William R. *Evaluating Training and Development Systems.* New York: American Management Associations, 1968.

Travers, Robert. *Second Handbook of Research on Teaching.* Chicago: Rand McNally, 1973.

Tuckman, Bruce W. *Evaluating Instructional Programs.* Rockleigh, N.J.: Allyn & Bacon, 1979.

Tyler, Ralph W. *Educational Evaluation: New Roles, New Means.* 68th Yearbook of the National Society for the Study of Education, Part 2. Chicago: University of Chicago Press, 1969.

Ulin, Jessie K. *Design to Evaluate Program and Administrative Effectiveness of Programs Funded Under the Adult Education Act of 1966.* Washington, D.C.: The National Advisory Council on Adult Education, 1975.

Van Maanen, John. *The Process of Program Evaluation.* Washington, D.C.: National Training and Development Service Press, 1973.

Weiss, C. H. (ed.). *Evaluating Action Programs: Readings in Social Action and Education.* Boston: Allyn & Bacon, 1972.

Worthen, Blaine R., and Sanders, James R. *Educational Evaluation: Theory and Practice.* Worthington, Ohio: Charles A. Jones Publishing Co., 1973.

Regarding Instruments, Statistics, and Techniques

Burros, Oscar K. *The Seventh Mental Measurement Yearbook.* Highland Park, N.J.: The Gryphon Press, 1972.

Cattel, Raymond B. *Personality and Mood by Questionnaire.* San Francisco: Jossey-Bass, 1973.

Cronbach, Lee J. *Essentials of Psychological Testing.* New York: Harper & Row, 1970.

DuBois, Philip H., and Mayo, Douglas G. *Research Strategies for Evaluating Training.* AERA Monograph Series on Curriculum Evaluation. Chicago: Rand McNally, 1970.

Edwards, Allen L. *Techniques of Attitude Scale Construction.* New York: Appleton-Century-Crofts, 1957.

Furst, Edward J. *Constructing Evaluation Instruments.* New York: Longmans, Green, 1958.

Griffith, Francis. *A Handbook for Observation of Teaching and Learning.* Midland, Mich.: Pendell, 1973.

Thurston, Louis L. *The Measurement of Values.* Chicago: University of Chicago Press, 1959.

Thyne, J. M. *The Principles of Examining.* New York: Halsted Press, 1974.

Walberg, Herbert J. (ed.). *Evaluating Educational Performance: A Sourcebook of Methods, Instruments, and Examples.* Berkeley, Cal.: McCutchan, 1974.

Wells, L. Edward, and Marwell, Gerald. *Self-Esteem: Its Conceptualization and Measurement.* Beverly Hills, Cal.: Sage Publications, 1975.

Helping Adults Learn

Part III

11
Designing and Managing Learning Activities

The Basic Process

The process for designing and operating particular learning activities according to the principles of andragogy in Chapter 4 is in general the same as the process for designing and operating comprehensive programs described in Chapters 5 to 10. Modifications in the application of the process have to be made, of course, owing to the more direct relationships among the parties involved and the greater specificity of the objectives in individual activities. But the adult-education process is a unitary system of assumptions, principles, and techniques that has integrity and is most effective when applied to the parts as well as to the whole.

I am proposing, therefore, that the same basic process should be applied to all types of learning activities—"learning activities" defined as separate units or sequences of the various formats of learning:

Formats for individual learning:
—An individual apprenticeship or internship arrangement;
—A correspondence-study course;
—A clinical counseling series with an individual;
—A directed study program with an individual;
—A programmed-instruction sequence;
—A coaching relationship between a supervisor and a subordinate.

Formats for group learning:
—An action project;
—A clinic, institute, or workshop;
—A club or organized group program;
—A conference or convention;
—A course;
—A demonstration program;
—An exhibit, fair, or festival;
—A large meeting or series of large meetings;
—A trip or tour.

The format of the community development project.
The process of designing and operating any of these learning activities involves these phases:
1) Setting a climate for learning;

2) Establishing a structure for mutual planning;
3) Diagnosing needs for learning;
4) Formulating directions (objectives) for learning;
5) Designing a pattern of learning experiences;
6) Managing the execution of the learning experiences;
7) Evaluating results and rediagnosing learning needs.

In the remainder of this chapter we shall explore some of the procedures and resources available to teachers and leaders in working through these phases.

Setting a Climate for Learning

Before getting into the procedures for setting a climate, let's see if we can agree on the characteristics of a climate that is conducive to learning. As I see it, these are the qualities of an environment that facilitate learning (with their opposites inhibiting learning):

1. *The physical environment*
—It is comfortable. Chairs are large enough and soft enough for adult bodies. "Smoking" and "nonsmoking" areas are designated if smoking is permitted. Temperature and ventilation are satisfactory.
—It is aesthetically pleasing. The decor is attractive and conveys human warmth; the closer it comes to looking like a living room in a home, the better. Colors are toward the bright side rather than the dull side of the rainbow.
—It is facilitative of interaction. (See Exhibits 20 and 21.)
—It is neither too crowded nor too spacious for the number of participants.

2. *The psychological environment*
—It exudes a spirit of mutual respect. The participants perceive one another, and sense that the instructor perceives them, as bringing into the environment a reservoir of experience that is itself a rich resource for one another's learning. They value the wide range of differences among themselves as enriching the environment. They listen attentively to one another.
—It is supportive and caring. People feel safe and unthreatened. They feel free to express themselves openly, to reveal their real feelings.
—It is warm and friendly. Not only do people feel respected, but they feel liked. People relate to one another as I-Thou human beings, not as It-It objects (in Martin Buber's terms). They know one another's names.
—It is collaborative rather than competitive. People are eager to share what they know and can do, rather than hold back for fear others might look "better" than they.
—It has a climate of mutual trust and mutual responsibility. The participants see the instructors or resource persons as fellow human beings—indeed, fellow learners—not as authority figures there to control or manipulate them. The participants accept responsibility to help in making decisions that affect their learning; they are not afraid to take initiative.
—It is a place in which the emphasis is on learning, not on teaching. If it were being televised, the cameras would be focused on what is happening to the learners, not what the teachers are doing.
The climate of a learning environment starts getting set long before the first

participant shows up—by the reputation an institution has gained over the years, by the location and external appearance of a building, and by other influences over which nobody has direct control. But the climate of a particular learning activity can be greatly affected by several kinds of direct intervention:

1. *Preparatory materials and activities.* The catalogs, flyers, form letters, and other announcements that are sent out in advance to recruit participants to an activity constitute the first conscious climate-setting opportunity. As was pointed out in Chapter 9, their appearance and spirit establish an image and set expectations in the minds of their readers.

In the case of those activities in which participants are registered in advance, as is frequently the situation with workshops, conferences, and club programs, it is often possible to get the participants involved in individual preliminary activity that puts them in a participatory frame of mind before they arrive. For example, they might be invited to submit a list of problems or concerns by mail or to do some preparatory reading or to collect some data about their job, their organization, or their community or to engage in a self-diagnostic exercise or to prepare a presentation of some sort. It is crucial, of course, that these preliminary activities have meaning and relevance to the participants and that they are actually made use of in the learning activity; if not, a climate of phoniness is likely to be the result.

2. *Physical arrangements.* Although the basic layout of a building often limits what leaders and instructors can do about the physical setting in which their groups will meet, they can usually improve on the typical custodian's notion of a good physical arrangement. If the chairs are placed in rows facing a podium, they can usually rearrange the chairs in a circle, semicircle, small circles, or other more interactive pattern, and can replace the podium with a small table (see Exhibit 21). If the blackboard is in an awkward position or is worn out, they can request an easel with newsprint (or bring their own). If the ventilation is poor, they can get to the room early and air it out before the participants arrive—and perhaps ask one of the participants to share responsibility for adjusting the windows. If the room is too hot, and the weather is nice outside, perhaps the group would do better sitting on the grass under a tree. In some conference centers, where the chairs are too hard for all-day meetings, I have seen people sit on the floors of small meeting rooms on pillows and mattresses, with much improvement in the social climate.

The social climate can be enhanced by such extra touches in the physical setting as tables to the side or the rear with books, materials, or an exhibit; maps, charts, or posters hung on the walls; a coffee urn with auxiliary supplies; a tape recorder playing soft music before the meetings start and at breaks; an adequate supply of ashtrays in one section of the room set aside for smokers; pitchers of ice water with plastic cups; and other touches that convey a sense of caring for the comfort of the participants.

It is my impression that instructors and activity leaders too often take for granted the physical setting they find when they arrive, without realizing the many simple things they can do to improve the impact it has on the social climate of their activity.

3. *The opening session.* I am convinced that what happens in the first hour or so of any learning activity (course, seminar, workshop, institute, tutorial, etc.) largely determines how productive the remaining hours will be. I see the setting of a climate that is conducive to learning as perhaps the single most critical thing I do as a facilitator of learning. What happens at the opening session will do more than anything else to set the climate for the entire activity. It is at this point that participants get the feeling that

they are seen as unique individuals who are respected and cared about for their individuality, or as a part of an anonymous mass. Several things can be done to contribute toward the former feeling:

The way they are greeted. In some situations, such as at workshops, conferences, and large meetings, it is possible to precede the opening session with an informal get-acquainted social period with coffee or cocktails. Hosts and hostesses could greet the new participants as they appear, give them pins or tags with their names printed in large letters, and introduce them to other participants and resource people. In situations where this is not possible, the instructor or activity leader, perhaps with the assistance of student-council members, can greet arriving participants, give them name tags, and introduce them to other participants.

The way they are oriented. Traditionally, the orientation of participants to the purpose and plan of work of an activity has been accomplished by a formal presentation of information by the instructor or leader. But more individualized orientation procedures may be possible. For example, each individual may be given an orientation statement to read and then question either in a general session or in small groups. Or the participants may be put into buzz groups and be invited to pool the questions they would like to have the instructor answer concerning the purpose and plan of work. Or, if it is an activity with which some of the participants have had previous experience (as is often the case with action projects, conferences, and club programs), old-timers may be paired or grouped with newcomers to orient them to the program. Whatever the form of the orientation, the substance should, of course, emphasize the role of the participants in a process of mutual self-directed inquiry.

The way they are introduced. It is critical in establishing a learning climate that each individual should feel closely related to at least a few other individuals early in the opening session. In a group of a dozen or fewer it is probably worthwhile to take the time for all participants to introduce themselves individually. In groups of over a dozen this procedure would be too time-consuming, so the preferred procedure is to put the participants into clusters of five or six, with the members of each cluster introducing themselves to one another. In either case, I like to have them share these things with one another: 1) *what* they are—their past and present work roles, their previous training, perhaps where they live; 2) *who* they are—one thing about themselves that makes them unique as individuals, such as unusual hobbies, interests, phobias, or other personality traits; 3) what special resources they bring to this learning experience from their previous training or experience that they would be willing to share with others; 4) what special problems, questions, or issues they are hoping to get help on in this activity.

Or, if a little more time is available, each group may be invited to develop a creative three- to five-minute presentation of the interests and resources of the collective membership of the group. When I have used this technique, groups have come up with poems, folk songs, skits, TV news broadcasts, statistical profiles, and other types of presentations that have set a tone of creative participation.

The most critical feature of this aspect of climate setting is that every face be capable of being attached to a name—by the instructor as well as by fellow participants. To facilitate this process, I make a point of having every participant write the name he or she likes to be called on a five-by-eight-inch card, using a large felt pen, with the card then folded like a tent and placed on a table or chair in front of the owner.

The way they are treated by the instructor. The behavior of the instructors is without doubt the single most potent force in establishing a social climate. The way they dress, for example, tends to set the norm for the entire group—and my general rule of thumb is to dress as informally and comfortably as is appropriate to a given situation. More important, the way they listen to participants will set the norm regarding how participants are to listen to one another; this, more than anything else, determines the degree of mutuality of respect that will prevail. In my own practice I make a point of listening attentively to every statement or question by students, and if there is any question about my understanding what they mean, I put what I think they said into my own words and ask them if that is what they meant. For the same reason, I work hard during the first session of an activity to get to know the names of the participants so that I can address them by name—preferably by first name; and I encourage them to call me by first name in order to reduce the social distance that traditionally exists between teachers and students.

The attitude instructors have toward themselves and their role is quickly conveyed to the participants and defines the nature of their relationship with them. If instructors nondefensively admit to not knowing the answer to some question, and invite the asker to get the answer and share it with the class, the role relationship soon becomes defined as that of mutual inquirers. If they give answers too glibly and dogmatically, even when they do know them, there will be a tendency for the students to become dependent upon them for information that would have more meaning for them if obtained through their own inquiry. Any behavior on the part of the instructors that is seen by the participants as being sarcastic, judgmental, degrading, belittling, or disrespectful toward a student—even if the participants themselves feel that way toward the student—would obviously interfere with a relationship of mutuality.

The social climate of an activity is affected by everything that happens during the course of the activity, but at no time with the potency of the impact of the opening session.

Establishing a Structure for Mutual Planning

The ideal situation is when a group is small enough for all participants to be involved in every aspect of planning every phase of a learning activity. The teacher, of course, retains responsibility for facilitating the planning by suggesting procedures and coordinating the process. But conditions are likely to be right for this maximum degree of participation only in small courses, action projects, workshops, and club programs. With larger groups the ideal situation can be approximated, however, by an imaginative use of subgroupings. For example, teams can be constituted for developing plans for various aspects of the program for the total group's consideration. Or a steering committee can be constituted consisting of representatives of random subgroups, and can meet in a theater-in-the-round arrangement, with the total group observing and reacting as they plan.

In a number of situations, however, such as in workshops, conferences, and large meetings, in which much of the planning has to be done before the participants assemble, a planning committee has to be appointed in advance. Under these conditions it is crucial that the committee be as representative of the participant population as possible and that it be replaced or augmented by participant-selected representatives at the earliest moment feasible. It also helps to preserve a sense of participation in planning if plans made by a planning committee are submitted to the participant body for modification and approval.

Diagnosing Needs for Learning

Certain judgments about general needs for learning were made in planning a total program of which a given learning activity is a part, as described in Chapter 6. But for the highest level of individual motivation to be achieved, it is imperative that the specific learning needs of the particular participants of a given learning activity be diagnosed—in fact, self-diagnosed.

The diagnostic process involves three steps: 1) the development of a model of desired behaviors or required competencies; 2) the assessment of the present level of performance by the individual in each of these behaviors or competencies; and 3) the assessment of the gaps between the model and the present performance.

Developing Competency Models

Models of desired behavior or required competence can be developed in several ways:

1. *Through research.* The Cooperative Extension Service, for example, has been able to develop rather specific models of the competencies required for successful farming by virtue of the research findings of state agricultural-experiment stations regarding which practices produce the best crops. Many state extension services have conducted research on required competencies for many other roles as well, such as homemaker, youth leader, community-change agent, and farm business manager. Considerable research has been done by government agencies, industry, and the universities on competencies required for supervision and executive management—indeed, leadership in general. The competencies required by teachers, doctors, hospital administrators, nurses, social workers, and other professional roles have been subjects of a good deal of research.[1] But for most of the nonvocational roles that are central in the lives of human beings there is little research regarding required competencies.

2. *Through the judgments of experts.* The literature abounds with judgments of experts regarding the required competencies for performing a variety of roles, ranging from a wide range of occupations to leisure-time user. Many institutions make use of their own experts—their executives, personnel staff, supervisors, and field workers—to construct models of required competencies for roles unique to their particular institutions. For example, Westinghouse Electric Corporation used task forces composed of selected line managers and staff specialists to construct competency models for its management development program.[2]

3. *Through task analysis.* By means of more or less elaborate observations, time study, and record-keeping of several people actually performing a given role, it is possible to construct a model of the competencies possessed by the most effective performers. A good task analysis consists of a categorization of the situations encountered in a role and descriptions of the types of action and related competencies required to cope with these situations successfully. Such a task analysis can be made by people associated with a role, such as supervisors, colleagues, and subordinates, but its value is likely to be greater if made by more objective observers. A comprehensive task analysis would

---

[1]Some of the best of this research is reported in the publications of the Institute for Competence Assessment, 137 Newbury Street, Boston, Massachusetts 02116.

[2]A description of the procedures used by Westinghouse is contained in my *The Adult Learner: A Neglected Species,* 2nd ed. (Houston: Gulf Publishing Co., 1978), pp. 180–197.

be too long to illustrate in a book this size, but a number have been made and can be obtained from the Public Health Service of the U.S. Department of Health, Education and Welfare.[3]

4. *Through group participation.* A fourth alternative is, of course, for a group to build its own model. And if time and circumstances permit, this is probably the alternative that will result in the greatest learning—for the process of building a model is itself a learning process, and the model that results, even though it will perhaps be cruder, is one to which the participants will have a deeper commitment. The sources of data available to a group in building its own model include: 1) research findings and judgments of experts as reported in the literature, 2) observation by the participants of role models in the field, 3) presentations by experts in the classroom, 4) interviews by the participants of experts in the community, 5) the participants' own experiences and observations, and 6) the experience of the instructors and leaders of the sponsoring institution.

For the task of model-building to be manageable by a total group, it is desirable that it be broken down into subtasks, with a separate team of participants for each subtask. For example, Westinghouse had one task force for each of the six functional categories of competencies deemed to be required for performance of the role of general manager: 1) marketing; 2) engineering; 3) manufacturing; 4) finance; 5) personnel; and 6) general management. Or, for a course on "Effective Human Relations," teams might be organized to develop lists of the required competencies of 1) knowledge, 2) insight, 3) attitude, 4) skill, 5) interest, and 6) value, for effective human-relations performance. The instructor would serve as a consultant and resource person to the teams in identifying sources of information about each type of required competence, and after a reasonable period of search the teams would pool their findings. For other subjects or roles a different set of subtasks may be desirable.

One more thing needs to be said about competency models at this point, and that is that the excellence of the model is not the most critical feature of the competency-based education process. A number of educators have expressed reluctance to experiment with using competency models because they do not have the time or money to get models constructed by experts or to have the models rigorously validated. It has been my experience that even relatively amateurish models constructed by the learners themselves, preferably with help from the instructors or other resource people, can help in producing a superior quality of learning. Westinghouse Electric Corporation, for example, has experimented with having the participants in their Executive Forum construct their own models—using the models developed by the "expert" task forces only as after-the-fact checklists—and has found that participants' models were not drastically different from the experts' models. The chief difference is the greater sense of ownership the participants feel toward their self-constructed models and, consequently, the greater investment of energy they put into accomplishing them. The Duke University School of Nursing has its third-year students develop models, with help from the faculty.

The most important effect of using competency models as a basis for diagnosing learning needs is the difference in attitude toward learning that it produces in the learners. I can illustrate this difference most sharply by describing my experience with graduate students. Before we started using competency models, students perceived their purpose to be to accumulate enough credits to earn a degree. When students

---

[3]See, for example, Public Health Service, *The Psychiatric Aide in State Mental Hospitals* (Washington, D.C.: Government Printing Office, 1965).

would enter a course and ask themselves, "Why am I here," they would answer, "To get three credits." They had what I think of as essentially a course-taking approach to education. But when we started experimenting with using competency models, students would enter a course knowing exactly what competencies it was designed to help them develop. They came to see the purpose of their taking a given course as being much more personal; they were there to develop their own competence, their personal equipment. I have seen similar changes take place in the attitudes of participants in competency-based workshops and staff-development programs in business and industry, government agencies, hospitals, and religious organizations.

Since the conditions and requirements for performing most roles are constantly changing, it is important that competency models be continuously reviewed and updated.

Assessing the Present Level of Performance

Here we enter relatively new and unexplored territory in the technology of adult education. Because adult education was tied so closely to pedagogy for so long, little attention was given to developing procedures and tools for helping adults diagnose their own needs—after all, if the teachers already know what they need, why waste time getting the students into the act? So the reservoir of experience and materials for student self-diagnosis of present level of performance is extremely limited. Indeed, there is probably no aspect of the technology of adult education that is in greater need of creative contributions by innovative practitioners. But there has been enough experience by a few innovators in the last few years to give evidence of the fruitfulness of energy spent in this direction and to provide some helpful guidelines and procedures.

Establishing a Self-diagnostic Attitude

Because competition for grades is such a strong element in the tradition of education, most adults enter into a learning activity in a defensive frame of mind. One of their strongest impulses is to show how good they are. So the notion of engaging in a self-diagnostic process for the purpose of revealing one's weaknesses—one's needs for additional learning—is both strange and threatening. It is crucial, therefore—particularly in the case of adults having their first andragogical experience—that ways be devised for helping participants get into a self-diagnostic frame of mind.

Certainly the establishment of a warm, supportive, nonthreatening climate as described above is a prerequisite condition to beginning work in this direction. I have found in my own experience that a brief presentation by the instructors of the rationale for self-diagnosis as an essential feature of self-directed learning helps to make the concept more intellectually acceptable—particularly if reinforced by the instructors' own example of seeking feedback regarding their own performance.

But probably the single most effective technique for inducing a self-diagnostic attitude is a human-relations laboratory experience. Where time permits, this could be a full-fledged one- or two-week workshop or a full-semester sensitivity training course. For example, in our graduate program in adult education at Boston University, we encouraged new entrants into the program to include our "Seminar in Group and Interpersonal Relations" in their first semester's program. Where time does not permit this depth of experience, a good beginning can be made in inducing a self-diagnostic attitude through a "microlab" or "minilab" (a one- or two-hour intensive group meeting in which observers or alter-egos give feedback to the participants on their behavior in the group, or participants give immediate feedback to one another) or a "marathon lab" (a group meeting extending without break for several hours—even overnight—

with continuous feedback on individuals' behavior). Certain nonverbal exercises have proved especially effective in opening people up to the examination of their own behavior nondefensively, and can be made available to the participants in any of the above laboratory patterns.

This self-diagnostic attitude can be reinforced and deepened throughout the activity by building into every group meeting that is held a procedure for analysis of the group's behavior. For example, at the end of each meeting of our learning-teaching teams at Boston University, the form reproduced in Exhibit K-1 was filled out by each member, the responses were quickly tallied, and the group discussed the meaning of the results. A similar procedure (perhaps using buzz groups instead of a written form) can be used at the end of meetings in which instructors have performed for their own self-diagnostic use (and role-modeling).

Providing Evidence of Present Performance

Let us be clear about one thing before proceeding with this matter of assessing performance. We are not talking here about a highly precise mathematical process of quantitative measurement of the full range of behaviors required for performing any set of functions. Such an aspiration would be totally unrealistic given the present state of the human sciences—and perhaps, given the complexity of human nature, it always will be. Rather, we are talking about a process that is more sensitizing than measuring, more concerned with setting broad directions of growth rather than defining terminal behaviors. The purpose of the process we are concerned with here is to help individual adults look objectively at their present level of performance of a relatively small sample of behaviors that are important to them at a given time in their development and to determine where they want to invest energy in improving their performance in the light of their models of desired behaviors.

Different kinds of performance call for different kinds of assessment procedures. Performance assessment in the area of *knowledge* requires the participants to demonstrate in some way what they know (or at least can recall). If the desired knowledge is in an established academic-subject field, or in any of several technical or vocational fields, one or more of the nationally standardized subject-knowledge tests mentioned in Chapter 10 may help participants to assess their present level of performance. If a standardized test is not available, a teacher-made test could be used. But I have found student-made tests to be generally more acceptable and usually just as effective.

Performance assessment in the area of *understanding and insight* requires that individuals demonstrate their ability to size up situations, see patterns, develop categories, figure out cause-and-effect relationships, and in general to apply knowledge and thought processes to the analysis and solution of problems. Some standardized tests of critical-thinking ability, as mentioned in Chapter 10, are designed to give evidence regarding this type of performance, as are teacher-made essay tests. But adults are likely to find simulation exercises, in which they act out their understanding and insight in handling "live" problems, to be more realistic and relevant. For example, in a supervisory-training program, groups of participants can take turns showing how they would handle various "critical incidents" supervisors typically face in dealing with subordinates, superiors, and colleagues. By comparing the various solutions tried and their effects, the trainees get some insight into their understanding of these kinds of problems. Role playing and, on a more elaborate scale, business games, are used for the same purpose.

Performance assessment in the area of *skills* requires that the participants do the action in question and have their proficiency rated in some way. The procedures and tools described under "performance tests" in Chapter 10 are as applicable to diagnostic purposes as to evaluation. A simple illustration of a skill-performance assessment procedure is provided by the device commonly used in public-speaking classes of having each participant make a short speech and have it rated by the other participants or a panel of speech experts on such scales as adequacy of vocabulary, clarity of expression, pacing, rhythm, gesturing, poise, conveying of sincerity, and other elements of the skill of speaking in public. The composite rating of the judges is then transposed onto a profile sheet such as is illustrated in Exhibit 30, giving the participant a quick perspective on the areas of skill needing most improvement. Similar profiles can be drawn up from observer-ratings of performance in real or simulated situations for such other skills as machine operating, instruction giving, interviewing, discussion leading, delegating, conflict handling, decision making, and any of the wide variety of skills involved in artistic and physical activities. For the assessment of certain basic skills, such as reading, computing, finger dexterity, etc., standardized tests are available, as indicated in Chapter 10.

Performance assessment in the areas of *attitudes, interests,* and *values* is much more difficult and even less precise than in the areas of knowledge, understanding, and skill. As was pointed out in Chapter 10, some standardized tests exist that can be used to get verbalizations about self-perceived attitudes, interests, and values, but there is little assurance that these are the ones that will be acted on in a particular situation when the chips are down. Role playing, and especially reverse role playing (as when a white person takes the role of a black person and vice versa), have been used extensively in human-relations training to help individuals get insight into their attitudes as they are revealed in action. And decision-making exercises, in which the individual has

---

Exhibit 30

PROFILE OF RATINGS OF PUBLIC SPEAKING SKILLS

Name of Student: _____   Date: _____

Mean Ratings

Skill Components	1 2 3 4 5 6 7 8 9 10 (Low — High)
Vocabulary	8
Clarity of expression	3
Pacing, pausing, emphasis	9
Voice projection	4
Gesturing	6
Logical development	4
Adequacy of supportive facts	10
Adequacy of illustrations	4
Appropriateness of humor	4
Quality of opening	8
Quality of closing	3
Rapport with audience	4
Conveying of sincerity	9
Pronunciation	9
Enunciation	3

to decide between two values (such as risky profit versus security), can help people discover which values they choose under pressure. But the technology has to advance much farther than it has before we can get very clear assessments in these areas.

Assessing Learning Needs

The final step in the self-diagnostic process is for individuals to assess the gaps that exist between their models of desired behaviors and their present level of performance. In a few situations, where the competencies involved are fairly simple and mechanical, the profile of gaps (which, of course, represent needs for further learning) may be quite precise and complete. But in most situations this process of self-diagnosis is more artistic than scientific. It is, realistically, merely a way of helping individuals make more sensitive judgments about which of many possible directions they might take in their continuing self-development at a given time.

Several examples of self-diagnostic tools are provided in this book. Appendix B reproduces the self-rating scale I use in my workshops for adult teachers and industrial trainers, and that I suggested in Chapter 1 that you might use in preparing yourself to read this book. In Appendix K, Exhibit K-2 is a diagnostic tool for a particular course in a School of Nursing, Exhibit K-3 is a diagnostic tool used by the Camp Fire Girls in its staff development program, and Exhibit K-4 is for a course in adult education.

The fact is that the very idea of self-diagnosis by learners is so new that the tools and procedures for helping them do it are primitive and inadequate. Clearly, this will be an area of great technological ferment in the next few years, and I urge my readers to put their creative energy to work on this great need and to share their innovations with me. If one thing stands out about adult learning, it is that a self-diagnosed need for learning produces much greater motivation to learn than an externally diagnosed need.

Formulating Directions (Objectives) for Learning

As was pointed out in Chapter 7, program objectives serve the purposes of determining what activities will be provided for what groups of participants and of providing benchmarks for evaluating the total program. Learning objectives serve the same purposes for particular activities. In the words of Ralph W. Tyler, one of the pioneer curriculum theorists, "Educational objectives become the criteria by which materials are selected, content is outlined, instructional procedures are developed, and tests and examinations are prepared."[4] It is important, therefore, that learning objectives be stated in a form that will be helpful to the instructor and participants in planning and conducting learning experiences and evaluating their outcomes.

In actual educational practice, learning objectives are stated in many ways. All too often they are stated as things which the instructor or the activity is going to do, as, for example, "to give information about . . ." "to demonstrate . . ." "to broaden appreciation of . . ." or "to create an awareness of. . . ." (These are, incidentally, direct quotes from activity announcements in my files.) These are not really statements of educational objectives, but rather of instructors' intentions. For education is not concerned with having the instructor perform certain activities; it is concerned with helping students achieve changes in behavior.

---

[4]Ralph W. Tyler, *Basic Principles of Curriculum and Instruction* (Chicago: University of Chicago Press, 1950), p. 3.

Objectives are sometimes stated in the form of lists of topics, concepts, or other content elements to be covered in an activity. Thus, a course in "Principles and Methods of Supervision" in a catalog in front of me at this moment states its objectives as being to cover "the role and responsibility of supervisors; planning; defining tasks; establishing standards and controls; delegation of responsibility; communication; motivation and morale. . . ." Objectives stated in the form of content elements may help students choose between activities, but they are not satisfactory learning objectives since they do not specify what the students are to do with the elements—memorize them, be able to apply them to life situations, feel differently about them, etc.

A third way in which objectives are often stated is in the form of generalized patterns of behavior without the content area to which the behavior applies being specified. For example, a brochure describing a library discussion program in front of me now states as its first objective "to develop critical thinking." But it doesn't say about what. Further down the list is "to develop broad interests" without any indication of the areas in which interests are to be aroused.

Tyler suggests that "the most useful form for stating objectives is to express them in terms which identify both the kind of behavior to be developed . . . and the content or area of life in which this behavior is to operate."[5]

In my own practice I have found that it helps me to discipline myself to include both behavioral and content components if I use the phraseology "to develop . . . [in the sense of 'to help participants develop'] in. . . ." I have found it useful, also, to have a general typology of behavioral aspects of objectives as a frame of reference for organizing a set of objectives for an activity. Hilda Taba proposes the following typology:

Knowledge: Facts, Ideas, Concepts
Reflective Thinking
—Interpretation of data
—Application of facts and principles
—Logical reasoning
Values and Attitudes
Sensitivities and Feelings
Skills[6]

A somewhat simpler typology is employed in Exhibit K-5 in Appendix K, which is a worksheet I have used in some of my courses for developing specific statements of objectives collaboratively with the students. After the students have experienced some of the kinds of self-diagnostic exercises described in the section above, they are able to specify quite concretely the content areas in which they need behavioral changes of each of the six types. One of the advantages of organizing objectives according to a typology of this sort is that it provides direct guidance in the selection of techniques for each learning experience; for, as will be shown later in this chapter, certain techniques are more effective in helping students achieve certain objectives than others.

The discussion of learning objectives up to this point has been in the broad humanistic sense of self-determined directions of self-development, with the instructor and the students participating mutually in the process of their formulation. But there is a rather substantial body of literature on objectives of a very different kind; and the discussion should not be ended without some acknowledgment of this other approach

[5]Ibid., p. 30.
[6]Hilda Taba, *Curriculum Development: Theory and Practice* (New York: Harcourt, Brace and World, 1962), pp. 211–228.

to the subject. As was mentioned previously in Chapter 8, programmed instruction is geared to a concept of "terminal behavior" objectives, with terminal behavior defined as "the behavior you would like your learner to be able to demonstrate at the time your influence over him ends."[7] The specifications for this type of objective are summarized by one of its proponents as follows:

1. A statement of instructional objectives is a collection of words or symbols describing one of your educational *intents*.

2. An objective will communicate your intent to the degree you have described what the learner will be DOING when demonstrating his achievement and how you will know when he is doing it.

3. To describe terminal behavior (what the learner will be DOING):

a. Identify the name of the over-all behavior act.

b. Define the important conditions under which the behavior is to occur (givens and/or restrictions and limitations).

c. Define the criterion of acceptable performance.

4. Write a separate statement for each objective; the more statements you have, the better chance you have of making clear your intent.

5. If you give each learner a copy of your objectives, you may not have to do much else. [*sic*].[8]

These statements are from a book entitled *Preparing Instructional Objectives*. But the educational philosophy expressed in the subtitle of the book—"A book for teachers and student teachers . . . for anyone interested in transmitting skills and knowledge to others"—explains why this approach to objectives is not given greater attention in this book about andragogy.

Humanistic educators, like Carl Rogers and Abraham Maslow, maintain that most human learning is far too complex to be described by observable, measurable, terminal behaviors. They suggest that objectives might more appropriately specify directions of growth, such as "to develop increasing self-confidence" or "to develop broader and deeper knowledge of. . . ."

My own position in this controversy is to acknowledge that there are certain kinds of learnings, particularly those that have to do with more or less routine operations (such as typing), that probably are facilitated by a specification of the terminal behaviors to be achieved, but that most learnings are, as the humanistic theorists maintain, too complex to be reduced to such mechanistic performances. Especially is this likely to be true whenever judgment, creativity, confidence, analytic ability, sensitivity, and the like, are components of the learning. But the important thing is that the objectives have meaning to the learners and provide them with directional guidance in their learning. In my own practice, therefore, I encourage the learners to state the objectives in the terms that have most meaning to them; for some this will be terminal objectives and for others, directions of growth.

Furthermore, one of the more significant findings of Tough's research regarding how adults learn naturally is that very often they will enter into a learning project with rather vague objectives and that as they become better informed about the content of their inquiry their objectives become sharper and clearer. For this reason, I authorize my students to revise their objectives repeatedly—which is hard to do with predetermined terminal behavioral objectives.

---

[7]Robert F. Mager, *Preparing Instructional Objectives* (Palo Alto, Cal.: Fearon Publishers, 1962), p. 2.

[8]Ibid., p. 53. The *sic* means that this is precisely what the author says, but I doubt that he means what I suspect—that by this time the students, if they are adult, will have disappeared.

Designing a Pattern of Learning Experiences

The task of this phase of the process of development of learning activities is to sketch out a pattern of learning experiences that will fulfill the objectives and will have the qualities of the art principles of line, space, tone, color, texture, and unity discussed in Chapter 8.

Organizing Principles

In works on curriculum theory in youth education this operation is referred to as "curriculum organization," and several standard "organizing principles" are suggested for patterning the learning experiences. For example, one standard textbook on curriculum development describes four such organizing principles for courses in which the exposition of content is the primary concern:

> The first is that which proceeds from the simple to the complex. The simple is defined as that which contains few elements or subordinate parts, as a one-celled animal is simpler than a many-celled animal, or as hydrogen and oxygen are simpler than chemical compounds. Chemistry and biology courses are frequently organized on this principle; and the organization of many other courses, such as grammar and foreign languages, is influenced by it in more or less degree.
>
> The second is an expository order based on prerequisite learnings. This principle is followed particularly in subjects consisting largely of laws and principles, such as physics, grammar, and geometry. Geometry is organized on the supposition that the theorems bear a particular logical relation to one another and are learned in that relation.
>
> The third form of exposition is that which proceeds from the whole to the part. Geography frequently begins with the globe, with the idea that the earth is a sphere, because this conception serves to interpret many geographic observations, such as differences in time and seasons.
>
> The fourth kind of exposition is chronological. Facts and ideas are arranged in a time sequence so that the presentation of later events is preceded by discussion of earlier ones. This is the organization followed in history courses—and frequently in literature courses, literary selections being arranged in time sequence.[9]

Where the development of behavior is the primary concern, other organizing principles are suggested, including increasing breadth of application, increasing range of activities included, from the part to the whole, a demonstration or direct experience followed by the development of principles, and many others.

These curriculum theorists emphasize that three major criteria must be met in building an effectively organized group of learning experiences. These are *continuity* (the vertical reiteration over time of major curriculum elements), *sequence* (higher levels of treatment with each successive learning experience), and *integration* (the horizontal relationship of curriculum elements so as to provide a unified view and unified behavior). Tyler points out that these criteria should be applied not to the logical organization of the subject matter, but to the psychological organization of the learner.

---

[9]B. O. Smith, W. O. Stanley, and H. J. Shores, *Fundamentals of Curriculum Development* (New York: World Book, 1957), p. 233.

In identifying important organizing principles, it is necessary to note that the criteria, continuity, sequence, and integration apply to the experiences of the learner and not to the way in which these matters may be viewed by someone already in command of the elements to be learned. Thus, continuity involves recurring emphasis in the learner's experience upon these particular elements; sequence refers to the increasing breadth and depth of the learner's development; and integration refers to the learner's increased unity of behavior in relating to the elements involved. This means that the organizing principles need to be considered in terms of their psychological significance to the learner.[10]

Learning-Design Models

In my own practice I have found it useful to go beyond the concept of curriculum organization—which conveys a sort of engineering flavor to me—and to superimpose on it a concept of *learning-design model,* which conveys more of the flavor of an art form. By "learning-design model" I simply mean a process plan—a projection of a flow of events—for accomplishing a given set of objectives in a sequence guided by a conceptual schema, such as the steps in an operation, the performance of a role, the functions of an organizational unit, or an integrating theme. My learning-design models use the natural processes of each particular learning situation as the organizing principle for the sequencing of learning experiences, in contrast to the use of the logic of a given body of subject matter as the organizing principle in the traditional *content-transmission models.*[11]

Components (Activity Units) of Learning-Design Models

A learning-design model is shaped by the arrangement of various types of activity units—the building blocks of educational architecture—in a pattern prescribed by the theme or process of the model. In keeping with the architectural analogy, this approach to the designing of learning is akin to the architectural doctrine that "form follows function."

The following six types of activity units are available to model designers:

1. *General sessions.* Meetings of all participants as a whole, with a variety of patterns of platform presentation and audience participation as described under "Large Meetings" in Chapter 8.

2. *Small groups* of various sizes and for a variety of purposes, including:
—*Topical discussion groups:* groups organized for the purpose of reacting to, testing the meaning of, or sharing ideas about informational inputs from reading or speakers on given topics;
—*Laboratory groups:* groups organized for the purpose of analyzing group behavior, experimenting with new behavior, and sharing feedback regarding the effects of various behaviors;
—*Special-interest groups:* groups organized according to categories of interests of participants for the purpose of sharing experiences and exploring common concerns;

---

[10]Ralph W. Tyler, op. cit., p. 63.
[11]For a more detailed treatment of the difference between a content-transmission plan and a process design, see my *Self-Directed Learning: A Guide for Learners and Teachers* (Chicago: Association Press/Follett Publishing Co., 1975), pp. 31–38.

—*Problem-solving groups:* groups organized to develop solutions to procedural or substantive problems of concern to the total assembly;

—*Planning groups:* groups organized to develop plans for activities within the design or for back-home application;

—*Instructional groups:* groups organized to receive instruction through the services of resource experts in specialized areas of knowledge, understanding, or skill;

—*Inquiry groups:* groups organized to search out information and report their findings to the total assembly;

—*Evaluation groups:* groups organized for the purpose of developing proposals for evaluating the results of the activity for the approval of the total assembly and perhaps executing the approved plans;

—*Skill practice groups:* groups organized for the purpose of practicing specified categories of skills;

—*Consultative groups:* groups organized for the purpose of giving consultative help to one another;

—*Operational groups:* groups organized for the purpose of carrying responsibilities for the operation of the activity, such as room arrangements, refreshments, materials preparation, equipment operation, etc.;

—*Learning-teaching teams:* groups which take responsibility for learning all they can about a content unit and sharing what they have learned with the total assembly;

—*Dyads:* two-person groups organized to share experiences, coach each other, plan strategies, or help each other in any other way;

—*Triads:* three-person groups organized for mutually helpful purposes;

—*Buzz groups:* randomly organized groups of three or four persons that meet in a general assembly to pool problems, ideas, or reactions and report them through a spokesman to the assembly.

3. *Individual consultation, counseling, or directed study:* in which the services of resource persons are made available to individual participants for personalized help.

4. *Reading:* the scheduling of special times (between meetings) for reading handout materials or a selection of references.

5. *Recreation, worship, or meditation:* periods of time set aside for socialization, religious activity, or creative solitude.

6. *Preparatory activity:* things the participants are invited to do before the learning activity starts, such as reading, self-analysis, data collection, etc.

Types of Learning-Design Models

The learning-design models I have developed so far in my own practice seem to group themselves into several types. I present them here not as a definitive set of typological categories, but as a way of illustrating the kinds of models that can be constructed. Actually, any conceptual schema is capable of providing the framework for building a model, and so the number of possible models is potentially infinite. The following types of models represent, therefore, what I hope is only the beginning of a rich ferment of innovation in our field.

Organic model. I have one basic model which I call my *organic* model. It can serve as a discrete model for a given learning activity, but it is also a sort of second-level aspect (or counterpoint melody) in all other models. The organic model consists of the andragogical steps of 1) climate setting, 2) establishing a structure for mutual planning, 3) diagnosing needs and interests, 4) formulating objectives, 5) designing a pattern of activities, 6) carrying out the activities, and 7) evaluating the results and rediagnosing needs and interests. Exhibit K-6 in Appendix K illustrates an organic model developed for a two-day course for corporation executives. Notice that the only preplanned elements are the broad learning objectives and a plan for involving the participants in diagnosing their own needs and collaborating with the resource people in planning and conducting learning activities. The workshop described in Exhibit I-5, in Appendix I, is another example of the organic model.

Operational model. The procedures involved in a particular operation, such as the operation of a machine, problem solving, decision making, scientific inquiry, program planning, the consultation process, or even the building of models, provide another kind of framework for constructing models. These models typically replicate the step-by-step flow of the procedures required by the operation.

Exhibit K-7 in Appendix K illustrates the development of a model based on the operation of a process of program evaluation in religious education. It is the work of a planning committee for a Consultation on the Place of Evaluation in Program Development of the National Council of Churches. The purpose of the consultation was to improve the competencies of denominational leaders in using evaluation procedures in religious-education programs. The committee first developed four alternative models: A) Model Building (designing models of evaluation); B) Technology Developing (the process of improving the technology of evaluation); C) Problem Clinic (solving current problems in evaluation); and D) Case Problem (using specific case problems as the basis of analysis and generalization). What happened is that the committee selected certain aspects of each design (indicated by the numbered brackets) and ended up with a modular design (E), by which is meant the combination of modules from several designs.

Exhibit K-8 in Appendix K reproduces a model of the decision-making operation developed in an executive-development workshop of five days' duration. The model was constructed by the pooling of several teams' ideas during the first day. Then a new set of teams was organized, one team for each of the five steps of decision making, with responsibility for devising diagnostic exercises to help individuals assess their level of performance in the "helping behavior" and "blocking behavior" aspects of each step, and this diagnostic phase was completed on the evening of the second day. On the third day each of these teams then planned a series of learning experiences—"work methods"—which were administered on the fourth and fifth days, with an evaluation of the workshop at the end of the fifth day.

Role model. The requirements for the performance of particular roles provide another framework for the construction of learning-design models. I have used the roles of trainer, manager, supervisor, nurse, YMCA secretary, change agent, teacher, parent, and school principal for this purpose. For example, Exhibit K-9 in Appendix K depicts a design developed with the staff of the Canadian National Council of YMCAs for a four-day inservice training conference based on the conception of the competencies required to perform the role of change agent.

Functional model. The functions of such organizational units as boards, committees, volunteers, staffs, members, departments, and the like, are often a useful basis for building learning-design models. Exhibit K-10 in Appendix K is an example of a design for a two-day workshop for members of the board of the Unitarian-Universalist Women's Federation which is based on the analysis of the functions of a board in this kind of organization.

Thematic model. Such themes as "Freedom and Authority," "Dealing with Conflict," "Creativity," and "Preparing for the Future" have served as the organizing concepts for other learning-design models.

Managing the Learning Experiences

The translation of a learning design into a sequence of activities involves making decisions about the most effective techniques and most useful materials for accomplishing the objectives of each unit, and then evolving strategies with the students for their sharing responsibility in the execution of the decisions. The role of the teacher in this phase, as I see it, is to serve both as a strong procedural technician—suggesting the most effective ways the students can help in executing the decisions—and as a resource person or coach, who provides substantive information regarding the subject matter of the unit, possible techniques, and available materials, when needed. The leader can also perform a useful "threading" function, providing the connective tissue or transitional commentary from one unit to the next.

Techniques

An attempt is made below to develop a typology or categorical checklist of the wide range of techniques available for helping adults to learn. It is not within the scope of this book to explain how to perform each technique, but for those who are unfamiliar with a particular technique, resources in the bibliography at the end of this chapter are provided.

1) Presentation techniques

—lecture	—demonstration	—slides
—debate	—colloquy	—dramatization
—dialogue	—audiocassette	—recording, radio
—interview	—programmed instruction	—exhibits
—symposium	—multimedia packages	—trips
—panel	—motion picture	—reading
—group interview		

2) Audience-participation techniques (large meetings)

—question-and-answer period	—reaction panel	—audience role playing
—forum	—buzz groups	—expanding panel
—listening teams		

3) Discussion techniques

—guided discussion	—group-centered discussion	—case discussion
—book-based discussion	—problem-solving discussion	—Socratic discussion

4) Simulation techniques

—role playing	—in-basket exercises	—action maze
—critical-incident process	—games	—participative cases
—case method		

5) T-group (sensitivity training)

6) Nonverbal exercises

7) Skill-practice exercises, drill, coaching

The task of selecting the right technique for the right occasion can be fraught with difficulties. For one thing, there is a curious tendency toward faddism in regard to techniques. During the 1930s discussion was the "in" technique; during the 1940s there was a wave of interest in presentation techniques supported by audiovisual aids; during the 1950s T-group techniques were fashionable; in the 1960s, simulation; in the 1970s, multimedia packages; and in the 1980s, electronic media. For another thing, there is a tendency on the part of individuals to go overboard on new techniques they have just mastered and to want to use them on every occasion; although the opposite tendency of individuals being reluctant to experiment with new techniques is probably even more prevalent.

The ability to select the most effective technique for a given purpose is probably best developed through well-evaluated experience, but two simple guidelines may help. The first guideline is to match the technique to the objective. Certain techniques are more effective in helping to bring about certain types of behavioral change than others. For example, a lecture may be an effective technique for increasing knowledge, but it has little impact on attitude. An attempt to indicate the most effective techniques for accomplishing particular types of behavioral changes is portrayed in Exhibit 31. The second guideline is the principle of participation: Given a choice between two techniques, choose the one involving the students in the most active participation.

Exhibit 31

MATCHING TECHNIQUES TO DESIRED BEHAVIORAL OUTCOMES

Type of Behavioral Outcome	Most Appropriate Techniques
Knowledge (Generalizations about experience; internalization of information)	Lecture, television, debate, dialog, interview, symposium, panel, group interview, colloquy, motion picture, slide film, recording, book-based discussion, reading.
Understanding (Application of information and generalizations)	Audience participation, demonstration, motion picture, dramatization, Socratic discussion, problem-solving discussion, case discussion, critical incident process, case method, games.
Skills (Incorporation of new ways of performing through practice)	Role playing, in-basket exercises, games, action mazes, participative cases, T-Group, nonverbal exercises, skill practice exercises, drill, coaching.
Attitudes (Adoption of new feelings through experiencing greater success with them than with old)	Experience-sharing discussion, group-centered discussion, role playing, critical incident process, case method, games, participative cases, T-Group, nonverbal exercises.
Values (The adoption and priority arrangement of beliefs)	Television, lecture (sermon), debate, dialog, symposium, colloquy, motion picture, dramatization, guided discussion, experience-sharing discussion, role playing, critical incident process, games, T-Group.
Interests (Satisfying exposure to new activities)	Television, demonstration, motion picture, slide film, dramatization, experience-sharing discussion, exhibits, trips, nonverbal exercises.

Materials and Devices

Probably no aspect of education is in such a state of technological ferment as that having to do with the materials and devices—audiovisual aids, training aids, media—of education. The range of materials and devices already developed is depicted succinctly in Edgar Dale's classic "Cone of Experience," which is reproduced with my adaptations in Exhibit 32. Dale explains his cone as follows:

> The cone is not offered as a perfect or mechanically flawless picture to be taken with absolute literalness in its simplified form. *It is merely a visual aid* in explaining the interrelationships of the various types of audio-visual materials, as well as their individual "positions" in the learning process.
>
> Looking at the cone, you see at once that each division represents a stage between the two extremes—between direct experience and pure abstraction. If you travel upward from the base, you move in the order of decreasing directness. . . . Similarly, if you travel downward from the pinnacle of the cone, you move in the order of increasing directness: "verbal symbols" are more abstract than "visual symbols"; and "visual symbols" are more abstract than such "one-sense aids" as recordings, radio, and still pictures.[12]

Dale does not imply a value hierarchy in his cone, that one level is better than another, that direct experience should be substituted for indirect experience; but he does maintain that "you can use indirect experiences wisely and well only when they are built on direct experiences."[13]

The selection and use of materials and devices is such a complex and rapidly changing aspect of educational technology that it would not be feasible to try to deal with it in detail in this book, and so a rather comprehensive list of resources is provided at the end of this chapter to which the reader can turn for specific instruction and information. But I should like to suggest several generalizations about the use of materials and devices with special reference to the principles of andragogy:

1. *In regard to textbooks.* The single most pervasive form of educational material, the textbook has been as much a liability as an asset to learning. It has been a liability by and large when it has been used as the basis of organization for a learning activity. In text-centered teaching the reading-assignment-followed-by-recitation-and-examination is the typical learning experience. It is obvious that such rigid adherence to a structure imposed by a textbook does not leave much room for individual differences, student needs and interests, consideration of issues and problems arising out of the experience of the students, or a spirit of self-directed inquiry. Textbooks—and all other sources of information—can be an asset to learning when used as resources to which students may go when the need for specific information arises in the process of inquiry.

2. *In regard to "homemade" materials.* In many instances published materials do not exist or are not available to fill a particular need in a learning activity. It is my observation that too often teachers feel a responsibility to fill the gap with something they produce, duplicate, and distribute to the students. I have found myself in recent years to be increasingly resisting this temptation and to be challenging the students to produce their own materials. And, frankly, the quality of the materials has improved—after all, a half-dozen students can give more energy to such a project than I can—and the process has been more educative for the students.

---

[12]Edgar Dale, *Audio-Visual Methods in Teaching* (New York: Dryden Press, 1954), p. 42.
[13]Ibid., p. 99.

3. *In regard to audiovisual aids.* There have been far too many errors in this aspect of educational practice owing to inadequate planning, selection, and student involvement. For what they may be worth, here are the steps I force myself to go through when using audiovisual aids:

a) *Planning by the instructor and students.* The introduction of audiovisual aids should be planned in conjunction with the techniques and content of a unit of learning. An aid should never (except in a course on audiovisual aids) be used simply because it is good in itself.

b) *Selection of the aid.* Available aids should be carefully reviewed (or previewed) by the instructor or a team of students, and only those that are clear, interesting, and directly on target should be selected.

c) *Preparation of equipment.* It is extremely important in the use of most teaching aids that whatever equipment is needed be set up and tested before it is used. For example, if films are to be used, the projector should be in place and threaded and focused, with volume set correctly (and with extra lamp bulbs handy).

d) *Preparation of the students.* The students should understand the purpose of the aid and should have an idea of what to look for in it.

Exhibit 32

THE CONE OF EXPERIENCE[14]

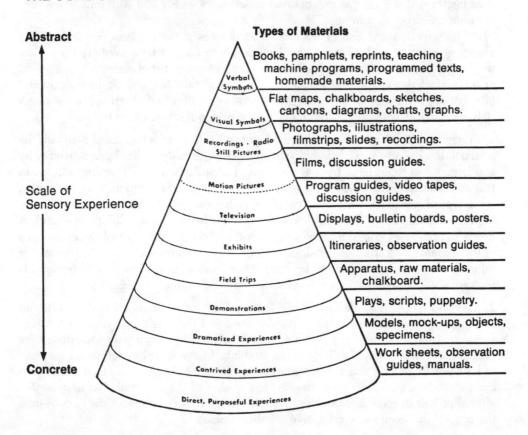

Abstract

Scale of Sensory Experience

Concrete

Types of Materials

Books, pamphlets, reprints, teaching machine programs, programmed texts, homemade materials.

Flat maps, chalkboards, sketches, cartoons, diagrams, charts, graphs.

Photographs, illustrations, filmstrips, slides, recordings.

Films, discussion guides.

Program guides, video tapes, discussion guides.

Displays, bulletin boards, posters.

Itineraries, observation guides.

Apparatus, raw materials, chalkboard.

Plays, scripts, puppetry.

Models, mock-ups, objects, specimens.

Work sheets, observation guides, manuals.

Verbal Symbols

Visual Symbols

Recordings · Radio Still Pictures

Motion Pictures

Television

Exhibits

Field Trips

Demonstrations

Dramatized Experiences

Contrived Experiences

Direct, Purposeful Experiences

[14]Adapted from Ibid., p. 43. By permission.

e) *Summary of the information.* When a large amount of information is presented, it will increase the aid's effectiveness if the points are summed up (preferably by a student) afterward.

f) *Discussion of the information.* In order to be sure that the information presented by the aid has meaning to the students it should be discussed and related to other aspects of their learning.

Up to now we have been talking about materials and devices that exist now. But a major revolution in this technology is imminent that may drastically transform the character of the learning-teaching transaction. Responsible scholars are predicting that such innovations will be introduced in the future as learning-center systems with stations placed in homes, offices, and dormitories (from which students can dial to a central computer facility for completely individualized instruction); pocket-size information-retrieval systems; a two-way visual-audio communicator; telepathic transmitters; and memory pills.[15]

Contract Learning

Finally, I would like to share with you a discovery that has solved more of the problems that have plagued me as a facilitator of learning over the years than all the other methods and techniques put together. It is a truly magical way to help learners structure their own learning—*the learning contract.*

First I want to talk about the problems it has helped me solve. At this point it would be helpful if you would turn to Exhibit K-11 in Appendix K to see what the learning contract form I use looks like, so that you can follow my reference to columns. For one thing, contract learning solves, or at least reduces, the problem of dealing with wide differences within any group of adult learners. It is characteristic of our field that we get people with widely varying backgrounds, previous experience, interests, learning styles, life patterns, outside commitments, and learning speeds. Didactic teachers usually cope with this situation by "aiming at the middle," with the hope that those at the lower end won't get too far behind and that those at the upper end won't get too bored—a hope that seldom is realized. In Column 1 of the learning contract the learners can state their objectives in their own words so as to take into account different emphases and can arrange them in different sequential orders. But even more important, in Column 2 they can identify learning resources and strategies that take into account different learning styles. I have had contracts in which five learners had identical objectives but identified five different ways of accomplishing them—one primarily by reading, another by interviewing experts, another by listening to audiotapes or viewing videotapes or films, another by engaging in a field project, and so on.

Another problem has to do with the learners clearly understanding the objectives of a learning activity. Traditionally we have relied on a course syllabus or program announcement to convey the instructors' objectives. The problem with this is that different learners will interpret the written objectives differently, often will not understand the instructors' language, and have little sense of ownership of the objectives. By having to write their objectives in their own words, using the instructors' objectives as a reference point, they are likely to understand them better and to have more of a sense of personal commitment to them.

Something wonderful often happens when learners start identifying resources for learning in Column 2; they discover a richer variety of resources than they would think

[15]Peter H. Rossi and Bruce J. Biddle, *The New Media and Education* (Chicago: Aldine Publishing Co., 1966).

of otherwise. Typically, learners come into a course or workshop with the preconception that the only resources are those of the instructors and printed materials they provide. When coaching learners on how to fill out Column 2, I challenge them to think of other resources—their own experience, their peers in the classroom, people they work with, professional library collections, and people in the community. This process opens up the learners' vistas to learning resources all around them in their environment.

Column 3 provides a self-disciplining device that helps the learners to schedule their time more efficiently by specifying target dates for completing each objective.

Columns 4 and 5 solve the most difficult problem of all for most teachers—evaluating the learning outcomes, or, in the case of academic settings, grading. Putting the responsibility on the learners to think for themselves what evidence they might collect to show that they have accomplished their objectives and how they can get that evidence judged, results in a sense of responsibility and a degree of creativity in the learners that is totally missing when the instructors take full responsibility for evaluation. But I must warn you that this is the point in the contracting process in which learners who are doing it for the first time become very anxious, for it is the first time in the lives of most of them that they have been asked (or allowed) to take this degree of responsibility for their own learning. Hence the need to provide strong support—both by the instructors and by peer groups.

Exhibit K-12 in Appendix K presents the "Guidelines" for using learning contracts which I hand out to participants in my workshops, inservice training sessions, and other "field-based" learning situations. A similar set of guidelines which I use in academic courses is reproduced in my *Self-Directed Learning: A Guide for Learners and Teachers* (Chicago: Association Press/Follett Publishing Co., 1975), pages 129–135. In that same book, on pages 44 to 58, I give a step-by-step description of how I go about performing the role of facilitator of learning in a graduate course based on the andragogical model. Exhibit K-13, Appendix K, reproduces an example of an actual contract by a student in my course, "History, Philosophy, and Contemporary Nature of Adult Education." Notice that this contract specifies what objectives will be accomplished for a grade of "B" (essentially the objectives contained in the course syllabus) and an "A" level objective that provides for superior performance in terms of the learner's unique interests, strengths, and professional goals.

An Example of Andragogy at Work

Since I have described elsewhere how I have applied the andragogical model in an academic course (*Self-Directed Learning*, pp. 44–58) and in a management development program (*The Adult Learner: A Neglected Species*, pp. 127–128 and 198–203), I will describe here how I use it in a short (one-day to five-day) workshop. I will follow the design contained in Appendix I, Exhibit I-5 to illustrate my procedures. Notice that it is a *process design* that can be used for any content area, since the participants identify the content they want to work on. I have used it with industrial trainers, government staff development officers, community college subject-matter teachers and administrators, religious educators, nurses, physicians, engineers, continuing dental educators, adult basic education teachers and administrators, cooperative extension workers, and others.

I arrange with the sponsors in advance for the meeting room to be set up with tables arranged as in Exhibit 21 (if at all possible; if the only room available is set up with rows of chairs, I quickly have the participants move their chairs into small circles of five or six persons each). Usually the participants have been asked to come a half hour before the starting time for registration, during which time coffee and rolls are available. As they register they are given a packet containing the handout materials (Appendix B, and Exhibits K–11, 12, 13, and 14 in Appendix K). The session starts at 9:00 A.M. with somebody welcoming the participants, reviewing the objectives, and introducing me (which I urge be kept as brief and personal as possible). I have a rule-of-thumb that there should be no more than ten minutes of front-end talking before the participants start participating. Here is what happens from then on:

9:00–10:00 A.M. Climate-setting Exercise

I need to find out some things about them so that I can make my resources relevant to them. I ask them to form groups of five or six persons each and share with one another their what's, who's, resources, and problems or concerns, as described earlier in this chapter. After twenty to thirty minutes I call them back together and retrieve the data by having them raise their hands if they fit into categories I call out (how many of you are administrators, how many are teachers, and so on). I ask a reporter for each group to summarize the problems and concerns that were expressed. I explain at this point that I will not undertake to solve their problems for them, but will provide some principles which they can later use in developing new solutions to their problems.

I like to take another fifteen to twenty minutes analyzing this experience in the light of the characteristics of a climate conducive to learning outlined at the beginning of this chapter, and getting feedback from them as to which of these characteristics they are experiencing in this environment.

10:30–11:30 A.M. Presentation of Pedagogical and Andragogical Models

After a coffee break I present my andragogical theory of adult learning, emphasizing that they should hear it not as "the word from on high," but as the framework of assumptions and principles that I am operating from—that it is more self-revelation than eternal revelation. I encourage them to test the theory in the light of their own experience, and to adopt only those aspects that make sense to them. I frequently use the chart in Exhibit K–14 in Appendix K as a handout so that the participants can follow along as I talk about the assumptions and process elements of the pedagogical and andragogical models and can raise questions or dialogue with me about them.

11:30 A.M.–Noon Group Meetings

During the half hour before lunch I have the participants get back into their small groups and apply the andragogical model to the problems and concerns they generated in their earlier meetings, identifying any questions they want to ask me after lunch.

1:00–2:00 P.M. Responses to Group's Questions

I have another rule-of-thumb, which is that I never schedule anything during the hour after lunch which puts the participants in a passive role, if I can help it. Teachers who have had lecture classes the hour after lunch know what I mean. (Actually, I prefer the Latin American solution to this problem better—the siesta; but our Calvinistic culture does not approve of this solution.) So I usually have the group raise the questions they generated before lunch, and I respond to them—often engaging in fairly lively dialogue about the issues and obstacles they expect to confront if they attempt to introduce the andragogical model back home.

2:00–2:45 P.M. Diagnosis of Learning Needs

Around two o'clock I introduce the idea of competency-based education, bringing out the points I make in Chapter 2. Then I have them make a self-rating of their competency-development needs, using the competency model in Appendix B. Actually, for the purpose of simply demonstrating this self-diagnostic process, they do not need to take the time to go through the whole model, so after about ten minutes I check to see if everybody has found at least one competency in which the "P" is two or more notches below the "R." If more time is needed to get everybody to that point, I give them another five or ten minutes.

Then we take another coffee break.

3:00–3:30 P.M. Drafting of Learning Contracts

When we reconvene I give a brief introduction to the idea and potency of contract learning, bringing out the points I make earlier in this chapter. Then I have them read the "Guidelines" (Exhibit K–12) that are in their packets and raise any questions of clarification. When I see that most participants are on the last page, I suggest that each one choose one of the competencies for which the "P" was below the "R," translate it into a learning objective in Column 1 of the learning contract form, and fill out the remaining columns of the form as suggested in the "Guidelines."

3:30–4:00 P.M. Sharing of Experience with Contracts

I call them back together now and explain that at this point when learners do this for the first time they are usually very anxious, since they have never before had to take this degree of responsibility for planning their learning, and so they need a support system. I ask each participant to turn to one or two nearby peers and form a "consultative team" which will review the work of each of its members and make helpful suggestions. I ask them to keep track of any problems or issues regarding the use of learning contracts in their back-home situations that they want to raise with me.

4:00–4:45 P.M. Problem Clinic

After about a half hour of mutual consulting I bring them back together again and invite them to raise any questions that have arisen, to which I respond.

4:45–5:00 P.M. Evaluation

Sometimes the sponsoring organization will have its own evaluation form, in which case I have the participants fill it out at this time. If this is not the case, I ask the participants to go back into their original groups of five or six, choose one person to be its recorder, and then agree on three or four statements they would like to make to me and the sponsors. I ask the recorder to turn in a sheet with these statements on it at the end of the period. In closing, I suggest that the participants complete diagnosing their competency-development needs and make out a complete learning contract after they get home, thus having a comprehensive plan for continuing self-development.

I use this same general design for longer workshops, allowing more time to go into more depth at each stage. Also, time is available in workshops of from three to five days for specific learning experiences called for in the contract to be structured.

Evaluating Results and Rediagnosing Learning Needs

This is the easiest section of this whole book to write, for all I really have to say is to go back to the earlier section of this chapter on "Providing Evidence of Present Performance" and review the procedures suggested there for diagnosing the gaps between desired behavior and present performance. Evaluation of learning consists of repeating these procedures (or equivalent forms of them) and measuring the changes that have occurred. Usually two results will flow from this activity: 1) the participants will have a perspective on their new level of strengths and weaknesses in the light of their original model of desired behaviors; and 2) they will discover that their notion of a model of desired behavior has been raised a notch or two, so that a new level of gaps between desired behavior and present performance has appeared.

And this is the central dynamic of the process of lifelong learning, continuing education, and andragogy.

For Your Continuing Inquiry . . .

Regarding Designing and Managing Learning in General

Craig, Robert L. (ed.). *Training and Development Handbook*. 2nd ed. New York: McGraw-Hill, 1976.

Davis, Larry N., and McCallon, Earl. *Planning, Conducting, Evaluating Workshops*. Austin, Texas: Learning Concepts, 1974.

Eble, Kenneth E. *The Craft of Teaching*. San Francisco: Jossey-Bass, 1976.

Garrison, Roger H. *Implementing Innovative Instruction*. New Directions for Community Colleges, No. 5. San Francisco: Jossey-Bass, 1974.

Godbey, Gordon C. *Applied Andragogy: A Practical Manual for the Continuing Education of Adults*. College Station, Penn.: Continuing Education Division, The Pennsylvania State University, 1978.

Hospital Continuing Education Project. *Training and Continuing Education: A Handbook for Health Care Institutions*. Chicago: Hospital Research and Educational Trust, 1970.

Houle, Cyril O. *The Design of Education*. San Francisco: Jossey-Bass, 1972.

Ingalls, John D., and Arceri, J. M. *A Trainers' Guide to Andragogy*. SRS 72–05301. U.S. Department of Health, Education and Welfare. Washington, D.C.: Government Printing Office, 1972.

Joyce, Bruce, and Weil, Marsha. *Models of Teaching*. Englewood Cliffs, N.J.: Prentice-Hall, 1972.

McKeachie, Wilbert J. *Teaching Tips: A Guidebook for the Beginning College Teacher*. Lexington, Mass.: D. C. Heath, 1969.

Miller, Harry L. *Teaching and Learning in Adult Education*. New York: Macmillan, 1964.

Nadler, Leonard, and Nadler, Zeace. *The Conference Book*. Houston: Gulf Publishing Co., 1977.

Regarding Competency Models and Self-directed Learning

(See bibliography at end of Chapter 2.)

Regarding Planning and Designing Learning Activities

Adams, R. E. *DACUM: Approach to Curriculum, Learning, and Evaluation in Occupational Training*. Yarmouth, Nova Scotia: Canada Newstart Program, 1972.

Curriculum Design and Development Course Team, the Open University. *Curriculum Innovation*. New York: Halsted Press, 1975.

Drum, David J., and Knott, J. Eugene. *Structured Groups for Facilitating Development: Acquiring Life Skills, Resolving Life Themes, and Making Life Transitions*. New York: Human Sciences Press, 1977.

Havelock, Ronald G., and Havelock, Mary. *Training for Change Agents: A Guide to the Design of Training Programs in Education and Other Fields*. Ann Arbor, Mich.: University of Michigan Institute for Social Research, 1973.

Jones, G. Brian, et al. *New Designs and Methods for Delivering Human Developmental Services*. New York: Human Sciences Press, 1977.

McLagan, Patricia A. *Helping Others Learn: Designing Programs for Adults*. Reading, Mass.: Addison-Wesley, 1978.

Regarding Educational Objectives

Baker, Eva L., and Popham, James. *Expanding Dimensions of Instructional Objectives*. Englewood Cliffs, N.J.: Prentice-Hall, 1973.

Bloom, Benjamin S. (ed.). *Taxonomy of Educational Objectives: Handbook I: Cognitive Domain*. New York: David McKay, 1956.

Cohen, Arthur M. *Objectives for College Courses*. Beverly Hills, Cal.: Glencoe Press, 1970.

French, Will. *Behavioral Goals of General Education in High School*. New York: Russell Sage Foundation, 1957.

Kibler, R. J., et al. *Behavioral Objectives and Instruction*. Boston: Allyn & Bacon, 1970.

Krathwohl, David R., et al. *Taxonomy of Educational Objectives: Handbook II: Affective Domain*. New York: David McKay, 1964.

Mager, Robert. *Goal Analysis*. Belmont, Cal.: Fearon Publishers, 1972.

_____. *Preparing Instructional Objectives*. Palo Alto, Cal.: Fearon Publishers, 1962.

Mager, Robert F., and Pipe, Peter. *Analyzing Performance Problems*. Belmont, Cal.: Fearon Publishers, 1970.

Regarding Methods, Techniques, and Materials

Aker, George F. *Adult Education Procedures, Methods and Techniques*. Syracuse, N.Y.: Library of Continuing Education, Syracuse University, 1965.

Baker, Robert L., and Schultz, Richard E. (eds.). *Instructional Product Development*. New York: Van Nostrand-Reinhold Co., 1965.

Benne, Kenneth; Bradford, Leland; and Lippitt, Ronald. *The Laboratory Method of Changing and Learning*. Palo Alto, Cal.: Science and Behavior Books, 1975.

Bergevin, Paul, et al. *Adult Education Procedures: A Handbook of Tested Patterns for Effective Participation*. Greenwich, Conn.: Seabury Press, 1963.

Bergevin, Paul, and McKinley, John. *Participation Training for Adult Education.* St. Louis, Mo.: Bethany Press, 1965.

Berte, Neal R. *Individualizing Education by Learning Contracts.* New Directions for Higher Education, No. 10. San Francisco: Jossey-Bass, 1975.

Carlson, Elliot. *Learning Through Games.* New York: Public Affairs Press, 1970.

Dickinson, Gary. *Teaching Adults: A Handbook for Instructors.* Toronto: New Press, 1973.

Otto, Herbert. *Group Methods to Actualize Human Potential.* La Jolla, Cal.: National Center for the Exploration of Human Potential, 1970.

Pfeiffer, William J., and Jones, John E. *A Handbook of Structured Experiences for Human Relations Training.* Issued periodically since 1969. La Jolla, Cal.: University Associates, 1969–1979.

Pigors, Paul. *Case Method in Human Relations: The Incident Process.* New York: McGraw-Hill, 1961.

Rogers, Carl. *Carl Rogers on Encounter Groups.* New York: Harper & Row, 1970.

Rossi, Peter, and Biddle, Bruce (eds.). *The New Media and Education.* Chicago: Aldine Publishing Co., 1966.

Russell, James D. *Modular Instruction.* Minneapolis: Burgess Press, 1974.

Schid, E. O., and Boocock, Sarane. *Simulation Games in Learning.* New York: Sage Publications, 1970.

Simon, Sydney B., et al. *Values Clarification.* New York: Hart Publishing Co., 1972.

Stroller, Frederick H. *The Use of Focused Feedback via Videotape in Small Groups.* Washington, D.C.: NTL Institute of Applied Behavioral Science, 1966.

Thayer, Louis (ed.). *Affective Education: Strategies for Experiential Learning.* La Jolla, Cal.: University Associates, 1976.

Verner, Coolie. *A Conceptual Schema for the Identification and Classification of Processes.* Washington, D.C.: Adult Education Association of the U.S.A., 1962.

Appendixes A–K

Appendix A

Correspondence with the Publishers of
Merriam-Webster Dictionaries Regarding "Andragogy"

Editorial Department
G. & C. Merriam Company
Springfield, Mass.

Gentlemen:

I am in the process of writing a book in which I feel
the need to coin a word, and I am hoping that you will have
some interest in helping to assure that it will be correct.

My book is on the emerging new technology of adult
education, which is based on a set of assumptions about
certain ways in which adults are different from youth as
learners.

It is important, therefore, to distinguish this new
technology from pedagogy, the art and science of teaching
children. As I understand it, "pedagogy" is derived from the
Greek <u>paid</u>, meaning child, and <u>agogos</u>, meaning leader. Some
European adult educators have been using the coined word
"andragogy" to describe the new technology of adult education. As I understand it, they are taking the Greek word
<u>andros</u>, meaning "man" as the stem for the new word. Since
I cannot find a Greek word for "adult," I take it that
<u>andros</u> is the nearest thing there is to a parallel for <u>paid</u>.

But I am inclined to emphasize the difference between
the two technologies by spelling the word andr<u>o</u>gogy rather
than andr<u>a</u>gogy. In combining two words of this sort, is
there a free choice between using the "o" in <u>andros</u> and the
"a" in <u>agogus</u>?

Since this book will be rather widely used in our field,
it may result in a new word being added to the lexicon of
adult education in this country. I would greatly appreciate
your advice.

Sincerely yours,

Malcolm S. Knowles
Professor

253

G. & C. MERRIAM COMPANY

PUBLISHERS OF MERRIAM-WEBSTER DICTIONARIES

SPRINGFIELD   MASS. 01101

February 29, 1968

Professor Malcolm S. Knowles
School of Education
Boston University
765 Commonwealth Avenue
Boston, Massachusetts 02215

Dear Professor Knowles:

We are glad to try to be of help to you in your search for a term to
denote "adult education", of which you wrote us on February 26. We have not
been able to find any record of previous use of <u>andragogy</u> in English. We have
however noted one instance of <u>androgogy</u>. This occurs in an abstract by R.
Lassner, no. 1487 in <u>Psychological Abstracts</u> 22 (April, 1948), of an article
in German by Heinrich Hanselmann in <u>Zeitschrift für Kinderpsychiatrie</u> 14 (1947),
53-60. Lassner writes, "If a person suffers as a result of speculation regarding metaphysical problems, he should be treated by the non-medical specialist.
This is the field of education (pedagogy) or re-education of the adult
(androgogy)." We assume that Lassner is here anglicizing a German <u>Androgogik</u>
found in Hanselmann.

We must, however, remark that while no exception can be taken to the formation <u>andragogy</u>, the spelling <u>androgogy</u> is difficult to defend on any grounds;
it violates the normal methods of forming compounds in Greek itself or in modern languages using Greek elements to form technical terms. The elements to
be joined are the stem <u>andr-</u> of the Greek word <u>anēr</u> "man", and the Greek word
<u>agōgos</u> "leader". The first element of a Greek compound is regularly the stem
(not the nominative or dictionary form). There is no <u>o</u> in the stem of the word
for "man"; the form <u>andr-os</u> is the genitive case, "man's", the <u>o</u> belonging to
the case ending. If, however, the stem of the first element ends in a consonant
and the second element begins with a consonant, an <u>o</u> is commonly inserted to
facilitate pronunciation. Hence we find such forms as <u>ped-o-baptism</u>, <u>andr-o-</u>
<u>gyne</u>, <u>metr-o-polis</u>. This <u>o</u> originated in imitation of the many compounds in
which the stem of the first element actually ended in this vowel (e.g. <u>mono-</u>,
<u>philo-</u>, <u>anthropo-</u>). But where the second element of a compound begins with a
vowel, not only is no connecting <u>o</u> needed after a consonant, but stems ending
in <u>o</u> or other vowels drop that vowel (e.g. <u>mon-archy</u>, <u>phil-ately</u>). What does
not happen in any circumstances is dropping the initial vowel of a second
element. We do not say <u>mono-rchy</u> or <u>philo-tely</u>; much less should we say <u>andr-o-</u>
<u>gogy</u>, dropping a vowel originally present and then inserting in its place one
not originally present. We therefore advise against using the proposed
<u>androgogy</u> as likely to cause raised eyebrows among those acquainted with the
principles governing the formation of compounds from Greek elements. To
<u>andragogy</u>, on the other hand, no such objections can be raised, and the close
parallel of <u>pedagogy</u> makes it seem a very suitable formation to denote the
contrasted discipline.

Very truly yours,
G. & C. MERRIAM COMPANY

By *F. Stuart Crawford*
F. Stuart Crawford

Appendix B

Competencies for the Role of Adult Educator:
Self-Diagnostic Rating Scale*

* Developed by Malcolm S. Knowles and students at North Carolina State University Department of Adult and Community College Education, 1978.

Name _____

Indicate on the six-point scale below: 1) the level of each competency required for performing the role you are in or are preparing for by placing an "R" (required level) at the appropriate point; 2) the level of your present development of each competency by placing a "P" (present level) at the appropriate point. For example, if your role is that of teacher, you might rate the required competencies for the role of learning facilitator as high and for the role of administrator as moderate or low; whereas if your role is that of administrator, you might do just the reverse. You will emerge with a profile of the gaps between where you are now and where you need to be in order to perform your role well.

	Absent	Low (awareness)	Moderate (conceptual understanding)		High (expert)
	0	1	2	3	4	5

I. As a Learning Facilitator

A. Regarding the conceptual and theoretical framework of adult learning:

1. Ability to describe and apply modern concepts and research findings regarding the needs, interests, motivations, capacities, and developmental characteristics of adults as learners.

   0   1   2   3   4   5

2. Ability to describe the differences between youth and adults as learners and the implications of these differences for teaching and learning.

   0   1   2   3   4   5

3. Ability to assess the effects on learning of forces impinging on learners from the larger environment (group, organizations, communities).

   0   1   2   3   4   5

4. Ability to describe the various theories of learning and assess their relevance to particular adult learning situations.

   0   1   2   3   4   5

	Absent	Low (awareness)	Moderate (conceptual understanding)		High (expert)

5. Ability to conceptualize and explain the role of teacher as a facilitator and resource to self-directed learners.

| 0 | 1 | 2 | 3 | 4 | 5 |

6.

| 0 | 1 | 2 | 3 | 4 | 5 |

B. Regarding the designing and implementing of learning experiences:

1. Ability to establish a warm, mutually respectful, facilitatlve relationship with learners.

| 0 | 1 | 2 | 3 | 4 | 5 |

2. Ability to engineer a physical and psychological climate of comfort, interactiveness, collaborativeness, openness, and mutual trust.

| 0 | 1 | 2 | 3 | 4 | 5 |

3. Ability to engage learners responsibly in self-diagnosis of needs for learning.

| 0 | 1 | 2 | 3 | 4 | 5 |

4. Ability to engage learners in formulating goals, objectives, and directions of growth in terms that are meaningful to them.

| 0 | 1 | 2 | 3 | 4 | 5 |

5. Knowledge of the rationales for selecting a variety of materials, methods, and techniques for achieving particular educational objectives.

| 0 | 1 | 2 | 3 | 4 | 5 |

6. Skill in using a broad range of materials, methods, and techniques and in inventing techniques to fit new situations.

| 0 | 1 | 2 | 3 | 4 | 5 |

7. Ability to involve learners appropriately in the planning, conducting, and evaluating of learning activities.

| 0 | 1 | 2 | 3 | 4 | 5 |

	Absent	Low (awareness)	Moderate (conceptual understanding)		High (expert)

8. Ability to design learning experiences for accomplishing a variety of purposes while taking into account individual differences among learners.

0	1	2	3	4	5

9. Ability to make use of small-group processes effectively.

0	1	2	3	4	5

10. Ability to evaluate learning procedures and outcomes and to select or construct appropriate instruments and procedures for this purpose.

0	1	2	3	4	5

11.

0	1	2	3	4	5

12.

0	1	2	3	4	5

II. As a Program Developer

A. Regarding the planning process:

1. Ability to describe and apply the foundational concepts (e.g., goal setting, forecasting, social mapping, social action, systems theory, leadership identification, needs assessment) that undergird the planning process in adult education.

0	1	2	3	4	5

2. Ability to involve community representatives appropriately in the planning process.

0	1	2	3	4	5

	Absent	Low (awareness)	Moderate (conceptual understanding)		High (expert)

3. Ability to develop and use instruments and procedures for assessing the needs of individuals, organizations, and subpopulations in communities.

    0   1   2   3   4   5

4. Ability to work effectively with various agencies in the community in collaborative program planning.

    0   1   2   3   4   5

5.

    0   1   2   3   4   5

B. Regarding the designing and operating of programs in adult education:

1. Ability to select and use procedures for constructing andragogical process designs.

    0   1   2   3   4   5

2. Ability to design programs with a creative variety of formats, activities, schedules, resources, and evaluative procedures.

    0   1   2   3   4   5

3. Ability to interpret census data, community surveys, needs assessments, etc., in adapting programs to specific clienteles.

    0   1   2   3   4   5

4. Ability to use planning mechanisms, such as advisory councils, committees, task forces, etc., effectively.

    0   1   2   3   4   5

5. Ability to develop and carry out a plan for program evaluation that will satisfy the requirements of institutional accountability and provide for program improvement.

    0   1   2   3   4   5

6.

    0   1   2   3   4   5

	Absent	Low (awareness)	Moderate (conceptual understanding)	High (expert)

III. As an Administrator

A. Regarding organizational development and maintenance:

1. Ability to describe and apply theories and research findings about organizational behavior, management, and renewal.

   0   1   2   3   4   5

2. Ability to formulate a personal philosophy of administration and adapt it to various organizational situations.

   0   1   2   3   4   5

3. Ability to formulate policies that clearly convey the definition of the mission, social philosophy, educational commitment, etc., of an organization.

   0   1   2   3   4   5

4. Ability to evaluate organizational effectiveness and guide its continuous self-renewal processes.

   0   1   2   3   4   5

5. Ability to plan effectively with and through others, sharing responsibilities and decision making with them when appropriate.

   0   1   2   3   4   5

6. Ability to select, supervise, and provide for inservice education of personnel.

   0   1   2   3   4   5

7. Ability to evaluate staff performance.   0   1   2   3   4   5

8. Ability to analyze and interpret legislation affecting adult education.

   0   1   2   3   4   5

9. Ability to describe financial policies and practices in the field of adult education and to identify a variety of funding sources.

   0   1   2   3   4   5

	Absent	Low (awareness)		Moderate (conceptual understanding)		High (expert)

10. Ability to perform the role of change agent vis-à-vis organizations and communities utilizing educational processes.

	0	1	2	3	4	5

11.

	0	1	2	3	4	5

B. Regarding program administration:

1. Ability to design and use promotion, publicity, and public-relations strategies appropriately and effectively.

	0	1	2	3	4	5

2. Ability to design and operate programs within the framework of a limited budget.

	0	1	2	3	4	5

3. Ability to make and monitor financial plans and procedures.

	0	1	2	3	4	5

4. Ability to prepare grant proposals and identify potential funding sources for them.

	0	1	2	3	4	5

5. Ability to make use of consultants appropriately.

	0	1	2	3	4	5

6. Ability and willingness to experiment with programmatic innovations and to assess their results.

	0	1	2	3	4	5

7.

	0	1	2	3	4	5

Appendix C
Life Tasks of American Adults

Vocation and Career

Early Adulthood (18–30)
Exploring career options
Choosing a career line
Getting a job
Being interviewed
Learning job skills
Getting along at work
Getting ahead at work
Getting job protection
Dealing with the issue of
  military service
Getting vocational counseling
Changing jobs

Middle Adulthood (30–65)
Learning advanced job skills
Supervising others
Changing careers
Dealing with unemployment
Planning for retirement
Making second careers for
  mothers

Older Adulthood (65 and over)
Adjusting to retirement
Finding new ways to be useful
Understanding social security,
  medicare, and welfare

Home and Family Living

Courting
Selecting a mate
Preparing for marriage
Family planning
Preparing for children
Raising children
Understanding children
Preparing children for school
Helping children in school
Solving marital problems
Using family counseling
Managing a home
Financial planning
Managing money
Buying goods and services
Making home repairs
Gardening

Helping teenage children become adults
Letting your children go
Relating to one's spouse as a person
Adjusting to aging parents
Learning to cook for two
Planning for retirement

Adjusting to reduced income
Establishing new living arrangements
Adjusting to death of spouse
Learning to live alone
Relating to grandchildren
Establishing new intimate relationships
Putting your estate in order

Personal Development

Improving your reading ability
Improving your writing ability
Improving your speaking ability
Improving your listening ability
Continuing your general education
Developing your religious faith
Improving problem-solving skills
Making better decisions
Understanding yourself
Finding your self-identity
Discovering your aptitudes
Clarifying your values
Understanding other people
Learning to be self-directing
Improving personal appearance
Establishing intimate relations
Making use of personal counseling

Finding new interests
Keeping out of a rut
Compensating for physiological changes
Dealing with change
Developing emotional flexibility
Learning to cope with crises
Developing a realistic time perspective

Developing compensatory abilities
Understanding the aging process
Re-examining your values
Keeping future-oriented
Keeping up your morale
Keeping up to date
Keeping in touch with young people
Keeping curious
Keeping up personal appearance
Keeping an open mind
Finding a new self-identity
Developing a new time perspective
Preparing for death

Enjoyment of Leisure Time

Early Adulthood
- Choosing hobbies
- Finding new friends
- Joining organizations
- Planning your time
- Buying equipment
- Planning family recreation
- Leading recreational activities

Middle Adulthood
- Finding less active hobbies
- Broadening your cultural interests
- Learning new recreational skills
- Finding new friends
- Joining new organizations
- Planning recreation for two

Older Adulthood
- Establishing affiliations with the older age group
- Finding new hobbies
- Learning new recreational skills
- Planning a balanced recreational program

Health

Early Adulthood
- Keeping fit
- Planning diets
- Finding and using health services
- Preventing accidents
- Using first aid
- Understanding children's diseases
- Understanding how the human body functions
- Buying and using drugs and medicines
- Developing a healthy life-style
- Recognizing the symptoms of physical and mental illness

Middle Adulthood
- Adjusting to physiological changes
- Changing diets
- Controlling weight
- Getting exercise
- Having annual medical exams
- Compensating for losses in strength

Older Adulthood
- Adjusting to decreasing strength and health
- Keeping fit
- Changing your diet
- Having regular medical exams
- Getting appropriate exercise
- Using drugs and medicines wisely
- Learning to deal with stress
- Maintaining your reserves

Community Living

Early Adulthood
- Relating to school and teachers
- Learning about community resources
- Learning how to get help
- Learning how to exert influence
- Preparing to vote
- Developing leadership skills
- Keeping up with the world
- Taking action in the community
- Organizing community activities for children and youth

Middle Adulthood
- Taking more social responsibility
- Taking leadership roles in organizations
- Working for the welfare of others
- Engaging in politics
- Organizing community improvement activities

Older Adulthood
- Working for improved conditions for the elderly
- Volunteering your service
- Maintaining organizational ties

Appendix D
Toward a Model of Lifelong Education*

* A working paper prepared for the Consultation on Lifelong Education, UNESCO Institute for Education, Hamburg, Germany, October, 1972, by Malcolm S. Knowles.

Alfred North Whitehead presented the insight about two generations ago that the reversal of the relationship between two basic dynamics of civilization in this century has required the redefinition of the purpose of education. Throughout history, until the first quarter of the twentieth century, the life-span of an individual was greater than the time-span of major cultural change. Under this condition it was appropriate to define education as a process of transmittal of what is known—of transmitting the culture. It was also appropriate to define the role of the teacher as that of transmitter of information and to regard education as an agency for youth.

But, Whitehead pointed out in a commencement address at Harvard University in 1930, "We are living in the first period of human history for which this assumption is false . . . today this time-span is considerably shorter than that of human life, and accordingly our training must prepare individuals to face a novelty of conditions."[1] In other words, as the time-span of major cultural change has become shorter than the life-span of the individual, it becomes necessary to redefine education as a process of continuing inquiry. The role of the teacher must shift from that of transmitter of information to facilitator and resource to self-directed inquiry, and to regard education as a lifelong process. For knowledge gained at any point of time will become increasingly obsolete in the course of time.

Two generations after this insight was presented, the schools around the world largely remain tied to the subject-matter transmittal framework of the medieval trivium and quadrivium (with some elaboration and the addition of vocational subjects). Accordingly, the educational establishment has come under increasing criticism from such social analysts as Saul Alinsky, Philippe Aries, Jerome Bruner, Jerry Farber, Paulo Freire, Paul Goodman, John Holt, Torsten Husen, Sidney Jourard, Ivan Illich, Rene Maheu, Margaret Mead, Jean Piaget, Neil Postman, Everett Reimer, Carl Rogers, Charles Silberman, Harold Taylor, and Alvin Toffler. The heart of much of the criticism is that the schools are out of touch with the reality of both human nature and the nature of a changing world. And one of the crucial new realities is that education must be lifelong to avoid the catastrophe of human obsolescence.

Clearly, therefore, new models of education as a lifelong process must be developed. I present the skeleton of such a model below in the hope that others will join me in strengthening it and putting flesh on it. The model consists of several assumptions and elements.

Competency Development for Life Roles

The first assumption is that the purpose of education is the development of competencies for performing the various roles required in human life. The first element in a new model would, therefore, be a taxonomy of these roles and their required competencies. Here is the beginning of such a taxonomy:

Roles	Competencies
Learner	Reading, writing, computing, perceiving, conceptualizing, evaluating, imagining, inquiring
Being a self (with unique self-identity)	Self-analyzing, sensing, goal building, objectivizing, value clarifying, expressing

---

[1] Alfred N. Whitehead, "Introduction," Wallace B. Donham, *Business Adrift* (New York: McGraw-Hill, 1931), pp. viii–xix.

Friend	Loving, empathizing, listening, collaborating, sharing, helping, giving feedback, supporting
Citizen	Caring, participating, leading, decision making, acting, "conscientizing," discussing, having perspective (historical and cultural)
Family member	Maintaining health, planning, managing, helping, sharing, buying, saving, loving, taking responsibility
Worker	Career planning, technical skills, using supervision, giving supervision, getting along with people, cooperating, planning, delegating, managing
Leisure-time user	Knowing resources, appreciating the arts and humanities, performing, playing, relaxing, reflecting, planning, risking

Obviously this list is not exhaustive; it is intended merely to illustrate some kinds of potential candidates for a taxonomic system.

Development of Skills of Learning

The second assumption is that the primary purpose of schooling is to help children and youth learn the skills of learning. The ultimate behavioral objective of schooling would be: The individual engages efficiently in collaborative self-directed inquiry in self-actualizing directions. I believe that these skills of learning include at least the following:

1. The ability to develop and be in touch with curiosities. Perhaps another way of describing this skill would be "the ability to engage in divergent thinking."

2. The ability to formulate questions, based on one's curiosities, that are answerable through inquiry (in contrast to questions that are answerable by authority or faith). This skill is the beginning of the ability to engage in convergent thinking or inductive-deductive reasoning.

3. The ability to identify the data required to answer the various kinds of questions.

4. The ability to locate the most relevant and reliable sources of the required data (including experts, teachers, colleagues, one's own experience, the various audiovisual media, and the community).

5. The ability to select and use the most efficient means for collecting the required data from the appropriate sources.

6. The ability to organize, analyze, and evaluate the data so as to get valid answers to questions.

7. The ability to generalize, apply, and communicate the answers to the questions raised.

The Development of a Spiral of "Learning Projects"

The third assumption is that the curriculum of organized education will most effectively achieve the objective of schooling if it is organized according to a spiraling series of individual learning projects,[2] with the understanding that several individuals with similar learning needs might engage in a learning project collaboratively. Under this assumption I visualize that the school would be presented to learners as a "learning-resource center" and that teachers would be presented as "learning-project consultants."

---

[2] For an elaboration on the concept of learning projects, see Allen Tough, *The Adult's Learning Projects* (Toronto: The Ontario Institute for Studies in Education, 1971), pp. 6–15.

In brief, the curricular process would work something like this:

Each individual's learning-project spiral would proceed according to his maturational process.

At each developmental stage (to be determined by diagnostic procedures) the learning-project consultant would expose the learner to appropriate role-competency models. For example, for early learners these might include the beginning competencies of the roles of learner, friend, family member, and leisure-time user. These roles might well be the focus for the next several years, with increasingly complex competencies being presented. In early adolescence the emphasis would gradually shift to the roles of unique self, citizen, and worker.

Following each exposure to a role-competency model the learner would select a set of competencies for which learning projects would then be developed with the help of learning-project consultants and other relevant resource specialists. Emphasis would be placed on the learner's making use of learning resources increasingly proactively and in widening circles out into the community.

At the completion of each learning project the consultant would engage with the learner in an analysis of the experience in a variety of dimensions, including cognitive gains, learning-skill gains, affective gains (and losses), and diagnosis of further needs.

I visualize that the learner would be gradually weaned away from the perception that he is engaged in schooling, and that when he has acquired the skills of learning appropriate to his aspirations he will come to see himself as a self-directed learner, making use of the learning-resources center as a resource that is available to him on his terms for the rest of his life. There will be no such thing as graduation. There will be no such thing as adult education. There will only be lifelong education.

Appendix E
Some Papers, Research Reports,
and Experiments on Andragogy

Abbott, William D. "An Experimental Study of Two Systems of College Dormitory Administration Comparing Andragogy and Pedagogy." Unpublished Ed.D. dissertation, Boston University, 1974.

"Andragogy and Tutored Videotape Instruction—A Significant Finding," PER Report, I, 21 (June 6, 1977), 2–3.

Becker, Steve. "Malcolm Knowles: An In-depth Interview with Steve Becker," an audiocassette series. Boston: Learncom, 1978.

Berle, Jill A. "Learning: A Life Experience," *Marine Corps Gazette,* December 1975, pp. 36–37.

Bernard, Jean L. "Perceived Constraints Operating on Adult Students, Teachers, and Directors in GEGEPS Regarding the Adoption of New Practices in Adult Education." Unpublished Ed.D. dissertation, Boston University, 1972.

Bowers, R. Dennis. "Testing the Validity of the Andragogical Theory of Education in Selected Situations." Unpublished Ph.D. dissertation, Boston University, 1977.

Bromley, James. "An Investigation of Some Changes That Take Place in Students as a Result of Their Participation in the Graduate Program of Adult Education at Boston University." Unpublished Ed.D. dissertation, Boston University, 1972.

Brown, F. Gerald, and Wedel, Kenneth R. *Assessing Training Needs.* Washington, D.C.: National Training and Development Service Press, 1974.

Brown, George C. "Planning for Adult Learners: An Introduction to Andragogy," Ecumenical Leadership Education Program, 1 Joy Street, Boston, 1977.

Brown, Leonard, et al. "Student-centered Teaching: The Analog to Client-centered Practice," *Journal of Education for Social Work,* Fall 1976.

Carson, David. "Analysis of Rationales Used to Justify Student Participation in Governance: A Philosophical Investigation of Their Relationship to the Concept of Andragogy." Unpublished Ed.D. dissertation, Boston University, 1972.

Cassara, Beverly. "A Study of Various Kinds of Educational Growth of Students in the Goddard College Degree Program." Unpublished Ed.D. dissertation, Boston University, 1970.

Cawood, Joe, and Stewart, Bev C. "The School Administrator: An Andragogue," *Education Canada,* Spring 1975, pp. 35–37.

Cooper, Signe, et al. "Self-directed Continuing Education in Nursing," American Nursing Association, Kansas City, Mo., 1978.

Cronkite, John W. "Andragogical Need Assessment Based on Projecting Images of the Future." Unpublished Ed.D. dissertation, Boston University, 1974.

Culbertson, William. "A Conceptual Model for In-Service Education for Community College and Technical Institute Occupational Instructors Who Have Not Participated in Traditional Teacher Education Programs." Unpublished Ed.D. dissertation, University of North Carolina at Greensboro, 1975.

Davia, Ralph A. "A Rationale and Assessment of Adult Education in the Department of Defense Schools, District III: An Exploratory Study." Unpublished Ph.D. dissertation, University of Santo Tomas, Manila, Philippines, 1976.

Decker, James T., et al. "In Search of a Consistency Model for Evaluation of Student Performance in Nontraditional Education," *Alternative Higher Education* II, 2 (1977), 145–150.

Dratz, Russell J. "The Effects of Programs Which Foster Self-directed Learning on the Drop-Out Rate, the Length of Stay, and the Preference for Self-directed Learning of Adult Basic Education Students." Unpublished Ed.D. dissertation, State University of New York, Albany, 1978.

Elias, John L. "Andragogy Revisited," *Adult Education* XXIX, 4 (Summer 1979), 252–256.

Estrine, Lewis. "The Effectiveness of Linear Versus Branching Programmed Instructional Methods in Adult Cognitive Learning." Unpublished Ed.D. dissertation, Boston University, 1975.

Fillinger, Robert E. "A Study of Factors Affecting Teaching in Protestant Theological Seminaries." Unpublished Ed.D. dissertation, Boston University, 1974.

Frey, Louise A., and DuBois, Eugene E. "Andragogy and Social Work Supervision: What They Can Learn from One Another." Unpublished paper, Boston University School of Social Work, 1972.

Gelford, Bernard, et al. "An Andragogical Application to the Training of Social Workers," *Journal of Education for Social Work,* Fall 1975.

Godbey, Gordon C. *Applied Andragogy: A Practical Manual for the Continuing Education of Adults.* State College, Penn.: The Pennsylvania State University Continuing Education Division, 1978.

Goodsir, Warwick W. "Andragogy and Its Implications," *Training and Development in Australia* V, 2 (June 1978), 12–19.

Grabowski, Marian Z. "Use of the Concept of Andragogy in Changing Presentation of Subject Materials Related to Body Integrative Controls." Practicum paper, Nova University for Higher Education, Fort Lauderdale, Fla., 1976.

Hadley, Herschel N. "Development of an Instrument to Determine Adult Educators' Orientation: Andragogical or Pedagogical." Unpublished Ed.D. dissertation, Boston University, 1975.

Healy, Grace M. "A Framework for Conceptualizing Lifelong Learning and Implications for Institutions of Higher Education Based upon the Philosophies of Kenneth D. Benne and Malcolm S. Knowles." Unpublished Ed.D. dissertation, Boston University, 1973.

Henschke, John. "Malcolm S. Knowles: His Contributions to the Theory and Practice of Adult Education." Unpublished Ed.D. dissertation, Boston University, 1973.

Ingalls, John D. *Human Energy: The Critical Factor for Individuals and Organizations.* Reading, Mass.: Addison-Wesley, 1976.

Ingalls, John, and Acceri, Joseph. *A Trainer's Guide to Andragogy.* (SRS 72–05301) U.S. Department of Health, Education, and Welfare. Washington, D.C.: Government Printing Office, 1972.

Kabuga, Charles. "Why Andragogy?" *Adult Education and Development.* Half-yearly journal for adult education in Africa, Asia, and Latin America, Bonn-Dad Godesberg, Federal Republic of Germany, September 1977.

Katz, Edna-Ann. "The Belief in Andragogy and the Development of Self-actualization." Unpublished Ed.D. dissertation, Boston University, 1976.

Kerwin, Michael A. "The Relationship of Selected Factors to the Educational Orientation of Andragogically- and Pedagogically-oriented Educators Teaching in Four of North Carolina's Two-Year Colleges." Unpublished Ed.D. dissertation, North Carolina State University, 1979.

Knights, Sue, and McDonald, Rod. "Adult Learners in University Courses," Educational Services and Teaching Resources Unit, Murdoch University, Australia, 1977.

Knowles, Malcolm S. "Adult Education: New Dimensions," *Educational Leadership,* November 1975.

———. *The Adult Learner: A Neglected Species.* 2d ed. Houston: Gulf Publishing Co., 1978.

———. "The Adult Learner is a Less Neglected Species," *Training* XIV, 9 (August 1977), 16–20.

———. "Adult Learning Processes: Pedagogy and Andragogy," *Religious Education* LXXII, 2 (March–April 1977), 202–211.

———. "Andragogy," a half-hour videotape. Nebraska Educational Television Council for Higher Education, 1972.

———. "Andragogy: Adult Learning Theory in Perspective," *Community College Review* V, 3 (Winter 1978), 1–5.

———. "Andragogy, Not Pedagogy," *Adult Leadership* XVI (April 1968).

————. "Human Resources Development in Organization Development," *Public Administration Review* XXXIV, 2 (March–April 1974), 118–122.

————. "An Experiment with Group Self-directed Learning: The Learning-Teaching Team." In Runkel, Harrison, and Runkel, *The Changing College Classroom*. San Francisco: Jossey-Bass, 1969.

————. "Innovations in Teaching Styles and Approaches Based upon Adult Learning," *Journal of Education for Social Work* VIII, 2 (Spring 1972).

————. "Issues in Adult Learning Psychology," *PRASAR* (University of Rajasthan, Janipur, India) I, 3 (October 1973), 36–47.

————. "Lifelong and Self-directed Learning," *Maryland* (University of Maryland Extension), X, 1 (Winter 1977), 11–13.

————. "The Manager as Educator." In James B. Lau, *Behavior in Organizations: An Experimental Approach*. Homewood, III.: Richard D. Irwin, 1975.

Komins, Alan S. "The Andragogy Workshop: Some Thoughts for the Profession," *International Journal of Continuing Education and Training,* Fall 1973.

Lebel, Jacques. "Beyond Andragogy to Gerogogy," *Lifelong Learning: The Adult Years,* May 1978 .

Levin, Rona F. "An Adventure in Andragogy." In Susan Mirin (ed.), *Teaching Tomorrow's Nurse: A Nurse Educator Reader*. Wakefield, Mass.: Nursing Resources, 1970.

Little, Thomas E. "Adult Learning in the Roman Catholic Church: A Discernment of Principles Through Analysis of the Documents of the Second Vatican Council and Selected Synods in the United States since 1965." Unpublished Ed.D. dissertation, North Carolina State University, 1979.

Mader, Sylvia S. "Junior College Biology Teaching: A Synergistic View," *American Biology Teacher,* October 1972.

Mahoney, Mary M. "A Comparison of Three Methods of Teaching Reading-Study Skills at the College Level." Unpublished Ed.D. dissertation, Boston University, 1974.

McKenzie, Leon. "The Issue of Andragogy," *Adult Education* XXVII, 4 (Summer 1977), 225–229.

Merirelles, Jose, and Batista, Margarida. "Executive Development: An Andragogical Approach," Center of Interdisciplinary Studies for the Public Sector, Federal University of Bahia, Salvador, Brazil, 1977.

Meyer, Sheldon L. "Andragogy and the Aging Adult Learner," *Educational Gerontology* II, 2 (April–June 1977), 115–122.

Newton, Eunice S. "Andragogy: Understanding the Adult as a Learner," *Journal of Reading,* February 1977.

Ross, Brenda B. "The Students' Self-perceived Position on the Continuum Between Childhood and Adulthood as a Determinant for Andragogy in the Eight Grade Inner City School." Unpublished Ed.D. dissertation, Boston University, 1974.

Rycus, Judith S. "Essentials of Inservice Training for Child Welfare Workers," *Child Welfare,* June 1978.

Savicevic, Dusan M. *The System of Adult Education in Yugoslavia.* Notes and Essays on Education for Adults, no. 59. Syracuse, N.Y.: Publications Program in Continuing Education, Syracuse University, 1968.

Schuttenberg, Ernest M. "An Andragogical Learning Approach to Graduate Professional Education," *Improving College and University Teaching Yearbook,* 1975, pp. 227–236.

Skiff, Dana A. "An Approach to Designing a Police Recruit Training Program Reflecting the Readiness to Learn and the Developmental Tasks of the Police Recruit." Unpublished Ed.D. dissertation, Boston University, 1975.

Tapper, Mildred. "The Relationship Between an Andragogical Model and Current Practice in University Schools of Nursing Continuing Education Departments." Unpublished Ed.D. dissertation, Boston University, 1973.

Thavilab, Vichien. "An Analysis of Andragogical Theory As Applied to In-service Education for Faculty Members of a School of Nursing in Thailand." Unpublished Ed.D. dissertation, Boston University, 1972.

Thorne, Edward H., and Marshall, Jean L. "Managerial Skills Development: An Experience in Program Design," *Personnel Journal* 55, 1 (January 1976), 15–38.

Tibbles, Lillian. "Theories of Adult Education: Implications for Developing a Philosophy for Continuing Education in Nursing," *Journal of Continuing Education in Nursing,* July–August 1977.

Torrence, Preston E. "A Study of the Relationship of Selected Teacher Behaviors to Teacher Effectiveness." Unpublished Ed.D. dissertation, Boston University, 1970.

Trester, Eugene F. "Biblical Andragogy: A Program in Biblical Education for Adults," the Dufferin-Peel Roman Catholic Separate School Board, Toronto, 1976.

Vorce, Armand E. "A Critical Analysis of Three Case Examples of Humanities Education Programs for Adults." Unpublished Ed.D. dissertation, Boston University, 1971.

Winterfield, Patricia. "Open Line: Community Colleges Should Develop Their Own Teaching Model," *American Sociological Association Teaching Newsletter* IV, 3 (February 1979), 10–12.

Wolfe, Delight. "The Concept of Authority and Its Implications for Nursing Education." Unpublished Ed.D. dissertation, Boston University, 1972.

Yodmani, Suvit. "An Evaluation of Community Development Practices of Development Volunteers in Five Universities in Thailand According to Criteria of a Validated Model." Unpublished Ed.D. dissertation, Boston University, 1972.

Appendix F

Chapter 5 Exhibits: Policy Statements

CORPORATE POLICY STATEMENTS

United Air Lines Corporate Training and Development Policy

United Air Lines is a service organization. Our value to customers and our success as a business depends on how effectively and efficiently the people of United carry out their responsibilities.

A people-centered organization like United must also be a people-developing organization. Management at every level must understand clearly that time and money spent wisely in training our personnel is an investment in the most crucial part of our system.

Each person in United is ultimately responsible for his own development to become an increasingly effective member of the United team.

Each manager and supervisor is responsible for providing the climate, conditions, and direction for the job-related development of his subordinates. (This responsibility cannot be delegated, since the most consistent training occurs day by day in the work situation.)

Each training specialist or training administrator is responsible for working with managers and supervisors to improve consistently the conditions and opportunities for developing subordinates' skills, knowledge, and attitudes.

United's operations must be flexible and adaptive to the increased tempo of change. This flexibility is directly dependent on our ability to train people promptly and effectively. It is therefore our policy to maintain a group of training specialists to insure that the training is well-planned, well-coordinated, well-conducted and utilizes the most appropriate methodology available.

Training is a costly investment and must be planned, budgeted and evaluated with care. The importance of this must be recognized at all levels of the company. To insure that the training function is carried on effectively we shall strive to develop with United Air Lines the following:

1. A corporate training policy that is understood throughout the system.

2. Managers and supervisors who understand, accept, and know how to fulfill their basic responsibility to train subordinates.

3. An approach to training which begins with clearly identified needs and ends with the measurable achievement of practical training objectives.

4. A clearly understood procedure which budgets, accounts for, and reports the cost of all training.

5. Systematic methods for assessing job performance and the effectiveness of training in improving that performance.

6. An organizational climate that encourages, recognizes and rewards inter-administration and inter-departmental planning and implementation of training programs.

7. Maintenance of a professional training unit responsible for the regular review of the qualifications of training personnel, technology, methodology, and media to keep United current with new developments in the training field.

8. Organizational mechanisms and procedures for effective inter-administration and inter-departmental planning of training programs and use of specialized training capabilities.

9. A system of recognition and rewards which attracts competent personnel to training positions and encourages them to develop their capability for a professional training career.

10. The early involvement of training personnel in planning those changes which have training implications.

Western Electric Policy for Corporate Education

The primary objective of corporate education is to keep managerial and professional people preeminent in their field and resolute in their self-development consistent with the needs of the business. Educational programs will be planned and administered to provide an effective deterrent to obsolescence of essential knowledge and a stimulus for self-development.

The responsibility for achieving these educational objectives must be shared by policy makers, educational organizations, functional staff organizations, line organizations, and the individual employee.

Responsibility for overall direction and guidance of the Company's education programs and the development of strategies to meet the Company's educational needs is assigned to the Corporate Education Board of Overseers.

With rapid change requiring continuous innovation in business and management skills and new technologies affecting our products, services and processes, the effectiveness of the Company's education depends on making the best choices of what *subjects to teach,* how *and* where *they should be taught, and* who *should be taught.*

In MANAGEMENT EDUCATION there are three general areas to be covered:
—Provide continuing education in the latest principles and techniques appropriate to the general responsibilities at each management level. This should include stimulating an awareness of a wide range of changes, e.g., technical, economic, social, legal, etc., which have the potential for substantial impact on the business and management.
—Provide specific education in areas of specialized management expertise. This recognizes that the art and science of management is also changing. To ensure specific knowledge, specialized subjects must be presented selectively to meet the need for in-depth skills by some managers and for a general understanding by others.
—Provide a clear understanding of the Company's structure and objectives. Through programs appropriate to different levels, using conventional course material and informal dialogue with higher management, provide a thorough understanding of the Company's policies, priorities, and procedures.

In PROFESSIONAL EDUCATION there are also three areas to be covered:
—Provide introductory education to orient new professional employees in the practical application and Company procedures necessary to make the earliest and most effective use of their academic education. This will include professional topics such as engineering and accounting in addition to providing an understanding of the professional role in the Company's structure and objectives.
—Provide specialized development to ensure the necessary competence to perform effectively in the emerging skill areas important to the Company's future.
—Provide selective development to renew the professional skills of employees whose expertise may otherwise become obsolete due to changes in the business and its technology.

It is the responsibility of the CORPORATE EDUCATION BOARD OF OVERSEERS:
—To ensure that appropriate procedures exist to manage the identification, scheduling, and administration of employee education.
—To establish the direction, develop the strategies, and guide the administration of corporate education.

—To review, periodically, corporate education plans and programs.

—To coordinate the involvement of policy makers, educational organizations, functional staff organizations, line organizations, and individual employees.

It is the responsibility of the CORPORATE EDUCATION ORGANIZATION:

—To plan and develop corporately funded education programs.

—To administer the Corporate Education Center and Western Electric extension education.

—To manage Western Electric's utilization of outside education.

—To provide overall direction of the Tuition Refund Plan.

—To develop standards and provide assistance in designing and administering local education programs.

It is the responsibility of FUNCTIONAL STAFF ORGANIZATIONS:

—To specify the standards of job knowledge for professionals and managers with specialized functional assignments.

—To support the development and implementation of educational programs to maintain and/or upgrade functional job skills and knowledge.

—To take an active part in planning and coordinating the attendance of functional professionals and managers at special functional educational programs.

It is the responsibility of LINE ORGANIZATIONS:

—To manage the procedure for identification, scheduling, and administration of employee education with vigor and thoroughness to support corporate goals and objectives.

—To allocate sufficient time and funds to meet the educational needs of the professional and managerial work force and be accountable for ensuring that the educational needs of each organization are achieved.

—To plan, develop, and administer local education programs in concert with the Corporate Education Organization.

It is the responsibility of the INDIVIDUAL EMPLOYEE:

—To ensure that one's job knowledge is up to date with the Company's current and emerging needs.

—To allocate a reasonable amount of time and effort, both on and off the job, to utilize the Company's education program.

—To include education in one's overall plan for self-development.

COLLEGE MISSION AND INSTITUTIONAL GOAL

Delaware County Community College, Pennsylvania*

Philosophy

The Delaware County Community College is committed to the comprehensive community college philosophy of meeting the post–high school educational needs of the community it serves. Within this area of responsibility and available resources, the College is dedicated to the policy of providing educational opportunities that will permit the youth and adults of the area to enrich their lives, develop themselves personally, and advance their careers to the limit of their desires and capabilities.

The role of the College is to offer programs and services for which it is particularly capable. It seeks to complement, not duplicate unnecessarily, those offered by other community institutions and agencies.

Mission

The mission of Delaware County Community College is to offer educational programs and services which are comprehensive, accessible, flexible, and community-centered in order to enhance the development of our community and its residents.

Accessibility

It is the goal of the College to be geographically, economically, socially, and educationally accessible to the citizens of the community.

Geographically	As a commuter-oriented institution, facilities should be located close to the geographic and population centers of the area served.
Economically	Every effort should be made, through sound management and the College's Financial Aid Program, to ensure that no applicant is denied admission due to the lack of funds.
Educationally	The College should maintain an "open-door policy" offering an educational opportunity to students with a wide diversity of backgrounds and abilities.
Socially	The College should remain socially accessible to those students who otherwise would not aspire to higher education.

Comprehensiveness

It is the goal of the College to be comprehensive in Instructional Programs, Educational Methods, and Student Services with an emphasis on the student rather than the institution.

Instructional Program	Designed to provide a broad range of offerings in response to student and community needs.
Educational Methods	Instruction should be presented in a manner designed to best serve the diverse backgrounds of individual students.
Student Services	An integrated and comprehensive program of student services should be available to assist each student in their maturity and personal development.
Management & Research Services	A continuing and comprehensive assessment of community and student needs shall be maintained to monitor the changing needs of the area.

* From the "Long Range Planning Document" approved by the Board of Trustees, June 1978.

Recognizing that the community college concept encourages the enrollment of students with differing abilities and objectives, the College should offer a comprehensive program of courses and curricula including:

Basic Education	Courses designed to provide basic skills and knowledge to enable students to qualify for admission to other programs.
Developmental Education	Courses of a remedial nature designed to qualify students for College and University Parallel, Occupational, or General programs.
General Education	One or two-year curricula designed for students who want additional education beyond secondary school but not necessarily with a particular occupational orientation.
Occupational Education	One or two-year curricula designed as individual educational experiences for students preparing for immediate employment in specialized areas for which there is a demonstrated need as well as an employment potential.
College and University Parallel Education	A two-year curricula of college instruction designed to assist those students planning to transfer to a four-year college or university to earn a baccalaureate degree.
Continuing Education	Opportunities for citizens of the community to enrich their lives, to increase their potential as wage earners, and to express themselves creatively and socially as individuals. In addition to the programs outlined above, these opportunities should be provided through specifically-designed courses, seminars, lecture series, workshops, and special educational and cultural activities.

Once a definite career direction has been identified, the College should assist the student, wherever possible, in creating an appropriate curriculum. As education is a uniquely individual process, the College should offer curricular patterns only as guidelines to assist students in reaching career objectives.

In view of the fact that the College accepts such a diverse population of applicants, each with a wide range of characteristics which will affect their performance, the College should provide a structured student service program designed to enhance the overall growth and development of the individual student. These programs should be designed to help students have a better understanding of self and others, both within the College community and in the larger society.

These programs should help each student to:
— acquire positive, realistic conceptions of their own abilities not only in the College environment but in the world at large as well.
— understand the structure and application of knowledge necessary to the process of forming judgments.
— equate the relevance of higher education to the quality of their lives.

The College accepts the responsibility for providing an instructional environment that is conducive to learning. This includes providing appropriate physical facilities where students and faculty meet, providing learning resources to complement classroom experiences, and organizing the instructional process to best further its goal of providing ways to reach individual students.

Community Centered

It is the goal of the College, as a locally sponsored two-year institution, to meet the postsecondary educational needs of the community it serves. It is essential that these needs be defined and recognized through communications between the College and the community.

The Board of Trustees, as elected representatives of the Local Sponsor, should serve as the main vehicles for coordinating communication with the Sponsor. In addition, two types of citizen committees should be used to facilitate communication: one to advise the College on program development; and the other, through liaison representatives from each school district, to advise on matters of concern to the Sponsor.

To further its goal of being community-centered, the College should invite community involvement on campus, encourage outside use of the College facilities, and strive to become a cultural center for the community.

Flexibility

It is the goal of the College to be a flexible and dynamic institution which can readily adapt to the changing needs, circumstances, and aspirations of the students it serves. Such flexibility implies not only a commitment to experimentation and innovation but also to an evaluation of the success of all projects initiated. In such a commitment, it is understood that some experimental projects may not be entirely successful.

The College should also be committed to regular evaluation of current offerings in terms of needs and effectiveness. To achieve the stated goal, the College should be flexible in allocating its resources through a planned program of educational emphasis and community development.

Goal Statements
Abstract of Goals

1.0 *Instructional*

The instructional goals are aimed at developing competency based curricula which infuse career education concepts and a general education core.

2.0 *Research*

The emphasis of the Research Program is to monitor the effectiveness of the College's programs and services.

3.0 *Public Service*

The focus of the Public Service Program will be on three diverse areas: increasing community awareness as to their educational needs, articulating with other educational institutions, and the programming of cultural affairs.

4.0 *Academic Support*

The basic thrust of the academic support program is to provide direct support to the instructional area while at the same time providing for the evaluation of courses, programs, instructional personnel, policy, and organization.

5.0 *Student Service*

Provide a balanced program of student services such as athletic/recreation, advising, counseling, placement, and activities that are accessible to all students.

6.0 *Institutional Support*

The aims of the institutional support program are as follows:

—to make more efficient, effective, equitable, and safe use of existing and potential resources—human, financial, physical, and operational—through ongoing planning and evaluation processes.

—to develop marketing strategies in reponse to identified community needs.

—to expand sponsorship to all residents of the College's service area.

7.0 *Student Access*

The major thrusts of the student access program are to recruit students, match them to courses and programs according to their interests and abilities, and to provide financial aid.

TRAINING POLICY, NATIONAL ENDOWMENT FOR THE ARTS*

1. PURPOSE: This Directive outlines the Endowment's policies, procedures, responsibilities and authorizations with respect to the training of employees through government or non-government facilities as prescribed in Chapter 41 of Title 5, U.S. Code.

2. POLICY: It is the policy of the National Endowment for the Arts to encourage and plan for the development of the skills, knowledges and abilities of its staff in the most equitable and efficient manner. To this end the Endowment:
—affirms support by top management for the goals of the program in all aspects;
—will systematically plan its training based on the short and long-term needs of the employees in furtherance of the agency's mission;
—coordinate its training program with other operating programs within the Endowment and, when possible, with the programs of other agencies with similar needs;
—will counsel with and inform its employees of the training opportunities available and the procedures used in selecting employees for training;
—will evaluate its program regularly to determine the extent to which training is contributing to the achievement of the Endowment's mission.

3. PROGRAM GOALS: The immediate goal of employee training is the development of employees to attain and maintain efficient performance in their current positions. The long-term goal is to develop their skills and knowledge so that they may advance to progressively more responsible positions. Each employee of the Endowment will be given equal opportunity to acquire the skills and knowledge he needs to learn his work quickly, to perform effectively, to meet changing conditions promptly and to advance his career opportunities.

Employee development will be accomplished through training on-the-job and by attendance at formal courses or seminars conducted in Government and non-Government facilities exclusively for NEA employees or in cooperation with other agencies and/or state and local governments. This training may be full-time or part-time, on- or off-duty, day or evening or any necessary combination of these. It may be accomplished through the use of methodology such as correspondence, lectures, conferences, workshops, supervised practice or other appropriate methods.

4. DEFINITION: "Training" means the process of providing for and making available to an employee, and placing or enrolling the employee in, a planned, prepared and coordinated program, course, curriculum, subject, system or routine of instruction or education, in scientific, professional, technical, mechanical, trade, clerical, fiscal, administrative, or other fields which are, or will be, directly related to the performance by the employee of official duties for the Government, in order to increase the knowledge, proficiency, ability, skill and qualifications of the employee in the performance of official duties.

5. EMPLOYEE COVERAGE: Employees serving under career, career-conditional or temporary appointments (or under appointments or details under the Intergovernmental Personnel Act of 1970) are eligible for training under the provisions of the Training Act.

6. APPROPRIATE TRAINING FACILITIES: Training shall be contracted for and conducted in the following facilities: a government facility, that is, property owned or substantially controlled by the government, or non-government facilities, including any instrumentality of state and local government, professional, commercial or international organization authorized by the President. No training facilities will be chosen that would place any restriction on trainees because of race, color, sex, handicap, religion or national origin.

---

* Administrative Directive P–410: Training, June 1978.

7. ALTERNATIVES TO TRAINING: Solutions to needs for particular skills may be found outside of training. Supervisors and managers should also investigate alternative solutions such as outside recruitment, the temporary use of experts or consultants, job restructuring, details or other management tools.

8. VETERANS' TRAINING: Persons appointed under the provisions of Public Laws 78–16 and 79–346 (Veterans' Readjustment Act) are obliged to undertake meaningful, job-related training. The requirements of the program are flexible to permit programs tailored to the needs of the Endowment. Developmental activities may include any of the following:
—planned on-the-job training;
—off-job classroom training;
—basic or remedial education, or both;
—high school or high school equivalency (GED);
—education beyond high school.

a. Training Eligibility: The Director of Administration may waive the one year of continuous service requirement on a case-by-case basis for persons under Veterans' Readjustment Appointment training agreements.

b. Outside Education: Veterans' Readjustment Appointment appointees may be allowed up to 10 hours of duty time per week to pursue creditable educational training. All such administrative leave must be approved in advance by the Training Officer, the pertinent supervisors and the Director of Administration. The employee must submit proof of enrollment and acceptance into the educational program for leave approval purposes.

9. LEAVE AND PAY DURING TRAINING PERIODS: Employees will remain in full pay status during approved training periods. Annual and sick leave policies will apply. However, no employee shall receive premium pay while in training, unless specifically authorized by the Civil Service Commission. Normal work periods which fall within a recess period will be charged to annual or sick leave as appropriate unless the employee is returned to work status or devotes recess periods to study or research directly related to the course of study.

10. COMPUTING LENGTH OF TRAINING: An employee is counted as being in training the same number of hours he is in a pay status if assigned to full-time training. (Full-time training is defined as training that is the only assignment of an employee during one or more workdays.) If an employee is assigned to part-time training, he is counted as being in the training the same number of hours he spends in class or with the instructor. Examples: An employee who normally works 40 hours a week and is sent to a special two-week seminar at a University as his only assignment for that period would be counted as being in training for 80 hours regardless of the number of hours he spends in actual instruction or study. An employee who is approved for training in a university course which meets three class hours a week for 15 weeks would be counted as receiving 45 hours of training.

11. AGREEMENT TO CONTINUE IN SERVICE:
a. Service agreements are required for all instances of non-government training in excess of 40 hours within a single program, i.e., two or more courses at an academic institution having a common purpose and occurring during the same term or instances of training having a common purpose and which are authorized at the same time. The minimum service obligation as established for Endowment employees is three (3) times the length of training or six (6) months, whichever is greater. "Length of training" means the number of hours a person spends in class or with the instructor in the facility.

b. Failure to Complete Service Agreement: An employee of the Endowment who leaves the Government shall pay to the government a sum equal to the expenses of the training and shall pay for any additional expenses incident to the training.

c. Transfer of Service Agreement: An employee who enters the service of another government agency or other organization in any branch of the government before fulfilling the service agreement will have the remainder of the service obligation transferred to the gaining agency when it would be against equity and good conscience or against public interest to require payment of the additional expenses at the time of transfer.

12. TRAINING THROUGH NON-GOVERNMENT FACILITIES: The Training Office will only approve training through non-government facilities when the following conditions are met:

a. The knowledges or skills gained would not be available from other available employees;

b. The training is not reasonably available from a government source or an existing source within the agency; and

c. the use of government facilities would be more expensive.

13. TRAINING FOR POSITIONS REQUIRING A DEGREE: The Training Office will not approve requests that are expressly intended to provide an employee training to receive an academic degree which subsequently would qualify the employee for a position which has a degree requirement. This does not preclude the approval of training courses which would improve an employee's performance of official duties.

14. MINIMUM SERVICE REQUIREMENTS: No employee having less than one year of current, continuous civilian service is eligible for training in non-government facilities unless the Director of Administration waives the requirement when the postponement of the training would be contrary to the public interest. Exceptions shall be made in accordance with the instructions in FPM Chapter 410, Subchapter 5–4.

15. MAXIMUM TRAINING IN A 10-YEAR PERIOD: Time spent in a non-government facility cannot exceed one year in the first 10-year period of an employee's continuous and non-continuous civilian service in Government following the date of his initial entrance into the civilian service and in each 10-year period of service thereafter. The one in 10 limitation for NEA employees does not include: (a) training that does not exceed 40 hours within a single program; (b) manufacturers' training; or (c) training through correspondence courses.

16. ATTENDANCE AT MEETINGS: Attendance at meetings which facilitate effective communication of ideas and information in areas of significance to the Endowment and which may have significant impact on the conduct, supervision or management of NEA functions may be authorized. Division or Office Heads are authorized to approve attendance at meetings involving no cost to the Endowment except travel and only minimal expenses such as taxi fares. Requests for attendance at meetings involving registration, tuition and similar expenses to the Endowment must be approved by the Division of Personnel.

17. PAYMENT OF TRAINING EXPENSES: Full or partial cost of training approved under this policy will normally be paid by the Endowment when the training is (1) directly or reasonably job-related; (2) required for more effective or improved performance of current duties; and/or (3) necessary for the economical and effective administration of the work of the Endowment resulting from an identified urgent training or staff resource capability need. Payment of the following expenses is authorized in addition to normal salary: transportation and per diem in accordance with existing regulations; tuition and matriculation fees; library and laboratory services; other service or facility fees directly related to training; and membership fees to the extent the fees are necessary costs directly related to the training itself or that payment of the fee is a condition precedent to undertaking the training.

Any individual who has been approved for training, which is being endorsed and paid for by NEA, has a very strong obligation to complete the training. Failure to successfully complete a training program makes the individual liable for the reimbursement (to NEA) of all training costs expended by the Endowment. If an individual feels compelled to withdraw from a training course, he/she must contact the Training Officer to discuss the specific reasons. UNDER NO CIRCUMSTANCES SHOULD ANY NEA EMPLOYEE JEOPARDIZE HIS/HER TRAINING STATUS BY MAKING AN ARBITRARY, UNILATERAL DECISION NOT TO COMPLETE THE TRAINING.

For those employees who take training at their own expense, the Endowment does not provide letters to file with their tax returns to justify tuition expenses claimed as deductions. However, if a deduction of this nature is challenged, the employee may request a supporting statement and the procedure below will be followed:

a. The employee should submit to the Division of Personnel a copy of the statement in support of the deduction that he/she filed originally with his/her tax form and a copy of the correspondence challenging the deduction.

b. The employee's Division/Office Head will be asked by the Division of Personnel for a memorandum stating whether or not he agrees with the employee that there is justification for the Endowment to support the claimed deduction.

c. If the Division/Office Head feels that claim is justified, the Division of Personnel will prepare the appropriate letter for the signature of the employee's Division/Office Head.

18. SUPERVISORY TRAINING:

a. Management Responsibility: Agency managers are charged with the responsibility of insuring that supervisors attain appropriate training in supervisory skills. It is the policy of NEA to fully support supervisory development to insure the highest level of effective management skills. To this end, managers are urged to periodically evaluate the training needs of its supervisors and plan appropriate training activities accordingly.

b. Training Requirements: Each new supervisor is required to have at least 40 hours of supervisory training either before or within six months of entry on duty as a supervisor. An additional 40 hours is required during the first two years of supervisory work. These requirements may be reduced when it is determined that (a) the supervisor possesses sufficient supervisory skills at the point of entry on duty as a supervisor; (b) the supervisor's academic preparation has been sufficient to prepare him/her for supervisory responsibilities. Recency of experience and training will be examined whenever a determination is made to reduce the training requirements.

19. REVIEW OF TRAINING NEEDS:

a. Division and Offices: Divisions and Offices must identify and report the realistic training needs of their employees at least annually to the Director of Personnel. In identifying needs, officials should consider the following: (1) individual employee needs as related to the Division or Office's program objectives; (2) significant needs regardless of whether these can be met with available resources; (3) future program and staffing needs; and (4) long-range as well as immediate needs.

b. Office of Personnel: The Division of Personnel will annually request comments from Division/Office Heads and individual employees with respect to their views on training needs. Such comments will be evaluated in formulating the overall training requirements of the Endowment and in reporting these needs, along with plans for meeting them, to the Deputy Chairman and the Director of Administration.

20. SELF-DEVELOPMENT: The Endowment will encourage employees to improve and increase their skills and knowledge through programs of self-development and will make every effort to foster an awareness in employees of their own responsibilities for self-development.

a. Publication of Training Information: Supervisory personnel and the Division of Personnel will be responsive to employee inquiries concerning the qualifications necessary for advancement in their current fields or other areas of interest.

Training opportunities will be made known to all employees by any of the following methods: (a) posting on bulletin boards; (b) articles in employee publications; (c) general circulation of training policies and regulations; and (d) reminders to record self-financed training in official personnel files.

b. Career Counselling: Career counselling will be provided to all employees upon request. As appropriate, the Training Officer will assist these employees in obtaining information on available training and advise them of the various means of attaining their career objectives.

The Division of Personnel will work with Divisions and Offices to develop plans and programs for meeting identified needs. Generally, Divisions and Offices will be responsible for preparing plans to deal with training in the technical and program work of the Endowment. However, these must be coordinated with the Division of Personnel before implementation to assure that all legal and policy requirements are met. The Division of Personnel has primary responsibility for developing plans to meet the agency's needs for training in personnel management, supervisory development, administrative abilities, secretarial and clerical skills and related areas.

The Division of Personnel is responsible for maintaining appropriate records as may be required under this Section.

21. EVALUATION OF TRAINING: Evaluation of training is an integral part of the entire training cycle. It is the responsibility of each employee receiving training to complete that portion of the Form OF-170 that will be provided to the employee for course evaluation and critique. Within three months of a completed course, the supervisor will be sent this same evaluation form. The supervisor should complete that portion of the form as designated; thus providing an opportunity for the supervisor and the employee to review the benefits of the training and their impact on the desired changes in employee knowledge, skills, and performance to determine whether the objectives of both the individual and the organization were met.

22. TRAINING REQUEST AND AUTHORIZATION PROCEDURES: All requests for training which exceed eight hours and involve the use of training funds must be effectuated on optional form 170 (10 part) "Request, Authorization, Agreement and Certification of Training." Instructions for the use of optional form 170 are contained in Appendix A of this Directive and obtainable from the Supply Room and in the Personnel Office.

PURPOSES AND OBJECTIVES OF THE COOPERATIVE EXTENSION SERVICE*

The purpose of the Cooperative Extension Service is to extend education to the people of the United States and in developing countries, as provided for by legislation and executive acts. In performing this function the Extension Service will help youth and adults to: (a) develop their full potential, (b) identify problems and take the steps necessary to solve them individually and collectively by utilizing research results when applicable, (c) increase their competency and willingness to assume leadership and citizenship responsibilities, and (d) acquire the ability to achieve higher incomes and levels of living on a continuing basis.

There are several major areas of program objectives which will receive high priority attention by the Extension Service. These are to develop the skills, attitudes, and understanding of people which will enable them to:

1. *Conserve and effectively use natural resources.*

The nation's natural resources, including soil, water, forest range, and fish and wildlife, provide the basis for economic growth and an adequate supply of farm and forest products. Essential natural resources must be maintained, developed, and used to meet production and general welfare needs. This involves reducing soil erosion and controlling water runoff and improving forest management. Population demands for leisure time use of natural resources will increase greatly because of population increase, urban sprawl, greater mobility, and expansion of leisure time.

2. *Efficiently produce range, farm and forest products.*

Improve the efficiency of production of range, farm, and forest products so as to enhance producer income and encourage production of an adequate supply of high-quality food and fiber products. Food and fiber supplies must be increased about 40 percent in order to meet domestic needs, 32 percent higher and an export goal 100 percent higher in 1980 than now. For the year 2000, these supplies must be increased 111 percent to meet 75 percent higher domestic needs and a 200 percent higher export goal. Domestic needs for forest products will be up an estimated 80 percent by 2000.

3. *Increase the effectiveness of the marketing distribution system.*

The larger share of the consumer dollar is being spent for marketing rather than producing farm and forest products. The potential is great for reducing marketing costs and for providing greater benefits and services for consumers. Greater efficiency of assembling, handling, processing, packaging, storing, transporting, wholesaling and retailing farm, forest, and range products increases consumer satisfaction, improves returns to farmers and marketers, and expands domestic and foreign markets.

It is the policy of the United States to expand international trade and to expand commercial export markets for U.S. agricultural commodities. Producers and marketers of farm, range, and forest products need much more knowledge of how to establish foreign markets, how to organize production and marketing to meet export demand, and determine the potential our products have in foreign markets. The USDA goal is to double farm product exports by 1980 and triple them by 2000.

Increasing domestic demand and improving markets abroad depend upon determining and satisfying consumer preferences for food, fiber, and forest products. This means developing products to meet consumer desires. More effort should be given to producing products with characteristics that meet consumer or processor needs and maintaining these qualities to point of use. New and improved uses and processes will result in more variety, reduced costs, and increased utilization of farm, forest, and range products.

---

* Prepared by a Joint Task Force of the Federal Extension Service, U.S. Department of Agriculture, February 15, 1967, mimeographed.

4. *Optimize their development (children, youth, and adults) as individuals and as members of the family and community.*

Virtually all family situations today embody social, economic, and technical factors. Adults, children, and youth need the understandings that enable them to effectively relate to others within and outside the family; the knowledge and skills related to maintaining optimum physical and mental health; opportunities to develop and practice citizenship and leadership; and incentives to strive for excellence in all human endeavors.

5. *Improve their community organization, services, and environment.*

Achievement of many aspirations depends upon group action at local, State, and federal levels to make desired public and private services and opportunities available. To a considerable measure, availability to individuals of utilities, health services, opportunities for education, employment, and recreation depend upon community action. Community groups, private and public, need facts as a basis for programs that lead to group satisfaction from planned use of economic and natural resources.

Effective control of diseases and pests, and the elimination of such environmental hazards as climatic extremes; air, water, and soil pollution; and food and feed contamination contribute to the well-being of the people and the security of the nation.

6. *Develop as informed leaders for identifying and solving problems in a democratic society.*

The power and influence of informed local leadership for bringing about change had been recognized by Extension workers since its beginning. The growth and accomplishments of Extension would have been seriously limited if it had not been for the new projects and proposals initiated by local leaders and the follow-up training and organizational work that they have done. To help individuals, groups, and communities to attain desired social and economic benefits through their own initiative and through the strategic processes of a democratic government, Extension must give greater emphasis to developing informed leaders.

7. *Raise their level of living and achieve their goals through wise resource management.*

Ways must be found to assist rural and urban people to improve their economic potential. Information on how to use money and other resources to achieve desired goals is needed. The ability to manage resources well is a means to improving the level of living for individuals and families, to providing greater opportunity for individual achievement, and to the abolition of poverty.

8. *Assist the people of other countries.*

The food crisis threatening the peace of the world leads to the development of a policy by the United States to use her abundant agricultural productivity to combat hunger and malnutrition and to encourage human and economic development in emerging nations. Our food, fiber, and agricultural technology represents our most effective instrument of foreign policy. Technical assistance in agriculture, forestry, and home economics will help developing nations produce more of their own food and fiber needs, improve their level of living, contribute to their economic growth, and lead to expanded export markets for the United States.

The Extension methodology is and will continue to contribute to the development of emerging nations and the welfare of the people in developing and more progressive countries.

CONTINUING EDUCATION FOR PERSONNEL IN HEALTH CARE INSTITUTIONS

In recent years, increasing emphasis has been given to the need for the continuing education of health care personnel. In some quarters, there is strong support for mandatory continuing education as a requirement for relicensure or recertification. Not enough attention has been given to the need to relate continuing education to job competency needs.

The American Hospital Association's Special Committee on Continuing Education developed this statement to emphasize three points: continuing education should be voluntary; continuing education required by employing institutions are legitimate costs of operation; continuing education should be competency related and objective job performance standards are needed if this relationship is to be meaningful. The statement was approved by the AHA House of Delegates August 19, 1975.

Introduction

The provision of high-quality health care is dependent upon competent performance by health personnel. Continuing education is one means by which health care personnel gain knowledge and skills so they can maintain and improve their performance in patient care or patient related activities.

The issues that surround the provision of continuing education for health personnel center on the need for, design of, provision of, and evaluation of continuing education activities.

These issues have been dealt with in the following ways, among others:

1. Some professional associations and governmental agencies have taken the position that participation in continuing education should be a condition of membership or must be mandated through renewal of licensure and certification. They propose that legal or quasi-legal requirements be used to induce participation by those professionals who must need continuing education.
2. Other professional groups prefer to develop self-assessment examinations that assist individuals to identify their needs for continuing education and then suggest a variety of ways in which the individuals can meet the needs that are identified.
3. Another approach identifies continuing education needs of health care personnel through the use of an emerging procedure known as patient care audit. Attainable standards of high-quality performance are being used as criteria for auditing the performance of health care personnel. Data are collected and analyzed to describe their practice patterns. The standards are then compared with actual practice to identify gaps or needs to be met by continuing education activities.

AHA's Recommendations

The American Hospital Association recognizes the need to ensure high-quality patient care and safety through careful personnel selection, preparation, and development and the need on the part of health care institutions to foster the growth and contribution of various health care personnel. The Association further recognizes that continuing education of health care personnel is also the concern of others, such as professional associations, educational institutions, accrediting agencies, governmental agencies, the public, and health care personnel themselves. Because of the need for commitment of health care institutions to continuing education to ensure personnel competence and in recognition of the related interests of various other groups, the American Hospital Association recommends the following to the membership:

1. The development of continuing education programs for health care personnel should include participation by health care institutions and by other groups with legitimate vested interests, such as professional associations, education institu-

tions, accrediting agencies, commercial organizations, governmental agencies, the public, and health care personnel. The role of these interests will vary in kind and intensity for various stages of program development. These stages include assessment of needs, setting of objectives, selection of activities, and evaluation.

2. Continuing education activities for all personnel in health care institutions should be relevant, accessible, and attainable and should represent a multidisciplinary approach, when appropriate.

3. Greater emphasis should be given to an assessment of competence in relation to job performance standards or through the process of patient care audit where appropriate. The results of such assessments should be used as one basis for developing continuing education activities.

4. Continuing education activities should be cost justified. With the need for responsible cost containment in the health care industry, cost effectiveness is a criterion of continuing education activities.

5. The financing of continuing education involves participation by professional organizations, employers, employees, and educational institutions. Health care institutions requiring continuing education of their employees as a means of improving specific job competencies should pay for it as part of their reimbursable operational expenses.

6. Where appropriate, health care institutions should collaborate with health care associations and other health care institutions to provide, as shared services, continuing education activities for all personnel. These efforts should be further expanded to include other appropriate groups, such as long-term care institutions, professional organizations, and health agencies.

7. Health care institutions should develop objective job performance standards so that continuing education needs may be determined by comparing actual performance against standards and so that practical suggestions and contributions to job performance needs may be made to curriculum planners in educational institutions which provide continuing education programs for health care workers.

In behalf of its membership, the American Hospital Association should:

1. Support voluntary approaches to continuing education.

2. Consider research and demonstration activities to develop effective procedures for needs assessment, performance appraisal, self-assessment examinations, and measures of cost effectiveness to help health care institutions, professional associations, educational institutions, and individuals in determining the need for continuing education and in designing, conducting, and evaluating various kinds of continuing education activities.

3. Assist in the development of more standardized reporting of participation by individuals in continuing education activities, both credit and noncredit. The development of continuing education registries would allow a record of participation in continuing education programs to be reported when the participant seeks employment in a new location or seeks promotion on the job. To the degree that results of performance appraisal and self-assessment are used to design and evaluate continuing education, the continuing education unit (CEU)† will more clearly relate to improved competence.

4. Provide leadership to its members and incorporate into its own program planning the recommendations made in this statement.

5. Encourage and work to improve the coordination of metropolitan, state, regional, and national hospital continuing education systems.

---

† The CEU was developed by the National Task Force to Study the Feasibility and Implementation of Uniform Unit for the Measurement of Noncredit Continuing Education Programs.

POLICY STATEMENT OF THE
UNIVERSITY OF WISCONSIN SYSTEM

Adopted by the Board of Regents, May 1973

Introduction

The Regents of the University of Wisconsin System reaffirm the historic commitment of the public universities of Wisconsin to public service and the public good.

This reaffirmation recognizes that the major contribution of the University System to the public good has been and will continue to be the contributions made by citizens who, through study with the University, learn more and bring increased knowledge and understanding to their work and lives. It also means, however, that the System will take those steps possible to it to make its resources of people, instruction, and knowledge available to the citizens, agencies, and institutions of Wisconsin who seek or have need for access to such resources, at the times and places, and in the forms most useful to them. It further means continuing assessment of University System resources, statewide need for access to such resources, and the coordinated planning of statewide outreach programs which make best use of available resources.

The Regents note that the public universities of Wisconsin have a tradition of public service and outreach activity equal or superior to that found in any part of the nation. But new times bring new needs and new opportunities. More citizens seek lifelong access to learning. Governmental and private agencies have increased need for access to the research products and knowledge base of the University System. Study, research, and information transfer focused on the major problems of our society lay urgent claim to attention from the University System. For all these reasons, invigoration of the "Wisconsin Idea" becomes a high priority mission for the University System as a whole in the decade of the 1970's.

The policies proposed in this document are intended to set the framework of purpose, organization, and relationship within which the vitalization of University Extension and outreach activity can be accomplished.

I. The Goals of Organization

The goals of organization are the following:

1. To establish the organization and administrative relationships which will make possible the coordination of University outreach activity on a statewide basis, with attention to continuing assessment of need, development of priorities, allocation of resources in terms of priorities, and elimination of duplicative or unproductive activity.

2. To facilitate maximum involvement in outreach activity by all Units of the University System, including arrangements which encourage initiative by Units and insofar as possible place decision-making in the hands of persons who develop and carry out programs.

3. To facilitate coordination of University outreach activity with the resources and activity of other agencies of the State.

4. To conserve the integrity of established, productive, and high priority outreach programs, such as those established with the counties through cooperative extension.

II. General Organizational Assumptions

1. There should be only one University Extension Unit for the System. This Unit has both unique responsibilities, and coordinate responsibilities with the campus Units for developing an effective, statewide, and coordinated University outreach program. University of Wisconsin Extension, which now carries its activity into all parts of the State, is designated as this Unit. Its responsibilities and the arrangements governing its relationship with other Units of the System are established in the sections of this document which follow.

2. Where campus Units now have separate divisions of Extension and/or Con-

tinuing Education, these divisions should continue their work within the limits of the campus entitlements provided in this document. To the extent that their work involves functions and responsibilities also held by University Extension, discussions between University Extension and the campus Unit should be undertaken promptly to the end of assimilating such functions and responsibilities into University Extension in cooperation with the campus Unit. As feasible, campus-based personnel who should also be working with and through the program activity of University Extension should become joint appointees of the campus and University Extension. Should problems develop in such arrangements which cannot be resolved between the campus Unit and University Extension, these should be brought to the Office of the Vice President, Academic Affairs, for resolution.

3. Continuing staffing for the outreach function of the University System should emphasize all steps to strengthen linkages between campus Units, University Extension, and other agencies with resources or outreach activity in the planning and conduct of outreach programs. To this end, it is assumed that the pattern of new appointments related to outreach functions, whether for new positions or for replacement of vacancies, will give first priority to the use of joint appointments, and that special approval must be obtained from the Office of the Vice President, Academic Affairs, for appointments either by campus Unit or University Extension which depart from this pattern.

III. Responsibility for Off-Campus, Credit-Bearing Courses

1. Campus Units have responsibility for developing and offering off-campus, credit-bearing courses, within their instructional mission, in their immediate service area.

a. This enables campus Units to have the option of developing extended day, extended week instructional programs as part of their regular residence instruction activity.

b. Units may also, at their option, agree to have such off-campus, extended day, extended week credit courses offered through or jointly with University Extension.

c. Immediate service area is defined as a first approximation as a geographic area which can be served by faculty teaching both on campus, and off campus on the same day. The Office of the Vice President, Academic Affairs, is authorized to designate further refinements of the immediate service areas of campuses after consultation with University Extension and the Unit or Units involved.

2. University Extension has responsibility for offering credit-bearing courses in the immediate service area of campus Units which respond to needs of the people of the area, but which represent the extension of resources not within the mission or the capability of the immediate campus Unit.

a. By specific delegation, campus Units with unique resources and teaching programs, have responsibility for working with and through University Extension for statewide dissemination of such programs, as needed.

3. An information system should be established to the end that University Extension has comprehensive information on the off-campus offerings scheduled by each campus Unit, and the campuses have comprehensive information on the Extension sponsored offerings in the State, with particular attention to the offerings in the immediate service area of any campus.

a. Extension should identify an office to monitor such information to the end that problems involved in programming gaps, or in programming duplications are identified. These problems should be resolved promptly by direct discussions between Extension and the campus or campuses involved, and in the event prompt resolution is not possible, should be referred to the Academic Vice President for resolution.

IV. Responsibility for Non-Credit Seminars, Short Courses, Conferences, etc.

1. Campus Units have responsibility for developing and offering non-credit instructional events, related to and supportive of their instructional mission, within their immediate service area.

    a. Campus Units may at their option work with and through University Extension in such offerings.

    b. The non-credit offerings developed should be on the basis of 100% cost-recovery—either based on the fact that they are provided without cost by the faculty involved, or that all costs are recovered from the participants.

    c. It is strongly recommended that campus Units work with and through University Extension as the fiscal manager for such events.

2. University Extension has responsibility for developing and offering non-credit instructional events in relation to planned statewide programs of continuing education.

    a. University Extension should provide on and close to campuses the non-credit events which are based on missions or resources not represented on the campus or provided by the campuses.

    b. By specific delegation, campus Units with unique resources and teaching programs should work with and through University Extension in the statewide dissemination of such programs, as needed.

3. The same information system used for credit offerings should be developed for non-credit offerings, and the same monitoring procedures followed to assure that gaps in programming or wasteful duplication does not occur.

4. As part of its statewide programming for University, non-credit outreach, University Extension should seek maximum involvement with campus Units to provide Extension-held resources for non-credit events which are not 100% cost recovery events.

    a. To the maximum extent consistent with fiscal responsibility, University Extension should support effective joint enterprise by campuses and Extension with budgets defined at the outset of the programming year. The end in view is to provide a consistent fiscal base for maximizing campus initiative on outreach programming in its immediate service area.

V. Statewide Assessment of Need and Program Planning

1. The arrangements specified in Sections III and IV, foregoing, require campus Units to assess instructional needs in their immediate service area as those needs relate to their missions, to join with Extension on assessing statewide needs for unique, campus-based programs, and to inform Extension concerning local and regional assessments and programs.

2. There is, additionally, a need to develop planning procedures which assure the production annually of work plans for statewide outreach programs related to: (a) information transfer relative to the identified needs of agencies, institutions and populations in the State; (b) coordinated educational support for effective engagement with identified State problems, such as economic development, health care, environmental use and protection, etc.

    a. University Extension, jointly with the Units, should create statewide planning committees involving participation from appropriate Units, agencies and field staff, for an identified list of on-going program areas to assess program needs and propose annual work plans.

    b. University Extension, jointly with the Units, should create a System Extension Administrative Council on outreach programming, involving representation from Units of the System, to advise concerning Extension policy, and to review and recommend concerning planning committee products, and the creation or elimination of planning committees.

c. In order to respond to emergencies, or identified short-term needs, University Extension should create, with the advice of the most appropriate instructional or research units, a task force to develop a University response.

VI. The Development of Mediated Instruction and Media Support for Instruction[1]

Recognizing the growing importance of mediated instruction to both campus-based instruction and University outreach, the Regents affirm the following policies concerning development of such instruction:

1. Units have responsibility for developing media support for their instruction, including mediated courses within their instructional mission and in support of their degree programs.

2. University Extension has responsibility for developing mediated and auto-tutorial courses supportive of its special statewide programming, and/or the needs of particular groups not otherwise served or effectively served.

a. Credit-bearing courses, including correspondence study courses sponsored by University Extension, should be developed cooperatively by Extension and one or more campus Units, with credit assignable to the sponsoring campus.

b. In the event of a need which cannot be filled in this way, University Extension, with the advice of an appropriate faculty Council and the approval of the Office of the Vice President, Academic Affairs, may proceed with development and dissemination of a course bearing Extension only credit.

3. Inter-institutional use of developed materials should be encouraged by:

a. Inter-institutional cooperation in planning and development of new courses, based on consortium arrangements for identifying needs and carrying out development tasks.

b. Systemwide dissemination through University Extension of information on developed courses and materials.

c. Continuing faculty evaluation of the quality and usefulness of available materials.

d. The establishment of System policy on user costs and copyright protection.

VII. External Degrees[2]

In order to facilitate access to higher education opportunity for citizens who do not now have appropriate access, including programs leading to appropriate degrees and certificates, the Regents provide the following:

1. There should be created in University Extension, coordinate with the Office of the Vice President, Academic Affairs, a new agency to be known as Regents Statewide University. This agency shall be charged with the following mission.

a. To establish an appropriate faculty-administrative task force drawn from Units of the System to establish the policy guidelines for any external degree program offered by the System, or any of its Units or consortia of Units.

b. On the basis of these guidelines, to establish an appropriate faculty task force or task forces from Units of the System to plan and design one or more undergraduate degree or certificate programs to be made available to Wisconsin citizens not now served or effectively served by higher educational programs offered by the System.

c. To review plans thus developed with one or several Units of the System, or consortia involving several Units, to the end of establishing the appropriate campus resource base for any proposed program.

---

[1] Plans are currently underway for the appointment by the President of a System Study Committee to examine problems and make recommendations in this area.

[2] This section has been modified by the Regents in the UW System recommendations in the 1974 annual budget review and the 1975–77 budget requests and means of implementation are still under administrative study.

d. To bring forward the plan, or plans, thus generated for review by the Office of Vice President, Academic Affairs, and recommendation to the Regents.

2. In initiating this planning program and goal, the Regents provide the following policy stipulations:

a. Programs proposed should be clearly designed for populations now not served or effectively served by the System, and therefore noncompetitive with existing programs.

b. Programs should make the maximum feasible use of existing resources, i.e., developed outreach courses of the campuses and University Extension.

c. Programs should be designated as experimental, and include provision for evaluation incident to decision on continuation, modification, or elimination.

d. Programs leading to degrees should provide the basis for assurance that degrees thus achieved will be qualitatively on a par with those now offered by the System.

VIII. Implementation

The Regents ask that System Administration issue the administrative guidelines needed to implement as rapidly as possible the policies stated in this document. Concerning implementation, the Regents observe:

1. That continuity of service for existing and effective programs should be assured, and that where transfer of the administrative location of a program or the personnel associated with it is needed to achieve the policy goals now affirmed, this be carried out only after full consultation with the units and people affected.

2. That it should be the goal of the System that credit instruction leading to a University degree, whether offered on campus or off, should be financed in the same state subsidy/student fee proportion as resident campus instruction. As a matter of equity, the University System should seek a condition where part-time students seeking educational goals through off-campus courses are neither disadvantaged nor advantaged in relation to resident students as to the quality and cost of their education. The Regents recognize that achievement of these goals will involve a series of transitional steps in University budgeting practices and procedures, and that this transitional process should be accomplished in such a way as to maintain and augment the current educational opportunities of Wisconsin citizens.

3. That a report on implementation steps and accomplishments be made to the Regents not later than December, 1973, to the end that progress may be assessed and any needed policy modifications or additions may be considered.

Appendix G
Chapter 7 Exhibits: Statements of Purposes and Objectives

PURPOSES AND OBJECTIVES OF PUBLIC SCHOOL CONTINUING PROGRAMS

Concord-Carlisle Regional School District, Massachusetts

The Advisory Committee affirms that as adult educators we are dedicated to finding the means whereby the goal of maintaining a currently educated citizenry throughout life in a changing democratic society can be fulfilled. We seek to establish practical and defensible programs which will be a demonstrable part of helping America grow and build for the future and we affirm the importance to society of making available rich educational opportunities for adults in the following areas:

In vocational, technical and professional education and training;

In education for the wholesome use of leisure time and the maintenance of mental and physical fitness;

In continuing education for adults having less than a high school education or its equivalent;

In a broadly based liberal education in the arts, sciences and humanities;

In education for civic understanding and participation—communitywide, state-wide, nationwide and worldwide;

In education for the later ages of life;

In family education and human relations.

Midway Adult High School, San Diego City Schools, California

The adult population in the United States faces day after day a broad variety of problems of adjustment to the changing industrial, agricultural, commercial, economic and cultural influences in our society. The rate at which our society is changing has increased with the coming of the Space Age. Technological unemployment is becoming more widespread and the responsibilities of a citizen in performing his duties are becoming more complex. The goal of adult education is to help the people of our society adjust more effectively to the rapidly increasing rate of cultural change. That segment of our population which is least able to adapt to the increasingly complex changes is the people who have not completed their high school education. This is the special province of Midway Adult High School. Midway is helping citizens to help themselves.

The specific objectives of this school are to:

1. Provide a high school curriculum to prepare adults and selected youth for more useful citizenship, employment, personal advancement and preparation for college.
2. Provide the opportunity for students to remove educational deficiencies.
3. Offer personnel services which will increase the student's self-understanding and help in his educational placement so that he may fully develop his potentialities.
4. Provide opportunities for adults to enrich their cultural life, become better parents and homemakers, increase civic knowledge and prepare for vocational improvement. In a free society dedicated to the worth of the individual and to the development of personality, the process of education becomes an end in itself.
5. Provide instruction in English and Citizenship for foreign born adults.
6. Provide instruction as required to meet special community needs.
7. Encourage enthusiastic support for a good overall public school program by giving good school experiences to the adults who attend. These same adults are our taxpayers, parents of school children and voting citizens.

The Des Moines, Iowa, Family Learning Project

The Des Moines Family Learning Project began in 1972 as a demonstration program in Family Education. Now operated by the Des Moines Public Schools, it continues to involve mothers and fathers, young adults and children in a process unique to both parent and elementary education. For the Parent Educator, the Family Learning Project can supply answers to the questions of recruitment and curriculum; for the Elementary Educator, it offers an effective means of involving, almost daily, parents in the education of their own children.

In its present scope, the program shows parents effective methods of helping their children learn to read and helps them discover solutions to many of the conflicts that occur in family situations. These central activities—human relations workshops and reading sessions for parents and children—form the nucleus around which can grow an educational program for all members of the community. In addition to pursuing a course in adult thinking skills or working toward a High School Equivalency Diploma, many parents are attending consumer homemaking seminars, toy safety sessions, and other "courses" supplied by resources external to the project. In dealing, fundamentally, with people and their needs, the Family Learning Project has the capacity to serve as a total "Center" for adults and children.

PURPOSES AND OBJECTIVES OF CONTINUING EDUCATION PROGRAMS IN COMMUNITY COLLEGES AND TECHNICAL INSTITUTES

Miami-Dade Community College, Florida (North Campus)

General Information

We're committed to the philosophy that learning is a lifetime process. The many years spent in formal education do not complete the learning experience, but become a foundation for the learning which is done every day of our lives. With the world of knowledge constantly growing and altering many of yesterday's concepts, continuing education is necessary for those who hope to stay in the mainstream of today's complex society. Therefore, Continuing Education non-credit courses are designed for adults who are not concerned with earning academic credit but who wish to enrich their cultural lives or improve their personal efficiencies and skills. No record of previous education is necessary, no grades are given, attendance standards are voluntary and little or no homework is required.

Comprehensive Program of Rehabilitative Education

The Continuing Education Department provides the non-credit Basic Skills component of the Comprehensive Program for Rehabilitative Education. "C-PORE" has developed the Basic Skills component as a means of meeting the needs of incarcerated persons in our county penal system. Study programs are designed to meet individual needs. These programs have as goals to offer mental stimulation, to improve attitudes, to teach skills and to provide motivation for those incarcerated to return to society with a positive attitude toward life. C-PORE is devoted to helping those in the penal system to become positive contributors to society. Classes are taught at various penal facilities in Dade County.

Institute for Urban Community Education

The Institute for Urban Community Education is a training program in leadership development and citizens education. Citizens are trained for participation and involvement in community growth and development. Community school advisory councils, advisory boards, developing community leaders, citizens participation groups, social programs, and lay citizens will benefit from the training provided. As new citizens' needs are determined, additional workshops will be developed. Funds for this program are provided by a grant from the U.S. Office of Education's Community Education Program.

The Institute's training design evolves from needs determined by citizens from throughout Dade County's multi-ethnic community. A series of community education workshops, seminars and short courses provide concentrated skill development in community problem-solving techniques.

Management and Professional Development Institute

This institute will be useful to aspiring managers, practicing business people, and other professionals in a variety of organizations. Management and Professional Development courses, workshops and seminars are designed to:

—Develop Improved Managerial Skills
—Help Managers Do a Better Job in Their Current Assignments
—Prepare Self Help For Small Businesses

Management Seminars

This series of community service seminars had been developed by professors of the Department of Management Development at Miami-Dade Community College. These seminars are specially designed to meet the training and development needs of men and women who are now in supervisory and middle management positions, as well as those who will be advancing to the supervisory level.

Tri-County Technical College, Pendleton, South Carolina

Adult Education Division

The Adult Education Division provides practical, individualized instruction of value for the everyday life of adults. Students in the Division of Adult Education may learn to read for the first time, prepare to successfully pass the General Educational Development Examination—GED EXAM—administered by the South Carolina Department of Education, continue post-secondary study, review and strengthen prior study or complete personal study goals.

Instruction is tailored to fit the need of the student. Students who have not recently been in school are given added assistance. Study may begin any Monday, day or night, with study schedules suitable to the student.

The Evening and Extension Division

The purpose of the Evening and Extension Division is to extend the educational opportunities to all who desire to enrich and fulfill their educational needs. Evening classes are scheduled specifically for those citizens whose work schedules, job commitments, or other conflicts prevent their enrolling in morning classes.

The aim of the Evening and Extension Division is to assess the needs of the community and to offer courses which enable the people to improve their business potential, stimulate their intellectual curiosity, and add value to their style of life. By offering College Transfer, Technical, Industrial, Vocational, General Education Development, Management Development and selected Community Interest programs, we reach the entire population of Anderson, Oconee, and Pickens counties.

The Evening and Extension Division publishes brochures of its offerings on the main TEC campus and in the satellite centers located throughout the Anderson, Oconee and Pickens counties. This brochure is available for the asking.

The Evening and Extension Division consists of three major departments: Community Service and Continuing Education, Career Development, and Management Development.

The purpose of the Community Service is to extend educational opportunities to all who desire to enrich and fulfill their educational needs. The courses are non-credit and are offered to stimulate the intellectual curiosity and to provide knowledge in subjects which are of the hobby nature.

Career Development courses are non-credit; however, CEU's are awarded to all participants who successfully complete the course. Career Development courses assist in developing a student in the knowledge and skill of many vocations and trades.

Quinsigamond Community College, Worcester, Massachusetts, Center for Continuing Education and Community Service

What is the purpose of the Center for Continuing Education?

The Center seeks to fulfill the educational needs of the adult community, whether in the area of personal fulfillment, social involvement, or business and professional skills. It seeks to make man whole by methods, techniques, and settings most suitable to his experience and his resources.

What do you mean by "Community Services"?

Community Services involve credit and non-credit educational experiences for the benefit of the Community—workshops, seminars, institutes and conferences, as well as long and short-term courses. The emphasis is directed toward the implementation of skills, attitudes, and behaviors in the student deemed to be helpful in increasing his concern for the welfare of the community.

What about the Community as a resource?

The resources of the Community and Quinsigamond are combined to embrace the needs of the full-time student as well as to fulfill the part-time needs of the entire population. The Center invites inquiries from business and industry, the trades and the professions, from local, state, and federal agencies, as well as the community-at-large.

Bunker Hill Community College, Charlestown, Massachusetts, The Open College

One of the primary purposes of the community college is to provide educational services to individuals and groups in the community who traditionally have not been served by higher education. To better serve these students and to provide flexible, innovative curricula for the traditional population, a special academic unit, the Open College, has been established as an integral part of Bunker Hill Community College.

The Open College is responsible for developing and administering highly personalized approaches to education, many involving the resources of the community outside the college. The objective of these efforts is to offer educational opportunities for personal and career development to individuals for whom alternative modes of education are appropriate.

Vital aspects of providing educational opportunities for intentionally diverse consumers are: to create an awareness of these opportunities and to develop and implement workable strategies for facilitating access to them. Consequently, the goals of the Open College blend two categories of activities: one designed to develop institutional capability, the other designed to broaden the base and facilitate the route of access.

The organizational goals of the Open College are to:
1. Develop and (as appropriate) maintain alternative educational services;
2. Deliver these alternative educational services to all students—with special emphasis on nontraditional students;
3. Establish and maintain relationships between the college and the community in order to improve access to education;
4. Identify and promote the utilization of community based educational resources;
5. Decentralize the educational delivery system into the community and, where possible, integrate it with existing community services.

Community College of Vermont (CCV)

Established in 1970 and now a full member of the Vermont State Colleges System, the Community College of Vermont (CCV) enables Vermonters to continue their education at home, taking courses nearby from instructors who often live in their own communities. The College is open to any resident of the state, regardless of age, financial situation, geographic location, or previous educational experience. CCV gears its services especially to people who have been discouraged in the past by high tuition costs, distance from campuses, family or job responsibilities, and limiting admissions policies.

By providing links between learners and learning resources, by effectively using talent and facilities already available, CCV is able to provide quality education at greater convenience and less cost to the consumer. Classes are held in local schools, offices, banks, factories, churches, and other community buildings.

Course leaders too, are drawn from the community. Hired on a part-time basis, they are generally local people who have full-time jobs practicing the skills they teach. It is thus common to find a secretary teaching office skills, a craftsman sharing his art, a lawyer teaching law, the director of a day care center tutoring students in child development, or a town official teaching a class in local government. In combining local classrooms and members of the community with the skills of Community College staff members, continuing education is created from within the community itself.

Because of its design, Community College places its greatest emphasis on the student. Through its field offices located in various geographical areas of the state, the College brings courses into Vermont communities, designing classes around people's needs. Course offerings vary greatly, from welding, home plumbing and heating, and basic automotive repair, to psychology, data processing, and principles of management. Among other ways of serving Vermont communities, college level education projects are underway which focus on the needs of men in the state prison, patients in the state's mental institution, and residents in homes for the aged.

Through low tuition costs, flexible class hours, open admissions, and use of existing resources, Community College brings increased educational opportunities to thousands of Vermonters previously isolated from continuing higher education.

The College believes that living, growing people come throughout their lives to take increasingly greater responsibility for their own actions. As an educational institution, CCV is obligated to help people realize that they are the ultimate source of their own growth and learning. We hold the conviction, therefore, that a successful educational experience should help people to become more self-reliant learners, capable of looking objectively at where they are, formulating goals for what they want to become, and acting to accomplish those goals.

We also believe that as people are made up of more than their intellects alone, and educational programs should help students develop not merely intellectually but should help them enhance their physical and social selves as well.

Finally, we believe that the ability to acquire and use information effectively is more fundamental than absorption of a set body of knowledge alone.

For these reasons, we place great emphasis on helping students to learn how to learn. This involves developing the skills of self-assessment, goal-setting, resource identification, implementation of a plan, and self-evaluation. It also means developing skills and knowledge related to one's whole relationship with the world—personal, social, manual/physical, and intellectual.

The College helps learners to identify and develop these characteristics through the competence-based curriculum and degree contract. By providing a broad outline of the competence that should result from a good education, the College enables students to design for themselves relevant and effective educational experiences. For this reason, most courses are planned mutually by students and teachers with clear learning outcomes in mind. Likewise, every degree student develops a learning plan and contract that focuses on the skills and knowledge to be acquired, rather than on courses to be taken.

Underlying this approach is the conviction that learning progresses through the constant interplay of thought and action, theory and practice. People learn both by doing and by reflecting on what they have done. Since learning is going on all the time, in or out of the classroom, it follows that a fundamental skill of the self-reliant learner is self-evaluation—the ability to identify what we have learned. For as we are able to recognize more readily what we have been learning in the past, we grow in our ability to expand our horizons and continue to learn into the future. And the more we come to view ourselves as continual learners, the more self-reliant we become.

PURPOSES AND OBJECTIVES OF COLLEGE AND UNIVERSITY CONTINUING EDUCATION PROGRAMS

University Extension, University of California, Davis, Continuing Education in Public Administration

A major function of University Extension, University of California, Davis, is to provide continuing education to professionals in the fields of public administration, environmental planning, management, health sciences, engineering, education and social sciences. Extension management programs offer supervisors and managers an opportunity to broaden and update their skills through a planned and coordinated program of study in specific fields of management. These programs are designed to provide information on continuous changes in the management field, explore effective techniques in applying them, and offer an atmosphere which encourages an exchange of ideas with other professionals. Certificate programs are particularly suited to those who cannot pursue a full-time degree program, or who hold degrees in other fields.

Each certificate program consists of a specifically developed sequence of courses, designed to provide depth in theory, fundamentals and applications. Those who successfully complete the series are awarded a certificate. Extension certificates have earned professional acceptance as evidence that participants are well-informed, interested and active members of their professions.

Scarritt College Center of Continuing Education, Nashville, Tennessee

Scarritt's Center of Continuing Education affords men and women the opportunity to increase their knowledge, understanding, skills, and sensitivity for ministry in the world. The overarching goal of the Center is to help equip Christians theologically and socially, spiritually and practically, personally and corporately, to engage in ministry and mission.

Of special present concern to the Center is the discovery of ways to enable people, in the spirit of Christ, to confront the struggle for justice and liberation, the need for increasing global consciousness, conflicts in values, emerging life styles, and related changes in church life and development.

Empire State College (State University of New York), Saratoga Springs, New York

Empire State College of the State University of New York was created in 1971 to meet the contemporary educational needs of persons in alternative, flexible, and human ways. The College was mandated to develop alternative approaches to higher education, building upon the existing strengths and resources of the entire State University system. The College must be understood, therefore, within the context of the entire system.

Empire State College identified four central purposes which would guide the development of college objectives and policies. 1. *Access:* The College would be responsive to the human and social circumstances of persons, especially to the need for flexibility of time and place, so that people previously unable or unwilling to attend a campus regularly could pursue an education. 2. *Content:* To be responsive to emerging social needs, and to meet the educational needs and purposes of diverse students, the College would provide initiative to each student in planning a nonprescriptive study program selected from many alternatives. 3. *Method:* The College would evaluate and utilize learning wherever it occurs, and develop such processes and resources as are necessary to respond flexibly to individual students in many locations. 4. *Cost/effectiveness:* The College would conduct research on these alternative models with particular attention given to cost/effectiveness.

Empire State College has no campus, no one central location. It has, instead, a variety of structural units—learning centers, learning units, satellites—which are used to "deliver" the College's educational concept to many different types of students across New York State. The College has planned for *change* in seven major areas or directions:

1. *Students.* The College is designed to serve increasing numbers of students who come from increasingly diverse backgrounds seeking to realize increasingly wide-ranging purposes. They are students who need alternatives to the traditional residential campus.

2. *Methods and Areas of Study: The College Curriculum.* Empire State College has developed a range of alternative methods for learning which are responsive to a variety of student needs. The range of areas for which students may develop study plans will include opportunities in education, and business; the broad range of opportunities in the liberal arts and sciences, especially interdisciplinary and problem-oriented areas; career ladder opportunities in the applied sciences, community services, and certain allied health programs.

3. *The College Faculty.* In order to provide varied educational alternatives to students, the Empire State College faculty include full-time and part-time mentors, part-time adjunct or community faculty, and tutors, field-supervisors, and non-teaching professionals. All work directly with students or with the development of learning resources for students. Substantial numbers of those persons come from other than academic backgrounds, and many of them continue to pursue their principal professional or vocational employment and interests while contributing significantly to the College.

4. *Learning Resources.* The learning resources available for students, including human resources, relationships with other institutions and organizations, opportunities for field experiences, independent study and modular learning materials, increase continually in variety and complexity so that students at every level can employ those most suited to their interests and abilities.

5. *College Organization.* The students, the faculty, and the learning resources they use are dispersed throughout the State and at other strategic locations through an expanded and diversified network of learning centers, units, mentors-on-location, and cooperative relationships with other institutions and organizations.

6. *Research.* Collection of data about educational contributions of varied approaches and concerning the educational progress of different students contributes significantly to short-range monitoring and modifications as well as to long-range planning. The research contribution to planning is enhanced by detailed analyses of the relative cost-effectiveness of various educational alternatives.

7. *Educational Objectives.* There is an increasing conceptual clarity concerning educational objectives as these relate to student purposes. The College has developed approaches to individual instruction through contract learning, independent study and modular programs, and the requirements and criteria for their initial approval and successful completion. The general framework for assuring the maintenance of the highest standards in granting advanced standing for prior learning and in the criteria for awarding associate and bachelor degrees will be continued and developed.

Metropolitan State University, St. Paul, Minnesota

Metropolitan State University, formerly Minnesota Metropolitan State College, is a competence-based upper-division institution designed expressly to serve adults in the Minneapolis–St. Paul metropolitan area whose needs were not being met by other post-secondary institutions. Authorized by the Minnesota State Legislature in May, 1971, Metro U admitted its first students in February, 1972. Metro U presently enrolls over 1,600 students and its graduates number over 1,000. The University which is the newest member of the Minnesota State University System, has received full accreditation by the North Central Association of Colleges and Secondary Schools.

Metro U has been self-consciously experimental in its approach to higher education. By design, the University has avoided replicating already existing educational opportunities and has focused on alternative approaches to educating adults. The educational program of the University is student centered, highly individualized, and competence-based.

Metro U, since its inception has focused on the outcomes rather than the inputs of the learning process. The recognition and assessment of experiential learning have been integral components of the University's educational program. The individualized aspect of Metropolitan State University allows students to design their own education and to complete it at their own pace. Many students attend on a part-time basis and use their jobs and home activities as part of their education. In addition to studying on their own time, students often have a choice of location. Metropolitan State University does not have a campus in the traditional sense but uses existing facilities throughout the metropolitan area as its campus. Classes are held in such places as the First National Bank of Minneapolis, the St. Paul YWCA, Brookside Community Center, and the Control Data Corporation. Students are also encouraged to include independent study and internships in their learning plans. Metropolitan State University has two centers where students may contact faculty members. They are located in Metro Square, St. Paul, and the IDS Center, Minneapolis.

Metro U's educational philosophy is embodied in the following tenets:

1. The University vests in each individual student responsibility for and authority over his or her education. The University vests in its officers and faculty responsibility for and authority over teaching and for determining whether or not a student has given adequate evidence that he or she has achieved his or her educational objectives.

2. The University records a student's educational progress in terms of the competencies the student achieves and *not* in terms of the number of courses or other units of experience which the student undertakes to achieve competencies.

3. The University believes that whenever appropriate, students should be encouraged to make use of community resources, including human resources and events controlled by agencies and organizations external to the University, to achieve their educational goals.

4. The University recommends that each student receiving a degree demonstrate a high level of competence in each of these areas of life: communications and basic learning, the responsibilities of being a member of a self-governing community; work; recreation; and personal development and social awareness. To achieve competence in the areas listed means that students must know and employ many of the arts, sciences, humanities, and applied disciplines. It also frequently means that students will require types of knowledge and understanding which vary significantly from the types usually associated with higher education, particularly experientially-based knowledge and affective knowledge; the University respects the broadening of the concept of what it means to be learned which is thereby implied.

5. The University expects that those upon whom it confers degrees will be life-long, self-directed learners committed to excellence in their learning.

PURPOSES AND OBJECTIVES OF PROGRAMS IN BUSINESS AND INDUSTRY

The Career Development Program of the General Electric Company

The objective of the career development program is to
—Help individuals who are actively exploring and establishing the next stage of their careers, on either their current position or in another position, thereby
Creating opportunities for you to
—Take a *thorough look at your career to date* and assure yourself that your manager is aware of your capabilities and accomplishments from past experiences through a prepared mutually rewarding face-to-face discussion with your manager.
—Think about your *immediate future* more thoroughly and realistically by
  —*analyzing your current position and your career path to date*
  —*inventorying your current job abilities*
  —*discussing and deciding with your manager what the* next *stage of your career planning and development should be*
  —*discussing problems and opportunities with your manager and other associates*
  —*projecting the characteristics and expected satisfactions from your future career*
  —*examining and then confirming or rejecting the assumptions you hold about yourself, others, or some aspect of your environment that influences your career planning*
—Convert the results of your thinking and discussions into *appropriate actions* which can be *planned* and are more likely to be *implemented.*
Creating opportunities for your manager to
—Shift "career talk" pressure from less productive questions about ultimate or long-term career goals of his people to more *productive attention* on the next *career stage* which may be development of greater *proficiency in a current position or preparation for another position.*
—Obtain *relevant information* to recommend or discourage a course of action, study, learning or career development planning.
—Find ways to identify a larger number of developmental opportunities for his people on-the-job which can be supplemented as appropriate with off-the-job training and education and more positions to which his people might move to develop their careers.

The Center for Creative Leadership, Greensboro, North Carolina

The mission of the center is to improve the practice of management by encouraging the identification and development of creative leaders. Our emphasis is on people—as individuals, as group members, and as constituents of organizations. Research is conducted from a behavioral science perspective aimed at answering fundamental questions about people as leaders. Training programs are designed with the conviction that people can learn the subtleties of leadership and that competent managers can become effective leaders. Communication, which involves the development of educational tools as well as the dissemination of information, is giving us the leverage to reach as many potential leaders as possible.

Appendix H
Chapter 8 Exhibits: Sample Program Designs

UCLA EXTENSION CATALOG CENTER SPREAD

ESPECIALLY FOR CAREER WOMEN

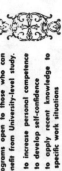

Programs open to those who can benefit from University-level study.

- to increase personal competence
- to develop self-confidence
- to apply recent knowledge to specific work situations

CLEARING COMMUNICATION LINES

Work-related communication skills necessary for efficient, effective operation. Demonstrations of newest methods for improving communication flow. Two Saturdays—in Downtown Los Angeles.
FEE: $20

ANATOMY OF PROGRAM PLANNING

The systems approach to planning adapted to community and business organizations, governmental and educational institutions. A Saturday workshop—in West Los Angeles.
FEE: $10

GROUP COUNSELING FOR WOMEN

Opportunities for Vocational, Educational and Community Activities
Individual tests, group counseling sessions, guest speakers from various fields. Ten evenings —in Downtown Los Angeles.
FEE: $45 includes testing.

MANAGEMENT METHODS FOR COMMUNITY ORGANIZATIONS

Application of principles and methods developed for the management of business and industry to the structure, operation and interpersonal relationships of community organizations. Four half-days—in West Los Angeles.
FEE: $30

DEVELOPING PERSONAL POTENTIAL

Part I, 814 Small group setting, informal yet structured, provides ways of establishing individual self-awareness and guidelines for self-development. Ten evenings—offered in Pasadena, West Los Angeles, and Downtown Los Angeles.
FEE: $45

Part II, 814A Continuation of Part I. Ten evenings—in West Los Angeles.
FEE: $45

BUILDING FAMILY STRENGTH 810

Increased effectiveness of family living through understanding roles and relationships, expectations and responses. Ten evenings—in West Los Angeles.
FEE: $45

DAYTIME PROGRAMS

For those with diversified interests who are seeking programs during convenient daytime hours on weekdays at locations throughout Los Angeles County

SIGNIFICANT RELATIONSHIPS FOR WOMEN

Cultivating perspective on one's current relationships and finding ways to build better relationships through spontaneity, empathy and trust. One afternoon through evening conference—offered in Long Beach and West Los Angeles.
FEE: $12.50, total conference, $3.50, evening only, for husbands. Dinner, optional.

THE CREATIVE APPROACH

In a seminar-type setting, discussion of attitudes and abilities which lead to freeing oneself for an innovative, independent life. Ten meetings—in West Los Angeles.
FEE: $30

BUILDING FAMILY STRENGTH 810

Increased effectiveness of family living through understanding roles and relationships, expectations and responses. Ten meetings—offered in Pasadena, West Los Angeles, Beverly Hills, Central Los Angeles, San Fernando Valley and Redondo Beach.
FEE: $45

GROUP COUNSELING FOR WOMEN

Opportunities in Educational, Vocational and Volunteer Activities
Individual tests, group counseling sessions, guest speakers from various fields. Ten meetings —offered in Torrance and West Los Angeles.
FEE: $45 includes tests.

CHOICE: CHALLENGE FOR MODERN WOMAN

Analysis of alternative roles and activities for women. Two films from the TV series, Choice: Challenge for Modern Women, plus group discussions. A one-day program—offered in Long Beach and San Fernando Valley.
FEE: $8

DEVELOPING PERSONAL POTENTIAL

Part I, 814 Small group setting, informal yet structured, provides ways of establishing individual self-awareness and guidelines for self-development. Ten meetings offered in West Los Angeles, Central Los Angeles, San Fernando Valley and San Gabriel Valley.
FEE: $45

Part II, 814 A Continuation of Part I. Ten meetings—in West Los Angeles.
FEE: $45

TRAINING FOR COUNSELOR ASSISTANTS

An introduction for persons with little professional training or experience in social work or the social sciences who want to become more knowledgeable and skillful helpers in community service. Ten meetings—in Pasadena.
FEE: $30

CONCORD-CARLISLE, MASSACHUSETTS, REGIONAL SCHOOL DISTRICT, SCHEDULE OF CLASSES BY DAY

DAY-HOUR SCHEDULE, CAMBRIDGE CENTER FOR ADULT EDUCATION

DAY HOUR SCHEDULE

Mon.

Morning
9:00-11:30
Basic Drawing 92
ESL 84
First Aid 48
Chinese Brush Painting ...99
Oil Painting 97
Illustration 96
Recorder 75
Stitchery 108
Weaving 109
Lunchtime
11:30-1:30
Color and Design 96
ESL 84

Interior Design 50
Modelling 102
Chinese Brush Painting ...99
Recorder 75
Weaving, Off Loom 109
Afternoon
1:30-4:00
Canoeing 119
Driver's Education 52
Painting, Japanese 100
Recorder 75
Sewing 111
Starting
4:00-5:30
Piano 76

Spring Spectacular 14
Woodcarving 102
Starting
5:30-7:30
Auto Maintenance 52
Arab Israeli 16
Better Hello 26
Bridge 81
Canoeing 119
Chinese Dinner 88
Crime Does Pay 56
Drawing, Basic 92
Exercise 112
Financial Planning 45
Hand Drums 77

Tues.

Morning
9:00-11:30
Baskets 107
Bible Tour 33
Birdwalks 25
Collage 98
Cooking, Easy 86
Drawing, Portrait 99
Flute 75
French 82
Freshwater Life 14
Italian 83
Piano 76
Sewing 111
Lunchtime
11:30-1:30
Art Anatomy 93

Bible 33
French 82
Italian 83
Life Drawing & Modeling ...94
Tolkien 59
Voice in Performance 75
Philosophy 32
Afternoon
1:30-4:00
BA's, MA's & PhD's 39
Ballet 113
Drawing Plants 95
Drawing for Teachers 95
Drawing, Pen & Ink 95
French 82
Philosophy 32
Photo 64

Writers in Progress 56
Starting
4:00-5:30
Chekhov 62
Mime 69
Spring Wildflowers 15
Travel Agent 46
Understanding Listener 79
Starting
5:30-7:30
Assertiveness Training 27
Astronomy 21
Batik 107
Bike Repair 51
Bookbinding 54
Camera Ready Copy 54
Canoeing 119

Wed.

Morning
9:00-11:30
Androgyny 59
Calligraphy 100
ESL 84
Exercise 112
French 82
Quilting 110
Short Story 59
Western Art 72
Lunchtime
11:30-1:30
Calligraphy 100
French Impressionism 73
Greece & Crete 18
Italy 18
Jung 31
Silkscreening 104
Theatre Workshop 70
Unconscious Processes 30
Zen Meditation 34

Afternoon
1:30-4:00
Art Workshop 104
Calligraphy 100
Needlepoint 110
Sightsinging 74
Silkscreening 104
Starting
4:00-5:00
Exercise 112
Hypnosis 30
Piano 76
Poetry for Teachers 64
Sign Language 48
Tree Identification 22
Starting
5:30-7:30
Bike Repair 51
Chinese Dining 90
Coastal Ecology 22
Cooking, Italian 87

Country Crafts 103
Craft Sampler 103
Empire of Number 21
Exercise 112
Family History 47
French 82
Funny Flick 67
Ground School 53
Harmonica 77
Hello 27
Homebuying 49
How to Buy a House 49
Interior Design 50
Investing 44
Jewelry 104
Layout & Design 55
Mixology 91
Old Books 54
Music, Classical 80
Photography, Basic 64
Poetry Workshop 63

Thurs.

Morning
9:00-11:30
Art Workshop 92
Drawing, Portrait 99
Dynamics of Investing 44
Jewelry 104
Painting, Vision &
  Expression 97
Piano 76
Primitive Firing 101
Stained Glass 104
Stitchery 108
Lunchtime
11:30-1:30

Drawing, Basic 92
Drawing, Life 93
Illustration Children's
  Books 54
Italic 100
Jewelry 104
Painting as Self-Expression .97
Afternoon
1:30-4:00
Cooking, Quick Gourmet ...86
Drawing, Landscape 96
Drawing, Life 93
Graphics 103
History of T.V. 51

Italic 100
Layout & Design 55
Sewing 111
Walking Tours of Boston ...20
Watercolor 99
Weaving, Floor-Loom 109
Writing for Children 54
Starting
4:00-5:30
Dulcimer 77
Ocean Environment 22
Painting 97
Painting, European 72
Women of Near East 19

Fri.

Morning
9:00-11:30
9:00-11:30
Country Crafts 103
Drawing, Life 93
ESL 84
Flute 75
Piano 76

Primitive Firing 101
Women, Options for 40
Lunchtime
11:30-1:30
Open Studio 100
Afternoon
1:30-4:00

English, Reading & Writing ..84
Piano Improvisation 78
Woodworking 51
Starting
4:00-5:30
Jewelry 104

Sat.

Morning
9:00-11:30
Business, Succeeding in ...42
Cathedral Windows 110
Camera Maintenance 66
Emotions & Eating 89

Embroidery, Russian 108
Fabric Wall Hanging 108
Film Animation 68
Framing and Matting 98
Guitar, Folk 76
Interviewing 39

Jazz, Blues Dance 114
Juggling 69
Non-Profit Organizations ...43
Photo, Basic 64
Photo, Intensive 65
Print Collecting 73

— SPRING 1979

ADULT PROGRAMS IN GREAT NECK, NEW YORK

The Public Schools

Humanities

Bible Commentary: Moses. 10 Mondays, 8–10 p.m.

Contemporary Fiction: by and about women. 7 Thursdays, 8–10 p.m.

The Novel in the 70's. 8 Fridays, 9:30–11:30 a.m.

Two Contemporary Novelists: Bellow and Fowles. 2 Saturdays, 9:30 a.m.–12:30 p.m.

Contemporary Poetry. 10 Tuesdays, 8–10 p.m.

Great Modern European Short Stories. 8 Mondays, 8–10 p.m., 8 Thursdays, 10 a.m.–noon.

Plays of Eugene O'Neill. 8 Thursdays, 10 a.m.–noon.

Philosophy: digging for its roots. 6 Mondays, 8–9:45 p.m.

The World Between the Wars. 8 Mondays, 10:30 a.m.–noon.

The Great Outdoors

Camping. 6 Mondays, 8–10 p.m.

Great Neck's Back Yard. 3 Mondays, 9:30 a.m.–noon.

Mathematics and Computers

Home Computers. 4 Mondays, 8–10 p.m.

Basic Programming. 8 Mondays, 8–10 p.m.

I Hate Math: clinic. 8 Mondays, 7:30–9 p.m.

Archeology

Archeological Lectures: views from the inside. 4 Wednesdays, 8–9:30 p.m.

Archeology and Origins of Western Civilization. 8 Mondays, 8–10 p.m.

Ancient Rome and Pompeii. 10 Wednesdays, 10 a.m.–noon.

A Trip to Pompeii: in New York. Monday, April 30, 9 a.m. sharp.

The Art and Archeology of Ancient China: China unearths her heritage. 5 Thursdays, 10 a.m.–noon.

Lifestyles

Assertiveness Training. 10 Thursdays, 8–10 p.m.

Behavior Modification: what is it and why are people talking about it? 5 Mondays, 8–10 p.m.

Cultivating Change: a lifestyle seminar. 10 Mondays, 8–10 p.m.

Meditation: beginners' workshop. 10 Tuesdays, 7:30–8:50 p.m.

Teachings in Mysticism: six paths to self-realization. 10 Tuesdays, 9–10 p.m.

Older Adults

REAP: academy for retired executives and professionals. Wednesdays and Fridays, 10 a.m.–noon.

Choral Group. 15 Wednesdays, 10 a.m.–noon.

Exploring Art Media. 15 Mondays, 9:30 a.m.–noon.

Folk Dancing. 4 Saturdays, 10:30 a.m.–noon.

Sculpture and Pottery Workshop. 10 Mondays, 1–3:30 p.m.

Writing: exploring the personal. 10 Wednesdays, 1:30–3 p.m.

Columbia University

China-Russia-America: superpower politics. 5 Wednesdays, 7:30–9:30 p.m.

New Cultural Trends in Africa. 5 Thursdays, 7:30–9:30 p.m.

Astronomy: gateway to the universe. 6 Wednesdays, 7:30–9:30 p.m.

The International Scene

Changing China. Saturday, May 12, 9 a.m.–4 p.m.

International Issues. 8 Mondays, 7:30–10:30 p.m.

Adult Learning Centers

English for Non-English Speaking. (7 time periods)

Basic-Intermediate-Advanced Instruction. (9 time periods)

Adult Learning Laboratory. (2 time periods)

Citizenship Education. Wednesdays, 7:30–10:30 p.m.

English Skills. 12 Thursdays, 10 a.m.–noon.

Preparing for College: as an adult. 8 Tuesdays and 8 Thursdays, 7:30–10 p.m.

And the following additional groupings of courses:

High School Credit Courses
College Credit Courses
Foreign Languages
Fine Arts
Antiques
Fine Crafts
Performing Arts
Business
Communication Skills
Office Practice
Interior Design as a Profession
Adventures in Cookery
Home Interests
Driver Education
Wheels
Personal Finance
Health Horizons
Sports and Physical Fitness
Games, Hobbies, and Pets
Boating and Piloting
Child Care

Appendix I
Chapter 9 Exhibits: Tools for Operating Programs

Exhibit I–1

LETTER OF APPOINTMENT

Mr. Joseph Smith
610 Main Street
Middleburg, Middlestate

Dear Mr. Smith:

This is to confirm your appointment (or reappointment) to the faculty of the Community Center Adult Education Program.

Your assignment is as follows:

    Courses: 1. Improving Your Speech
               2. Speaking for Radio

    First session: January 17

    Room: 215

    Compensation: $150 for each eight-week course, totaling $300
                   for the term, payable one-half January 31 and
                   one-half February 28

As you know, this assignment is contingent upon the development of an adequate enrollment. I shall appreciate your signing and returning the attached duplicate of this letter, agreeing to these conditions.

I am looking forward to working with you during the coming term and sincerely hope that your experience will be a fruitful one.

                                    Yours very truly,

                                    John R. Doe
                                    Director of Adult Education

_____

Instructor's Agreement:
    This will acknowledge receipt of the above letter and my agreement to the terms stated in it.

        (Signed)_____

Exhibit I–2

FACULTY ORIENTATION MEMO

Cambridge Center for Adult Education

Dear Faculty:

Welcome to this next term at the Cambridge Center for Adult Education. Let me just remind you of a number of items:

BEFORE CLASSES START:

For supplies, please see David Tickton in the office. Please check with him before the term begins, allowing ample time for ordering materials and/or sending out supply lists to students. Please prepare these lists for materials not obtainable at the Center.
For language books, see Jim Smith. For all other books check with David Tickton.

If there is none or minimal registration for your class you will be notified of the cancellation of your course and of your appointment before the term starts.

WHEN CLASSES START:

At the first meeting please introduce yourself and tell your students a bit about your background and experience. Then have all students introduce themselves plus any information you may want from your students (expectations, interests, experiences, etc.). One ice-breaking technique is to have each student introduce his or her neighbor after people are given time to chat together for 3 or 4 minutes. Please inform your students at this time of what you expect to cover in your course and how you intend to do so, thus preparing your students for what is to come in the next weeks or sessions. Ins and outs of supplies, materials and reading lists should also be discussed at this time.
Last but not least -- please IMPRESS upon your students the importance of keeping purses, handbags, etc. with them at all times -- unfortunately there have been a number of thefts so people should be careful.

REGISTRATION:

If there is not sufficient registration to run a viable class at the first meeting you will receive payment for this one meeting. Students will be told at this time that the class will be cancelled and they will be given the option to register for another class or receive a refund.

Please sign up in the office ahead of time for equipment you need to use for your class. First come, first served!

We have no duplicating machine in the office. If materials need xeroxing . . . copy (not more than 5 pages) MUST be left in the office by Thursday of the preceding week. Please, if you charge xeroxing, write clearly on the slip title of course for which xeroxing was done.

Please notify the office immediately if the model has not shown up on time.

As a rule, children and animals should not be permitted in class. In exceptional cases, do check with all other students whether or not such presences are acceptable (some students may be allergic to

Exhibit I–2

animals for instance). Also it is a good idea to check whether or not smoking in class is acceptable.

Please note: Definitely <u>no smoking</u> in any room where flammable materials are being used.

Before leaving your classroom at the end of class, please <u>straighten things up</u> for a moment so the next class can be comfortable.

IMPORTANT: CANCELLATIONS AND MAKE-UPS

Call 547-6789 the moment you know you cannot teach a class -- we will accept a substitute you may have lined up -- <u>you</u> will be responsible for appropriately reimbursing your substitute. If you do not have a substitute, we will try to find one or else cancel your class and try to reach all students by postcard or telephone. If a class has to be cancelled due to illness or holidays you will be expected to make-up during the week after the end of the term on the regular class day and time -- unless you make other arrangements with your students. If you do, <u>let the Office know ahead of time. For that matter, any time a class is held outside the Center -- field trip or make-up -- let us know as soon as you know the date and place so we can tell students who may have been absent, have forgotten, etc.</u>

ALSO NOTE:

<u>Mail</u>, notes and packages for faculty will be left in the faculty message box in the office. Please check <u>at least</u> once a week.

<u>Checks</u> -- faculty will be paid twice a term, half-way through and at the end of the term. Your <u>check</u> will be ready to pick up in the office if you teach at Brattle House or Blacksmith House. Otherwise your check will be mailed unless you request to pick it up.

<u>Telephones</u>: As we do not have unlimited service we would appreciate your limiting office calls to matters concerning your class only.

We do <u>not</u> give out your telephone number -- if you wish to authorize us to give out yours, leave word with the office or tell Johnnie Scheff.

Suggestions for lectures, concerts, etc., should be given to Jim Smith.

<u>Exhibits</u>: For both faculty and students, both fine arts and crafts, please see Barry Jacobson for scheduling.

If you have any interesting information about your class or students for our in-house paper, please tell Katherine Kuhns.

Do let us know <u>immediately</u> of any changes in your address or telephone. <u>Please!</u>

Have a wonderful term -- do let me know about any comments you have.

<u>IMPORTANT!!</u> IF ANY STUDENT IS INJURED IN YOUR CLASS, AS A RESULT OF THAT CLASS OR NOT, PLEASE NOTIFY THE CAMBRIDGE CENTER OFFICE IMMEDIATELY.

Alida J. O'Loughlin
Director

Exhibit I–2

Cambridge Center for Adult Education | 42 Brattle Street | Cambridge, Mass. 02138 | Tel. 547-6789

TEACHING SUGGESTIONS FOR FACULTY

If this is your first time teaching at the Center, these comments and suggestions may be helpful. Some of these ideas have come from reviewing the evaluations by students of courses taught in the past. Your course, as a new course, will be evaluated and you may find looking at the evaluations helpful. In general, these evaluations show how positive the response is to classes at the Center and why students return year after year.

1. Students at the Center differ widely in background, ability and age. You may have to go more slowly than you planned or vary the assignments for different individuals. It may be necessary to encourage the hesitant students as well as to keep the stronger students from dominating the class.

2. Classes at the Center are informal and enjoyable yet students have high expectations. Complaints in the evaluations usually relate to lack of organization of class materials. Be sure that you plan your classes to make full use of the time and that your instructions for procedures and assignments are clear.

3. You may want to stop after the class has met several times and talk over how things are going with the group. This kind of discussion can 'clear the air' as well as produce some good ideas for teaching. It also permits differences of opinion to come up early enough to be easily solved.

4. In 'how to' courses, students sometimes feel that they are not getting enough personal instruction. Obviously, you cannot be everywhere at once, but try to see that no one waits too long for some help with his/her particular problem.

5. You can stop in at the office any time for advice or assistance: Jim Smith, David Tickton, Barry Jacobson or Johnnie Scheff are ready to answer questions or talk about your class with you.

Exhibit I–3

TEACHER'S PROCESS PLAN

Course:_____ Teacher:_____

Semester:_____

AT THE OPENING SESSION:

1. How will you introduce yourself? How will you describe your
    perception of your role, your special resources and limita-
    tions, your availability for consultation, etc.?

2. What procedures will you use to engage the students in becoming
    acquainted with one another in terms of their work, experience,
    resources, interests, etc.?

3. What other procedures will you use to establish a climate of
    mutual respect, collaborativeness rather than competitiveness,
    informality, security, warmth of relationship with you,
    supportiveness, etc.?

4. How will you engage the students in examining, clarifying, and
    influencing the objectives of the course?

5. How will you acquaint the students with your plan of work for
    the course and their responsibilities in it?

6. How will you help them prepare to carry the responsibilities
    you expect of them?

7. How will you acquaint the students with the resources (material
    and human) available to them for accomplishing their learning
    objectives?

8. What learning activities will you suggest the students engage
    in between the first and second sessions of the course?

9. What physical arrangement of your meeting room do you prefer
    to facilitate interaction among the students and between them
    and you?

IN SUBSEQUENT SESSIONS (indicate which session when appropriate):

1. How will you engage the students in diagnosing their individual
    and collective needs and interests regarding the content of
    the course?

2. How will you engage the students in formulating learning
    objectives based on their diagnosed needs and interests?

3. What specific learning strategies (methods, techniques, devices,
    materials, etc.) do you propose using in this course?

4. How will the students be involved in selecting and participa-
    ting in these strategies?

5. What procedures and tools will you use for helping students
    assess their progress toward their objectives?

Exhibit I–3

6. What procedures and tools will you use for evaluating learning outcomes at the end of the course?

7. If appropriate, how will grades be arrived at?

8. What procedures and tools will you use for getting feedback from the students periodically and at the end regarding the quality of this learning experience?

9. What content do you expect to be acquired through this course (including knowledge, understanding, skills, attitudes, and values)?

Exhibit I–4

FACULTY INSTITUTE, UNIVERSITY COLLEGE
NORTHEASTERN UNIVERSITY

Friday and Saturday Evenings

7:30–8:00 Orientation (Dean Allen)
—Introduction of new faculty members
—Administrative announcements
—New program developments
—Objectives of this Institute

8:00–8:20 Problem Census (Dr. Malcolm Knowles)
—Buzz groups of faculty members share problems, difficulties, frustrations they experience in helping adults to learn, arrange them in priority order, and report them out through a spokesman.
—Priority concerns are listed on blackboard and clustered into categories.

8:20–8:30 Organization of Group Works
—Faculty members are asked to indicate by a show of hands which category of concerns each wishes to work on, thus constituting a work group for each category.

8:30–9:00 Resource Input (Dr. Knowles)
—Members of the work groups are asked to consider how principles of andragogy as summarized by Dr. Knowles might be applied to the solution of the problems in their areas of concern.

9:00–9:45 Work Group Meetings
—Work groups meet in assigned rooms to pool their thinking about solutions to their problems in the light of the principles of andragogy. Each group selects a spokesman to report their findings.

9:45–10:30 Closing Session
—Work group spokesmen report findings.
—Dean Allen and Dr. Knowles dialogue on reactions and further suggestions.

Exhibit I–5

PROCESS DESIGN FOR A ONE-DAY WORKSHOP

Andragogy, Self-directed, and Contract Learning

Competency-Development Objectives

   1.   An understanding of the modern concepts of adult learning and how these differ from traditional concepts of youth learning.

   2.   An understanding of the role of educator as facilitator and resource for self-directed learners.

   3.   The ability to apply these concepts to the designing of learning experiences for one's self and others through the use of learning contracts.

Schedule

9:00-10:00 a.m.   Climate-setting exercise

   --Sharing of information in small groups about participants' whats, whos, resources, and questions, problems, and issues.

10:00-10:15 a.m.   Analysis of this experience

10:15-10:30 a.m.   Break

10:30-11:30 a.m.   Dialogic presentation of the theoretical framework of Andragogy.

11:30-noon   Table groups apply this model to their questions, problems, and issues, and pool questions requiring further examination.

12:00-1:00 p.m.   Lunch

1:00-2:00 p.m.   Response to groups' questions

2:00-2:45 p.m.   Diagnosis of competency-development needs.

   --Introduction to competency-based education and the model of competencies for facilitators of learning.

   --Self-diagnosis of competency-development needs by individual participants.

2:45-3:00 p.m.   Break

3:00-3:30 p.m.   Drafting of learning contracts

   --Individual participants draft contracts for their two or three highest-priority learning objectives.

3:30-4:00 p.m.   Sharing of experience with learning contracts

   --Groups share learning contracts and identify questions requiring further examination

4:00-4:45 p.m.   --Response to groups' questions

4:45-5:00 p.m.   Evaluation of this workshop

Exhibit I–6

CERTIFICATE OF COMPLETION

CERTIFICATE OF COMPLETION

CENTRAL YMCA COMMUNITY COLLEGE

1960

PATET OMNIBUS · CHICAGO

CONTINUING EDUCATION
CENTRAL YMCA COMMUNITY COLLEGE

has successfully completed the following course:

_____ Term

_____ Instructor

Date_____   _____
                                   Director, Continuing Education

29 WEST RANDOLPH STREET • CHICAGO, ILLINOIS • 60601 / 211 WEST WACKER DRIVE • CHICAGO, ILLINOIS • 60606

Exhibit I–7

A PERSONAL CAREER PLANNING PROCESS

For Managing the Controllable Parts
of One's Career Development

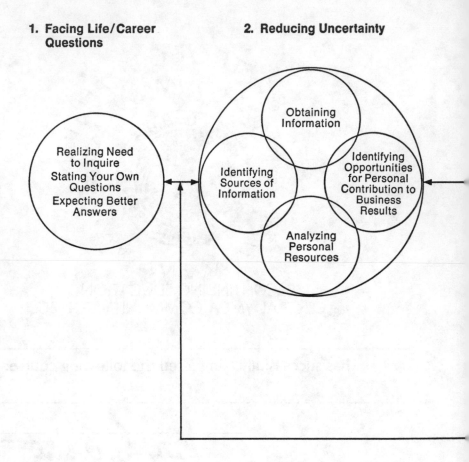

1. Facing Life/Career Questions

Realizing Need
to Inquire
Stating Your Own
Questions
Expecting Better
Answers

2. Reducing Uncertainty

Obtaining
Information

Identifying
Sources of
Information

Identifying
Opportunities
for Personal
Contribution to
Business
Results

Analyzing
Personal
Resources

Key Features

Key features of *Career Dimensions,* a self-directed approach to career planning at General Electric, are:

- Voluntary Participation: Free choice in use of the program and in the sharing of thoughts, documented or otherwise.

- Discipline for Continuous Learning: Guides for learning how and what to learn, including the discovery and testing of perceived realities (self, plans, situation, assumptions, and conclusions).

- Focus on the Next Step: The emphasis is on the next step or activity necessary to improve professional development, whether or not any kind of a job change or movement is involved.

- Coordinated with Life Planning.

- Guides for Preparing Actionable Professional and Career Development Plans.

Exhibit I–7

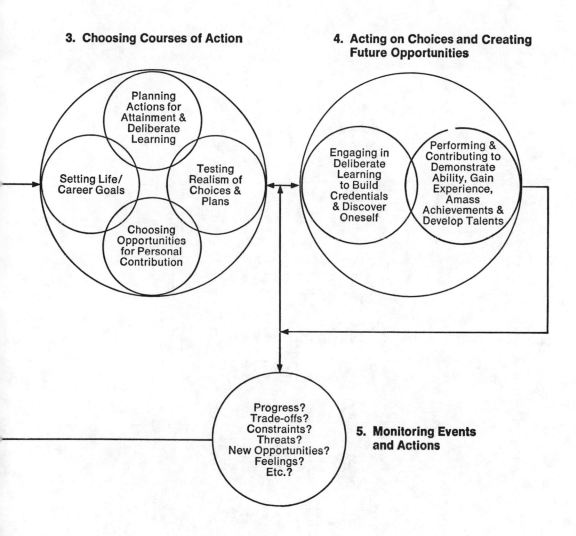

3. Choosing Courses of Action

Planning Actions for Attainment & Deliberate Learning

Setting Life/Career Goals

Testing Realism of Choices & Plans

Choosing Opportunities for Personal Contribution

4. Acting on Choices and Creating Future Opportunities

Engaging in Deliberate Learning to Build Credentials & Discover Oneself

Performing & Contributing to Demonstrate Ability, Gain Experience, Amass Achievements & Develop Talents

Progress? Trade-offs? Constraints? Threats? New Opportunities? Feelings? Etc.?

5. Monitoring Events and Actions

- Flexibility:
    - —Individual may choose, sequence and pace what he or she does.
    - —The process may be done alone, with a partner, or in a small group; some parts do require one to interview another person.
    - —Relevant parts may be repeated without returning to "go."
    - —The discipline of learning and the results may be transferred to a variety of employment and personal situations.

- Integrated with managerial guidelines for career coaching.

- Supplemented and integrated with a handbook for human resource specialists.

Storey, W. D. Self-directed career planning at the General Electric Company. Working paper. © General Electric Company, 1976.

Exhibit I–8

DIRECT MAIL PROMOTION – ADULT EDUCATION PROGRAM

Central YMCA, Chicago, Illinois
Spring (starting April 6)

MAILING LIST	DATE	LETTER	ENVELOPES NO.		CATALOGS NO.		POSTERS NO.	FLIERS	REMARKS
Institutional List	Mar. 1	#1	9 by 12	40		400	100	None	Addressograph
Personnel Managers	Mar. 1	#2	9 by 12	125		675	300	None	Addressograph
YMCA Executives	Mar. 8	#1	9 by 12	24		300	100	None	Addressograph
Present Ad. Ed. Students	Mar. 15	None	Permit	900	1 ea.	900	None	None	Addressograph
Former Ad. Ed. Students	Mar. 15	None	Permit	3950	1 ea.	3950	None	None	Addressograph
Ad. Ed. Prospects	Mar. 15	None	Permit	2200	1 ea.	2200	None	None	Addressograph
YMCA Members & La Salle Club	Mar. 15	#5	Permit	1650	1 ea.	1650	None	None	Addressograph
Nurses Homes	Mar. 15	#4	Cat. Size	124	5 ea.	625	None	None	Hand address from Red Book "Hospitals"
Eleanor Clubs	Mar. 15	None	Cat. Size	7	5 ea.	35	None	None	Hand address from Red Book "Clubs"
Public Libraries	Mar. 8	#1	9 by 12	54	2 ea.	108	2 ea. 108	2000	Addressograph
Book Stores	Mar. 11	#1	Cat. Size	60	1 ea.	60	None	1000	Hand address special list
Ad. Ed. Council Bd. of Directors	Mar. 15	None	1st class	17	1 ea.	17	None	None	Addressograph
YMCA Bd. of Directors	Mar. 15	#3	1st class	30	1 ea.	30	None	None	Addressograph
Ad. Ed. Committee	Mar. 15	#3	1st class	20	1 ea.	20	None	None	Addressograph
Reminder Postcard to A. E. Students & Prospects	Mar. 29—10,970 cards								
						10,970	608	3,000	

Exhibit I-9

SCHEDULE OF SPECIAL FORM LETTERS

Central YMCA Adult Education Program
Spring Term (starting April 6)

	DATE	LETTER	ENVELOPES	AMT.	ENC.
Former Dancing Students	Mar. 22	#10	1st class	414	None
Former Painting Students	Mar. 22	#11	1st class	168	None
Former Photography Students	Mar. 22	#12	1st class	125	None
Former Public Speaking Students (re Parliamentary Law and Using Good English)	Mar. 22	#6	1st class	107	None
Social Agency Directors and YMCA Exec. Sec. (re Promotion & Publicity)	Mar. 22	#7	1st class	95	"Blurbs" and catalogs
Real Estate Students, former (re Starting Your Own Bus. and Accounting)	Mar. 22	#8	1st class	680	Return Post Card
Former Income Tax Students	Mar. 22	#9	1st class	54	None
Former Music Students	Mar. 30	#13	1st class	83	None
Former Reading Students	Mar. 30	#14	1st class	62	None

Exhibit I–10

PUBLICITY SCHEDULE

Central YMCA Adult Education Program
Spring Term (starting April 6)

PRIMARY SUBJECT	MEDIUM	DATE
General Announcement	City Press, House Organs, Com. Papers	March 1
Reading Courses	City Editors	March 25
Business Courses	Business Editors and Bar Ass'n, Law Review, Ass'n of Commerce, J. of Commerce	March 30
Interior Decoration	Woman's Page Editors	March 26
Photography	City Editors	March 29
Music Courses	Music Editors	March 31
Automobile Driving	Travel Editors	April 1
General Announcement	City Editors	April 4
Housing Course (General Plans)	Real Estate Editors, daily papers and Real Estate weeklies	March 26
Housing Course (General Plans)	Community Papers and House Organs	March 26
Housing Course (Instructors appointed)	City Editors	April 4
Housing Course (Topics Treated)	City Editors	April 18
Human Interest Stories	Feature Writers	During Term
Radio Interviews	Stations WGN, WMAQ	During Term

Exhibit I–11

NEWSPAPER ADVERTISING SCHEDULE

Central YMCA Adult Education Program
Spring

Tribune classified ad, 1 mo.		400.00
Community Newspapers		200.00
General ad—24 lines—Schools section		
Tribune ..... Sunday	3 times—March 7, 28, April 4	400.00
Sun-Times ... Sunday	1 time—March 28	100.00
Dancing ads—14 lines—Run of paper		
Tribune ..... Daily	2 times—March 24, April 5	150.00
Sun-Times ... Daily	2 times—March 23, 29	100.00
Salesmanship ad—14 lines—Business section		
Tribune ..... Daily	1 time—March 17	50.00
Contract Bridge—14 lines—on same page as bridge column		
Tribune ..... Daily	1 time—March 22	50.00
Sun-Times ... Daily	1 time—March 23	40.00
Interior Decoration—14 lines—On home furnishing page		
Sun-Times ... Daily	1 time—March 23	40.00
Accounting ad—14 lines—Business section		
Tribune ..... Daily	1 time—March 25	50.00
Sun-Times ... Daily	1 time—March 24	40.00
	TOTAL	1,620.00

Exhibit I–12

SAMPLE PUBLICITY RELEASES

FOR IMMEDIATE RELEASE   ADULT EDUCATION
                                               Concord
                                               369-9500, ext. 218

NEW COURSES, OLD FAVORITES APPEAR IN ADULT ED BROCHURE

Brochures for the fall term of the Concord-Carlisle Adult and
Continuing Education program are now in the mail. Each year more
than 4,000 persons of high school age and older participate in a
potpourri of courses ranging from accounting to yoga.

This fall, in addition to favorites which will be repeated, a
number of new courses are offered. To assure broad-based appeal,
these will appear in all areas of the Adult Education program:
Practical Skills, Personal Dynamics, Business and Careers, Creative
Arts, Outdoor Bound, Parent and Family Education, Home and Garden,
Gourmet, Crafts, Language and Literature, Fashion and Sewing, Music,
Dance and Exercise, and Special Opportunities.

Film buffs can look forward to Non-Fiction Film, a sequence of
12 Wednesday evening showings of films carefully chosen to demonstrate
the development of non-fiction film as a medium. Dancers and would-be
dancers have lots to choose from, as Disco and Greek Dancing classes
join Jazz, Tap, Ballroom and Square Dancing in the course roster.
New and exciting adventures await the travellers in the ARMCHAIR
TRAVEL series. For all citizens THE LEARNING WHEEL, an in-depth look
at the workings of our public school system, and THE TAXPAYERS REVOLT,
a one-evening look at the implications for Concord and Carlisle of
the current movement to limit taxes, offer pertinent information and
varying opinions on current important issues.

New and exciting experiences are available to all who wish to
enhance their interests and skills or to gain new ones. For further
information contact the Adult Education Office in Concord at
369-9500, extension 218.

Exhibit I–12

PUBLICITY RELEASE:

From: The Department of Continuing Education
        Division of Community Services
        Miami-Dade Community College North Campus

In a unique move generated by the favorable response to its Senior
Citizens' Cultural Arts Festival, the Division of Community Services
at Miami-Dade Community College's North Campus is sponsoring a series
of on-campus programs geared to Senior Citizens and their lifestyles,
beginning January 11.

These courses will be part of the Winter Term at the North Campus, and
are comprised of the following: "Exercise and Self Improvement,"
Thursdays, 1:30 to 3:00 P.M.; "Crime Prevention Workshop," Thursdays,
3:00 to 4:30 P.M.; "Body Dynamics and Rhythmic Dancing," Fridays,
1:30 to 3:00 P.M. and "Current Events," Fridays, 3:00 to 4:30 P.M.
There is a $5.00 fee per course.

Because the courses are offered during daytime hours, an opportunity
for communication between young students and Senior Citizens takes
place. In this, the senior and young students can exchange ideas and
information on cultural backgrounds, ethnic heritage, professional
experiences and social styles.

Senior Citizens' Agencies, groups or individuals are encouraged to
enroll their seniors in this program, giving the seniors an excellent
opportunity to become involved with the young adults enrolled at
Miami-Dade Community College. Transportation to these courses must
be provided by the agency or group. Instructions will be geared
toward the abilities of the seniors enrolled. The Student Government
Association (SGA) on the North Campus is looking forward to this
interaction with Dade County's older adults.

Exhibit I–12

 University of Southern California News Service

University Park, Los Angeles, CA 90007

For use: Upon Receipt   Contact: Lucy Mack
                                          741-7750

"The History of Organized Crime in America" will be taught by
attorney Michael J. Aguirre, former assistant counsel to the Senate
Permanent Investigations Subcommittee, at the University of Southern
California's College of Continuing Education.

Beginning Feb. 6 for credit and March 13 for noncredit, the
course is designed for professionals who may encounter organized
crime and for the general public. Among those who will be particularly interested are attorneys, social workers, clergy, journalists,
government officials and law enforcement personnel.

Aguirre's classes will cover both the history and current operations of the crime syndicate, as well as problems in attacking it.

Film relating to the Joe Valachi hearings will be shown, and
guest lectures will be given by key Senate investigators Laverne Duffy
of Iowa and Phillip Manuel of Washington, D.C., and by crime reporters
James Drinkhall of San Francisco and Jack Tobin of Los Angeles.

Other participants in the course will include Ed Meese, director
of the Center for Criminal Justice, Policy and Management at the
University of San Diego School of Law; Thomas Kotoske, chief of the
Justice Department Strike Force, San Francisco; Desmond Hakethal of
Los Angeles (91202), special agent supervisor for the U.S. Department
of Labor; and Brian Michaels, deputy district attorney of San Diego.

Information on the course, which may be taken for academic credit
or for its informational value only, is available at (213) 741-2410.

Exhibit I–12

News Release

Cambridge Center for Adult Education
42 Brattle Street / Cambridge, Mass. 02138
telephone 547-6789

EDITORIAL FEATURE (Release) 500 wds

With twenty-five thousand annual enrollments, the Cambridge Center
for Adult Education is setting records in the popular business of
extra-curricular learning. Although founded 122 years ago, only
recently did the Center blossom in popularity swelling its
enrollment to 10,000 in 1970 and now to the current high mark.

"The catalogue is a gem," said one student, "I love just reading it.
I don't think there's a subject that hasn't been offered some time
or other." The current catalogue fills its pages each semester with
350 course offerings from Botany for Plant Lovers to study trips to
Guatemala to a course on a Therapeutic Approach to Stress.

With the Harvard University area as a steady resource for class
teachers, the Center brings to its students a quality of teaching
that excels over many other equivalent programs. "This is done,"
says Alida O'Loughlin, the Center's energetic director, "without
sacrificing one of our primary aims. This is to offer adult education
at the lowest possible cost. We want the Center to be affordable to
anyone." An average series of classes costs between $35 and $40
per student.

Exhibit I-12

The bee-hive activity of the Center is not readily visible if one
looked only at the facilities. The Center's main building is a
revolutionary period house on Brattle Street. Newly renovated, its
exterior stands out as a significant historic resource in the bustle
of Harvard Square. A few doors down is the Blacksmith House made
famous by the poet Henry Wadsworth Longfellow in the verses of "The
Village Blacksmith" written in 1839. Purchased by the Center in 1972,
this house was spared from demolition, remodeled, and a modern
extension is now being added to accommodate a pressing need for art,
photography, and meeting space. This old historic building is also
the home of the Blacksmith Bakery which maintains a mouth-watering
reputation for providing the best Viennese pastries anywhere in
greater Boston.

"The list of shoppers at our bakery counter is like a who's who of
Cambridge personalities," says the manager, Jill Bloom. "On many days
it's hard to even get a seat for breakfast or for day-time goodies
now that we are known as a quiet refuge from the noise and rush in
the Square."

A glance at the counter is enough to disarm the staunchest dessert
diet. A six-layer Dobos Torte (Hungarian) waits. And a Linzer Torte
(Viennese). Or a hazelnut Mozart Torte. Rum Balls. Petit Fours.
Cherry Streudel. And even a Rum Malakov.

While for some the Center may be a particularly appetizing dessert,
to most the Center is what the students want it to be. And for each
of them it is a special place that fulfills needs that can only be
served by the informal personality of the teachers and staff. There
is Carol, a mother at seventeen, now thirty, eagerly taking every

Exhibit I—12

literature course offered to make up for an education that ended in High School. Or Stuart, an established lawyer, who discovered after a difficult divorce an emotional outlet in painting which can be shared with friends. And Barbara, a secretary downtown, became an avid collector of mushrooms and shares her enthusiasm in a mycology class. And there is Nathan, who spent most of his life in an institution and is now old, taking pride in following courses at the Center in sewing and weaving.

If you live anywhere in Boston, you may be close enough to discover this uniquely dynamic place. Its special personality has attracted tens of thousands over the years. To discover for yourself pick up a catalogue or call for one at 547-6789. You may then find it hard to resist taking a course in Preparing for Spring, or Disco-Dancing, or in joining a class to learn about Tutankhamun and his treasures.

Exhibit I–13

REQUEST TO FACULTY FOR PUBLICITY PICTURES

Concord Public Schools
Concord-Carlisle Regional School District

MEMORANDUM

TO: Adult and Continuing Education Teachers

FROM: Evelyn Zuk, Director

SUBJECT: PUBLICITY PICTURES

During the past three years, we have been blessed with exceptional
growth in our adult education program. The community has received
the brochure with enthusiasm and looks forward to the new offerings
and old favorites each term.

This January, however, because of the Energy Crisis, winter term will
have to be postponed until after the February vacation. The new regulations on heating public buildings will make it too cold for classes
in the school buildings in the evenings.

In order to insure continued interest in the program when we reconvene
in late February or early March, we are planning an extensive picture
spread in the local papers in January. To help us prepare this
publicity, will you please provide two or three pictures which will
capture the activity and excitement of your class. Each picture need
contain no more than yourself and one or two students "doing something." People just sitting in chairs or listening will not convey
the atmosphere of the class nearly as effectively as one or two students actively engaged in a project or even in an animated discussion.

If you have no camera yourself, one of your students, perhaps with a
Polaroid, may be able to help you. The newspapers remind us nearly
every week to keep the news stories short and to provide good action
pictures. We know from the many calls we receive in the office that
this kind of publicity is effective. Just seeing someone familiar in
a class often brings new students. Your cooperation then in providing
us with prints will ensure that our program will continue and that
your class will receive the publicity it deserves. We are trying to
build a "picture library" for any future publicity. If you have
questions or problems, call the office, 369-9500, exts. 218,283.

OFFICE OF
ADULT AND CONTINUING EDUCATION
115 STOW STREET
CONCORD, MASSACHUSETTS 01742
(617) 369-9500 Ext. 283

Exhibit I-14

SAMPLE CATALOG COVERS

University Cincinnati
ALUMNI COLLEGE

350 FRENCH HALL
CINCINNATI, OHIO 45221

COOKING WITH
MICROWAVE OVENS

OPEN FORUM
ON PHOTOGRAPHY
AND GRAPHIC ARTS

HOW TO CARE FOR
YOUR HOUSE PLANTS

Bet they never had classes like these when you were in school...

MEN & DIVORCE
PANEL DISCUSSION

WOMEN & DIVORCE
PANEL DISCUSSION

TOUR OF TRUDY HAUSER'S
MINERAL COLLECTION

NIGHT LIFE!

• ADULT EDUCATION •

WORCESTER PUBLIC SCHOOLS
WORCESTER MASSACHUSETTS

WINTER SPRING '79

CONCORD-CARLISLE
ADULT & CONTINUING EDUCATION

Exhibit I–14

PERFORMING AND FINE ARTS
and, to a certain degree, Other Great Adventures

University of Southern California
Spring 1979   **College of Continuing Education**   Spring 1979

Exhibit I-15

A SAMPLE OF FLYERS BY THE UNIVERSITY OF CALIFORNIA RIVERSIDE EXTENSION

Courses in

PLANT SCIENCES

SPRING 1979

UNIVERSITY OF CALIFORNIA
EXTENSION/RIVERSIDE

Introduction to

Micro Computers

Ask what

your computer

can do for you.

University of California Extension, Riverside

University of California,
Riverside
University Extension

Human Services and Health Sciences

Courses for Late Spring 1979

starting dates

Apr. 27...Understanding the Homosexual

Apr. 27...Dreams and Conflicts

Apr. 27...The "Right" to Live and Die

Apr. 28...Group Work With Elderly

May 4.....Assertion Training

May 4.....Massage and Relaxation

May 11....Psychosynthesis for People Helpers

May 18....The Person You Were Meant to Be

June 1....Creativity and Problem Solving

June 2....Obstetrical Care and Childbirth

June 2....Juvenile Diabetes

GOURMET TREATS

ADVENTURES IN GOURMET
FOOD AND WINE

INTERNATIONAL DINING
AT HOME

GOURMET BEERS:
A One-Day Tasting Seminar

APPRECIATION OF
CALIFORNIA WINES

University of California Extension, Riverside

Exhibit I–16

CONCORD-CARLISLE REGIONAL SCHOOL DISTRICT
ADULT AND CONTINUING EDUCATION BUDGET

	1976-77				1977-78				
	TOTAL	APPROP.	CASH FUNDS		TOTAL	APPROP.	(CHANGE)	CASH FUNDS	
Director	$22,410	$11,205	$11,205	50%	$22,410	$11,205		$11,205	50%
Secretaries	19,110	12,485	6,635	37%	19,885	13,250	$765+	6,635	33.4%
Print-Mail	4,500	2,000	2,500	55.6%	5,000	2,400	400+	2,600	52%
Office Supp.	450	225	225	50%	600	300	75+	300	50%
Publications	125	125			125	125	(NC)		
Teachers	69,440	21,125	48,315	69.6%	72,390	22,390	1,265+	50,000	69.2%
Classroom Supp.	5,430	570	4,860	89.5%	5,700	700	130+	5,000	87.7%
Travel in St.	50	50			50	50	(NC)		
Travel out St.	400	300	100	25%	400	300	(NC)	100	25%
Custodians	2,800	2,800			1,250	1,250	1,550-		
Equip. Main.	175	175			175	175	(NC)		
Liab. Ins.	230	50	180	78%	230	75	25+	155	67.3%
Rentals	2,450	2,000	450	18%	3,000	2,500	500+	500	16.6%
Equip. New	400	300	100	25%	400	300	(NC)	100	25%
Equip. Replace	200	200			200	200	(NC)		
Energy Charge								2,300	100%
TOTALS	$128,180	$53,610	$74,570	58.1%	$132,830	$55,220	$1,610+	$78,895	59.3%

Exhibit I–17

BUDGET REPORT
UNIVERSITY OF SOUTHERN CALIFORNIA

BUDGET REPORT   UNIVERSITY OF SOUTHERN CALIFORNIA
DIVORCING FAMILY CONFERENCE
JANUARY 26-27, 1971   COLLEGE OF CONTINUING EDUCATION

Account #: 82-2808-0045

	PROJECTED BUDGET	ACTUAL BUDGET	
Income	100 @ 35 -- 3500	146 @ 35 26 @ 26 -- 5867.50 9 @ 9	
Expenses			
Honorarium	200	250	(most speakers donated services)
Promotion	850	814	(sponsors provided free mailing lists)
Facility Rental (coffee included)	900	1397	(includes free center admission for 20 of 35 complimentaries)
Parking	---	18	
CCE Support	210	461	
Lunches	800	1512	(includes 35 complimentary lunches)
Travel	---	454	
CECH	---	67.50	
USC Overhead	540	894	
TOTAL	3500	5867.50	

Subsidy
Travel guaranteed by Bar if needed	454	From Title XX grant Honorarium 250 Xerox 100 Plus travel expense and tuition for 19 Title XX attendances

Exhibit I–18

COST ANALYSIS SHEET
GREAT NECK PUBLIC SCHOOLS

Course #_____

              COST ANALYSIS

Session_____

Faculty_____   Course_____

Contract hours	_____
Total fee	_____
Minimum enrollment	_____
Maximum enrollment	_____
Min. fee total	_____
Max. fee total	_____

<u>Expenses, personnel</u>
    Salary
    Transportation   _____
    Faculty   _____
    Aids/models   _____
    Guest speakers   _____

Total Personnel   _____   _____

<u>Expenses, other</u>
    Materials   _____
    Supplies   _____
    Books   _____
    Equipment   _____
    Food/Meals   _____
    Xerox   _____
    Chartered coach   _____
    Hotel   _____
    Tickets   _____
    Museum admissions   _____
    Memberships   _____
    Subscriptions   _____
    Long distance tel.   _____

Total other expenses   _____   _____

<u>Promotional costs</u>
    Flyers   _____
    Advertising   _____
    Graphics   _____
    Brochure   _____
    Postage   _____

Total promotional   _____   _____

Total costs of course   _____

Combined costs of course **+** Fee Per Registrant **=** Minimum Registration

_____   _____   _____

Actual costs of course **-** Income from fees **=**   **+ OR -**

Exhibit I–19

FINANCIAL POLICIES OF THE CAMBRIDGE CENTER FOR ADULT EDUCATION

GENERAL INFORMATION

APPLICATION—For each course, mail a separate application form together with a separate check or money order made payable to the Cambridge Center for Adult Education. All applications received before the first day of "Mail Registration" will be considered on the first day of mail registration. Thereafter mail applications will be processed in the order in which they are received. No one may register in-person before the "In-Person Registration" period. However, registrations with checks—no cash—left in the office will be considered with the next day's mail. Early mail registration is encouraged to help avoid disappointment. Please list on the application form alternative time sections when available and other alternative courses. All Center classes are limited in enrollment as designated in the course descriptions.

The Cambridge Center reserves the right to change or cancel courses and times or to substitute instructors.

TUITION—FULL TUITION MUST ACCOMPANY THE APPLICATION—Checks will be returned promptly and your name put on the waiting list if courses are filled. Tuition paid for one term may not be credited to another. A charge of $2.00 will be made for checks returned for insufficient funds.

NO REFUNDS—You may transfer to another course in the current term if there is an opening, or ask that your ticket be sold. If sold the Center will deduct $3 from the sales price. No tickets will be sold for unfilled courses or after the second meeting. If a ticket is sold after the first class, a proportional percentage of the course fee will also be deducted.

SINGLE ADMISSION—In some exceptional cases in courses in which registration has not been filled single admission may be purchased but do not hold a place in the course. Prices range from $3 to $5.

COURSE INFORMATION—For a complete listing of courses offered in the Boston area the Center suggests you contact the Educational Exchange, 17 Dunster Street, Cambridge (876–3080).

SUPPLIES—Except where noted, art supplies and study materials are not included in the fee.

SCHOLARSHIPS—Partial and full scholarships are available. People 65 and over may pay half fees for any classes.

MAKE-UPS—There is no provision for individual make-ups. Meetings will be made up for those postponed by holidays, extreme weather conditions, or to accommodate the instructor. Students may not make up absences by attending classes other than their own.

VISITORS AND GUESTS—Guests are not permitted to attend classes unless advance permission has been granted by the Office. Substitutions will not be permitted.

THE CENTER ASSUMES NO RESPONSIBILITY FOR PERSONAL PROPERTY LEFT IN THE HALL, CLASSES OR STOREROOMS, BOTH DURING AND AFTER THE TERM.

Appendix J
Chapter 10 Exhibits: Evaluation Materials

PROGRAM EVALUATION: FOR REALITY*

By Laverne B. Forest
Department of Continuing and Vocational Education
Division of Program and Staff Development, University of Wisconsin

Background

As an academician and practitioner of adult education program evaluation, I must act consistently with my underlying values, beliefs, and assumptions. I am thus alarmed to look at the current status of adult education program evaluation. It is not consistent. Little relationship exists between the basic philosophies and concepts we profess, and the actual evaluations practiced and found useful in the real world.

I want to talk about these inconsistencies by presenting some basic assumptions related to evaluation, by briefly reviewing evaluation literature and practice, by suggesting an alternative concept of evaluation, and by suggesting several remedies for the illness that exists.

Some Basic Assumptions

First our basic concepts ought to stand up to reality. Theory and practice ought to be synonymous. We must operate from assumptions which recognize the basic nature of adults, adult education programs, and the real world in which they operate. Adult education programs involve a variety of adults: learners, funders, administrators, politicians, planners, and peers. We continually interact socially with adults as educational programs are developed, implemented, and recycled.

Adults involved in our programs vary in their experiences, communities, responsibilities, roles, expectations, values, and assumptions. Adult education programs and related systems vary by as many ways as there are adults.

So what? Let's think of adult education program evaluation literally. It is simply the determination of the goodness, worth, or value of programs (defined as systems of social interaction with both experiences and outcomes). Let us further presume that the real value of an experience varies, depending on its consequences and outcomes. The more useful the outcomes, the more valuable the experience. If so, the value of program outcomes must also vary according to a person's experiences related to the program. The relationship goes both ways. The value of program outcomes and the value of program experiences are interdependent.

This reasoning leads to only one conclusion. All people related to adult education programs will place varying values on that program's outcomes, depending on their experiences with it, and whether the program met their own concerns and expectations.

The ways people involved in a program evaluate it must therefore also vary infinitely. A program will have multiple values and the concept of evaluation must be broad enough to encompass them. It must allow people related to an adult education program to determine how the program's experiences and outcomes are evaluated, and its values to them. Program evaluation must be designed by the program situation and the people in it if real value is to be determined.

Do our present program evaluation concepts allow this? If not, why not? To answer these questions, let me retrace how evaluation literature and practice have developed.

---

* Reprinted by permission from *Adult Education* XXVI, 3 (Spring 1976), 167–177.

Present Literature Themes

Six interrelated themes in program evaluation literature have developed and led us away from reality:

1. Increasing importance and pressure for accountability.
2. Educator control of evaluation.
3. More formalized and systematic evaluation.
4. Too much reliance on and direct imitation of evaluation models developed for other educational systems.
5. Dependence on educational objectives.
6. Increased quantification and measurement.

Parallel with these six themes (or because of them) is a seventh: increasing frustration over the lack of usable, decision-related evaluation, a frustration which sometimes leads to no use at all.

Theme 1: Accountability

Life continues to become more complex. Adult education programs (their participants, experiences, and outcomes) have never existed in a vacuum. They're interrelated with other small and large social systems (families, legislatures, business firms, administrators). These other systems and institutions provide support, resources and the right to exist. In turn they demand the program be accountable. It's only a fair proposition.

Accountability is increasingly important. Specific references on educational accountability as a reason for evaluation are much more evident since 1970 (1)(9)(17)(18).

Exceptions to the general theme exist and other reasons for program evaluation are emphasized (21)(25), but the most dramatic increase in interest in evaluation is due to accountability. The best proof of this is the built in evaluation requirements of federally-supported projects. Accountability to other systems has become the dominant basis for, and influence on, program evaluation.

Theme 2: Educator Control

With the increasing importance of accountability, literature and practice have naturally inclined to emphasize the need for professional educators and/or evaluators to "take control" of evaluation.

Without exception, conceptual models written for professional educators suggest tasks for them to more completely control the process: design evaluations, set objectives, decide data to collect. Supposedly these tasks are too complex for anyone except professional educators and researchers to perform (2)(5)(21)(24)(25)(28). Review of evaluation practice reveals few examples where educators did not try to control the process.

Theme 3: Systematizing and Formalizing Evaluation

Parallel with taking control of the evaluation process is the notion that program evaluation must be more formal and systematic. Almost universally, education program evaluation experts advocate increased formal evaluation (8)(21)(25)(27)(29).

Most important are those writings which recognize the existence and usefulness of both informal and formal evaluation but then dismiss informal evaluation and advocate moving towards formalizing evaluation because of its advantages in dealing with accountability (12)(15)(16)(24)(28).

Theme 4: Direct Transfer of Evaluation Models to Adult Education

Much evaluation literature is related to elementary and secondary formal school settings, which is a big part of the problem. Because most evaluation models have developed in systems where educators "control" the learning situation, it has been natural for adult education programs to adapt or actually imitate those models.

Several bright spots exist. Rippey (20), Sjogren (23), Brack (6), and others provide some ideas more appropriate to informal adult education programs, but these are exceptions.

Theme 5: Educational Objectives

The most basic theme of evaluation literature related to other formal education originally was defined by Bobbit (4), and later by Tyler:

The process of evaluation is essentially the process of determining to what extent the educational objectives are actually being realized by the curriculum and instruction. (27:105–06)

Others (3)(19) have amplified, clarified, and made the idea more specific. Such adult educators as Boyle and Jahns (5), Knowles (15), Houle (14), and Thiede (26) agree.

Other points of view exist (10)(20)(22), but generally the concern for accountability, educator control, more formal evaluation, and resulting reliance on already developed models of evaluation, has led to the almost universal use of educational objectives (established at the beginning of a program) as the basis for program evaluation.

Theme 6: Quantification, Measurement and Data Collection

The previous themes, particularly the emphasis on educational objectives, are tied to another development: measurement and data collection on whether or not objectives are achieved. Computer technology has also provided impetus to this trend. Faster computers with larger memory systems can store and analyze more data.

Because we must determine whether objectives have been achieved, and because of the increased capability to gather, handle, and analyze data, we've built more and more quantification with accompanying reliability, objectivity, and control into program evaluations. Many equate evaluation with measurement. Others say data must be *the* basis for evaluation (14)(25). The most direct application of data collection as evaluation is the Cooperative Extension Service's Management Information System (SEMIS).

Theme 7: Evaluation As Unused and Useless

Program evaluation literature, primarily because of accountability, advocates that adult education professionals control the evaluation process, systematize it, determine if achievements meet objectives, and collect more data about the program. With few exceptions, this concept guides the practice of adult education program evaluation.

Yet, paradoxically, the practice of this concept of evaluation has led to role confusion, frustration, ineffectiveness, pessimism, apathy, neglect of evaluation and disregard for evaluation results. For examples, see Hampton (12), Sjogren (23), or Udell (28). In making the point, Sjogren says:

The situation is almost a comedy. An "evaluator" is hired to play the role while both he and the project director know the evaluation activity will make little difference to anybody . . . While the evaluation role is being played, the *real* evaluations that do make a difference are being made by the project staff, and the constituents. The evaluator is often not even aware of their judgments. (23:267)

The best evidence of pessimism and apathy is that practitioners either don't make formal evaluations or dislike doing them.

Program evaluation literature and practice contain a paradox. Pressure increases for accountability and formal systematic evaluations based on educational objectives (5)(12)(14)(15)(16)(28). At the same time such evaluations are irrelevant to program decision-making in the real world. They are simply unable to capture "the value of programs" for those deciding about them.

The literature has developed irrespective of reality. Current models and their applications are impractical impositions on actual program situations and people's experiences. What can we do about it?

Is There an Alternative?

We have three ways to deal with this paradox:

1. We can ignore it and let the inconsistency stand.
2. We can continue to try to bring actual practice into line with the current concept by professing and prescribing what practice should be and by forcing theory onto reality.
3. We can redefine adult education program evaluation to fit the existing program realities and their value to people.

A redefined concept that applies to reality will be not only easier, but more valuable in practice than one written in isolation from reality.

I do not see the first or second choices as at all viable. How can we close our minds to the paradox and ignore it? And who are we to prescribe and force upon reality what isn't there? I thus see only the third choice (re-defining) as a viable path towards logical, ethical, and pragmatic program evaluation in spite of the difficulties and challenges.

What is this re-definition? In essence, the potential for redefining program evaluation lies at the opposite end of the seven themes I have described. Figure 1 illustrates this potential. The alternatives in Figure 1 are a composite of present and more realistic ways of thinking about and doing evaluation.

To be more specific, our programs are accountable not only to others but to ourselves. Furthermore, the evaluation process itself must be accountable and do what it says—determine the value of the program.

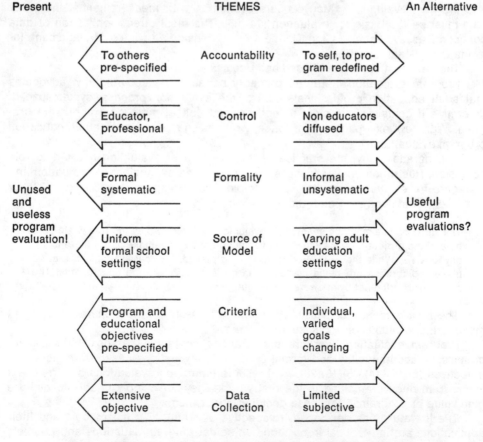

Figure 1.   Alternatives To Present Evaluation Themes.

Second, others related to our program cannot be excluded from the evaluation process, no matter how hard we try to take control of it. It is natural for people to judge the value of things in their lives; how naive are we to think we can be in control? Instead, let us recognize the central role of others in the evaluation process.

Third, and integral to the first two points, is that the diffused evaluations are going on naturally, continuously, and informally, regardless of how formal we try to make them. Interestingly, ample research indicates that these informal evaluations are pervasive and influence further evaluations. Thus, not only do informal evaluations exist (as most educators recognize), but because of their pervasiveness, they are as or more powerful, and possibly more important than the formal evaluations we continue to advocate. In fact, these informal evaluations are the barrier to acceptance of more formal evaluation reports. We should recognize their crucial importance.

Fourth, let us allow the informal adult education setting, and people related to it, to define the evaluation models. Though such exciting ideas as grounded theory, inductive research, and transactional evaluation are beacons of light, we have not yet allowed noneducator control, informal evaluation, and non-data collection.

Fifth, educational and program objectives cannot serve as *the* criteria for evaluation. How can they, when Houle (13), and many others since, have shown adults to have unique, complex, and varying motives for participation in programs? How can initial objectives serve as *the* criteria when Dewey (7), Friere (11) and others have shown the value of an experience or an outcome to depend on the perspective of the person(s) involved? How can we use only program objectives that external systems may not even be aware of? We *must* allow for informal, diffused evaluations, utilizing varied, dynamic criteria, from all people related to the program.

Sixth, extensive data do not represent the value or worth of a program. We need to take our cues from the existing, pervasive, informal evaluations. These most prevalent, and thus most powerful, evaluations do not seem to need tables of data and computer printout for making judgments. These informal evaluations by participants, funders, politicians, and other decision-makers are also causing much frustration among data collectors and researchers. Let us recognize the intuitive good sense of adults related to our programs.

Finally, these current informal, uncontrolled, varied-criteria, nondata evaluations are the ones being used in practice and reality. Redefining our evaluation concept thus unites theory and practice.

I stated earlier, this evaluation alternative presents its own difficulties and challenges. However, these challenges have to do not so much with program evaluation, as with communication and adult learning. Though not all of the answers are now apparent, several directions are implied regarding how we can deal with evaluation and accountability, yet avoid creating structured systems only because we are accountable.

Getting Practice and Concept Together

If all programs are being evaluated continually by many people related to them, and if these informal evaluations are used to make decisions, is there anything an adult education program evaluator can or should do?

From one perspective, we should do nothing. The process will take care of itself. But adult education as a system is not isolated from other systems and institutions. Interrelated with other systems, adult education is accountable regardless of the nature of the program. We can deal with accountability in one of two ways, depending on whether the decision making and evaluation are internal to the program, or whether evaluations are used by others outside the program to make decisions about it.

Decision Making Internal To Program

When we adult educators have contact with participants, we should increase our powers of observation and listening to discover the value of a program. Repeat participants, increased participation, grapevine feedback from non-participants, and pressure to do something different all tell us something about how others value the program.

If we hear a comment like "That was a good meeting!" and ask "Why do you say that?" we'll ascertain a variety of criteria and goals people use to judge the program. If we note people's overt characteristics, questions and comments, we can get a fix on their motives and criteria without imposing formal data collection on them. (Note: these are all ways of improving communication skills, not ways of evaluation.)

What is critical in effectively using informal evaluations, however, is to *recognize their existence, their varied nature, their control and influence over future decisions,* and *therefore their importance.* We should make it obvious to participants that we recognize their informal judgments and expect their feedback.

There is an educational obligation also. We can help program participants become more aware of their own informal judgments, their criteria, and how they make decisions about adult education programming. It is a good way to help adults involved in the program (including ourselves) mature, grow, and increase their power and control over their own experiences.

Involving participants and others in program evaluation is now a trite and meaningless phrase. We can make it meaningful by *using* the informal evaluations of others in our decisions.

Decision Making External To Program

Accountability is a sticky issue when those outside the program situation are making the decisions. Most are saying that formal evaluation and extensive, objective data collection are needed in these cases to help others understand our achievements. I am not convinced. First, if those to whom our programs are accountable read reports at all, they do not have time for extensive summaries of data. Furthermore, informal, grapevine feedback and pressures from other people influence their decisions at least as much as the data we can present. Accountability to others is not a question of evaluation, but of good communication. Our program results must instead become better known through informal evaluation feedback to decision-makers. Let's not fight the natural inclinations of people; let us instead be part of the reality and encourage more of it.

We have another challenge. We have too often created our own accountability traps. How can we help external decision makers better understand what we can realistically achieve, and the natural indicators of whether or not we achieved it? Do we invite and expect external decision makers to actively evaluate our programs while they are going on? Do we ask them to talk to participants? Do we know their criteria, or do we simply assume they use the criteria we stated in a program proposal? All these questions offer clues about how we can use the ongoing informal evaluations external to our programs.

Better informal communication with decision-makers is needed if they are to learn the real value of our programs. The types of communication will vary by group, program, and pressures. The only risk involved is that some programs might be more justifiable on paper than in actuality.

I do not intend to completely reject formal, educator controlled program evaluations, but informal evaluation controlled by non-educator decision makers is far more crucial than we have recognized. We can use these natural and powerful evaluation processes to improve our programs and our accountability if we recognize that they exist, and relate to them more imaginatively than we have. This can mean moving far to the right in Figure 1 on all themes in some programs, or moving slightly to the right on some and more on others. How imaginatively we use the right side of the continuum depends on the program, the people related to it, the type of accountability needed, and the decisions to be made.

References

1. Alkin, Marvin G. "Accountability Defined." *Evaluation Comment,* III (May, 1972), 1–5.
2. Bernstein, Ilene, and Freeman, Howard. *Academic and Entrepreneurial Research.* New York: Russell Sage, 1975.
3. Bloom, Benjamin; Englehart, Max; Furst, Edward; Hill, Walter; and Krathwohl, David. *Taxonomy of Educational Objectives, Handbook I: Cognitive Domain.* New York: David McKay, Inc., 1956.
4. Bobbit, Franklin. *How to Make a Curriculum.* Boston: Houghton Mifflin, 1924.
5. Boyle, Patrick, and Jahns, Irvin. "Program Development and Evaluation." *Handbook of Adult Education.* Edited by Robert Smith and George Aker. New York: MacMillan, 1970.
6. Brack, Robert. "Innovative Projects Evaluation." *Journal of Extension,* XIII (March/April, 1975), 39–47.
7. Dewey, John. *Theory of Valuation.* Foundations of the Unity of Science, International Encyclopedia of Unified Science XI, No. 4, Chicago: University of Chicago Press, 1939.
8. Duft, Ken D. "Systems Planning for Extension." *Journal of Cooperative Extension,* VII (Fall, 1969), 168–78.
9. *Educational Technology,* XI (January, 1971).
10. Eisner, Eliot W. "Educational Objectives: Help or Hindrance." *The School Review,* (Autumn, 1967), 250–60.
11. Friere, Paulo. *The Pedagogy of the Oppressed.* New York: Herder and Herder, 1971.
12. Hampton, Leonard A. "Evaluating Continuing Education Programs." *Adult Leadership,* (September, 1973), 105–07.
13. Houle, Cyril. *The Inquiring Mind.* Madison, Wis.: University of Wisconsin Press, 1961.
14. Houle, Cyril. *The Design of Education.* San Francisco: Jossey-Bass, 1972.
15. Knowles, Malcolm. *The Modern Practice of Adult Education.* New York: Association Press, 1970.
16. Knox, Alan. "Continuous Program Evaluation." *Administration of Continuing Education.* Edited by Nathan Shaw. Washington, D. C.: National Association for Public School Adult Education, 1969.
17. Lutz, Arlen, and Swoboda, Don W. "Accountability in Extension." *Journal of Extension,* X (Winter, 1972), 45–48.
18. Mondale, Walter F. "Social Accounting, Evaluation, and the Future of the Human Services." *Evaluation,* I (Fall, 1972), 29–34.
19. Popham, James W., and Baker, Eva. *Establishing Instructional Goals.* Englewood Cliffs, N. J.: Prentice Hall, 1970.
20. Rippey, Robert. *Studies in Transactional Evaluation.* Berkeley: McCutchan Publishing, 1973.
21. Scriven, Michael. "The Methodology of Evaluation." *Perspectives of Curriculum Evaluation.* Edited by Robert Tyler, Robert Gagney, and Michael Scriven. Chicago: Rand McNally and Co., 1967.
22. Scriven, Michael. "Pro's and Cons about Goal-Free Evaluation." *Evaluation Comment,* III (December, 1972), 1–4.
23. Sjogren, Douglas. "Program Evaluation in Schools." *Studies in Transactional Evaluation.* Edited by Robert Rippey. Berkeley: McCutchan Publishing, 1973.
24. Stake, Robert, "The Countenance of Educational Evaluation." *Teachers College Record,* LXVIII (April, 1967), 523–40.

25. Stufflebeam, Daniel, and the PDK National Study Committee on Education. *Educational Evaluation and Decision Making.* Itasca, Ill.: F. E. Peacock Publishers, 1971.
26. Thiede, Wilson. "Evaluation and Adult Education." *Adult Education: Design of an Emerging Field.* Edited by Gale Jensen, A. A. Liveright and Wilbur Hallenbeck. Washington, D. C.: Adult Education Association of the U.S.A., 1964.
27. Tyler, Ralph W. *Basic Principles of Curriculum and Instruction.* Chicago: University of Chicago Press, 1950.
28. Udell, Gerald. "Yes, A Change Agent Can Evaluate." *Journal of Extension,* XIII (Sept./Oct., 1975), 14–21.
29. Worthen, Blain, and Sanders, James. *Educational Evaluation: Theory and Practice.* Worthington, Ohio: Charles A. Jones, 1973.

STUDENT EVALUATION QUESTIONNAIRES

THE ADULT PROGRAM
Great Neck Public Schools
10 Arrandale Avenue
Great Neck, New York

COURSE _____

FACULTY _____

Dear Participant:

We are evaluating many of our courses. Will you check this evaluation sheet as it applies to your experience in the course listed above? Your prompt reply will assist us in planning for the coming semester. Thank you.

---

1. How many sessions have you attended up to now? 1 2 3 4 5 6 7
   Please circle.   8 9 10 11 12 13 14 15

2. Up to this point, how would you rate this course?
   ___ Excellent ___ Good ___ Fair ___ Poor

3. What one thing do you feel is <u>most effective</u> in this course?

   _____

4. What one thing do you think has been <u>least helpful</u>?

   _____

5. Please use <u>E</u> for excellent, <u>G</u> for good, <u>F</u> for fair, <u>P.</u> for poor.

   _____ Room facilities   _____ Material covered
   _____ Personality of Instructor _____ Your own participation
   _____ Discussion of Students   _____ Way course was planned

6. Do you think we should offer this course again in Great Neck? _ Yes _]

7. Put a check in front of each statement that you feel describes your own attitude toward this course. You may check more than one.

   __ I have learned a great deal that is helpful.
   __ I have learned many things, but the course is not designed to be permanently helpful.
   __ The subject is too difficult for me, but I am trying to absorb it.
   __ I find the course too juvenile, but am learning something.
   __ I would not keep coming, but I hate to waste the registration fee.
   __ The instructor is wonderful, but I don't think I'm learning anythin
   __ The instructor is poor, but I am learning a few things anyway.
   __ There is too much talk from the students.
   __ The students don't get a chance to talk enough.
   __ I am very satisfied with the course.

8. Please write in any suggestions or criticisms that you feel would be interesting or helpful. (Use the reverse side of the sheet.)

   YOU DO NOT NEED TO SIGN THIS

TERM EVALUATION

Please complete and return to the Cambridge Center. Your comments will help us evaluate and improve our program.

Name and Time of course_____

Please check:

Instructor's knowledge of content:

excellent_____good_____fair_____poor_____

Instructor's presentation of content:

excellent_____good_____fair_____poor_____

Format and organization of course:

excellent_____good_____fair_____poor_____

Does the class meet with your expectations? If yes, how? If no, why not?

What is the best aspect of the class for you? What is the worst?

Why did you take the course?

_____interested in the subject?

_____subject sounded interesting?

_____wanted to meet people interested in the same thing?

_____could not get into first choice?

_____other

What do you think you are learning in the course?

How did you hear about the Cambridge Center?

What other courses would you like to see us offer?

Comments: (Use the back of this sheet if necessary)

COURSE AND INSTRUCTOR EVALUATION

Department of Adult and Community College Education

Course No. _____

Semester _____

RESPONDENT INFORMATION

1. Major Curriculum: _____

2. Graduate: Master _____ Doctoral _____

_____

PART A. QUALITY OF TOTAL LEARNING EXPERIENCE	Superior	Above Average	Average	Below Average	Poor	No Opinion
1. Instructor stimulates curiosity, independent thinking, and student participation in class.	5	4	3	2	1	--
2. Teaching strategies employed are appropriate for you in facilitating your learning.	5	4	3	2	1	--

	Superior	Above Average	Average	Below Average	Poor	No Opinion
3. To what extent did the course meet your needs and expectations.	5	4	3	2	1	--
PART B. QUALITIES OR CHARACTERISTICS OF THE INSTRUCTOR						
4. Instructor possesses and effectively utilizes human relations skills in providing individual attention to students.	5	4	3	2	1	--
5. To the best of your ability, give your overall judgment of your instructor as an effective teacher.	5	4	3	2	1	--
6. Instructor appears to have a thorough and current knowledge of the subject matter.	5	4	3	2	1	--

PART C. PHYSICAL ASPECTS

7. Learning materials presented are appropriate and useful in facilitating your learning.

    5   4   3   2   1   --

8. The physical characteristics of the learning environment (classroom, conditions, comfort, freedom from outside distractions) are conducive to learning.

    5   4   3   2   1   --

PART D. EVALUATION

9. You are adequately kept informed of your progress toward the attaining of course objectives.

    5   4   3   2   1   --

10. Evaluation of your learning is explicitly related to the specified course objectives.

    5   4   3   2   1   --

PART E. COURSE OBJECTIVES

	Superior	Above Average	Average	Below Average	Poor	No Opinion
11. The objectives of the course are clear.	5	4	3	2	1	--
12. The subject matter chosen for instruction is clearly related to course objectives.	5	4	3	2	1	--
13. You are adequately involved in setting course objectives.	5	4	3	2	1	--
14. To which extent were the course objectives obtained.	5	4	3	2	1	--

PART F. COMMENTS

LEADER'S EVALUATION FORM

Name of Activity _____

Name of Leader _____

Time and place of meeting _____ Date _____

I. Nature of the group
   A. Composition
      1. Enrollment, total: _____

         Men _____

         Women _____
      2. Age range
      3. Educational background
      4. Occupational representation
      5. Percentage of attendance for the term _____%
   B. Needs and interests
      1. What did the participants expect to get out of the activity?
      2. What do you feel were the real reasons for their joining?
   C. What, in your opinion, were the outstanding characteristics of this group? What was your reaction to it?

II. Aims
   A. General
      1. What did you conceive the objectives of this activity to be at the beginning of the term?
      2. In view of your experience, how would you alter these objectives for the future?
   B. Specific
      1. What specific results did you hope to achieve with individuals?
      2. To what extent were these results accomplished?

III. Methods and Content
   A. Methods
      1. Describe briefly the principal methods you employed in this activity.
      2. To which of these did the participants respond best?
      3. Appraise the interest of the participants in this activity. Did it fluctuate significantly? (If so, can you cite specific causes?)
      4. What suggestions for improvement can you make?
   B. Content
      1. Describe briefly the material covered in this activity.
      2. What changes in content would you suggest if the activity is repeated?

IV. Evaluation
   A. To what extent do you feel this activity fulfilled its objectives?
   B. What specific results were accomplished with individuals—what changes in behavior took place? (Cite cases.)
   C. What general recommendations would you make for the improvement of this activity? For the improvement of the program as a whole?

Appendix K

Chapter 11 Exhibits: Some Tools for
Conducting Learning Activities

PROCESS RATING SHEET FOR INQUIRY TEAMS

(Circle one number in each scale)

1. What is the degree of your feelings
   of satisfaction with this meeting?   1 2 3 4 5

2. How clear is the team about its goals
   and tasks?   1 2 3 4 5

3. How well are team members listening
   to one another?   1 2 3 4 5

4. To what extent did you contribute to
   the work of the team today?   1 2 3 4 5

5. To what extent were your ideas accepted
   and used by the team?   1 2 3 4 5

6. To what extent did one or two team members
   dominate the discussion?   1 2 3 4 5

7. To what extent did you personally resent
   overparticipation by other members?   1 2 3 4 5

8. To what extent did team members prepare
   themselves (do background reading, etc.)
   for the meeting?   1 2 3 4 5

9. How well is the team organizing itself
   for its work?   1 2 3 4 5

10. To what extent do you think the team should
    make better use of outside resources?   1 2 3 4 5

11. To what extent does the team recognize its
    problems and conflicts and deal with them
    openly?   1 2 3 4 5

What suggestions would you like to make to improve the
team's operation?

_____

_____

_____

_____

PRELIMINARY SELF-DIAGNOSIS FOR PROGRAM PLANNING FORM

The University of Western Ontario, Faculty of Nursing

Recommended Competencies	Self-Rating				Recommended Learning Experiences
	Don't Know	Weak	Fair	Strong	
Understands role of nursing on the health team					
Understands the phenomena of health and illness					
Understands the rationale of assessment and existing assessment tools					
Understands the meaning of process in nursing					
Understands the dynamics of the nurse-patient relationship					
Understands the nature of planned change as it relates to improving nursing practice					
Has knowledge of psychosocial determinants of illness					
Has knowledge of concepts and principles from related sciences useful in nursing practice					
Has broad overview knowledge of the research done in relationship to nursing practice					
Has knowledge of trends and emerging roles in nursing practice					
Has ability to identify and think philosophically about nursing practice issues					
Has ability to evaluate effectiveness of nursing measures					
Has ability to involve others in decision-making processes					

Criteria						
Uses a theoretical framework in her own practice of nursing which can be described, discussed and tested out in practice						
Has empathic attitude toward patients and skill in forming nurse-patient relationships						
Has skill in assessing patient's needs						
Has ability to form nursing care objectives						
Has ability to plan nursing intervention which takes into consideration the individual's "phenomenal field"						
Has ability to use explanatory concepts from related sciences and nursing in explaining the basis for her nursing diagnosis and intervention						
Has ability to gain understanding of how the patient perceives his condition or situation						
Has ability to interpret and apply research findings in nursing practice						
Has ability to communicate orally and in writing at a professional level						
OTHER						

CAMP FIRE GIRLS: SELF-DIAGNOSTIC FORM

CAMP FIRE GIRLS, INC.
NATIONAL TRAINING DEPARTMENT

Explanation for use of Preliminary Self-Diagnosis for Training Form

The form which is attached has been designed so that training and learning experiences that are made available through the National Training Department of Camp Fire Girls can be geared to building the kind of strength that you feel you need in order to do your job more effectively. It also is an attempt to identify some of the general functions that seem to be required of professional Camp Fire staff and some of the specific competencies needed to perform those functions. There is space provided on the form for other functions and competencies which you feel need to be applied to your particular situation and that you would like to strengthen.

No one could ever be expected to be strong in every last area indicated on the form. Learning and developing new skills is a lifelong task. As soon as we achieve learning or skill at a certain level, then our goals for achieving more are naturally set at the next highest level. Therefore, all of us will always be needing new kinds of learning experiences to learn new kinds of skills and competencies.

The self-diagnosis form is not a job performance appraisal. Your responses are not to be used for "Am I going to keep my job?" questions. What is important here is your helping the training team build a creative and meaningful training program based on areas you objectively think need to be strengthened. The challenge is to achieve objective appraisal of your own skills and to build strength in areas where you feel it is needed.

As you read through the form, it would be very helpful to your training team if you would indicate three things:

1) What is your self-rating with regard to the specific competency that is indicated?

   a) The column labelled "Don't Know" on the form is to indicate that you're not sure whether you can state that you have a given understanding or ability or skill. If you check this column, the training program will try to help you find out whether that understanding of ability is present and what you feel the strength of it to be. It could be that there are strengths that each of us has that we are, ourselves, not aware of. Finding this out could be a very important learning. Also, you may need to check "Don't Know" if a certain competency is unclear to you. Where this is the case, your checking "Don't Know" will help the training team know that time needs to be spent in the conference on that item.

   b) The columns labelled "Weak," "Fair," "Strong" on the form are for you to indicate the relative strength that you feel you have in a given competency. These also will help identify the most helpful learning areas that the training conference should focus on.

2) The column "Recommended Learning/Training Experiences" on the form is provided for you to indicate the kind of experiences in a training program that you feel would help you strengthen

a competency in yourself. Please interpret the phrase "training program" very liberally and not in the traditional sense. For example, if you feel that your self-rating for "Understanding of the Role of a Social Agency in Society" would be in the "Fair" category, some possible learning experiences that you might suggest could include:

a) Reading The Godfather.

b) Interviewing three other social agency leaders around the question "What do you feel is the role of a social agency in society?"

c) Participating in a discussion group with others in the social agencies field discussing the same question.

d) Other experiences that you might think of.

3) Add your own training ideas to those already included. Please be as specific as possible as to the kinds of problems you would like to work on and the additional strengths you want to build.

All of the items included on the form are there to help you understand your job more thoroughly and to help you work at doing your job more effectively. There is no such thing as a right or a wrong answer to anything on the form. What is important is how you see yourself performing and learning how to strengthen the areas that you feel you need to grow in. Today you may feel that you have a competency that is very strong in a certain area. That being the case, perhaps you ignore working on building the competency. A very helpful learning could be that that competency isn't as strong as you thought it was. Therefore, you work at making it stronger where before you were ignoring it. By the same token, it may be that you feel that you have not very much strength in a certain area only to discover in training that your competency in that area is, in fact, very effective. This could lead to your making use of your resource more frequently and in more places than you have used it before. The greatest likelihood is that if you feel you're strong, you are in fact strong. If you feel you need to strengthen a certain area, then you can work to do so. This will confirm your own effectiveness.

You can help make your training experience be a useful one for yourself by filling out the form and sending a copy back to the National Training Department Office. An extra form is included so that you can have a record of what you say to bring with you to the training event itself. You may want to keep your copy on file so that, two years from now, you can look back at it and ask "Having been involved in training, how would I fill this form out today?" Over a period of time a collection of these forms could provide you with an overall picture of your professional growth and your ability to plan specific experiences for your own continuing learning.

Many thanks for your help.

PRELIMINARY SELF-DIAGNOSIS FOR TRAINING

NAME _____   LOCATION _____   TITLE _____   DATE _____

In order to help your training team help you in developing a training program of learning experiences that will build on your present strengths and develop needed new strengths in the competencies required of professional staff, please rate your own assessment of your present level of performance in each of the following competencies:

REQUIRED FUNCTIONS	RELEVANT COMPETENCIES	SELF-RATING					RECOMMENDED LEARNING/ TRAINING EXPERIENCES
		Don't Know	Weak	Fair	Strong		
A. Formulating policies, objectives, program	Understanding of the role of a social agency in society						
	Ability to identify and think philosophically about social issues						
	An understanding of the process of human growth and learning						
	Ability to evaluate institutional effectiveness and program/ administrative outcomes						
	Ability to involve others in decision-making processes						
	Understanding of professional staff/ volunteer relationships						
	Understanding of Camp Fire Girls as an agency and as a program						
	Understanding of the nature of "leadership" in a voluntary agency						
	Ability to identify and use resources effectively						
	Others: (Please use extra sheet if needed.)						

B. Obtaining public understanding and support	Understanding of the dynamics of community behavior and structure					
	Skill in planning and executing strategies of community involvement and communication					
	Ability to plan and carry out community surveys					
	Ability to identify and involve community leadership effectively					
	Ability to conceive and project a relevant agency image and program					
	Ability to collaborate effectively with other community agencies					
	Others: (Please use extra sheet if needed.)					
C. Planning, supervising, and evaluating program and administrative activities	Understanding of principles of program development					
	Understanding of principles of administration and management					
	Ability to translate general objectives into specific plans					
	Skill in performing a helping role in supervision and collaboration					
	Ability to select and use a variety of methods to achieve particular goals					
	An accepting attitude toward others and skill in motivating and guiding their activities					

REQUIRED FUNCTIONS	RELEVANT COMPETENCIES	SELF-RATING				RECOMMENDED LEARNING/ TRAINING EXPERIENCES
		Don't Know	Weak	Fair	Strong	
	Understanding of and skill in using group processes in goal setting and problem solving					
	Ability to perceive and skill in making creative use of conflict					
	Ability to utilize both positive and negative feedback to strengthen program and administrative activities					
	Others: (Please use extra sheet if needed.)					
D. Participating in the advancement of the social agency field	Ability to interpret and apply reports and research findings from leaders in the social agency field					
	Ability to conduct and report on innovative programs and activities					
	Ability to communicate orally and in writing at a professional level					
	Skill in providing professional leadership					
	Interest in reading professional literature and in participating in professional associations					
	Others: (Please use extra sheet if needed.)					
E. Other functions related to performance of particular roles in your community (Please use extra sheet if needed.)						

SELF-DIAGNOSTIC GUIDE

ED 510 Adult Education:
History, Philosophy, and Contemporary Nature

Competencies	Importance to My Career			Importance to My Self-actualization			Level of Present Development			
	None	Medium	High	None	Medium	High	Low	Fair	Good	Excel.
A. Regarding adult education's characteristics as a social movement and its role in society:										
1. Ability to perceive and interpret the adult education movement in the perspective of its historical evolution and present status.										
a. Ability to describe and evaluate the various values, aims, and assumptions that have guided (and could guide) adult education as an instrument for accomplishing social goals.										
b. Ability to assess the contributions and shortcomings of adult education in influencing the development of American society.										
c. Ability to assess the contemporary issues, problems, and needs in society and to prescribe what adult education's responses to them should be.										
2. Ability to express a personal point of view regarding potential future societal needs and what adult education's responses to them should be.										

Competencies	Importance to My Career			Importance to My Self-actualization			Level of Present Development			
	None	Medium	High	None	Medium	High	Low	Fair	Good	Excel.
a. Ability to identify the relevance of adult education to the problems and needs of diverse subpopulations in our society.										
b. A personal commitment to the belief that adults can take responsibility for their own learning.										
B. Regarding the contemporary scope and structure of adult education as a field of operation:										
1. Ability to describe and interpret the societal roles, objectives, clienteles, policies, programs, and operational procedures of institutions providing adult educational services.										
2. Ability to describe the various roles performed by adult educators and the conditions, requirements, and bases of compensation for these roles.										
3. Ability to explain the locations and characteristics of graduate degree programs and continuing professional development opportunities for adult educators.										
4. Ability to describe and assess collaborative efforts to provide for the coordination of resources in the field.										

5. Ability to describe the ways in which adults engage in nonformal learning and the ways in which experiential learning is assessed for academic credit.							
6. Ability to describe efforts at international cooperation and patterns of adult education around the world.							
C. Regarding adult education as a discipline and field of study:							
1. Ability to describe modern concepts of adult learning and their implications for program development and operation.							
2. Ability to identify and apply the contributions of the various social sciences and the humanities to the conceptual foundations of adult education.							
3. Ability to think philosophically about the issues confronting adult education as an emerging discipline and field of study.							
4. Ability to describe and utilize past and present research investigations in the field of adult education and cognate disciplines.							
5. Ability to describe and interpret adult education as a discipline and field of study to professional and lay audiences.							

WORKSHEET FOR STATING LEARNING OBJECTIVES

Behavioral Aspect	Content Areas
To develop *knowledge* about	1. 2. 3. 4. 5. 6. 7.
To develop *understanding* of	1. 2. 3. 4. 5. 6. 7.
To develop *skill* in	1. 2. 3. 4. 5. 6. 7.
To develop *attitudes* toward	1. 2. 3. 4. 5. 6. 7.
To develop *interest* in	1. 2. 3. 4. 5. 6. 7.
To develop *values* of	1. 2. 3. 4. 5. 6. 7.

ORGANIC MODEL

**Young Presidents' Organization
"University for Presidents" Management of
Community Activities Course**

Objectives:

> To help participants clarify the roles they and their wives can perform as participants and leaders in community activities; to develop knowledge, understanding, skills, and attitudes required for effective performance of these roles.

Design:

1. Climate setting: introduction of participants by spokesmen giving composite picture of present community roles of members of table groups of six persons each.

2. Diagnostic phase: each table group constructs a critical incident in which a president or his wife has to make a choice regarding taking a community responsibility; table groups exchange incidents in pairs and each group discusses issues that would be confronted in making such a choice; members at each table pool problems and concerns with which they want help.

3. Planning phase: spokesmen for tables report out problems and concerns and a master list is built on newsprint by resource person;

problems are categorized (e.g., [a] planning a meaningful pattern of community activities; [b] differentiating between roles of volunteers and professionals; [c] motivating volunteers; [d] conducting board meetings; [e] leading discussions; [f] getting committees to work; [g] fund raising; [h] planning organizational change; [i] gaining public understanding; [j] planning better programs; [k] revitalizing annual meetings, etc.); delegates organize themselves into learning-teaching teams for highest-priority categories.

4. Learning activity phase: each team plans a presentation, skill exercise, group discussion, or simulation exercise to exploit the experience of the participants in solving the problems in its category, with the resource persons serving as consultants. Each team makes its presentation, with short critique by total group.

5. Evaluation phase: teams meet to pool their assessment of the extent to which the objectives have been accomplished, and report out their findings, with suggestions for improvement in future designs.

OPERATIONAL MODEL

National Council of Churches Consultation on Evaluation

Design A
(model building)

MON eve	Separate work groups —design models of evaluation for:

TUES am	1. measuring behavioral outcomes
aft	2. steering program operation
eve	3. assessing program effectiveness
WED am	4. program standard setting 5. evaluating this conference

⑦

—with periodic progress reports in general sessions

aft	FREE
eve	General session: Reports of workgroups, with reactions and suggestions

⑧

THURS am	Denominational teams —assessment of gaps between models and practice —strategy proposals
aft	FREE
eve	Reports of denominational teams
FRI am	Evaluation of this program

Design B
(technology-developing)

MON eve	Input: formulating program objectives: cognitive, affective, and operational

①

TUES	Work groups: "What should our objectives be?" 1. In church schools 2. In auxiliary organizations
am	3. In adult education programs 4. In social action 5. In congregational activities 6. Evaluation of this conference
aft	Sharing of work group findings
eve	FREE

WED am	Input: how to get data for measuring progress toward cognitive, affective, and operational objectives
aft	FREE
eve	Work groups (same as Tues. a.m.): "Techniques we now have and new techniques we need for getting these data."

THURS am	Reports of work groups
aft	Table groups and general session —issues and needs requiring future action: proposals ⎬ ②
eve	FREE

FRI am	Evaluation of this conference

Design C
(problem clinic)

MON eve	Problem census by table groups —Organization of work groups by type of problems

TUES am	Work groups identify: 1. What solutions to these problems are now known? 2. What new resources are needed?
aft	3. What lines of action might be taken?
eve	FREE

WED am	—Progress reports by work groups —Input of information & suggestions by consultants
aft	FREE
eve	—work groups finalize findings and ditto reports

⑥

THURS am	Denominational teams: —strategies for solving these problems ⎬ ⑨
aft	General session: sharing of strategy proposals ⎬ ⑩
eve	FREE

FRI am, eve	Evaluation of this conference

Design D
(case problems)

MON
eve
Description & analysis of non-church cases
(agric. ext., youth agency, industry)

⟩ ④

TUES
am
Description & analysis of selected church cases
(small, large, local council, denominational agency)

aft
Consultant panel: Some generalizations about
evaluation based on these cases

⟩ ③

eve
FREE

WED

am
Work groups: Design of evaluation programs for
typical case situations:
1. small church
2. large church

aft
3. church council
4. district agency

eve
5. national agency
6. this conference

⟩ ⑤

THURS
am
Reports of work groups, with identification of:
1. gaps in knowledge and techniques
2. problems and issues faced

aft
FREE

eve
Denominational teams: proposals for future action

⟩ ⑩

FRI
am
Reports of teams
Evaluation of this conference

Design E
(modular)

SUN eve	Introduction and orientation (1) Input: Planning as a necessary condition for evaluation (2) Table groups identify issues and concerns
MON am	Reports of issues and concerns from table groups (3) Input: Criteria for evaluation
aft	(4) Case descriptions of three evaluation experiences (5) Table groups analyze these case descriptions in light of the above criteria Consultant panel reacts to table groups' critiques
eve	Individual study and reflection
TUES am	(6) Input: Available resources and their use Functional work groups identify questions regarding use of resources by churches
aft	Dialog between work groups and consultant panel on questions about resources (7) Identification of special interests (e.g., tools for evaluation, supervision of evaluation, implementation, etc.) Organization of special interest groups
eve	FREE
WED am	Special interest groups meet
aft	(8) Reports of findings of special interest groups Reactions by consultant panel
eve	Informal groups
THURS am	(9) Organization of strategy planning groups by denominations and National Council Meeting of strategy planning groups on requirements for change in the evaluation practices of denominations and councils
aft	Strategy planning groups meet Input: Bringing about readiness for change
eve	Strategy planning groups meet
FRI am	(10) Recommendation of strategy planning groups Plans for the future Evaluation of this consultation

OPERATIONAL MODEL

Steps in Decision Making Model

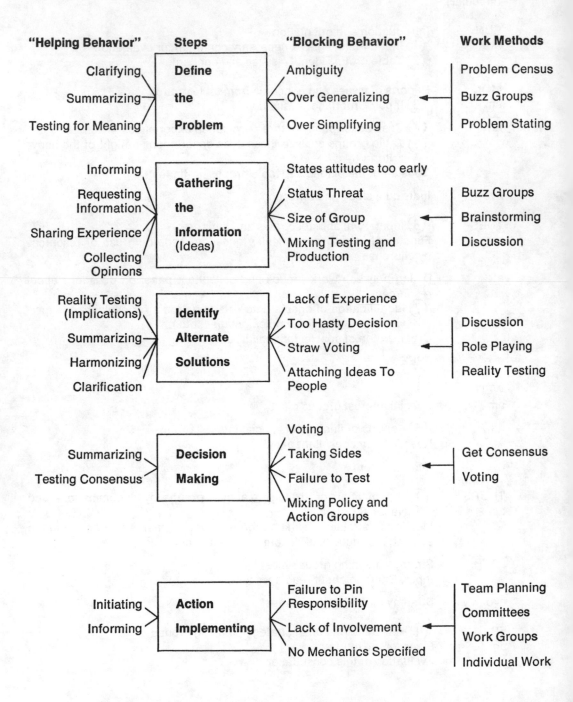

"Helping Behavior"	Steps	"Blocking Behavior"	Work Methods
Clarifying Summarizing Testing for Meaning	**Define the Problem**	Ambiguity Over Generalizing Over Simplifying	Problem Census Buzz Groups Problem Stating
Informing Requesting Information Sharing Experience Collecting Opinions	**Gathering the Information** (Ideas)	States attitudes too early Status Threat Size of Group Mixing Testing and Production	Buzz Groups Brainstorming Discussion
Reality Testing (Implications) Summarizing Harmonizing Clarification	**Identify Alternate Solutions**	Lack of Experience Too Hasty Decision Straw Voting Attaching Ideas To People	Discussion Role Playing Reality Testing
Summarizing Testing Consensus	**Decision Making**	Voting Taking Sides Failure to Test Mixing Policy and Action Groups	Get Consensus Voting
Initiating Informing	**Action Implementing**	Failure to Pin Responsibility Lack of Involvement No Mechanics Specified	Team Planning Committees Work Groups Individual Work

ROLE OF CHANGE AGENT MODEL

Canadian YMCA Staff Conference
Tentative Design

Pre-Conference Activity:

1. Each individual staff member will develop a list of personal objectives for his work in the immediate future.

2. Each individual will prepare a force-field analysis, identifying the forces aiding and impeding him in accomplishing these objectives.

3. Each individual will develop a list of obstacles (derived from the impeding forces in the force-field analysis) in the way of his accomplishing his objectives.

Conference Planning of Change
Strategies for Present

4. Sub-groups of staff will develop list of objectives for work of national staff in the immediate future, then pool them into a composite list.

5. Sub-groups of staff will develop obstacles (via force-field analysis) to accomplishment of staff objectives, then pool them into a composite list.

6. Sub-groups of staff will develop strategies for overcoming obstacles, then pool them into composite list.

7. Individual members of staff will rate self and one another on "Openness to Change" Scale, then share perceptions.

8. Each individual, in collaboration with two staff consultants, will develop personal strategies for change.

Conference Planning of Change
Strategies for Future

9. Sub-groups of staff will develop list of objectives for national staff for next five years, then pool.

10. Sub-groups of staff will develop change strategies (via a force-field analysis) for accomplishing these five-year objectives.

FUNCTIONAL MODEL

Unitarian-Universalist Women's Federation
Tentative Design, Board Training Workshop

Tuesday, Sept. 29

9:00–9:45	"The Organization as a Structure for Getting Work Done" —Responsibilities of board, committees, staff —Concepts of role delineation —Principles of effective operation
9:45–10:30	Assessment of UUWF in the light of these principles —Diagnosis of problems and deficiencies by small groups
10:30–10:45	Coffee break
10:45–12:00	Reports from small groups and problem clinic
12:15–1:30	Lunch
1:30–2:15	"More Effective Committees" —Observation of a hypothetical committee meeting —Generalizations about typical symptoms of committee ills and their causes —Some guiding principles and techniques
2:15–2:30	Coffee break
2:30–3:45	Observed practice of above principles and techniques by three ad hoc committees (composition and tasks to be formulated by executive secretary)
3:45–4:30	Observers' reports and clinic
4:30–6:00	Free time
6:00–7:15	Dinner
7:15–8:00	"Making Better Use of Our Resources"

	—Types of resources available (members, staff, outsiders, other committees, etc.) —How to give and receive help
8:00–9:15	Observed practice by the continuing ad hoc committees
9:15–10:00	Observers' reports and clinic

Wednesday, Sept. 30

9:00–9:45	"The Art of Reporting" —Some barriers to communication —Formats and techniques for committee reports
9:45–10:00	Coffee break
10:00–11:15	Observed practice by the three continuing ad hoc committees
11:15–12:00	Observers' reports and clinic
12:00–1:30	Lunch
1:30–2:15	"Making Organizational Decisions" —Theory of democratic decision-making —Division of responsibility for decision-making —Conditions and procedures for better decisions
2:15–2:30	Coffee break
2:30–3:45	Observation of Board (or Executive Committee?) making decisions on the recommendations of the ad hoc committees
3:45–4:30	Observers' reports, clinic, and closing generalizations

LEARNING CONTRACT FORM

Learner _____

Learning experience _____

Learning Objectives	Learning Resources and Strategies	Target Date for Completion	Evidence of Accomplishment of Objectives	Criteria and Means for Validating Evidence

SOME GUIDELINES FOR THE USE OF LEARNING CONTRACTS IN FIELD-BASED LEARNING

Why Use Learning Contracts?

One of the most significant findings from research about adult learning (e.g., Allen Tough's *The Adult's Learning Projects,* Ontario Institute for Studies in Education, Toronto, 1971) is that when adults go about learning something naturally (as contrasted with being taught something), they are highly self-directing. Evidence is beginning to accumulate, too, that what adults learn on their own initiative they learn more deeply and permanently than what they learn by being taught.

Those kinds of learning that are engaged in for purely personal development can perhaps be planned and carried out completely by an individual on his own terms and with only a loose structure. But those kinds of learning that have as their purpose improving one's competence to perform in a job or in a profession must take into account the needs and expectations of organizations, professions, and society. Learning contracts provide a means for negotiating a reconciliation between these external needs and expectations and the learner's internal needs and interests.

Furthermore, in traditional education the learning activity is structured by the teacher and the institution. The learner is told what objectives he is to work toward, what resources he is to use and how (and when) he is to use them, and how his accomplishment of the objectives will be evaluated. This imposed structure conflicts with the adult's deep psychological need to be self-directing and may induce resistance, apathy, or withdrawal. Learning contracts provide a vehicle for making the planning of learning experiences a mutual undertaking between a learner and his helper, mentor, teacher, and often, peers. By participating in the process of diagnosing his needs, formulating his objectives, identifying resources, choosing strategies, and evaluating his accomplishments, the learner develops a sense of ownership of (and commitment to) the plan.

Finally, in field-based learning particularly, there is a strong possibility that what is to be learned from the experience will be less clear to both the learner and the field supervisor than what work is to be done. There is a long tradition of field-experience-learners being exploited for the performance of menial tasks. The learning contract is a means for making the *learning objectives* of the field experience clear and explicit for both the learner and the field supervisor.

How Do You Develop a Learning Contract?

Step 1: Diagnose Your Learning Needs.

A learning need is the gap between where you are now and where you want to be in regard to a particular set of competencies.

You may already be aware of certain learning needs as a result of a personnel appraisal process or the long accumulation of evidence for yourself of the gaps between where you are now and where you would like to be.

If not (or even so), it might be worth your while to go through this process: First, construct a model of the competencies required to perform excellently the role (e.g., parent, teacher, civic leader, manager, consumer, professional worker, etc.) you are concerned about. There may be a competency model already in existence that you can use as a thought-starter and checklist; many professions are developing such models. If not, you can build your own, with help from friends, colleagues, supervisors, and expert resource people. A competency can be thought of as the ability to do something at some level of proficiency, and is usually composed of some combination of knowledge, understanding, skill, attitude, and values. For example, "ability to ride a bicycle from my home to the store" is a competency that involves some knowledge of how a bicycle operates and the route to the store;

an understanding of some of the dangers inherent in riding a bicycle; skill in mounting, pedaling, steering, and stopping a bicycle; an attitude of desire to ride a bicycle; and a valuing of the exercise it will yield. "Ability to ride a bicycle in cross-country race" would be a higher-level competency that would require greater knowledge, understanding, skill, etc. It is useful to produce a competency model even if it is crude and subjective because of the clearer sense of direction it will give you.

Having constructed a competency model, your next task is to assess the gap between where you are now and where the model says you should be in regard to each competency. You can do this alone or with the help of people who have been observing your performance. The chances are that you will find that you have already developed some competencies to a level of excellence, so that you can concentrate on those you haven't. An example of a part of a competency model showing how needs have been diagnosed is shown below.

Step 2: Specify Your Learning Objectives.

You are now ready to start filling out the first column of the learning contract, "Learning Objectives." Each of the learning needs diagnosed in step 1 should be translated into a learning objective. Be sure that your objectives describe what you will *learn*. (For example, "To read the following books . . ." is not a learning objective; a learning objective will describe what you want to learn from those books. State them in terms that are most meaningful to you—content acquisition, terminal behaviors, or directions of growth.)

Step 3: Specify Learning Resources and Strategies.

When you have finished listing your objectives, move over to the second column of the contract, "Learning Resources and Strategies," and describe how you propose to go about accomplishing *each* objective. Identify the resources (material and human) you plan to use in your field experience and the strategies (techniques, tools) you will employ in making use of them. Here is an example:

Learning Objective	*Learning Resources and Strategies*
Improve my ability to organize my work efficiently so that I can accomplish 20 percent more work in a day.	1. Find books and articles in library on how to organize my work and manage time, and read them.
	2. Interview three executives on how they organize their work, then observe them for one day each, noting techniques they use.
	3. Select the best techniques from each, plan a day's work, and have a colleague observe me for a day, giving me feedback.

Step 4: Specify Target Dates.

This column provides a self-disciplining device that enables you to schedule your time more efficiently by specifying target dates for completing each of your learning objectives.

Step 5: Specify Evidence of Accomplishment.

After completing the third column, move over to the fourth column, "Evidence of Accomplishment of Objectives," and describe what evidence you will collect to indicate the degree to which you have achieved each objective. Perhaps the following examples of evidence for different types of objectives will stimulate your thinking about what evidence you might accumulate.

Type of Objective	Examples of Evidence
Knowledge	Reports of knowledge acquired, as in essays, examinations, oral presentations, audiovisual presentations; annotated bibliographies.
Understanding	Examples of utilization of knowledge in solving problems, as in action projects, research projects with conclusions and recommendations, plans for curriculum change, etc.
Skills	Performance exercises, videotaped performances, etc., with ratings by observers.
Attitudes	Attitudinal rating scales; performance in real situations, role playing, simulation games, critical incident cases, etc., with feedback from participants and/or observers.
Values	Value rating scales; performance in value clarification groups, critical incident cases, simulation exercises, etc., with feedback from participants and/or observers.

Step 6: Specify How the Evidence Will Be Validated.

After you have specified what evidence you will gather for each objective in column four, move over to column five, "Criteria and Means for Validating Evidence." For each objective, first specify what criteria you propose the evidence will be judged by. The criteria will vary according to the type of objective. For example, appropriate criteria for knowledge objectives might include comprehensiveness, depth, precision, clarity, authentication usefulness, scholarliness, etc. For skill objectives more appropriate criteria may be poise, speed, flexibility, gracefulness, precision, imaginativeness, etc. After you have specified the criteria, indicate the means you propose to use to have the evidence judged according to these criteria. For example, if you produce a paper or report, who will you have read it and what are their qualifications? Will they express their judgments by rating scales, descriptive reports, evaluative reports? One of the actions that helps to differentiate "distinguished" from "adequate" performance in self-directed learning is the wisdom with which a learner selects his or her validators.

Step 7: Review Your Contract with Consultants.

After you have completed the first draft of your contract, you will find it useful to review it with two or three friends, supervisors, or other expert resource people to get their reactions and suggestions. Here are some questions you might have them ask about the contract to get optimal benefit from their help:

—Are the learning objectives clear, understandable, and realistic; do they describe what you propose to learn?
—Can they think of other objectives you might consider?
—Do the learning strategies and resources seem reasonable, appropriate, and efficient?
—Can they think of other resources and strategies you might consider?
—Does the evidence seem relevant to the various objectives, and would it convince them?
—Can they suggest other evidence you might consider?

—Are the criteria and means for validating the evidence clear, relevant, and convincing?

—Can they think of other ways to validate the evidence that you might consider?

Step 8: Carry Out the Contract.

You now simply do what the contract calls for. But keep in mind that as you work on it you may find that your notions about what you want to learn and how you want to learn it may change. So don't hesitate to revise your contract as you go along.

Step 9: Evaluate Your Learning.

When you have completed your contract you will want to get some assurance that you have in fact learned what you set out to learn. Perhaps the simplest way to do this is to ask the consultants you used in step 6 to examine your evidence and validation data and give you their judgment about their adequacy.

Learning-Need Diagnostic Guide

Indicate on the six-point scale below the level of each competency required for performing the role you are interested in by placing an "R" at the appropriate point. Then indicate your present level of development of each competency by placing a "P" at the appropriate point. The gaps between the Rs and the Ps will indicate your learning needs.

Essential Competencies	Absent	Low (awareness)	Moderate (conceptual understanding)		High (expert)
	0	1	2	3	4	5

As a Learning Facilitator

Regarding the theoretical framework of adult learning:

1. Knowledge of the current concepts and research knowledge regarding the needs, interests, motivations, capacities, and developmental characteristics of adults as learners.	0	1	2	3	4	5
2. Understanding of the differences between youth and adults as learners and of the implications of these differences for teaching and learning.	0	1	2	3	4	5
3. Understanding the processes and conditions of adult learning and the forces that affect learning in the dynamics of individual, group, and organizational behavior.	0	1	2	3	4	5
4. Knowledge of the various theories of learning and a personal theory about their application to particular adult learning situations.	0	1	2	3	4	5

SAMPLE COMPLETED CONTRACT

LEARNING CONTRACT FOR __ED 510: History, Philosophy, Contemporary Nature of Adult Education__

Student: _____ Soc. Sec. # __260__ __74__ __8334__ Instructor __Malcolm Knowles__

Learning Objectives B-Level	Learning Resources and Strategies	Evidence of Accomplishment of Objectives	Criteria and Means for Validating Evidence
To acquire knowledge of the characteristics of adult education as a social movement and adult education's role in society. (Meet this objective for all 6 competencies listed under objective A in the course syllabus.)	A. Read the specific references suggested on the course syllabus in the Inquiry Units section. If additional reading is necessary or desired, review the references listed in the Master Bibliography. Review notes from first class session. Attend and participate in inquiry team presentations. Interview one or more of the following persons: Dr. Epps Ready, Dr. William Gragg, Dr. Kenneth Segner, Dr. Malcolm Knowles.	A. In a notebook, prepare a section of information for each of the 6 competencies listed under learning objective A. The types of information to be contained in the notebook include: appropriate notes from references, notes from first class session and other sessions, materials from inquiry team presentations, learning diary-type summaries of understandings gained from the inquiry team presentations, reports from interview(s).	A. Final assessment of the notebook will be by consultation team. Each consultation member will be asked to complete the following rating scale: 1. The organization of the notebook was easy to understand. yes to some degree no 2. The notebook contains sufficient information for acquiring knowledge in all 6 competencies for objective A. yes some additional no info. is needed 3. The notebook can be useful to others seeking to understand the characteristics of adult education as a social movement and adult education's role in society. very useful somewhat not useful useful

To acquire knowledge and understanding of the scope and structure of adult education as a field of operations. (Meet at least a minimum standard of achievement for all 6 competencies listed under objective B and competency 6 listed under objective C in the course syllabus.)

B. Read the specific references suggested on the course syllabus in the Inquiry Units section. If additional reading is necessary or desired, review the references listed in the Master Bibliography. As a member of an inquiry team, assist in preparing a class presentation on competencies 1, 2, and 5 under B and 6 under C. Meet with inquiry team members to discuss information collected and ways of presenting information. Decide on most appropriate presentation for competency 3 and presentations by Dr. Malcolm Knowles for competencies 4 and 6. Interview Dr. Lin Compton.

A middle or positive rating will indicate this objective has been met. (Prior to final assessment, I will ask 2 adult education graduate students who are not in ED 510 this semester to examine the notebook, complete the rating scale, and after suggestions for improvement, I will include the ratings and suggestions in the back of the notebook.)

B. Participate in the Inquiry Team class presentation. Participation will include preparation, presentation, and evaluation. In the notebook used for learning objective A, prepare a section of information for each of the 6 competencies listed under learning objective B and competency 6 under learning objective C. The types of information to be contained are the same as for learning objective A.

B. An evaluation of the inquiry team presentation will be made by the class members. The evaluation device should include items for the following criteria: value, effectiveness, organization. An average or better rating will indicate this objective has been met.

Final assessment of the notebook will be the same as for learning objective A.

Learning Objectives B-Level	Learning Resources and Strategies	Evidence of Accomplishment of Objectives	Criteria and Means for Validating Evidence

To acquire knowledge and understanding of character-istics of adult education as a field of operations and tech-nology. (Meet at least a mini-mum standard of achievement for competencies 1–5 listed under objective C in the course syllabus. Competency 6 was included under objec-tive B.)	C. Read the specific references suggested on the course syllabus in the Inquiry Units section. If ad-ditional reading is necessary or desired, review the references listed in the Master Bibliography. Attend and participate in team presentations for competencies 1 and 2 and presentations by Dr. Malcolm Knowles for competen-cies 3, 4, and 5. Prepare a packet of information to identify and ex-plain the characteristics of adult education as a field of operations and study.	C. In the notebook used for learn-ing objectives A and B, prepare a section of information for com-petencies 1–5 listed under learn-ing objective C. The types of information to be contained are the same as for learning objective A with the exception of interviews. Completion and presentation of a packet of information to identify and explain the characteristics of adult education as a field of operations and study.	C. The persons who use the packet of information will com-plete the following rating scale *before* reading the packet:
			
			 1. I teach adults.
			     yes no
			
			 2. I am knowledgeable of the *field of adult education* (i.e., con-ceptual foundations, philosoph-ical issues, financial policies and practices, the effects of physical environment on learning, the major areas of research).
			 yes several areas one area no
			
			   The persons who read the packet of information will com-plete the following rating scale *after* reading the packet.
			
			   1. This packet of information helped me gain information about the *field of adult education.*
			 all areas several areas
			 one area none
			
			   2. This packet of information was organized for easy under-standing.
			 yes yes—some parts difficult
			 no—some parts easy no

388

Learning Objectives A-Level	Learning Resources and Strategies	Evidence of Accomplishment of Objectives	Criteria and Means for Validating Evidence

To gain knowledge and understanding in how the self-directed learning approach can be used in articulation of the Clarke Central High School Child Development Occupational Training Program and the Athens Area Vocational Technical School Child Development Occupational Training Program. (Both institutions are located in Athens, Georgia.)	Review the literature on articulation of secondary and post-secondary occupational training programs. Seek help from other resources (i.e., examples of program(s) in North Carolina successful in articulation, faculty members in the Occupational Education Department, Dr. Malcolm Knowles, etc.). Develop a position paper describing self-directed learning and its implication(s) in articulation.	Request that Dr. Malcolm Knowles and Dr. Joseph Clary review the paper, evaluate the content for logical applications and impact on the reader, and offer suggestions for improvements, present paper (in combination with packet of information developed for objective C) to the Clarke County Secondary Home Economics supervisor and to the two instructors in the Athens area Vocational-Technical School Child Development Department.	Request that all 3 persons in the Clarke County School system rate the paper, using the following items:
			
			1. After reading this paper, I am interested in investigating further the possibility of achieving articulation through self-directed learning.
			
			yes somewhat no
			
			2. The position of this paper was clearly presented.
			
			yes some points no
			     need to be
			     clarified
			
			A rating by 2 of the 3 persons in either of the highest 2 categories in both questions will indicate the objective has been met.

A rating by 2 persons of either of the highest two categories in both questions will indicate the objective has been met.

Final assessment of the notebook will be the same as for learning objective A.

THE ASSUMPTIONS AND PROCESS ELEMENTS OF THE PEDAGOGICAL AND ANDRAGOGICAL MODELS OF LEARNING

ASSUMPTIONS

About:	Pedagogical	Andragogical
Concept of the learner	Dependent personality	Increasingly self-directing
Role of learner's experience	To be built on more than used as a resource	A rich resource for learning by self and others
Readiness to learn	Uniform by age-level & curriculum	Develops from life tasks & problems
Orientation to learning	Subject-centered	Task- or problem-centered
Motivation	By external rewards and punishments	By internal incentives, curiosity

PROCESS ELEMENTS

Elements	Pedagogical	Andragogical
Climate	Tense, low trust Formal, cold, aloof Authority-oriented Competitive, judgmental	Relaxed, trusting Mutually respectful Informal, warm Collaborative, supportive
Planning	Primarily by teacher	Mutually by learners and facilitator
Diagnosis of needs	Primarily by teacher	By mutual assessment
Setting of objectives	Primarily by teacher	By mutual negotiation
Designing learning plans	Teachers' content plans Course syllabus Logical sequence	Learning contracts Learning projects Sequenced by readiness
Learning activities	Transmittal techniques Assigned readings	Inquiry projects Independent study Experiential techniques
Evaluation	By teacher Norm-referenced (on a curve) With grades	By learner-collected evidence validated by peers, facilitators, experts Criterion-referenced

The body of theory and practice on which teacher-directed learning is based is often given the label "pedagogy," from the Greek words *paid* (meaning child) and *agogus* (meaning guide or leader)—thus being defined as the art and science of teaching children.

The body of theory and practice on which self-directed learning is based is coming to be labeled "andragogy," from the Greek word *aner* (meaning adult)—thus being defined as the art and science of helping adults (or, even better, maturing human beings) learn.

These two models do not represent bad/good or child/adult dichotomies, but rather a continuum of assumptions to be checked out in terms of their rightness for particular learners in particular situations. If a pedagogical assumption is realistic for a particular situation, then pedagogical strategies are appropriate. For example, if a learner is entering into a totally strange content area, he or she will be dependent on a teacher until enough content has been acquired to enable self-directed inquiry to begin.